D0430588

THE TRAVELER'S KEY TO
SACRED ENGLAND

SACRED ENGLAND

A GUIDE TO
THE LEGENDS, LORE, AND LANDSCAPE
OF ENGLAND'S SACRED PLACES

JOHN MICHELL

Alfred A. Knopf   New York   1988

THIS IS A BORZOI BOOK
PUBLISHED BY ALFRED A. KNOPF, INC.

Grateful acknowledgment is made to the following for the use of
photographs in this book:

English Heritage: Westminster Abbey Chapter House; Wal-
tham Abbey; Maison Dieu, Ospringe; Avebury; Silbury Hill;
Knowlton; Glastonbury Abbey; Tintagel Castle; Belas Knap;
Castlerigg Stone Circle; Housesteads Roman Fort; Lindisfarne
Priory; Warkworth Hermitage; Studley Royal; Rievaulx Abbey;
Bury St. Edmunds Abbey.

The National Trust: Avebury; St. Michael's Mount; Chedworth;
Lindisfarne Castle; Farne Islands; Studley Royal Church; Rievaulx, the Doric Temple.

British Tourist Authority: Ely Cathedral (two photographs)

Ministry of Works: The Hurlers; Birdoswald, Hadrian's Wall;
Mt. Grace Priory.

Department of the Environment: Old Sarum; Abbotsbury, St.
Catherine's Chapel.

Paul Broadhurst: Duloe Stone Circle, Liskeard; Castle Treryn,
Land's End.

R.W. Hammond/Edwin Gardner: Tintagel.

William Fix: Glastonbury Tor.

Fredric Lehrman: St. Michael's Church, Brentor.

Library of Congress Cataloging-in-Publication Data

Michell, John [date]
   Traveler's key to sacred England.

   Bibliography: p.
   Includes index.
   1. England—Antiquities—Guidebooks.   2. England—
Description and travel—1971-   —Guidebooks.
3. Christian antiquities—England—Guidebooks.
4. Christian shrines—England—Guidebooks.   5. Christian
pilgrims and pilgrimages—England—Guidebooks.   6. Man,
Prehistoric—England.   7. Legends—England.   8. Folklore—England.   I. Title.
DA90.M5   1988   914.2'04858   87-46041
ISBN 0-394-55573-2 (pbk.)

First Edition

CONTENTS

Acknowledgments   ix
Introduction   xi
Hints to Pilgrims   xiii

1   THE MAKING OF THE SACRED LANDSCAPE   3

2   LONDON: The City of King Brutus   17
    Westminster Abbey   19
    St. Paul's Cathedral   27
    The City of London Churches   30
    Some Other London Places of Worship   46

3   AROUND LONDON: Essex, Hertfordshire,
        Buckinghamshire, Oxfordshire, Hampshire, Kent   53
    St. Albans   53
    Waltham Abbey   57
    The Chiltern Hills   60
        Jordans   60
        Milton's Cottage   61
        Stoke Poges   62
        Stonor Park   65
    Winchester   68
    Canterbury   77

4   THE SOUTHWEST: Wiltshire, Dorset, Somerset   89
    Avebury   89
    Stonehenge   96
    Old Sarum   106
    Salisbury   108
    Knowlton   111
    Wimborne Minster   111
    Milton Abbas   115
    Dorchester   117
    Abbotsbury   120

Cerne Abbas   122
Sherborne   125
Glastonbury   128
Wells   144
Bath   152

5   THE WESTERN PENINSULA: Devon and
      Cornwall   160
Exeter   160
A la Ronde   164
Dartmoor   166
Cornish Holy Wells   172
Morwenstow   182
Tintagel   184
St. Michael's Mount   185
The Land's End   188

6   THE WELSH BORDER: Gloucestershire,
      Worcestershire, Herefordshire, Cheshire   194
Gloucester   194
Cotswold Long Barrows   200
Chedworth   202
Deerhurst   204
Worcester   206
Hereford   209
Kilpeck   215
Chester   216
St. Winifred's Wells   221

7   THE NORTH: Cumbria, Northumberland,
      Durham   223
Stone Circles of Cumbria   223
Carlisle   228
Arthurian Cumbria   231
Lindisfarne   235
Bamburgh   241
Warkworth   243
Hexham   244
Durham   247

8   YORKSHIRE   254
York   254
Ruined Abbeys of Yorkshire   262
Fountains Abbey and Studley Royal   263
Rievaulx Abbey   267
Byland Abbey   270
Jervaulx Abbey   271
Mount Grace Priory   272

Ripon   273
Sacred and Curious Rocks   277
  Knaresborough   277
  Brimham Rocks   280
  Boroughbridge   282

9 EASTERN ENGLAND: Lincolnshire,
   Cambridgeshire, Norfolk, Suffolk   284
Lincoln   284
The Isle of Ely   289
Peterborough   296
Island Sanctuaries of Fenland   301
Walsingham   304
East Dereham   308
Bury St. Edmunds   309

Further Reading   315
Index   317

ACKNOWLEDGMENTS

Gratitude and affection to all who have helped in the making of this book as hosts, guides, or good companions, particularly Su and Alan Bleakley, Paul Broadhurst, Chung Yee Chong, Margaret Hickey, Evelyn Honig, Jane Rainey, Christine Rhone, Jean Ruzicka; to John Anthony West who suggested it and Toinette Lippe who patiently edited it.

INTRODUCTION

There are many good guidebooks to England and its various regions and aspects, and this one is not intended as a rival to any of the others. Its aim is to provide a good-natured, quietly informative companion to those travelers in England who seek the ancient spirit of the land. There is a saying in India that "every river is as sacred as the Ganges," and the truth of that is apparent to everyone at certain times, as when a whole landscape is made glorious by sunrise or a shaft of evening light. Yet there are places which have an attractive, numinous quality that marks them out as natural sanctuaries. "It is certain," said Sir Thomas More in the sixteenth century, "that God wishes to be worshipped in particular places." These are the places we shall seek out and visit. Some of them are famous, drawing pilgrims and tourists throughout the year; others are quiet and secluded. There are cathedrals and abbeys, historic churches, revivalist centers, shrines of saints and poets, pagan sanctuaries, megalithic temples, holy wells, rocks, and trees. The one thing they have in common is that they are all in different ways centers of spiritual energy, places to experience. Their legends, histories, and points of interest are related here. How one experiences them is a personal matter.

The places described in this book are only a sample; everyone who knows England will have favorite sites which have been omitted. If every worthy site were to be included, however, this book would be a mere list. In England there are forty-four cathedrals and a greater number of ruined abbeys which are worth visiting, as well as some fifteen thousand parish churches and countless old chapels, shrines, hermitages, holy wells, and other types of religious site or monument. Of an earlier period, England contains several hundred stone circles and megalithic sanctuaries, from the great temples of Stonehenge and Avebury to the humbler relics of an ancient faith which still sanctify the wilder parts of the countryside. Despite the depredations of centuries—especially our own twentieth century—it is quite remarkable how much of sacred England has survived. All that can be done in the space of one book is to hint at the richness of experience which the English countryside offers to pilgrims, historians, and antiquarian travelers. To illustrate this, there are certain places which absolutely demand inclusion—Stonehenge, Walsingham, Durham cathedral, for example—and others are chosen because they are characteristic of their areas. Thus there is a concentration of City churches in London, holy wells in Cornwall, St. Catherine's shrines in the south, Saxon lady saints in the Fenlands, ruined abbeys in Yorkshire, and Arthurian sites in Cumbria. These by no means limit the interesting features of their districts. Almost every old village church has something to reward the pilgrim, and every feature in the landscape has its sacred legend. In a few weeks one can visit the great sanctuaries of England, or one can explore a single district without exhausting its store of sacred places and monuments.

This tour through some of England's sanctuaries proceeds in a generally clockwise direction, starting from London and its surroundings, then westward to Cornwall, along the Welsh border to the north and back to London by the east coast. It is thus somewhat in the nature of a fringe tour, providing an outline which dedicated pilgrims can fill in according to their own interests, inclinations, and guidance.

The modern tendency is to conserve historic sites, and many of the places visited are now maintained and displayed by official custodians. Discerning visitors may regret that in some cases the process of "tidying up" has been taken too far, with the result that sites once surrounded by romantic wilderness are now set more prosaically in landscapes of tended lawns and pathways. It may be that in future years a more harmonious balance will be struck between natural beauty and the interests of conservation. Inevitably, however, the cost of maintenance means limited opening hours and the levying of entrance fees. All churches and cathedrals, apart from Ely, can still be entered without payment, though a fee is sometimes charged for seeing parts of their interiors. Their times of opening and closing, and the entrance fees to other sites, are given in the text. They are, of course, subject to change. In most cases there are reduced fees for children, and special arrangements can be made by visiting parties. Up-to-date information about bookings and accommodation can be obtained from local tourist information centers, whose addresses and telephone numbers are listed under the relevant towns or districts.

In traveling between these sacred places, one not only refreshes one's own spirit but assists in the work of reviving the latent spirit of the earth, whose renaissance brings peace and contentment in and among nations. May all who take the pilgrim's path find blessings, health, and good cheer and enjoy a safe, delightful journey.

HINTS TO PILGRIMS

The following notes were written in about 1950 by the late Major Wellesley Tudor Pole, the widely respected mystic and author, who founded the Chalice Well Gardens at Glastonbury as a resting place for pilgrims on their way to the shrines of St. Michael in the West of England.

Honor your holy places once more and let them and their unseen Guardians be remembered in your hearts and minds and prayers. It is in such ways that the road will be made straight for One who will surely come if there are sufficient of those who have made themselves worthy of His coming.

Whenever a centre is found to be neglected or in disrepair, do not leave that spot without doing something, however small, to improve the situation, in the spirit of loving service. Whether conscious of his presence or no, always salute the Guardian on arriving and on leaving each centre visited.

Do not fear to proclaim your faith or to make your reasons for pilgrimage known, whenever the opportunity *naturally* occurs.

Do no harm to life in any form whilst on your pilgrim way, showing particular regard for animals, flowers and children.

Pray daily for the peace of the world, for true fellowship among men and for the realisation of the fact that *all* Life lives and moves and has its being within the infinite and universal Mind of the Creator.

Darkness can not overwhelm the world so long as Light continues to radiate by reflection from the hearts and minds of all who dedicate themselves to this high purpose. Learn also to reflect the Light from each holy place to which your pilgrim steps are led.

Look within for your guidance and inspiration; go forth in faith and courage; and return in peace.

PILGRIMAGE TOURS, RETREATS, CHORAL SERVICES

Medieval pilgrims often journeyed in groups organized by a travel agent who provided them with security, food, lodgings, and transport to and from their destination. The pilgrimage trade is enjoying a current revival, and there are several reputable tour operators (recommended by the British Tourist Authority) who specialize in Christian pilgrimages.

British Heritage Tours The tours they offer include: the John Wesley Methodist Round; Presbyterian Heritage Tours;

Birthplace of Whitefield and Evangelicalism; Quaker Tours.

British Heritage Tours
314 Linen Hall
162–168 Regent Street
London W1R 5TB
Telephone: London (01) 437 9461

Summer Academy Among their special interest holidays:
Monastic Buildings in Northern England; Castle and Abbey
in Medieval Scotland.

Summer Academy
The University
Canterbury, Kent CT2 7NX
Telephone: Canterbury (0227) 470402

Highway Holidays A Parish Holiday gives one a week in an
English country village and an opportunity of sharing in the
life that revolves around the parish church.

Highway Holidays Ltd.
Avon Close
95 Crane Street, Salisbury
Wiltshire SP1 2PU
Telephone: Salisbury (0722) 338733

Inter-Church Travel Their tours include: Ely Cathedral and
the Fens; Northumberland, Cradle of Christianity; Pastoral
Places throughout Britain; York, the Northwest, and the
Dales; Festivals of Music and Arts. They also organize visits
to cathedrals, abbeys, and parish churches.

Inter-Church Travel
45 Berkeley Street
London W1A 1EB
Telephone: London (01) 734 0942

Visit Northumbria From the Holy Island of Lindisfarne one
can explore the sacred places associated with the history of
the early Celtic church in northeast England.

Visit Northumbria
69 Newbottle Street
Houghton-le-Spring
Tyne and Wear
Telephone: Houghton (0783) 845146

Holiday Fellowship Their special interest tours include:
Brasses and Brass Rubbing; Religion in England; the Abbeys
and Cathedrals of North Yorkshire; In the Steps of St.
Cuthbert and the Venerable Bede.

HF Holidays Ltd.
142–144 Great North Way
London NW4 1EG
Telephone: London (01) 203 0433

Tours of megalithic and ancient spiritual sites are offered by:

Gothic Image Ltd.
7 High Street, Glastonbury
Somerset BA6 9DP
Telephone: Glastonbury (0458) 31453

The British Institute of Earth Mysteries
The Coach House
Mount Street, Brecon
Powys LD3 7DU
Telephone: Brecon (0874) 5164

The following places are notable among the active pilgrimage centers of England:

Aylesford Priory Catholic pilgrims attend the Shrine of Our Lady of Mount Carmel and St. Simon Stock. The priory has accommodation in its retreat house.

The Pilgrimage Secretary
Carmelite Priory
Aylesford, Maidstone, Kent
Telephone: Maidstone (0622) 77272

Glastonbury Abbey The Anglican pilgrimage takes place on the last Saturday in June.

The Abbey Gatehouse
Glastonbury, Somerset
Telephone: Glastonbury (0458) 32267

There is also an annual Catholic pilgrimage to Glastonbury on the first Sunday in June, and there is a Druid gathering on May 1.

St. Albans Abbey An Easter Monday pilgrimage goes annually from St. Paul's Church, Hoddesdon, to the abbey, where a service is held near the shrine of England's first Christian martyr.

Pilgrimage Secretary
Deanery Office
St. Albans Abbey
St. Albans, Hertfordshire
Telephone: St. Albans (0727) 52120

Whalley Abbey The abbey is once more, as in medieval times, a leading place of pilgrimage in the north of England. Pilgrims are received and retreats are held in the old manor house built in the ruins of the Cistercian monastery.

Whalley Abbey
Blackburn, Lancashire
Telephone: Whalley (025482) 2268

Walsingham The season for pilgrimages to the Shrine of Our Lady of Walsingham runs from Easter through October. A pilgrims' hospice offers accommodation.

The Administrator
The College
Walsingham, Norfolk
No telephone.

Many religious houses in England offer accommodation
and facilities for retreats of various kinds, from solitary
meditation to organized courses and community activities.
An ecumenical journal about retreats, including lists of
places, is obtainable for 80p from:

The Association for Promoting Retreats
Liddon House
24 South Audley Street
London W1Y 5DL

In many cathedrals and collegiate churches there is a regular choral service, sometimes daily, to which visitors are
welcome. These great buildings were designed to be filled
with music, and in them today can be heard the finest English
choirs chanting the liturgical works of British and foreign
composers. Details concerning these places, with the times of
their choral and other services, can be obtained from:

Australia
British Tourist Authority
Midland House
171 Clarence Street
Sydney, N.S.W. 2000
T: (02) 29-8627

Belgium
British Tourist Authority
Rue de la Montagne 52
Bergstraat, B2
1000 Brussels
T: 02/511.43.90

Brazil
British Tourist Authority
Avenida Ipiranga 318A, 12°
Andar,
conj. 1201
Edificio Vila Normanda
01046 São Paulo=Sp
T: 257-1834

Canada
British Tourist Authority
94 Cumberland Street, Suite 600
Toronto, Ontario
M5R 3N3
T: (416) 925-6326

Denmark
British Tourist Authority
Møntergade 3
DK-1116 Copenhagen
T: (01) 12 07 93

France
British Tourist Authority
63 Rue Pierre Charron
75008 Paris
T: (1) 42 89 11 11

Germany
British Tourist Authority
Neue Mainzer Str. 22
6000 Frankfurt am Main 1
T: (069) 2380750

Hong Kong
British Tourist Authority
Suite 903
1 Hysan Avenue
Hong Kong
T: 5-764366

Ireland
British Tourist Authority
123 Lr Baggot Street,
Dublin 2
T: 614188

Italy
British Tourist Authority
Via S. Eufemia 5
00187 Rome
T: 678 4998 or 678.5548

Japan
British Tourist Authority
Tokyo Club Building
3-2-6 Kasumigaseki, Chiyoda-ku
Tokyo 100
T: (03) 581-3603

Mexico
British Tourist Authority
Edificio Alber
Paseo de la Reforma 332–5 Piso
06600 Mexico DF
T: 533 6375

Netherlands
British Tourist Authority
Aurora Gebouw (5e)
Stadhouder-Skade 2
1054ES Amsterdam
T: (020) 855051

New Zealand
British Tourist Authority
Norwich Insurance House
8th Floor
Queen & Durham Streets
Auckland 1
T: 31446

Norway
British Tourist Authority
Mariboes gt 11
0183 Oslo 1
T: (02) 41 18 49

Singapore
British Tourist Authority
14 Collyer Quay 05-03
Singapore Rubber House
Singapore 0104
T: Singapore 2242966/7

South Africa
British Tourist Authority
7th Floor JBS Building
107 Commissioner Street
Johannesburg 2001
PO Box 6256
Johannesburg 2000
T: (011) 29 6770

Spain
British Tourist Authority
Torre de Madrid 6/4
Plaza de España
Madrid 28008
T: (91) 241 1396

Sweden
British Tourist Authority
For visitors: Malmskillnadsg 42
1st Floor
For Mail: Box 7293
S-103 90 Stockholm
T: 08-21 24 44

Switzerland
British Tourist Authority
Limmatquai 78
8001 Zurich
T: 01/47 42 77 or 47 42 97

United Kingdom
British Tourist Authority
Thames Tower
Black's Road
London W6 9EL
T: (01) 846-9000

USA Chicago
British Tourist Authority
John Hancock Center Suite 3320
875 N. Michigan Avenue
Chicago, Illinois 60611
T: (312) 787-0490

USA Dallas
British Tourist Authority
Cedar Maple Plaza Suite 210
2305 Cedar Springs Road
Dallas, Texas 75201-1814
T: (214) 720-4040

USA Los Angeles
British Tourist Authority
World Trade Center
350 South Figueroa Street
Suite 450
Los Angeles, California 90071
T: (213) 628-3525

USA New York
British Tourist Authority
40 West 57th Street
New York, New York 10019
T: (212) 581-4700

SACRED
ENGLAND

1
THE MAKING OF THE SACRED LANDSCAPE

Before the Protestant Reformation in the sixteenth century, England was very obviously a sacred land. In both town and country the church steeple was the dominant symbol of the landscape, while the Church calendar with its feasts and saints' days dominated the pattern of the year. Stone crosses by the roadside guided travelers to the famous places of pilgrimage, where shrines and holy relics gave miraculous cures and other blessings. At innumerable lesser shrines about the countryside, by rocks, hills, and holy wells, crowds gathered on certain days to perpetuate rites and customs which, though often of pagan origin, were sanctioned by the Church. These occasions were marked by fairs, festivals, and markets where all kinds of local business were conducted. Every corner of the landscape had its sacred and legendary associations, and these were constantly added to as successive generations contributed new tales of marvels and miracles. Thus the face of the country was like a storybook, illustrated by the monuments and natural features which preserved its history. This book could be read by country people who, being generally illiterate, could read no other. It was the source of their education and culture and enabled them to live fully human lives in their own native surroundings.

The Puritans' destruction of religious relics and "idols," and the suppression of festivals and popular assemblies, coincided with the growth of centralized political and economic power. These developments had a crushing effect on local independence and culture. The rural population declined, and whole chapters of its traditional lore were erased from the face of the landscape. Modern industry and the methods of modern agriculture and communications have since hastened the process of deculturization; but that process has at the same time brought about a reaction. It is now widely apparent that the future of the earth as a living system is in many ways threatened, and that the basic cause is modern alienation from nature. There is a very essential difference between the present scientific way of regarding the earth, as a mass of inert matter, and the traditional view of it as a living, spiritual entity. It may be that, out of sheer necessity, the traditional view will once again become popular. In that case, the proper understanding of the earth, including its spiritual aspect, will be the priority of future science. That implies the future reconsecration of the earth, as a whole and in all its parts, to the spirit which gives it life. How that is done can be discovered through study of the landscape and the history of its sacred places, to which the following is an introduction.

THE PRIMEVAL GARDEN

Everything about prehistoric times is by the nature of things uncertain. No one knows who were the first inhabitants of England or when they appeared. The earliest known stone implements are dated to about 300,000 years ago, after which successive ice ages are said to have driven everyone out of the country. The date of about 10,000 B.C. is given as the end of the last ice age, when England again became comfortably habitable. It was then occupied by groups of nomadic people, each group ranging over a particular region and living on the natural resources of its territory.

These people lived well and simply and made so little impression upon the earth that what chiefly remains from their time is the debris of their feasts. Feasting played a large part in their lives. Following the necessary fast of early spring (corresponding perhaps to our Lenten fasting), they began the yearly ritual journey around their country. As nomadic people have always done, they took the accustomed routes and stopped at familiar places. These places were marked by some natural feature, a tree, a rock, or a spring of water, wherein dwelt a spirit, and the nature of that spirit determined what should be done there. Some places were for gathering herbs or nuts, others for hunting a particular game. With these substantial gifts of the local spirit came others of a different order: healing, fertility, and oracular dreams. At certain places other traveling groups were regularly encountered, leading to ceremonies and exchanges of gifts which later became festivals and markets.

Thus, from the very beginning of their history, the sacred places of a country accumulate a wide variety of lore and custom. Nomadic people, such as the Australian Aborigines today, perform their annual journeys in the footsteps of the creative spirits who first shaped the hills, rivers, and other features of the landscape. The paths they took, the places where they stopped, and the locations of episodes on their journey form the sacred geography of the nomads, who ritually imitate the actions of the creative spirits at the appropriate spots. The places where a certain animal or plant was first created are made sacred to that species, and whatever member of the tribe has a special affinity for it is charged with performing the proper ceremony. Other places are scenes of mythical adventures, where a divine ancestor did some heroic act which ever afterward has been commemorated there. It was no doubt by a similar process that certain British landmarks first became associated with the prototypes of Arthur, Merlin, and other native heroes.

This picture of Mesolithic or Middle Stone Age life in Britain emphasizes its most essential feature, the intensely spiritual relationship between people and landscape. It shows how successfully the ancient people communicated with the local spirits of the country and how well they were able to live as a result. Dr. Richard Muir (*Reading the Celtic Landscapes*, 1985) gives detail to the picture:

> As long as these hunting and fishing folk did not upset the natural balances, each valley, strand and lake basin could sustain a clan of hunter-gatherers, which migrated around an eternal circuit, harvesting each resource which the changing seasons provided. There were salmon in the rivers, eggs to be gathered on the sea cliffs, fish, seals and stranded whales along the coast and limpets on the rocks, while the rich woodlands harboured wild cattle, deer and horses, fungi, fruit, roots and shoots. . . . To live well under the Mesolithic economy one needed to have an intense awareness and understanding of Nature, know the habits and behaviour of the intended prey and when each edible plant would release its fruits and where it could be found.

All that survives of Mesolithic craftwork are the beautifully formed flint implements known as microliths, which include saws and delicate arrowheads. These fine objects were exchanged as gifts between tribes and have often been found far from their original sources.

The pattern of life at that time was closely in accord with the pattern of human nature (which was no doubt formed under similar conditions) and with the requirements of human spirit. Every aspect of life was celebrated. This was the innocent Golden Age yearned for by poets, the Garden of Eden or lost paradise. People felt secure in their own country, a sacred landscape inhabited by familiar spirits, each of which was visited in the course of the annual pilgrimage. Though it has left scarcely any physical mark upon the landscape, that way of life laid the foundations of native culture, which rest in the sacred places of the country. Certain spots, where the old British nomads gathered at the shrine of some nature spirit, are now marked by cathedrals and churches. Many have retained sacred and legendary associations from the old times. Thus the basic pattern of the English landscape, still discernible beneath its modern accretions, was laid down in times before settlement as a network of sacred centers with pilgrimage paths between them.

SHRINES AND SETTLEMENTS

In a book with the amusing title *Civilization: Its Cause and Cure,* the nineteenth-century sage Edward Carpenter suggested that civilization was a "disease which the various races of man have to pass through—as children pass through measles or whooping cough." There is no knowing what it is that causes a people, who for thousands of years have been living satisfactorily in the same nomadic pattern, to move toward a settled life-style. An elderly person may sometimes have been left by the traveling group to shelter by a sacred spring, later to become its resident priest, priestess, or oracle. Certainly the first settlements were by springs and traditional shrines.

The change from nomadic to settled life coincided with the beginning of agriculture, and the first traces of cultivation in England are from about 5000 B.C. That time, therefore, was the beginning of serious warfare, which occurred first between settled and wandering people—as in the story of Cain and Abel or the farmers-against-the-cowboys tradition in the American West—and was perpetuated in disputes between settled communities over property and possessions.

With settlement came formal religion and science. They were required for the organization of society and to preserve contact with the spirits of nature, theologized as gods, on which life still depends. Settlement involves guilt. In the exchange of the delights and hardships of the road for the more even life of domestic comfort, certain things were lost. Human nature is no longer as fully satisfied as it was in the old wandering days; the distant shrines are no longer visited, and the sacred landscape has shrunk to the district around the homestead. The feeling of guilt is expressed by prophets who urge a return to the sacred journey. Their voice rings through the Old Testament, as in Jeremiah's reproach to the Tribes that they "stumble in their ways from the ancient paths" (18:15) and in "Thus saith the Lord, stand ye in the ways, and see, and ask for the old paths, where is the good way, and walk therein, and ye shall find rest for your souls" (6:16).

The way to compensate for giving up the sacred journey is to ritualize it. Plato's advice to colonists in the *Laws* was to seek out the sacred places of the old inhabitants, rededicate them to familiar gods, and reinstitute festivals there on the appropriate days. There should be, he said, at least 365 festivals in the course of a year. Thus the shrines of the local spirits in the country were to be attended and honored at the proper seasons in imitation of nomadic times.

Plato looked for the best possible social order, one combining the advantages of settled life with the spiritual values of nomadism. That is the ideal of every civilization, and early religion and science were designed to realize it. Religious systems reduced the wide-ranging sacred landscape of the nomadic people to the proportions of a settled district. No longer did seasonal festivals occur spontaneously, as the old wanderers reached the customary site; their times were now determined by a priestly calendar based on astronomy. The round of festivals still reflected the rhythm of nomadic life. Each was dedicated to a particular god who corresponded to an aspect of human mentality and instinct and presided over one of the stages in the farmer's and the hunter's year. Life thereby was made rich and varied, less so than under the free spirit of primeval times, but with the comfortable compensations of settled life.

Civilization demands hierarchies and specialization in functions. A priestly profession comes into being, whose tasks include keeping the calendar and the record of events and officiating at rituals. The overall purpose of the priests is to keep the life of their communities in harmony with the seasons and ways of nature. In many parts of the world, including the British Isles, a comprehensive code of science was developed with the object of regulating the dealings between humanity, the earth, and the cosmos. Much is still to be learned about its methods and achievements; the following summarizes the present state of knowledge on the subject.

SACRED SCIENCE AND THE MEGALITHS

Not long after the beginning of Stone Age agriculture, something dramatic but mysterious took place along the western coasts of Europe. From the Canary Islands, Spain, and Portugal to Brittany, Ireland, Britain up to the northern Scottish isles, and parts of Scandinavia, large, skillfully built stone structures began to appear from early in the fifth millennium B.C. Among the oldest and most impressive are great chambered mounds, such as New Grange in Ireland, Maes Howe on the main Orkney island, and the smaller Bryn Celli Ddu in Anglesea. Their main feature is a passage-way, walled and roofed with large stones, leading to an inner stone cavern, sometimes with side chambers, buried deep within a dome-shaped mound of earth and stone. Archaeologists refer to them as tombs, but that was certainly not the limit of their function. Westminster Abbey, for example, is full of old bones but cannot be described as a mere tomb or reliquary. Particularly in Ireland, some of the stones within and around the mounds are inscribed with patterns or symbols. Their meaning is unknown, but in Martin Brennan's book *The Stars and the Stones*, it is shown that some of the symbols are picked out by rays of light or shadow at particular times of the year. Brennan also shows that the passages into the mounds are so oriented that at a certain date they allow a light beam from the sun or moon to penetrate into the inner recesses of the chamber. New Grange, for example, receives the light of the rising sun at midwinter. This interplay of light and darkness with the carved symbols on the walls of the inner chamber suggests that the buildings were used for purposes other than burials: for recording seasons and astronomical cycles and as places of vigil and initiation. Rather than tombs, perhaps, they might be called temples.

According to the revised method of radiocarbon dating, the

earliest known mound is at Kercado in Brittany, which was
built in about 4800 B.C. Others range from about that time to
3000 B.C or later. In the same period and into the second
millennium B.C. many thousands of great stone or megalithic
structures were built, together with vast stretches of earthworks. Regional variations are found between those in
different lands, Britain having by far the greatest number of
stone circles—almost a thousand are known—but the simi-
larities between them are so striking that they must surely
have had a common origin and purpose.   .

Until a few years ago it was believed that the megalith
builders must have spread to the northwest fringes of
Europe, as conquerors or missionaries, from some original
seat of civilization on the Mediterranean. However, that
theory was disproved by the discovery of radiocarbon dating,
which established that the monuments on the Atlantic
coastline were considerably older than their supposed Mediterranean prototypes. Academic patterns of prehistory were
thereby upset, but attention was drawn to certain earlier
writers, long ignored, who had anticipated this development.
One of them was J. Foster Forbes, an antiquarian mystic and
the author of several books on ancient Britain, such as *The
Unchronicled Past* (1938). On the subject of stone circles he
wrote that:

> They were made from about 8000 B.C. by people from the West, priests
> who survived the Atlantis cataclysm.
> Their overall purpose was to establish and maintain social order.
> They functioned both as lunar observatories and as receiving stations
> for celestial influences at certain seasons.
> They were instrumental in augmenting the earth's fertility and the
> prosperity of the people by controlling the earth's field of vital and
> magnetic energies.

Several of these ideas, such as the western origin of the
megalith builders, are in accordance with the later evidence,
and others have since been verified. The use of stone circles
for measuring the complicated cycles of the moon was
demonstrated in Alexander Thom's *Megalithic Lunar
Observatories* in 1971, and in his earlier work, *Megalithic
Sites in Britain*. Through statistical analysis of the numerous surveys he took of stone circles and neighboring monuments, Thom was able to show that:

> Stone circles were precisely planned and laid out in accordance with
> certain geometric figures in the classic Pythagorean tradition. The
> unit of measure in their designs was the "megalithic yard" of 2.72 feet.
> Stones within and beyond the circles lined up to indicate a natural or
> artificial mark on the horizon where the moon or sun reached one of
> the extreme positions in their cycles, as at a solstice. The megalith
> builders had a highly developed, unified code of science based on
> number and geometry, and they were expert surveyors, engineers, and
> astronomers.

These conclusions indicate that the ancient dwellers in
Britain were not, as had previously been thought, savages

and simple peasants, but people who lived in ordered societies governed by a religious-scientific priesthood.

From the 1970s, research into the hidden properties of stone circles has produced some remarkable results which, though not yet conclusive, tend to support the ideas of J. Foster Forbes. The investigation of anomalous energies at the old sites has attracted dowsers, engineers, and scientists. Tom Graves's *Needles of Stone* gives a dowser's view of the connection between megalithic sites and magnetic earth currents. The use of Geiger counters and ultrasonic detectors has revealed abnormal patterns of pulsations within stone circles that vary throughout the year. One effect which has been widely recorded is that the levels of ultrasound and radiation inside the circles is significantly lower than outside; hence the title of Don Robins's book on megalithic energies, *Circles of Silence*.

From the apparent fact that the megalith builders placed their circles and other stone monuments on sites with peculiar dynamic properties, it seems likely that they were aware of and made use of certain natural energies for practical purposes connected with their way of life. Early settled societies were concerned above all with the fertility of land and livestock and communication with the local and ancestral spirits who were presumed to be the cause of human prosperity. The megalithic science is certain, therefore, to have been spiritually based. In simple nomadic times, communication with spirit was made naturally and spontaneously in the course of the annual journey; the science of early settled times was designed to make up for the loss of natural communication by a system of ritualized invocation. It was a form of magical technology. The power of the ancient shrines was augmented by the erection of stone monuments or temples, where the local spirit was induced to dwell and follow human example by becoming domestic. Where in the old wandering days the shrines had been active only during the short period when they were visited, their season of potency was now extended. How this was done is told symbolically in the heroic legends of the dragons or serpent killers. The serpent is an image of the mercurial earth currents by which the country is made fertile; transfixing the serpent's head with a stake or stone pillar is the traditional method of arresting and tapping its flow of energy. At Delphi, where in archaic times the Pythoness or earth serpent had dwelt and given oracles for a brief season in the year, the piercing of her head by Apollo's staff lengthened her period of efficacy by several months. The spot where her energies were centered was marked thereafter by the *omphalos* stone at the center of the shrine. Further information on the ancient sacred science and its perception of the nature and use of earth energies can be found in *The Decline of Oracles*, a work by Plutarch, who was a priest at Delphi in the first century A.D.

The religious-scientific works of the megalith builders,

along with domestic building and agriculture, produced a dramatic change in the appearance of the landscape. Yet the new pattern of temples, roads, and settlements was firmly based on the sacred geography of nomadic times. Temples and oratories were built on the old nature shrines, and the paths between them were still trodden by pilgrims or used for religious processions. On their straight course between the sacred places, the people erected stones and other landmarks, and thus were created the straight alignments of ancient monuments, known as "leys," which have been the subject of much modern research in the British landscape. These lines across the country were as sacred as the temples and shrines they linked, and evidently they played an essential part in the mystical megalithic science. Memories of the old times, preserved in the folklore record, identify the paths between the old shrines as ways of the dead and spirit paths, where at certain times of the year strange lights and phantom creatures are seen. Where the paths intersect, the old stone monuments have a variety of strange reputations, as the scenes of supernatural events or for powers of healing and fertility. The folklore of megalithic monuments forms a significant background to the modern scientific discoveries of abnormal energy patterns at the old sites.

In creating their sacred landscape, the Stone Age priests of settled times were careful to preserve the old pattern and the spiritual values attached to it. The temples and natural shrines about the country were seen as forming the body of one great temple, the native holy land. By a round of feasts and rituals throughout the year, the spirit of the earth was made content and bountiful, allowing the settled communities to grow and prosper. Archaeologists now reckon that the population of England in the second millennium B.C. was at least as large as the two to three million it was at the time of the Norman Conquest. Prehistoric standards of craftsmanship, science, and general culture were many degrees higher than those of medieval England.

THE CELTIC DRUIDS

The question of who invaded Britain in prehistoric times, and when these incursions took place, was much debated by earlier generations of scholars. Bloody battles were imagined, in which one race virtually exterminated another and populated the country anew. Mysterious "Beaker" folk were said to have arrived in the third millennium B.C., introducing metalwork and burying their chiefs in barrow tombs along with their favorite beakers. After them came the Celts; around 600 B.C. was the accepted date for their appearance in Britain.

The nature of these invasions and their supposed dates are all now disputed. Archaeological science earlier in this century was much concerned with racial types, and it was fashionable to argue that successive invaders prevailed because they were of superior stock to the natives. At the root of these theories were Darwin's theory of evolution and belief in progress. The influence of such theories has now waned, and scholars are more inclined to regard social changes as being produced by migrations of culture at least as much as by warfare. In ancient times, as today, new ideas spread quickly enough around the world without violence. Nor is there any more certainty about the date of the Celts' arrival. One can speak of Celtic culture and languages, but there is no single Celtic race; Celtic speakers vary in appearance from short and swarthy to tall and fair. Evidence of Celtic culture appears in Britain from the second millennium B.C., and it is now suggested that the Celtic priesthood could have been responsible for the Stonehenge temple, built in about 2000 B.C..

Celtic society in Britain preserved many features from the previous order, including shrines and feast days. Its calendar combined lunar and solar cycles, as in megalithic times. The social structure was similar to that advocated by Plato, based on a religious cosmology and democratic idealism. Each tribe had its own territory with fixed borders, and that land, held by the tribe as a whole, consisted of forest and wilderness, common lands and agricultural holdings. Under a complicated system of land tenure, everyone's rights and obligations were carefully defined. Some of the land was worked in common for the chieftain, the priests, and the old, poor, and sick tribesfolk; the rest was apportioned as family farms. Grazing and foraging rights were shared on the common lands. Much of the tribal business was conducted at annual assemblies, where land disputes were decided, petty offenders were tried, and chiefs and officials, both male and female, were appointed by popular vote. A great many old farmsteads in Britain today are on Celtic sites. During his raid on Celtic Britain in 55 B.C., Julius Caesar commented on its high population and numerous farms and cattle.

The unifying bond between all the Celtic tribes was their common priesthood, the Druids. Their efforts preserved common culture, religion, history, laws, scholarship, and science. They had paramount authority over every tribal chief and, since their office was sacred, they could move where they wanted, settling disputes and stopping battles by compelling the rival parties to arbitration. They managed the higher legal system and the courts of appeal, and their colleges in Britain were famous throughout the Continent. Up to twenty years of oral instruction and memorizing was required of a pupil before being admitted into their order. Minstrels and bards were educated by the Druids for similar periods.

Knowledge of the Druids comes directly from classical writers of their time. They were compared to the learned priesthoods of antiquity, the Indian Brahmins, the Pythagoreans, and the Chaldean astronomers of Babylon. Caesar wrote that they "know much about the stars and celestial

*A British Druid:
An eighteenth-century
image.*

motions, and about the size of the earth and universe, and
about the essential nature of things, and about the powers
and authority of the immortal gods; and these things they
teach to their pupils." They also taught the traditional
doctrine of the soul's immortality. They must have professed
detailed knowledge of the workings of reincarnation, for one
writer said that they allowed debts incurred in one lifetime to
be repaid in the next.

A significant remark of Caesar's was that Druidism originated in Britain, which was its stronghold. Indeed, it has all
the appearance of a native religion, being deeply rooted in
the primeval native culture. Its myths and heroic legends are
related to the ancient holy places of Britain, and they may
largely have been adapted from much earlier traditions. In
Celtic as in all previous times, the same holy wells and
nature shrines were visited on certain days for their spiritual
virtues. The overall pattern of life was scarcely changed. In
the course of time, society became more structured and
elaborate and the Druid laws more rigid, but the beginning
of the Celtic period in Britain was evidently not marked by
any major break in tradition. Nor was there any great shift in
population; the British today, even in the so-called Celtic
lands, are predominantly of native Mesolithic ancestry. The
Druids' religion and science also have the appearance of
belonging to an earlier Britain. Their knowledge of astronomy may have descended from the priests of megalithic
times, together with the spiritual secrets of the landscape.

Yet there is an obvious difference between the Celtic
Druids and the megalithic priests before them. The Druids

abandoned the great stone temples and reverted to the old natural shrines, the springs and groves where they held their rituals. A religious reformation is here implied. It is characteristic of state priesthoods that their spiritual powers wane as their temporal authority grows, and the less confidence they inspire, the more tributes and sacrifices they demand of the people. In its latter days the rule of the megalithic priesthood probably became so onerous that it was overthrown. Whether as a native development or prompted by outside influences, a spiritual revival seems to have occurred in Britain in about 2000 B.C., with the building of the cosmic temple of Stonehenge and the first evidences of Celtic culture. Stonehenge is a unique monument, a symbol of a new revelation. The tendency in modern scholarship is to see it once more as the temple of the Druids. If so, it proclaims the high ideals on which Druidism in Britain was founded.

ENGLAND'S FIRST CHRISTIANS

The date and circumstances of Christianity's origin in England are unknown. According to the legend of St. Joseph of Arimathea's missionary journey to Glastonbury, it was shortly after the Crucifixion. Bran the Blessed is credited by the Welsh with bringing Christianity to the British Isles in the first century, and there is a record of King Lucius's receiving missionaries from Rome in 167.

Although the Romans persecuted the early Church and made St. Alban the first English martyr at the end of the third century, their soldiers and officials in Britain were susceptible to the new religion and no doubt helped to spread it among the natives. Yet it was recorded by Tertullian in about 200 that there were Christian colonies in parts of Britain which the Romans never reached. Many other old writers remark on the early beginnings of Christianity in Britain, implying that it was never imposed on the Celtic culture but developed naturally from the existing religion as a reformation of Druidism.

The original institution of British Christianity was the Celtic Church. Its history, rituals, and above all its spirit were essentially different from those of the Roman Church. Its saints, as the early priests and holy men were called, were heirs to the Druid tradition, often literally so, in that many of them were children of Druids or former Druid priests themselves. Like the nonconformists of modern times, they rejected the formalism of the established religion and returned to the source of religious spirit in the wild places of the countryside. The doctrines of Christianity were not unfamiliar to them, for the Druids recognized the mystical Trinity, and the image of Divinity sacrificed on a cross or tree was significant in their own theology. Thus the Celtic Druids readily adopted Christianity in its original, gnostic form. Their Celtic Church was that of St. John the Divine, visionary and spiritual, rather than that of St. Peter in Rome.

In many ways the Celtic Church perpetuated the customs of the Druid religion from which it sprang. The Celtic monks adopted the Druid tonsure, shaving their heads across the crown from ear to ear and leaving it long behind. That was the tonsure of St. John rather than that of St. Peter, where the head is shaved on the crown. The Celts celebrated Easter on a day calculated by the Jewish lunar calendar, also used by the eastern churches, while the Roman calendar, as amended by a succession of popes, produced a different Easter Day.

As successors to the Druids, the Celtic bishops and priests were appointed by their own tribes and ministered to their own tribal districts. Their monasteries replaced the Druid colleges, which had been suppressed by the Romans, as centers of learning. In them were preserved the native traditions of philosophy, craftsmanship, and bardic lore. The wisdom and scholarship of the ancient world survived in the Celtic monasteries during the Dark Ages, when missionaries from Britain and Ireland spread the light of Christianized culture throughout Europe.

The Celtic Church was distinguished by its close relationship to nature, its belief in immortality and individual free will, its married priests and women saints, and its tolerance. These were also features of Druidism. Religious fanaticism was alien to the Celtic spirit. For several centuries Christians and pagans lived side by side, warring among themselves for traditional tribal reasons rather than for ideology. One of the last of the old-fashioned pagan kings, Penda of Mercia in the seventh century, fought his rivals, pagan and Christian alike, without rancor, and said that he had nothing against Christians except bad ones. Pagan kings married Christian princesses and allowed them to practice their own religion, and the Christians refrained from aggressive proselytizing. One complaint the Roman Church brought against the Celts was that they were not active enough in the missionary field.

When the Roman legions withdrew from Britain at the end of the fourth century, leaving cities, temples, and great country houses to fall into ruin, the only cultural institution remaining in these islands was the Celtic Church. Native and classical learning was upheld in its monasteries, which were the sole providers of higher education. Pagan nobles sent their children to them, and thus Christianity began to prevail in the ruling families. Pagan customs were long maintained throughout the countryside, but among educated people paganism was regarded as outmoded and provincial. Christianity had become the religion of modern international culture.

THE END OF THE CELTIC CHURCH

The Church of Rome was long jealous of Celtic independence and disapproved of the pagan customs and doctrines that the Celtic Church had adopted. When St. Augustine was sent to England by the pope in 597, his mission was both to convert the pagan kingdoms of the Anglo-Saxons and to bring the native church under Roman discipline. The Celtic bishops refused to oblige him, but Roman influence nevertheless began to prevail. Rome was the world center of power and scholarship and was thus naturally attractive to ambitious clerics. Rome's constant appeal was for worldwide Christian unity, by which it meant total subservience to Rome. Some of the Celtic clergy thought the price was worth paying, while others were firm in preserving the traditional rites of their church.

The two sides met in 664 at a synod or church council in Whitby, a town on the east coast of Yorkshire with a Celtic abbey founded by St. Hilda. The immediate point at issue was the date of Easter and whether it should properly be calculated by the Celtic or the Roman method. Attached to this was the whole question of whether the Celts should keep their independent rites or whether they should reject them in favor of Rome's.

At the Synod of Whitby, Bishop Colman of Lindisfarne spoke for the Celtic Church. Being Irish, he was not fluent in the Saxon English language of the debate. Opposing him was Bishop Wilfrid, a man of formidable intellect and ambition with powerful connections in Rome. His patron, King Oswy of Northumbria, presided over the debate. He may not have understood the subtle arguments which both sides produced, for he settled the issue on one simple point. Colman claimed the apostolic descent of his church from St. John. Wilfrid asserted the seniority of the Roman Church's founder, St. Peter. King Oswy knew of St. Peter as the keeper of the gates to heaven and said that he would not dare to offend him for fear of being refused admittance. He therefore awarded victory to the Roman party.

Bishop Colman resigned his see at Lindisfarne and retired with a few followers to the old Celtic monastery at Iona. Even there the Roman influence was soon apparent, and the Celtic diehards found their last refuge on an island off the Irish coast.

The absorption of the Celtic Church by the Roman caused pain and resentment but no bloodshed. The Celtic virtue of tolerance was displayed by many priests of the old church who accepted with good grace the new order and worked peacefully to implement it. One example was St. Cuthbert, who obeyed the Synod by converting to Rome and was then sent as prior to Lindisfarne, where he tactfully persuaded the monks to abandon their Celtic practices. Compromises were allowed and local customs were often respected, with the result that the Roman Church in Britain became subject to Celtic influence. That influence can be seen most clearly today in Ireland, where feast days and pilgrimages from Celtic and pagan times are patronized by the Church.

In England the traditions of Celtic Christianity were

inherited by the Saxons whom the Celtic saints converted. Their churches were built on the old sanctuaries, and their sacred art followed Celtic models. The Celtic spirits survived the Norman invasion. Medieval kings boasted of their Celtic lineage from King Arthur, and Celtic ideals were revived in the age of chivalry. In churches and cathedrals the medieval craftsmen carved symbolic figures that had nothing to do with Roman Christianity but reflected the Celtic love of nature and humanity. Mystics in all ages have been inspired by the memory of Celtic Christianity.

CONTINUITY AND REFORMATION

Stability and change are the two opposing principles in nature that lie behind the world of appearances. In English religious history they are represented by the two themes which govern its entire course: continuity and reformation.

Continuity is demonstrated by the ancient, enduring sanctity of many of the great religious centers. It is illustrated, for example, by the prehistoric holy wells which are found beneath such cathedrals as York, Winchester, Carlisle, and Ely and at innumerable parish churches.

Reformation plays a necessary part in religious history because spiritual powers can never adequately be confined, codified, or institutionalized. All man-made systems are imperfect and doomed sooner or later to fail. The more powerful and elaborate they become, the nearer they are to collapse. Religion expresses the communion between the human spirit and the divine spirit in nature. That communion can be achieved through various forms of magical or religious techniques, by invocation in appropriately designed temples, or through sacred architecture, chants, music, incense, and images in dimly lit cathedrals. These methods are of course artificial, and the more ritualized they become, the more they diverge from the simple, natural processes of spiritual communion. When a religious system becomes too formal and oppressive, religious people abandon it and return to the natural sources of spirit in the wild places of the countryside. There they build shrines and oratories, thus beginning a new cycle of religious development.

Sacred places are not fixed and permanent. Formerly great shrines are abandoned and desecrated; others spring up with the cult of a saint or a memorable person and fade away with it. Then there are places such as Stonehenge, which retain their reputation for sanctity but, through losing their local populations, or for some other reason, fall aside from the mainstream of religious continuity. Yet many of the sites described in this book have been religious centers since before the dawn of history, and they illustrate the themes of continuity and reformation.

2

LONDON: THE CITY OF KING BRUTUS

Most visitors to Britain arrive first in London, and they are likely to spend at least a few days in that great and marvelous city. There are many good reasons for doing so. As an international center of business and finance, of art, fashion, and entertainment, London has attractions for everyone. Yet despite its popularity and the masses who flock to it every year, London is still the most secretive of cities. Even to its seven million inhabitants it is largely unknown territory, and its strange, complicated character is but slowly revealed to visitors. Its very origins are rooted in mystery. Modern scholarship attributes its foundation to the Romans, but its traditional history goes back to at least a thousand years before the invasion of the legions, to the time of the legendary first king of Britain, Brutus the Trojan, who set up his capital in London and gave it its first known name, New Troy, latinized as Tri-Novantum. Thus on Caesar's second incursion into Britain, in 54 B.C., the people he found occupying London and the territory to the north were called the Tri-Novantes.

According to the old British chronicles, King Lud, the sixty-eighth ruler after Brutus, fortified London in about 70 B.C. and gave it its present name, a corruption of Lud-Dun, Lud's fortress. His name is also remembered in Ludgate Circus and Ludgate Hill, the site of St. Paul's Cathedral. The old Lud Gate itself, the western entrance through the city walls, displayed heroic statues of King Lud and his two sons. When the gate was taken down in 1760, the statues were preserved and are now to be seen in the Church of St. Dunstan in Fleet Street.

The legendary burial place of King Brutus is the Bryn Gwyn or White Mound on which the Tower of London now stands. There also, in the fifth century B.C., was interred Molmutius, the twenty-first king in line, who built highways across the length and breadth of Britain and first codified the native British laws. His Molmutian Code, defining the rights, duties, and privileges of a citizen, was incorporated in the Anglo-Saxon laws and is thus at the foundation of

English law today. Drawn up as triads in the Druidic manner, it reflects the simple dignity of its age. The following are some extracts.

> There are three tests of civil liberty: equality of rights; equality of taxation; freedom to come and go.
>
> There are three causes which ruin a state: inordinate privileges; corruption of justice; national apathy.
>
> There are three guarantees of society: security for life and limb; security for property; security of the rights of nature.
>
> There are three things free to every man, Briton or foreigner: water from spring, river, or well; firewood from a decayed tree; a block of stone not in use.
>
> There are three persons entitled to public maintenance: the old; the babe; the foreigner who cannot speak the British tongue.

Other provisions included the right of suffrage, male and female. In those days, it was claimed, a stranger not speaking the language could pass unmolested through Britain, meeting hospitality wherever he went.

Shakespeare in his play *Cymbeline* (Kymbelin, the seventy-first British king, in 22 B.C.) says that "Molmutius made our laws" and calls him the first to be crowned king. His source was probably Holinshed's *Chronicles* of 1577, where it is said that previous rulers were known as chiefs. Therein also is the story of the magical ruler Bladud, who flew with artificial wings and crashed upon the present site of St. Paul's, and the tragedy of the son who succeeded him as Leir II (Shakespeare's King Lear).

Molmutius is also credited with instituting the Law of Sanctuary, whereby the holy places were made inviolable refuge for criminals, fugitives, and victims of persecution. That law, reaffirmed by the first Christian rulers, survived up to the Reformation in the sixteenth century. Its pagan origin was not then openly acknowledged, but its great antiquity was made the basis of a plea before the House of Commons in 1555, when Abbot Fackenham tried unsuccessfully to defend the sanctuary at Westminster, threatened by Henry VIII. It had first been instituted, he claimed, by the Christian convert King Lucius early in the second century A.D., after he had destroyed a pagan temple on the same site.

The enlightened policies of Molmutius were followed by his son, Belinus, who has left his name in Billingsgate (Belin's Gate). He extended the sanctity of the holy places to the ways of travel and pilgrimage between them by land and water. The proclamation was framed in traditional style: "There are three things free to a country and its borders: the rivers, the roads, and the places of worship. These are under the protection of God and His peace. Whoever on or within them draws weapons against anyone is a criminal." We still remember this law in the designation Queen's (or King's) Highway, which should ensure free and unmolested passage on public thoroughfares. Footpads, muggers, and highwaymen have historically been punished with extra severity because, in violating the sanctuary of the highroad, they added sacrilege to crime.

Every Londoner in Shakespeare's day was familiar with the legends of the old Trojan kings and with the spots associated with them. Such popular knowledge has since been educated away, and children can no longer delight in the tales of a Brutus who conquered Britain from the giants, of Bladud the aeronaut, and the rest of their fabulous dynasty. The first important historian to deny their authenticity was William Camden, whose *Britannia* of 1607 omitted their entire record. Thereby, said one of his critics, he "blew off 60 kings at one blast." Camden's skepticism was reasonable in his time because the antiquity of London was then unknown. Since the 1940s, however, when German wartime bombing destroyed much of London's old City area and allowed archaeologists to investigate beneath the ruins, it has become recognized that many of its churches and monuments were built over sites which go back to Roman and earlier times. This has caused renewed interest in the histories of the old kings and their legendary links with the sacred places of their former capital. In the following descriptions of London's churches and pilgrimage places, the antiquity of their foundations is emphasized. Centuries of history are reflected in their architecture and monuments, but their main attraction to pilgrims is the atmosphere of peace and sanctity which in some cases they have retained from prehistoric times.

WESTMINSTER ABBEY

There is no more hallowed ground in England than the site of Westminster Abbey on the old Isle of Thorns, or Thorney Island. Formerly it was insulated by the Thames, and by two arms of the River Tyburn now buried in pipes. According to its earliest legends, it was a sacred island in prehistoric times, the site of a royal palace, a Druid college, and religious monuments, the last of which, a conical mound of assembly called Tothill, was destroyed some centuries ago. There is no written or archaeological record of those times or of the first Christian foundation there. The tradition is that the Christian convert King Lucius, early in the second century, built the first church on Thorney in place of an older temple to Apollo. The Saxon King Sebert in the seventh century is also claimed as the founder, but all traces of previous churches on the site of Westminster Abbey were obliterated by King Edward the Confessor, whose magnificent church to St. Peter, much the same size as the present abbey, was consecrated in 1065 on the eve of the Norman Conquest. This saintly king was canonized in 1161, and his shrine within the abbey became famous as a place of miracles and pilgrimage. When, after the Conquest, the Saxon bishops

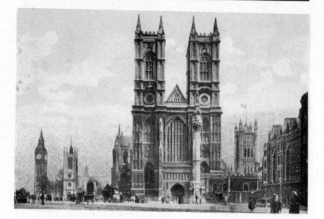

The west front of Westminster Abbey with Big Ben on the left (1922 postcard).

were required to resign their sees, one of them, Wulfstan of Worcester, refused to do so. Appealing to the spirit of the Confessor, he thrust his staff into the old king's tomb, where it remained upright and immovable. Hearing of this wonder, King William admitted that the bishop had made good his case and allowed him to continue in office.

Nothing but the foundation now remains of King Edward's church, which was rebuilt entirely in the thirteenth century and achieved its present form in 1745, when the west towers, designed by Sir Christopher Wren, were finally completed.

Among the holy relics that once attracted pilgrims to the abbey were the Virgin Mary's girdle (presented by the Confessor), some blood of Christ in a crystal vase, a print of His foot on a stone, and a piece of the True Cross. Today these relics are no longer counted among the abbey's treasures, but in their place is an awesome collection of tombs and monuments illustrating every aspect and period of England's history. Their combined effect, together with the natural and accumulated sanctity of the place, is profoundly moving. Every visitor will find a great deal more of interest in the abbey than can be mentioned here; all that can be described below are some of those sights which no one will want to miss.

The Nave

Entering the nave through the western entrance between Wren's towers, one is struck immediately by the solemn atmosphere and the profusion of monuments on all sides. Some are noble and beautiful while others, to modern eyes, may seem absurdly elaborate and garish, though no doubt all were thought appropriate in their time. Straight ahead in the center is the tomb of the Unknown Warrior, containing the remains of an unidentified British soldier brought back from a French battlefield of World War I. He stands for all the victims of that dreadful massacre and has come to represent for many people the hosts of humble warriors from all nations who have given their lives in subsequent conflicts. Above the west door is the monument to William Pitt, England's youngest-ever prime minister at the age of twenty-four, and at the far end of the nave lie the great physicists William Kelvin, Ernest Rutherford, and J. J. Thompson, near the very fine marble monument to Sir Isaac Newton.

Beyond the nave are the aisles to the choir, with many monuments to great people of the eighteenth and nineteenth centuries. The musicians Edward Elgar, Henry Purcell, and Ralph Vaughan Williams are also commemorated; so are John Wesley, the founder of Methodism; the antislavery campaigner William Wilberforce; and Admiral Sir Cloudsley Shovell, who distinguished himself in 1707 by running his ship aground on one of the Scilly Isles, whereupon a local woman murdered him on the rocks and chopped off his fingers to steal an emerald ring. His elaborate monument was carved by Grinling Gibbons. Also to be seen are the heads of Charles Darwin and Alfred Wallace, whose theory of evolution set up a rival creation myth to that of the Church.

The Choir and Sanctuary
Since the time of Harold, the last Saxon king, the monarchs of England have always been crowned within the inner sanctuary of the abbey. On its floor is a pavement of Cosmati

*The choir of
Westminster Abbey*

mosaic work, geometrically designed to represent the Ptole-
maic, geocentric view of the world. It is thought that the
mosaic and porphyry materials for the work were the gift of
the pope in 1268. The stalls and pews in the choir are of no
antiquity, having been made in 1848, but they are impres-
sively ornamental and in the Gothic style.

St. Edward the Confessor's Chapel

This is the sacred heart of the abbey, the site of its most
precious relics. At the center, behind the altar, is the shrine
of the Confessor. It has lost its former splendor, the jewels
and golden images that once bedecked it having been
wrenched away during the dissolution of the monasteries in
1540. The saintly king died in 1066, and when his tomb was
reopened in 1102 the body was found to be entire, yellow-
bearded, and with its limbs still supple. So many pilgrims
used to flock to the shrine that the stone floor to the niches
at its base has been worn down by people kneeling there in
search of cures. On the fifteenth-century stone screen at the
west end of the chapel are carved scenes from St. Edward's
life and visionary experiences. Around him lie five other
kings and four queens, mostly represented by wonderful
effigies. Among them are Edward I, who brought the
Coronation Stone to the abbey, and his queen, Eleanor of
Castile. They were crowned together in the abbey after they
returned from the Crusades, where Eleanor is said to have
saved her husband's life by sucking poison from his wound.
After she died at Harby, Nottinghamshire, in 1209, it took

*The reconstructed
shrine of St. Edward
the Confessor.*

several days to bear her embalmed body to the abbey; wherever her body rested on the journey, tall stone crosses were erected and various of her organs were deposited beneath them.

The Coronation Stone   At the west end of St. Edward's Chapel is the Coronation Chair, containing England's most sacred stone. Next to it is a huge sword, eighteen pounds in weight, which belonged to Edward III.

The Coronation Chair and the Stone of Scone lodged within it.

The Coronation Stone is lodged beneath the seat of the chair and is fixed to it by iron clamps. Legend identifies it as the stone, described in Genesis 28:18, that Jacob used for a pillow during his prophetic dream at Bethel, after which he set it up as a monument and anointed it. Jacob's sons are said to have carried it to Egypt, and thence it was taken to Spain. When Simon Brech, the son of the Spanish king, invaded Ireland in about 700 B.C., he took the stone with him. It was placed on the holy hill of Tara and became known as the Lia-Fail, the Stone of Destiny. For about a thousand years the kings of Ireland were crowned upon it. When a king of the royal line sat upon it, the stone groaned aloud, but for false pretenders it remained silent. During the fifth century it was taken to Scotland and became the coronation seat of the Scottish monarchy. For some four and a half centuries it was kept at the monastery of Scone (for which it is known as the Stone of Scone—pronounced "scoon") until in 1296 Edward I of England seized it and placed it beneath the seat of the Coronation Chair, on which the monarchs of England have ever since been crowned. An early Scottish king, Kenneth, composed a Latin verse upon it, translated as:

> If Fates go right, where'er this stone is found,
> The Scots shall monarchs of that realm be found.

The prophecy was fulfilled by the accession of James VI of Scotland as James I of England. The present queen, Elizabeth II, lays stress upon her Scottish ancestry, as a token of her legitimacy through the stone, which links the British monarchy with the old kings of Israel.

Only twice in almost seven hundred years has the stone been taken out of the abbey. The first occasion was in 1653, when Oliver Cromwell had himself installed as Lord Protector upon it in Westminster Hall. The second was in 1950, when a party of young Scots raided the abbey by night and succeeded in removing it. They attempted to find a refuge for it in a Scottish cathedral, but none of the authorities they approached would have anything to do with it. Meanwhile, the coronation of Elizabeth II was almost due, and there was great consternation about the missing stone. Just in time its captors relented and revealed its hiding place to the police, by whom it was restored to the abbey.

The Chapels
The ambulatory north of the sanctuary leads to a number of chapels, each with its own peculiar history and monuments. Most remarkable among them is the Nightingale monument to a lady of that name who died in childbirth. The fine allegorical sculpture by Roubiliac in 1761 shows a husband trying to shield his wife from the sword of Death. It stands in the St. Michael Chapel. In the ambulatory adjoining it is the colossal monument to General James Wolfe, who took Quebec. Particularly rich is the Chapel of St. John the Baptist, where stands the tallest monument in the abbey, to Lord Hunsdon, cousin and chief bodyguard to Elizabeth I. He is said to have died of grief when his promotion to the title Earl of Wiltshire was temporarily delayed. In the center of the chapel lies the effigy of the queen's favorite, the Earl of Essex, and on the south wall appears the kneeling figure of Mrs. Mary Kendall, whose claim to fame is that she "liv'd with the Lady Catherine Jones."

The theme of octagonal geometry in the chapter house of Westminster Abbey is most purely expressed in the pattern which springs from the top of the central pillar.

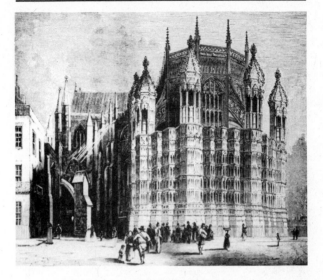

The exterior of Henry VII's Chapel.

Henry VII's Chapel

Situated at the east end of the abbey, the glorious Henry VII's Chapel has been called one of the wonders of the world. Even though its original stained glass was destroyed, the light and atmosphere within it are superb. Around it are royal and noble tombs and statues of saints, and beneath its magnificent fan-vaulted roof hang the colorful banners of the knights of the Order of the Bath, whose members are installed here.

In the north aisle, where one first enters, is the tomb of Elizabeth I, who presided over an heroic age of poetry and invention. Her effigy is thought to be a lifelike portrait. Next to her and below is her half sister and royal predecessor, Queen Mary. During the reigns of these two ladies, many good Christians, Protestant and Catholic, were tortured, burned alive, or cruelly executed. Yet here they lie in peace together, and a touching inscription refers to the two sisters hoping for the one resurrection. Beyond them, at the east end of the aisle, is Innocents' Corner, where, between monuments to infant daughters of James I, a sarcophagus contains bones unearthed in the Tower of London during Charles II's reign. He believed them to be the remains of the tragic young "princes in the tower," supposedly murdered in 1483 by order of their uncle, Richard III.

Opposite, in the south aisle, is the splendid tomb of Mary, Queen of Scots, who, as an unsuccessful rival to Queen Elizabeth for the throne, suffered the consequences and was beheaded in 1587. Next to her is the romantic "Winter Queen," Elizabeth of Bohemia, daughter of James I. After the tragic death of her husband, Frederick, whose ambition

Henry VII's Chapel, Westminster Abbey.

was to turn his realm into an ideal kingdom, she retired to London and died there in peace.

Poets' Corner
The south transept of the abbey is where literary visitors linger, for there is the famous Poets' Corner, where writers of the greatest genius or reputation are commemorated on every side. Here is a roll call of English letters. The senior occupant is the poet Chaucer, who died in 1400, and after him come Shakespeare, Dryden, Spenser, Jonson, Milton, Blake, Keats, Shelley, Burns, the Brontës, Wordsworth, Tennyson, Coleridge, Thackeray, Dickens, Kipling, Hardy, Henry James, Auden. The effect of all these great names crowded together, as at a dream literary party, is overpowering. It is a relief to step aside into the peaceful Chapel of St. Faith, to the south of Poets' Corner, which is furnished for rest and meditation.

The Cloisters and Museum
A walk around the cool, dimly lighted cloisters, with a glance at the many curious monuments displayed on its walls, makes an agreeable end to one's progress through the abbey. Steps from its north side lead down to the crypt, where, among heavy Norman pillars, is the abbey museum. Among its exhibits is an astounding collection of royal and other effigies. It was the custom from at least the fourteenth century for a dressed, lifelike effigy to be exhibited at a great person's funeral and after the burial. Those in the museum include accurate representations of Charles II, Elizabeth I, Anne, and William and Mary. Admiral Nelson is there with

his face and dress as in life, and there are actual death masks of Edward III and Henry VII. By these relics English history is brought to life in the imagination.

Beyond the cloisters and the abbey is Dean's Yard, the ancient Westminster boys' school, and the many historic buildings which occupy the area of the former sanctuary, where those who took refuge were free from persecution. To violate the sanctuary by harassing its inmates was an act of sacrilege. A scandalous episode in the fourteenth century, when blood was shed within the sanctuary, resulted in the abbey's being closed for four months for cleansing and reconsecration.

WESTMINSTER ABBEY is open to visitors Monday through Friday, 9 to 4, and Saturdays, 9 to 2. Admission to royal chapels £1.50, to museum 50p. Underground station: Westminster.

ST. PAUL'S CATHEDRAL

Rising 365 feet above the summit of Ludgate Hill, the dome and lantern of St. Paul's were designed to dominate the City, and they form one of the most familiar symbols of London. From times unknown this has been a sacred spot. The great Roman temple there, said to have been dedicated to Diana, supplanted an earlier shrine traditionally associated with Brutus, Lud, and the old Trojan dynasty. At the northeast corner of the present churchyard stood the famous Paul Cross, marking a hallowed place of assembly where London citizens once exercised their democratic rights to discuss and legislate the affairs of their city. Adjoining it was a tower for the bell that summoned the people to meetings. In later times the cross was a popular resort for preachers and

St. Paul's Cathedral, London.

orators. The public's rights there were jealously guarded for centuries; there was outrage in 1321 when the St. Paul's authorities tried to seize the common land, and nearly three hundred years later the Lord Mayor asserted the City's rights to an area around the cross which, he said, had belonged to the London people "time out of mind."

The Roman temple had long crumbled when, in the seventh century, a Saxon church and monastery were built on its site and Mellitus, a companion of St. Augustine, became the first Bishop of London. Little is known of these buildings, which were destroyed by fire in about 1088. "Old St. Paul's" was then built, a cathedral even larger than the present one, with a spire in excess of 460 feet tall. This was one of the great churches of Christendom, filled with monuments to the important and noble people buried there. One of the Saxon tombs preserved in it was that of the memorably named Ethelred the Unready. He is listed, along with many other ancient notables whose monuments have since been destroyed, on the wall of the crypt below the present cathedral.

Old St. Paul's was so badly damaged by the Great Fire of London in 1666 that it was considered beyond repair. Sir Christopher Wren was made principal architect, not only for the new cathedral but for the entire city. The St. Paul's which he first planned can be seen today, in the form of a large wooden model, in the cathedral crypt. He described it as "something coloss and beautiful, conforming to the best style of Greek and Roman architecture." When this design was rejected, he drew up another in the same classical style. King Charles approved it, and construction began in 1675. Not until 1710 was the dome completed. It is not surprising that, with so many other churches and important building works to attend to, Wren was sometimes distracted from his major project, but the slowness of the work gave his rivals an opportunity to air their jealousy. Wren was accused of delaying the finish of St. Paul's in order to retain his annual salary (which was no more than £200). The commissioners who employed him began to obstruct and meddle with his work. One of their requirements was that the side walls of the cathedral be topped by a balustrade, which, said Wren, was done to suit the ladies, "who think nothing well without an edging." At the age of eighty-five he was forced to resign his post as architect. Yet he bore no resentment; retiring to the country, he spent his last four years quietly studying philosophy. On his death he was given the honor due to him, burial in St. Paul's. Above his tomb, in the southeast corner of the crypt, is the Latin inscription *Si monumentum requiris circumspice,* "If you wish to see his monument, look around you."

Even on a summer day, when crowded with visitors, the interior of St. Paul's has a sobering, awesome effect that is experienced most fully in early morning and at dusk. Those who stand beneath and look up into the dome may feel themselves to be an integral part of a vast, ordered universe. By a winding stone staircase one can climb aloft, first to the Whispering Gallery, famous for its strange acoustical properties, and then, if weather permits, to the very summit of the dome, where one can see the great bulk of the cathedral as a whole and gaze out for miles and miles across London to the distant country.

The custom of memorializing great people within St. Paul's was not started again until about a century after its rebuilding, but in the nineteenth century it was carried on with a vengeance, and the place is now thronged with tombs and monuments. Great warriors abound. In the subterranean crypt, the largest in Europe, Admiral Horatio Nelson holds the place of honor directly below the dome. Around him lie his commanders, accompanied by a veritable army of heroes. The black marble sarcophagus containing Nelson's body has a curious history. Originally it was constructed to hold Cardinal Wolsey within the chapel at Windsor, but he died in disgrace and was buried somewhere less important, leaving his funeral container without a tenant until the victor of Trafalgar was deemed worthy of occupying it. East of Nelson is the even more splendid tomb of the Duke of Wellington, made of a rare Cornish marble, dark purple and studded with quartz. Along with the military men are many other heroes, of literature, art, and music. Near Wren's tomb is the painters' corner, where lie Reynolds, West, Opie, Lawrence, Turner, Landseer, Millais, and Holman Hunt, whose picture of Christ, *The Light of the World,* hangs above in the south aisle. A rare feast of monumental sculpture is

St. Paul's Cathedral. The view through the choir to beneath the dome has now been opened by the removal of the screen, shown here as Wren designed it.

St. Faith, the church below Old St. Paul's.

offered throughout the building, from the grandiose tomb of Lord Melbourne, Queen Victoria's first prime minister, to the suitably humane statue for Florence Nightingale. Many of these objects are immensely elaborate. Often they serve to illustrate the transience of fame; for it is frequently the case that the most pompous monuments are to people of whom one has heard absolutely nothing at all.

The spot which has the greatest air of sanctity within the whole of St. Paul's is at the east end of the crypt. Above it was once a parish church, pulled down in the thirteenth century when the old cathedral was enlarged to cover its site. The crypt of that church preserved its memory as the church of St. Faith-below-St. Paul. Now it is the chapel of the Order of the British Empire, for those judged to have given outstanding service to their country. Its furnishings are modern, but its atmosphere is that of a Grail chapel. Intimate and family ceremonies of baptism, confirmation, marriage, and memorial are now held there.

ST. PAUL'S is open Monday through Friday, 8 to 7 (to 5 in winter), and Saturday, 11 to 3:15. Admission is free, but donations are solicited and small charges are made for entry to the east end, upper galleries, and crypt (open 10 to 3:15). Underground station: St. Paul's.

THE CITY OF LONDON CHURCHES

The oldest part of London, known as the City or the Square Mile, is the area around St. Paul's formerly enclosed by the Roman wall. Today it is the business center, dominated by monstrous office buildings and with very few residents, but up to the nineteenth century it was densely populated, and before the Great Fire of 1666 it contained about a hundred tiny parishes, each with its own church. Only a few of them survived the fire, of which eight remain intact. Sir Christopher Wren rebuilt fifty-one of them, mostly on the old foundations, while he was planning the new St. Paul's. Many have since been demolished—shamefully—to make room for offices, and one of them, St. Mary Aldermanbury, was packed off to America in the 1940s to be reerected on the Westminster College campus in Fulton, Missouri. All the City churches were damaged and some were destroyed by the bombing of London during World War II. After the war, those which could be saved were lovingly restored by their parishioners, aided by benefactors and skilled craftsmen. There are now thirty-nine old churches in the City, together with a number of towers and graveyards marking former sites.

For all the damage it caused to London's historic sanctuaries, the bombing had one useful consequence. By exposing foundations, it allowed archaeologists to investigate previous buildings on the sites. The results were astonishing. Over and again it was found that sites which had previously been thought of as medieval were in fact far older, going back to Saxon, Roman, and even earlier times. Examples of previous buildings below existing churches can be seen at the Church of All Hallows by the Tower and St. Bride in Fleet Street, which is built over a prehistoric holy well, as is St. Olave in Hart Street. Reputedly the oldest of London

The dome of St. Paul's rising behind an assembly of towers and steeples designed by Sir Christopher Wren for the City churches.

churches, St. Peter, Cornhill, stands on the highest ground in the City, probably over a pagan shrine.

From the proportion of City church sites which, upon investigation, have proved to be ancient, it seems likely that most churches were founded, like St. Paul's, on places of pre-Christian sanctity. No city is more tenacious in its traditions than London, where parishes still exist which for centuries have had no church of their own. They have odd names—St. Dionis Backchurch, St. Peter-le-Poer, St. Benet Fink—whose meanings in some cases are now unknown and may have pagan references. This archaic pattern of church sites and parish boundaries is a relic of prehistoric London, a link between today's mighty center of commerce and the pre-Roman metropolis of King Brutus's dynasty.

LONDON STONE

While visiting City churches, one is likely to go down Cannon Street. On its north side, opposite Cannon Street Station, is a monument of such insignificance that most passersby do not even glance at it. It is nothing more than a gnarled, blackened lump of limestone, about eighteen inches square, lodged within a niche in a wall of a bank and protected from touch by a stout iron grating. This is the famous London Stone, which marks the centerpoint of the City.

Once it was part of something larger, a pillar or cross that stood on the other side of the street. The building of the station was the cause of its removal in the nineteenth century. The stone was then placed in the wall of St. Swithun's churchyard, but the church was ruined by bombing in World War II and was demolished in 1962 to make way for commercial development. London Stone was kept on the same spot within the wall of the new building.

Nothing is known of its early history and only traces of its legend have survived, but according to them, London Stone is mystically connected to the whole destiny of the city: The fate of the stone is the fate of London. For that reason it has been preserved and protected. When Jack Cade entered the city in 1450, leading his rebellious band of Kentish peasants, the first thing he did was to ride up to the stone and strike it with his sword. By that gesture, he claimed, he became the rightful lord of London. The populace at that time must certainly have been aware of the significance of his act.

The name of a twelfth-century Lord Mayor, Fitzaylwin of Londonstone, prompted a theory that the stone was originally from his house, but scholars place it's origin much earlier than that time. Cannon Street is on the line of a Roman or possibly pre-Roman road, and London Stone is thought to have been the omphalos or sacred center of London, where all roads to the City met and from which distances were measured. The antiquarian Sir Lawrence Gomme supposed that it marked the site of a folk moot, "where the suiters of an open-air assembly were accustomed to gather together and legislate for the government of the City." The wall into which the stone is built is that of a Chinese banking corporation, which may not be by chance since the Chinese are adept at locating their houses and businesses at spots of mystical significance which attract good luck and prosperity.

It is hardly worth a special visit, but if one is passing London Stone, one might pause to consider the crowds who flock to Piccadilly Circus in the belief that it is the center of London, whereas the true center is exactly where one is standing.

THE OLD CITY CHURCHES

The City churches are the hidden shrines of London. Each has its peculiar character and atmosphere, developed over many centuries. Their individuality is not impaired by the fact that most of the existing buildings were designed by one man, Sir Christopher Wren. His policy was to rebuild on their old foundations the churches destroyed by the Great Fire, often reproducing their former features. The parishioners usually wanted their new church to retain the spirit of the old, and Wren was able to oblige them. With the aid of expert craftsmen he created an astonishing range of architectural forms, designed in the classical manner according to the ancient principles of harmonic proportion that had been rediscovered at the Renaissance. The exteriors of Wren's churches are generally plain and simple, for they were originally hidden by shops and houses, but his towers and steeples, which once formed the London skyline, were given elaborate detail and symbolism. Often they were meant to be seen from certain vantage points in relation to each other; one example is the dome of St. Paul's, which from Fleet Street is seen perfectly bisected by the spire of St. Martin.

Since the nineteenth century Wren's grand design of the City has been blotted out by commercial development and is now apparent only in glimpses. Many of its details, however, can still be appreciated. All over the City, Wren's little churches continue to defy the monopoly of the office buildings, and where they have been destroyed there is often a tower, a graveyard, or a secluded garden to mark the site. Such places are much valued by City workers who meet, meditate, and eat sandwiches there, and the surviving churches are as active as they have ever been. Daytime services, talks, concerts, and exhibitions are held in them, and each one has a special function, from sheltering the homeless to accommodating the rich and secretive City guilds. The following directory of the remaining City churches gives brief notes; further details can be found in the guides which are available in most of the churches. Opening times are given here as advertised, but they are subject to variation and can be confirmed by telephoning the office of the Area Dean: 623 6970.

CHURCHES IN THE CITY OF LONDON

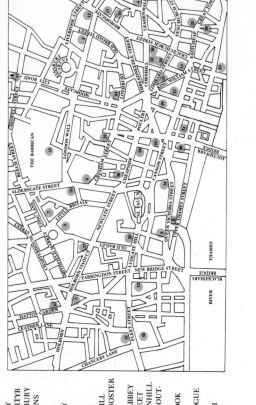

1. ALL HALLOWS-BY-THE-TOWER
2. ALL HALLOWS-ON-THE-WALL
3. ST. ANDREW, HOLBORN
4. ST. ANDREW UNDERSHAFT
5. ST. ANDREW-BY-THE-
   WARDROBE
6. ST. ANNE AND ST. AGNES
7. ST. BARTHOLOMEW-THE-
   GREAT
8. ST. BARTHOLOMEW-THE-LESS
9. ST. BENET
10. ST. BOTOLPH, ALDERSGATE
    STREET
11. ST. BOTOLPH, ALDGATE
12. ST. BOTOLPH, BISHOPSGATE
13. ST. BRIDE
14. ST. CLEMENT
15. ST. DUNSTAN-IN-THE-WEST
16. ST. EDMUND, KING AND
    MARTYR
17. ST. ETHELBURGA
18. ST. GILES, CRIPPLEGATE
19. ST. HELEN, BISHOPSGATE
20. ST. JAMES, GARLICKHYTHE
21. ST. KATHERINE CREE
22. ST. LAWRENCE JEWRY
23. ST. MAGNUS-THE-MARTYR
24. ST. MARGARET LOTHBURY
25. ST. MARGARET PATTENS
26. ST. MARTIN
27. ST. MARY ABCHURCH
28. ST. MARY ALDERMARY
29. ST. MARY-LE-BOW
30. ST. MARY-AT-HILL
31. ST. MARY WOOLNOTH
32. ST. MICHAEL, CORNHILL
33. ST. MICHAEL, PATERNOSTER
    ROYAL
34. ST. NICHOLAS COLE ABBEY
35. ST. OLAVE, HART STREET
36. ST. PETER-UPON-CORNHILL
37. ST. SEPULCHRE-WITHOUT-
    NEWGATE
38. ST. STEPHEN WALBROOK
39. ST. VEDAST
40. BEVIS MARKS SYNAGOGUE
41. WESLEY'S CHAPEL
42. THE TEMPLE CHURCH
43. ST. ETHELDREDA

All Hallows-by-the-Tower This church, which stands opposite the Tower of London, survived the Great Fire but was
destroyed (except for the tower) by the bombing in World
War II. Beneath the ruins were found the remains of a Saxon
church, a stone cross, and other relics. Below the tower is a
Roman pavement laid over earlier foundations; the site is
evidently very ancient. In the museum below the church are
Roman and other valuable objects, and there is a model of
Roman London. William Penn was baptized in the church,
and President John Quincy Adams was married there. It was
rebuilt after the war. Open daily, 9 to 6; Saturday and
Sunday, 10 to 6.

All Hallows-on-the-Wall, London Wall. The north wall, with
steps to the pulpit, is on the old City wall. There was
probably a shrine here in ancient times. The medieval
church served a local colony of hermits. Bombed during the
war, the church was restored in 1962 and has regained its
beautiful interior. Open Monday through Friday, 9 to 5.

St. Andrew, Holborn, Holborn Circus. Located on the site of
a Saxon church recorded in 951, restored after the fire and
once again after being bombed in the war, the present
church has a large, light, galleried interior. The chapel below
the tower is more intimate. A tomb surmounted by a
weeping cherub is that of Thomas Coram, who in 1741
started the Foundling Hospital to rear and educate abandoned children. Open Monday through Friday, 8:15 to 5:30.

*The traditional maypole formerly erected in front of the
church of St. Andrew Undershaft.*

St. Andrew Undershaft, Leadenhall Street. The name refers to a shaft or maypole erected annually at a festival in front of the church until the sixteenth century, when the maypole was burned as a pagan survival. A monument in the northeast corner is to the London historian John Stow (died 1605); the quill pen in his hand is renewed at a service held annually on April 5 by the Lord Mayor of London. The church dates to 1268. Open Monday through Friday, 10:15 to 2:15.

St. Andrew-by-the-Wardrobe, Queen Victoria Street. So called for being near the royal storerooms or wardrobe, the church is hidden in alleys south of St. Paul's. It was bombed in 1940, then rebuilt and furnished with pieces from other City churches. Open Monday through Friday, 7 to 6.

St. Anne and St. Agnes, Gresham Street. Here one finds a lovely interior with columns. Long neglected, it is now a Lutheran church with services in Latvian and Estonian. Evidence of antiquity appears in its former name, "by-the-willows," implying that it was once near a stream. Open Sundays.

St. Bartholomew-the-Great, Smithfield. The church was first built in 1123 by Rahere, a courtier of Henry I, who had a vision of hell from which he was saved by the intervention of St. Bartholomew. His fine monument is north of the altar. A healer in his lifetime, his tomb was later visited for cures. On a window opposite is a rebus (punning image) on Prior

The nave of St. Bartholomew-the-Great.

Bolton, consisting of a dart (bolt) piercing a barrel (tun). Up
to the Reformation the church was much larger and had a
monastery beside it. The present church is the old Norman
choir with later additions. One side of the cloisters remains.
A marble monument to Edward Cooke in the south aisle asks
visitors to weep for him, "or else stay and see the marble
weep." In humid weather the effigy sometimes appears to
shed tears. The tiny churchyard, entered through a medieval
gatehouse, is hemmed in by houses. At one time the church
was almost hidden by buildings leaning against it. Open
daily, 8 to 5.

St. Bartholomew-the-Less, Smithfield. This is a pre-fire
church, much rebuilt, now small and neat with lovely
monuments. It adjoins St. Bartholomew's Hospital (Bart's)
and serves as its chapel and as a parish church. Entrance to
church and hospital is through a gatehouse of 1702 with a
statue of Henry VIII above it. Here at Smithfield many
Protestant martyrs were burned to death, and there are
memorials to them in front of the hospital. Open daily, 6 a.m.
to midnight.

St. Benet, Paul's Wharf, Upper Thames Street. For more
than a hundred years this has been a Welsh Episcopalian
church with services in Welsh. The most unspoiled of
Wren's City churches, it retains its original galleries, carvings, and pillars. Stone for building St. Paul's was unloaded
at Paul's Wharf nearby. Open by special arrangement only.
Telephone: 723 3104.

St. Botolph, Aldersgate Street. The churches of St. Botolph,
of which this and two others remain, were placed at the
gates of the City as oratories for those about to undertake a
journey. St. Botolph was a seventh-century Saxon abbot who
became the patron saint of travelers. Rebuilt in the eighteenth century, this church is plain and dark outside, but
within are many interesting features, including a pulpit on a
carved palm tree and a stained-glass window of Christ's
Agony in the Garden. The churchyard to the south, once
shared by three parishes and now called Postman's Park, has
a memorial cloister designed by G. F. Watts that commemorates heroic deeds in everyday life. Open Monday, Tuesday,
Wednesday, 10:30 to 3; Thursday, 1 to 2; Saturday and
Sunday, 2 to 3.

St. Botolph, Aldgate. This large brick church on the old City
wall was rebuilt in the 1740s on Saxon foundations with an
unusual orientation, north-south. On the pulpit five inlaid
panels display interesting religious symbolism. The head of
Lady Jane Grey's father, the Earl of Suffolk, executed in
1554 on Tower Hill, is kept in the church but is not on view
to visitors. Homeless vagrants are given hospitality in the

crypt. Open Monday through Friday, 10 to 5; Sunday, 10 to noon.

St. Botolph, Bishopsgate. John Keats was baptized in this church, which was rebuilt in 1725. It is light and classical inside with fine Victorian furnishings. In the large churchyard surrounding it is a former school, now the hall of the Fan Makers' Company, with statues of children in niches outside it. Open Monday through Friday, 7 to 6; Sunday (first in month only), 10:30 to 12:45.

St. Bride, Fleet Street. This is the most fascinating of the London churches because its site has been sanctified from pagan times. By the northwest corner of the present church and within the walls of an earlier building was the holy well of St. Bride or Bridget, a fifth-century Irish saint, to which pilgrimages were made on her feast day. The Wren church with its elaborate "wedding cake" steeple was bombed in the war and rebuilt in the 1950s. Excavations in the ruins uncovered a succession of previous shrines and churches, Saxon, Roman, and Celtic. The prehistoric holy well is the oldest feature, but it has been covered over. Foundations of the early buildings can be seen in the crypt, which is now a museum. Being in Fleet Street, famous for its newspaper offices, St. Bride has been adopted as the journalists' church. The east wall, which is skillfully painted to appear curved, is actually flat. On the south wall is a terra-cotta head of Virginia Dare, the first child of English parents to be born in North America. Open daily, 9 to 5; Sunday, 9:30 to 6:30.

St. Clement, Eastcheap. This is the church whose bells, according to the nursery rhyme, peal "Oranges and lemons," recalling the days when the parish had a fruit market. The interior, light and plain, has lovely eighteenth-century carvings on the pulpit, its canopy, and the font cover, where the Holy Spirit is represented as a dove. Open Monday through Friday, 9 to 5.

St. Dunstan-in-the-West, Fleet Street. The dark, octagonal interior with fine early monuments dates to 1831, when the old church, which jutted into Fleet Street and blocked traffic, was rebuilt further back. The clock is from the earlier church, and so are the figures of Gog and Magog, legendary giants, who strike a bell. Over the side entrance is a contemporary statue of Elizabeth I that stood over the Lud Gate before its demolition in 1760. Also from the gate are the curious statues of King Lud and his sons, now in the porch. Today the church is used by a Rumanian Orthodox congregation. Open Tuesday, Thursday, Friday, 11 to 2:30.

St. Edmund, King and Martyr, Lombard Street. The legend of St. Edmund, the Saxon king of East Anglia martyred by the Danes in 870, is told at Bury St. Edmunds (page 310). The Wren church was bombed by an airship in World War I and was extensively restored in the 1950s and 1960s. Furnishings include a richly carved pulpit and a font cover with figures of the Apostles (only four of the twelve remain). Open daily, 8:30 to 4.

St. Ethelburga, Bishopsgate. This ancient, pre-fire church is the smallest in the City. Hemmed in by buildings and fronting a busy street, it has an air of peace and sanctity, and the secret churchyard behind it would suit a hermit. The delicate screen, loft, and other furnishings were made in 1912. Three of the four stained glass windows illustrate the 1607 expedition of Henry Hudson in search of the northwest passage. The dedication to a seventh-century abbess of Barking indicates a Saxon foundation. Open Monday through Friday, 11 to 3.

St. Giles, Cripplegate. The church, founded in the eleventh century, survived the Great Fire but was bombed in the war together with its surroundings. Rebuilt in 1960, its square, brick tower is the central feature in a landscaped area that incorporates parts of the old Roman City wall. Busts of Oliver Cromwell, who was married in the church in 1620; Milton, who was buried here; Bunyan, and Defoe stand at the west end. Open Monday through Friday, 10 to 2; Saturday, 2 to 5; Sunday, 7:30 to 6.

Inside St. Giles's Church.

St. Helen.

St. Helen, Bishopsgate. In 1212 a Benedictine nunnery was placed beside the church, which is probably a Saxon foundation. It is a grand old church, thronged with tombs and rich monuments. There are two parallel naves, the northern one formerly used by the nuns and the other by the parish. A screen separated the two, but in the fourteenth century, a complaint was made that the nuns waved at and even kissed the parishioners over the screen, dressed ostentatiously, and kept little dogs. At the east end of their nave is a squint to give the nuns a view of the altar. Open Monday through Friday, 9 to 5; Saturday, 2 to 4:30; Sunday, 9:30 to 8.

St. James, Garlickhythe, Upper Thames Street. The church was burned in the Great Fire, and the replacement by Wren was bombed in the war. Wren's design has since been finely restored. A church was recorded here in the twelfth century, and the site is probably of much earlier sanctity. Around it, on the bank of the Thames, was once London's garlic market. A mummified corpse, found in a vault and now in a cupboard of the church, may be a relic of one of the six Lord Mayors of London buried here. Open Monday through Friday, 9 to 5.

St. Katherine Cree, Leadenhall Street. The old church was rebuilt a few years before the fire, which it survived. After the war it was restored as headquarters of the Industrial Christian Fellowship. The interior is splendid, with classical columns and roof bosses painted with the arms of the City Livery Companies. In the east window is a large catherine wheel. The secluded churchyard once belonged to the priory of Christchurch, of which Cree church is a corrupted form. Open Monday through Friday, 9 to 5.

St. Lawrence Jewry, Gresham Street. The name commemorates a colony of Jews who lived hereabouts until their expulsion from England in 1290. The church is near the Guildhall, the seat of the City's government, and belongs to the City Corporation, which accounts for its solemnity and grandeur. The Wren interior was completely destroyed in the war and has since been recreated. A sixteenth-century painting in the vestibule shows the martyrdom of St. Lawrence, who was roasted over a gridiron at Rome in 258 A.D. Ordered by the emperor to yield up the treasures of his church, St. Lawrence had brought to him the old, sick, and indigent of the parish, saying that they were the Church's greatest treasure. For that he was made to suffer his agonizing death. On the spire of the church is his symbol, a gridiron, together with a model of the bomb that hit the building in 1940. Open Monday through Friday, 7:45 to 5; Saturday and Sunday, 2 to 5.

St. Magnus-the-Martyr, Lower Thames Street. The fine steeple was designed by Wren as a landmark for travelers crossing the old London Bridge, since rebuilt. Now it is almost hidden by modern buildings, but its interior is one of the most splendid in the City. The services are "high" Anglo-Catholic, and the church has a holy relic, a piece of the True Cross that is displayed to the faithful every Good Friday. Open Tuesday through Saturday, 11 to 3:30; Sunday, 10 to 1.

St. Margaret Lothbury A church on this site was first recorded in the twelfth century, and since then the meaning of Lothbury has been forgotten. The present Wren building, damaged in the war, contains monuments and furnishings from several nearby churches that were destroyed. Open Monday through Friday, 8 to 5.

St. Margaret's Pattens, Eastcheap. The name probably refers to the pattens or iron clogs which were once sold nearby. Wren's church has a lovely west gallery and a beadle's pew in the northeast corner. In front of it is a "punishment chair" to which naughty children were brought so as to be under the beadle's eye. Open Monday through Friday, 9 to 4.

St. Martin, Ludgate Hill. Traditionally founded in the seventh century, the church has many interesting features and legends. It is probably on a pagan site associated with the former Temple of Diana on Ludgate Hill, where St. Paul's now stands. This relationship was emphasized by Sir Christopher Wren, who built St. Martin's steeple so that, seen from the north side of Fleet Street to the west, it exactly bisects the dome of St. Paul's. The church is used by City and Masonic guilds and is being restored. Open Monday through Friday, 10 to 4.

St. Mary Abchurch, Cannon Street. The origin of the name may be Saxon, but its meaning is lost. There was a church here by the twelfth century. The interior is one of Wren's finest and has been little changed apart from postwar restorations. Beneath a painted dome there is much beautifully crafted furniture, notably the reredos behind the altar, which is the work of the incomparable Grinling Gibbons (1648–1721), who collaborated with Wren after the fire. Bombing during the war revealed a medieval crypt below the churchyard. Open Monday, Wednesday, Friday, 10 to 4; Tuesday and Thursday, 12 to 2.

St. Mary Aldermary, Queen Victoria Street. The name "Elder Mary" implies that the church here was the first in the City to be dedicated to St. Mary. The site must therefore be of ancient sanctity, though the first record of a church here was in the eleventh century. The tower survived the fire and was given pinnacles by Wren, who built the present large church in Gothic style with a decorative fan-vaulted ceiling. Open Tuesday through Friday, 10:30 to 3:30.

St. Mary-le-Bow, Cheapside. Those born within the sound of Bow bells are entitled to call themselves Cockneys. The site is very ancient, and the church was rebuilt by Wren as the grandest in the City. It was demolished after being bombed in 1941, apart from the tower, one of Wren's finest, which is surmounted by a flying dragon. Below the modern church, nobly reconstructed in 1964, is a crypt with Norman masonry that is possibly of earlier origin. Part of it is used for meetings of the Court of Arches, which legislates on ecclesiastical matters. Open Monday through Friday, 9 to 4 (crypt, 9:30 to 1).

St. Mary-at-Hill, Lovat Lane, Eastcheap. This was a favorite church of the late poet laureate Sir John Betjeman. It has, he wrote, "the least spoilt and most gorgeous interior in the City, all the more exciting for being hidden away among cobbled alleys, paved passages and brick walls overhung by a plane tree." With its pale light, old carved woodwork, and box pews (the only examples remaining in the City), it recalls the London of Charles Dickens and even earlier times. Wren repaired it after the fire, and the tower was rebuilt in the following century. Open Tuesday, 1:15 to 1:45; Wednesday and Thursday, 1 to 2.

St. Mary Woolnoth, Lombard Street. As is so often the case with the old City churches, the original meaning of the name is lost. It is probably Saxon and implies an early foundation on the site. The old church, repaired by Wren after the fire, was pulled down in 1716, when the present church was built by Wren's pupil, Nicholas Hawksmoor. It is one of his finest works. The Bank Underground station was built directly beneath it in 1897. Open Monday through Friday, 8 to 4:30.

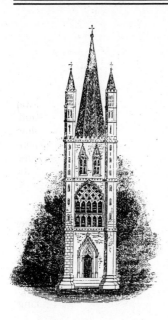

The tower of St. Michael, Cornhill, rebuilt in its former style after the Great Fire.

St. Michael, Cornhill St. Michael's churches are usually on high ground, and this church is near the highest spot in the City, which is occupied by St. Peter's Church a few yards to the east. A Saxon church of St. Michael was recorded on the present site before the Norman Invasion, and excavation would probably reveal a Roman temple beneath it, for here was once the Forum, the center of Roman London. Wren rebuilt the church after the fire, and Hawksmoor added the pinnacled tower, which in earlier times had a spire. The interior was refurnished in Gothic style in the nineteenth century. Open Monday through Friday, 8:30 to 5.

St. Michael, Paternoster Royal, College Street. The one Lord Mayor of London whom everyone has heard of is Dick Whittington, who rose to prominence through the guidance of his famous cat (the story occurs in universal folklore). In 1423 he was buried in this church, of which he was a benefactor. It was badly damaged by a V-1 rocket in 1944, but its pulpit, reredos, and other fittings had been removed to safety. They were replaced in the church in 1968, when it was restored and reopened as headquarters of the Missions to Seamen. The old Lord Mayor and his cat are shown in a modern stained glass window. The name refers to the paternosters or rosaries formerly made nearby, and to the town of La Reole near Bordeaux, with which local wine merchants once traded. Open Monday through Friday, 9:30 to 5:30.

St. Nicholas Cole Abbey, Queen Victoria Street. The origin of the name Cole is a classic puzzle among etymologists. It often appears in the form Cold, as in Coldharbour, which is a common placename and occurs repeatedly (though not exclusively) beside old roads and trackways, suggesting a

derivation from "cold arbor," an overnight shelter for travelers. The name of this church, formerly Cold Abbey, may
possibly come from a cold arbor which once stood here. The
earliest reference to a church on the site was in 1144. Wren's
church was bombed in the war and refashioned internally
with modern stained glass windows in 1960. Open Monday
through Friday, 8:30 to 5.

St. Olave, Hart Street, near Fenchurch Street. The church
survived the fire but was largely rebuilt after being bombed
in 1941. It is entered through a quiet old churchyard and a
gate decorated with skulls and crossbones. Victims of the
plague were buried here. In the church is a monument to
Samuel Pepys and his wife, whose bones are here. Nearby,
according to the parish records, Mother Goose was buried in
1586. St. Olaf, to whom the church is dedicated, was a Norse
king martyred in 1030. A stone in front of the sanctuary was
laid by King Haakon VII of Norway when the church was
restored in 1951. In the lower crypt is a tiny chapel and a
holy well with medieval masonry which was probably the
center of a prehistoric shrine. The discovery of Roman ritual
objects on the site proves its antiquity. Open daily, 8 to 6:30.

St. Peter-upon-Cornhill This claims to be the oldest church
in the City and to have been the most important in the time
of King Lucius, who founded it in 179 A.D. The site is likely
to be of ancient sanctity, for it is the highest point in the City
and was contained within the Roman Forum. As a mark of

*The tower of
St. Peter-upon-Cornhill.*

BEE IT KNOWNE TO ALL MEN THAT IN THE YEARE OF OVR LORD GOD 179, LVCIVS THE FIRST CHRISTIAN KING OF THIS LAND, THEN CALLED BRITAINE, FOVNDED Ý FIRST CHVRCH IN LONDON, THAT IS TO SAY Ý CHVRCH OF S.PETER VPON CORNEHILL: AND HEE FOVNDED THERE AN ARCHBIS-HOPS SEE, AND MADE THAT CHVRCH Ý METROPOLITANE AND CHEIFE CHVRCH OF THIS KINGDOME, AND SO IT INDVRED Ý SPACE OF 400 YEARES AND MORE, VNTO THE COMING OF S. AVSTIN THE APOSTLE OF ENGLAND, THE WHICH WAS SENT INTO THIS LAND BY S.GREGORIE, Ý DOCTOR OF Ý CHVRCH IN THE TIME OF KING ETHELBERT. AND THEN WAS THE ARCH-BISHOPS SEE & PALL REMOVED FROM Ý FORESAID CHVRCH OF S. PETER VPON CORNEHILL, VNTO DOROBERNIA, THAT NOW IS CALLED CANTERBVRIE, & THERE IT REMAINETH TO THIS DAY, AND MILLET A MONKE WHICH CAME INTO THIS LAND WITH S.AVSTIN, HEE WAS MADE THE FIRST BISHOP OF LONDON, AND HIS SEE WAS MADE IN PAL'S CHVRCH. AND THIS LVCIVS KING WAS THE FIRST FOVNDER OF S.PETERS CHVRCH VPON CORNEHILL, & HEE REIGNED KING IN THIS LAND AFTER BRVTE 1245 YEARES. AND IN THE YEARE OF OVR LORD GOD 124 · LVCIVS WAS CROWNED KING: AND THE YEARES OF HIS REIGNE WERE 77 YEARES. AND HEE WAS BV-RIED (AFTER SOME CHRONICLES) AT LONDON: AND AFTER SOME CHRONICLES HEE WAS BVRIED AT GLOCESTER, IN THAT PLACE WHERE Ý ORDER OF S.FRANCIS STANDETH NOW.

An inscription within St. Peter's Church records the early foundation of the church there.

its antiquity, St. Peter retains certain old customs and privileges. It was rebuilt by Wren after the fire and contains a carved screen and much seventeenth-century woodwork. Overhung by grandiose City buildings, the church with its tiny churchyard is like a secret, spiritual shrine within the Temple of Mammon. Open Monday through Friday, 8 to 4.

St. Sepulchre-without-Newgate, Holburn Viaduct. There was a Saxon church here, built of wood and dedicated to St. Edmund, the East Anglian martyr king. A Norman stone church succeeded it, and in 1450 it was rebuilt as the largest parish church in the City. It was given its present dedication at the time of the Crusades. Much of the exterior survived the fire. A tablet behind a choir stall in the south aisle commemorates the adventurous Captain John Smith, one of the founders of Virginia, who was buried nearby in 1631. A window opposite depicts the little ships in which his party set out for America in 1606. A picture of Pocahontas, the American Indian princess who, according to Smith, saved his life while he was a captive of the Indians, is sold in the church; she married another colonist, John Rolfe, and died in England. There was formerly a tunnel from the church to Newgate Prison across the road on the present site of the Old Bailey criminal court. On the eve of executions the church's watchman would proceed through the tunnel to ring a bell outside the condemned cell and recite a gruesome verse calling for repentance. The bell and verse are displayed on a pillar near the Smith monument. Open Monday through Friday, 9 to 4.

St. Stephen Walbrook   The Walbrook stream once ran nearby, and the church was originally on its west bank. It was rebuilt on the present site east of the Walbrook in the fifteenth century and now stands beside the Mansion House, the official residence of London's Lord Mayor. The interior of the church is reckoned to be one of Wren's masterpieces. The splendid dome was his experimental model for St. Paul's. In the church is the headquarters of the Samaritans, who give advice and comfort by telephone to those contemplating suicide. Open Monday through Friday, 10 to 3; Sunday, 12:30 to 1:30.

St. Vedast, Foster Lane. Twelve local parishes were amalgamated after the fire, and the parishioners were accommodated in St. Vedast's Church, rebuilt by Wren. It was bombed in 1940 and restored in 1962 with furnishings from other churches. The dedication is to a sixth-century French bishop. Open Monday through Friday, 10 to 6; Sunday, 10 to noon.

SOME OTHER LONDON PLACES OF WORSHIP

Sir Christopher Wren built three churches in London outside the boundaries of the City. All three were bombed in the war. St. Anne, Soho, was totally destroyed except for its tower, which still stands. The other two, St. James, Piccadilly, and St. Clement Danes, were restored.

St. James, Piccadilly. Here is one of the liveliest of London churches. Apart from regular services, it offers concerts, lectures, and meetings, and there is a weekly crafts and antiques market in the forecourt on Piccadilly.

St. Clement Danes, Fleet Street. Like a great ship, the church stands in the middle of Fleet Street. Its site is very ancient, with indications that it was once a pagan sanctuary. A Roman graveyard occupied it, and there was a holy well here when Christian missionaries built a wooden church on it in the sixth century. It was reconsecrated by the Danes in the time of King Canute, hence the name. As a further sign of its antiquity, the church is situated in alignments with several other old sites, as described below.

Bevis Marks Synagogue, EC3. At the time of the Commonwealth under Oliver Cromwell, the Jews—who had been expelled from England in 1290—were invited to return. The first comers were Sephardic Jews from the Netherlands who had earlier been expelled from Spain. Over the years a large

Jewish community grew up in London's East End and parts of the City. The Bevis Marks Synagogue was built in 1701. It is a charming old red-brick building, hidden away in a courtyard off Bevis Marks in the heart of the City. It can be visited on Sunday, 10:30 to noon.

Wesley's Chapel, 49 City Road, EC1. Known as the Mother Church of World Methodism, this is the center of Methodist pilgrimage. John Wesley bought the land from the City Corporation in 1776 and appealed for funds to build the chapel, which was completed two years later. Exactly two hundred years after it was first opened, on All Saints Day 1978, the newly restored chapel was reopened by the Queen. Wesley's house, where he spent his last years, adjoins the chapel and has also been restored and opened. Below the chapel, the Museum of Methodism offers a large display of objects illustrating the worldwide development of the Methodist Church. Opposite the chapel is the old burial ground on Bunhill Fields. In this peaceful spot, shaded by trees, one can see the tombs of England's pilgrim John Bunyan and the prophetic poet and artist William Blake. Wesley's Chapel, the house, and the museum are open daily, 10 to 4. Admission £1.50.

The Temple Church (St. Mary), Fleet Street. An alley off the south side of Fleet Street leads to the church in a small courtyard. Adjoining it are two of the four Inns of the Court, inhabited by lawyers and law students. They have owned the church since the fourteenth century. Previously it belonged

Interior of the Temple Church.

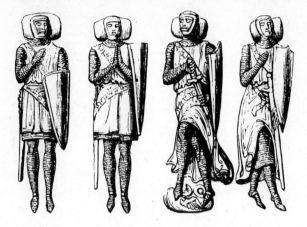

Effigies of Knights Templar in the Temple Church.

to the Order of Knights Templar, who built it in 1185. They were warrior monks who undertook the protection of pilgrims on the routes to the Holy Land. The rebuilding of the Temple at Jerusalem was their ultimate goal, and to that end they studied the esoteric and masonic sciences then taught in the ancient mystery schools. The Templars are thought to have been responsible for introducing the principles of Gothic architecture into Europe. Their churches were built as circular temples in imitation of the Holy Sepulchre in Jerusalem. Other examples are at Cambridge, Northampton, and Little Maplestead in Essex.

To the west of the round church is a Norman porch and doorway carved with knights and demons. Above the stone seats around the inside of the wall are sixty-four fantastically carved heads of people and beasts. There is a gallery above and a crypt below in which Templar initiation ceremonies were held. In 1240 a beautiful eastern extension was built as the choir. The ratio between the longer and shorter sides of its rectangular plan was made to equal $1:\sqrt{2}$, which is the ratio between the side and the diagonal of a square. Thus the square and the circle, symbols respectively of matter and spirit, were united in one building. Famous among antiquarians are the effigies in the church; one of them, a thirteenth-century marble figure on the south wall, is believed to represent Heraclius, patriarch of Jerusalem, who consecrated the round church. Open daily, 10 to 4; Sunday, 1 to 4.

St. Etheldreda, (Roman Catholic), Ely Place, Holborn Circus. In 1873 the church was sold at auction and became the first ancient place of worship since the Reformation to be regained by the Roman Catholics. Ely Place is just outside the old wall of the City, and until recently it was an administrative anomaly, belonging to Cambridgeshire rather than to

London. Criminals and debtors who took sanctuary there were safe from the London authorities. From the thirteenth century it belonged to the princely bishops of Ely, who had their palace there and used the present church as their chapel. Elizabeth I confiscated the entire property to give to her favorite, Sir Christopher Hatton, and when the bishop objected she quelled him with a blunt note:

> Proud Prelate,
>   You know what you was before I made you what you are now: if you do not immediately comply with my request, by God I will unfrock you.
>   Elizabeth

Antiquarians have claimed that the church rests on the foundations of a third-century Roman-British temple. The present building, finished in about 1260, is one of London's finest Gothic survivals. It was saved from the Great Fire by a providential change of wind. It is on two floors, with a large crypt below the main church. The beautiful traceried windows, damaged in the war, are filled with modern stained glass; the design at the west end shows English Catholic martyrs. The theme of martyrdom is repeated in the statues of Catholics executed during the Tudor reigns. Secluded in Ely Court, a little alley off Ely Place, is the historic Mitre Tavern with some interesting relics. The church is open daily, 8 to 7. Further information and details of guided walking tours of the area are available from the Clerkenwell Heritage Centre, 33 St. John's Square, EC1. Telephone: 250 1039.

The Chapels in the Tower of London
The Tower of London is England's most popular tourist attraction. Its character as a fortress puts it outside the subject of this book, but its site is bound up with the sacred

The Norman pillars of the chapel in the White Tower.

history of London, and its unique Norman chapel gives it the right of inclusion. The Tower is steeped in English history and in the blood of many of its leading participants. Since the time when William the Conqueror built it to repress his unwilling London subjects, it has been the scene of state and private violence, of torture, murder, and execution. Its main exhibits now are galleries of arms, armor, and instruments of punishment. Electronic devices protect the Crown Jewels. Their symbolic guardians, the famous Beefeaters or Yeomen of the Guard, stalk the grounds of the Tower in their Tudor uniforms, and with them stalk six gaunt ravens, their wings clipped to prevent their escape, for it is said that when the ravens leave the Tower the citadel will crumble.

The White Tower   The ravens belong to the Tower as the sacred birds of Bran the Blessed, a legendary Welsh hero whose talismanic head was brought to London for burial within the Bryn Gwyn or White Mound on which the White Tower was later built. Bran's head was the magical protector of London from prehistoric times to the days of King Arthur, who is supposed to have dug it up in order that he alone might defend the kingdom. Thereupon followed the onslaught of the Anglo-Saxons. The White Mound is also the traditional burial place of the kings Brutus the Trojan and Molmutius the Lawgiver. As a sacred hill, it was never built upon by the British, but Julius Caesar is believed by some to have erected a fort on it, and now it is almost obliterated by the Normans' White Tower, the central stronghold. Part of its sloping base on the south side is all that is now visible of it.

   In the basement of the White Tower, where suits of armor are displayed on the walls, is a deep well with masonry which the authorities say is Roman but which could be of an earlier period. It has even been claimed as a prehistoric astronomical well, as used by the ancients for observing the stars by daylight.

St. John the Evangelist This chapel is on an upper floor in the southeast corner of the Tower. Built in 1080, it has remained unchanged apart from being stripped of its fittings and ornaments. Huge Norman pillars separate the nave from two aisles and a sanctuary. This has been a place of solemn vigil, oath taking, and knightly ceremonies. There is much that could be experienced here by the solitary dreamer, but the stream of visitors constantly passing through dissipates the atmosphere and makes it chiefly appealing to students of architecture.

St. Peter-ad-Vincula This is another chapel within the precincts of the Tower, on Tower Green to the northwest. Its interior can be seen by joining a Yeoman of the Guard tour, and there are public services in it every Sunday (except during August) at 11 a.m. Henry VIII built it on the site of a previous church in 1519, and in it were buried his second wife, Anne Boleyn, and his fifth, Catherine Howard, both of whom he had beheaded on the Green a few yards away. Also killed there and buried ignominiously below the chapel were the old Countess of Salisbury, Lady Jane Grey, the Elizabethan Earl of Essex, the rebel Duke of Monmouth, and a host of others. The associations of the place make it oppressive; old terrors and miseries seem to hang in the air, and those who are sensitive to impressions from the past might do well to avoid it.

THE TOWER OF LONDON is opposite Tower Hill Underground station. Its opening hours in summer are: Monday through Saturday, 9:30 to 5; Sunday, 2 to 5. The winter hours are Monday through Saturday, 9:30 to 4; closed Sunday. Admission £4.

ALIGNMENTS OF LONDON CHURCHES

A feature of ancient religious monuments worldwide is their location on series of straight alignments. In some parts of the world, notably Bolivia and elsewhere in South America, the lines connecting native and Christianized sacred sites are still visible as dead straight pathways. In England the principle of aligned sites was rediscovered in the 1920s by Alfred Watkins of Hereford, who called them "leys." Where churches occur on these alignments it may be that they stand on sites of pre-Christian sanctity. It was the declared policy of the early Church to build over pagan sanctuaries. St. Paul's and other City churches have pagan shrines below their foundations. It has also been suggested that the traditional practice of aligning sacred sites may have been carried on into the Middle Ages by masonic architects initiated into the esoteric doctrines. York, Norwich, Bristol, and Cambridge are among the old English cities where

St. Martin-in-the-Fields.

alignments of churches and other monuments have been noted. Two examples in London are described by Paul Devereux and Ian Thompson in their book *The Ley Hunter's Companion* (1979). These lines link several of the churches named above:

I. St. Clement Danes; the Temple Church; St. Paul's Cathedral; St. Helen, Bishopsgate; St. Dunstan, Stepney. The history of the site of the Temple Church is unknown before the twelfth century. The other churches on the line have evidence of Saxon or earlier foundations.

II. St. Martin-in-the-Fields; St. Mary-le-Strand; St. Clement Danes; St. Dunstan, Fleet Street; Arnold Circus. There are no records of churches on these sites, apart from that of St. Clement Danes, before the eleventh or twelfth century, but Roman remains have been found on the site of St. Martin. Arnold Circus is the former site of an artificial mound which has long been destroyed and was once occupied by a monastic building. This line coincides with the present course of the Strand.

3

AROUND LONDON

ESSEX, HERTFORDSHIRE, BUCKINGHAMSHIRE, OXFORDSHIRE, HAMPSHIRE, KENT

ST. ALBANS, *The Shrine of England's First Martyr*

The great cathedral church or abbey of St. Albans in Hertfordshire stands on hallowed ground, for there in about the year 289 England's first Christian martyr was beheaded by the pagan Romans. The legend says that Alban was a Roman citizen who gave shelter to a fugitive Christian priest, was converted by him, and when the man was about to be arrested, took his place, allowing him to escape. Places of execution were often on high points where the punishment would be widely visible, and St. Alban's shrine, placed on the highest ground within the hilltop abbey, is probably the site of his martyrdom.

Alban's gesture must have seemed vain at the time, for the priest, Amphibalus, was soon captured and tortured to death. Yet from the time of Alban's death, stories of miracles began to circulate. Roman Christians built a chapel over his remains, and a church succeeded it. The church was destroyed by heathen marauders, and for some time the site lay derelict until, in the eighth century, King Offa founded an abbey there. The martyr's bones were revealed miraculously by a guiding star, and a monastery of Benedictine monks was established to honor the relics.

The city of Verulamium, where Alban lived, was originally the capital of a British nation whose ruler at the time of the Roman invasion was Cassivelaunus. It was stormed by Caesar's legions and grew to become the greatest Roman city in Britain, even though Boadicea captured and burned it in 61 A.D. With the decline of Roman power it fell into ruins, and by the end of the fifth century it was almost deserted, most of the population having moved to the new town which grew up around St. Alban's place of martyrdom on the hill above it. Just before and after the Norman Conquest the remaining buildings of old Verulamium were demolished to provide materials for a new, enlarged abbey. The work was carried out by the Norman abbot, Paul of Caen. Much of it can still be seen in the massive central tower, the transepts,

*The cathedral on the hill where St. Alban was martyred,
seen from the old Roman city of Verulamium.*

and the eastern part of the nave. The abbey has since been
extended, altered, or patched up in every century up to the
present, and the result is a pleasantly eccentric mixture of
styles and materials, from the Roman bricks in the old parts
to the new chapter house opened in 1982. One of its glories
is the colorful fifteenth-century high screen near the center
of the abbey. The splendid western front, begun in the
twelfth century, was completed anew in the nineteenth. By
that time the whole building was in danger of collapse, and
extensive restorations were undertaken, largely through the
generosity of Lord Grimthorpe. These works were much
criticized as being too drastic, and indeed many of the
abbey's ancient features were destroyed by the restorers. Yet
the history of the abbey has been one of constant renewal,
and the Victorians' confident craftmanship is seen today as
adding to its splendor and interest.

The Saint's Shrine

At the dissolution of the monasteries by Henry VIII in the
sixteenth century, St. Albans Abbey suffered badly from
Puritan iconoclasm. The monastic buildings were mostly
demolished, leaving only a great gateway to the west of the
cathedral. Worst of all, the beautiful fourteenth-century
shrine of St. Alban, built of carved and painted Purbeck
marble, was torn down and smashed to pieces. For three
centuries only the base remained to mark the site. Then, in
the middle of the nineteenth century, some marble fragments were discovered in a blocked-up recess within the
abbey. They were recognized as parts of the old shrine, and
a search was instituted for the remainder. Other pieces
emerged from beneath walls and floors. Sir Gilbert Scott,
who was in charge of restoration at the time, fitted them

together like a jigsaw, making good the missing parts, and St. Alban's shrine rose again.

Today the shrine is once more a popular resort of pilgrims, and the atmosphere around it is intensely religious. Here undoubtedly beats the heart of the abbey, an unforgettable spot. Beside and above the shrine is the ancient Watching Gallery of richly carved oak, where in former times a succession of monks kept constant vigil over the relics of the saint.

Old Verulamium
The door at the end of the abbey's south transept gives onto a lawn and the site of the old monastic foundation. A path leads downhill through an orchard to the crossing of the River Ver where, opposite the bridge and at the end of Abbey Mill Lane, stands a curious octagonal public house, the Fighting Cocks, one of the oldest inns in England. On the other side of the Ver and the ornamental lake which has been formed from its waters is the site of the Roman city of Verulamium.

Apart from some earthworks and bits of flint wall, there is little at first to be seen on the surface, but a right turn past the lake and a walk of a few hundred yards takes one to the Verulamium Museum opposite St. Michael's Church. The museum brings the whole site to life. Excavations have been going on at Verulamium throughout this century, and the remarkable finds exhibited here include artifacts from ancient British and Roman times, statues and religious objects, and some fine mosaic floors. Verulamium was clearly a great city. Near the museum is the Roman theater, now excavated and restored, with seats for 1600 people. South of it are the foundations of a temple and a mosaic floor with traces of a central heating system.

St. Alban's reconstructed shrine and the Watching Gallery beyond.

Sir Francis Bacon and the Shakespeare Mystery

Chief among the famous people associated with St. Albans is Sir Francis Bacon, who lived about 25 miles north of the town in Gorhambury, a great Tudor mansion built by his father, Sir Nicholas, in 1568. The house was entirely rebuilt in 1777, but some of the old building survives in ruins, and the park with its ancient oak trees retains many features that would have been familiar to Sir Francis. Gorhambury House, with its fine collections of paintings, furniture, and glass, is now the seat of the Earl of Verulam, who opens it to the public on Thursday afternoons, May through September.

An interesting marble sculpture of Francis Bacon in St. Michael's Church, near the Verulamium Museum, shows him in characteristic pose, leaning thoughtfully on his elbow. *Sic sedebat,* "Thus he would sit," the inscription says. This monument has long been an attraction to Baconians, those who believe that Francis Bacon secretly wrote the plays and verse attributed to William Shakespeare, the actor from Stratford-on-Avon. The first such pilgrim was the New England scholar Delia Bacon, who came to England in 1853 in an unsuccessful attempt to excavate Shakespeare's tomb at Stratford for documents she believed were buried there. Another American, United States Representative Ignatius Donnelly of Minnesota, founder of the Populist Party and author of books on Atlantis, Bacon-as-Shakespeare, and other unorthodox theories, journeyed to St. Albans in the 1890s, hoping to gain insight into the true authorship of Shakespeare's works by investigating the Bacon monument with his dowser's pendulum. In one of his books, *The Great Cryptogram,* he claimed to have found a cipher in the Shakespeare plays that proved that Bacon wrote them. Scholars have remained skeptical about his conclusions, but in 1985 a fascinating piece of evidence turned up which apparently links the author of Shakespeare's works with St. Albans.

The new evidence was discovered in the medieval White Hart Inn on Holywell Street, opposite the east end of the abbey. During restorations to an ancient room in the inn, previously used for some years as an antique shop, a remarkable painting, long hidden by paneling, was found on one of the walls. Measuring some ten by thirty feet, it has been identified as an illustration of the death of Adonis as described in Shakespeare's poem, *Venus and Adonis,* his first published work, of 1593. Experts say that the White Hart wall painting was done within a few years of that date. It is the only known contemporary illustration of a Shakespearean subject. Baconians theorize that the room in which it was found was once used for Rosicrucian masonic meetings that were attended by Sir Francis Bacon.

A visit to the White Hart in the spring of 1986 found restoration work still under way. Further paintings may be exposed as the rest of the paneling is removed. It is promised that the room will be shown to the public beginning in 1987.

ST. ALBANS is situated in Hertfordshire, about 20 miles north of London. There are regular trains from St. Pancras and King's Cross Stations, London (fastest journey, twenty minutes). St. Albans City Station is about fifteen minutes walk from the abbey, and there are buses.

The abbey is open daily to 5:45 in winter and to 6:45 in summer.

The Verulamium Museum is open daily, April through October, 10 to 5:30; Sunday, 2 to 5:30. In winter, 10 to 4. Admission 70p.

The admission fee to Gorhambury House is £1.20.

The Tourist Information Centre is at 37 Chequer Street, St. Albans. Telephone: St. Albans (0727) 64511.

WALTHAM ABBEY

Bordering London to the northeast are six thousand acres of public land covered by Epping Forest. It is a great place to explore on foot or on horseback, and in spite of its attractions for artists, naturalists, and picnickers one can easily find solitude in its deep woodland glades. Rural villages and old inns lie sheltered among the forest trees.

West of the forest the land descends to the valley of the River Lea, which is a flat area, messily industrialized and without obvious interest. Waltham is one of its small towns. The automobile age has dealt harshly with it, but there are still medieval streets near its battered old abbey, which was once famous among pilgrims for the miracles performed there. The Holy Rood that was the instrument of those miracles vanished at the Reformation, but the abbey is still much visited for its antiquarian features. After Durham and Norwich it has the finest and most extensive range of Norman architecture in England. Its eastern end has been destroyed, and so have the former monastic buildings to its north. In their place are gardens and a tidy lawn from which bits of old masonry protrude. The site of the former chancel, to the east of the abbey, is sacred ground to English traditionalists who still resent the imposition of the "Norman yoke," for somewhere there—the exact site is no longer known—Harold, the last king of Saxon England, was buried after his defeat and death at the battle of Hastings.

The Finding of the Miraculous Cross

During the reign of King Canute (or Cnut), between 1017 and 1035, a remarkable discovery was made in Somerset. A man dreamed that on a hilltop at Montacute, about 15 miles south of Glastonbury, a treasure would be found. Excavations were made there, and a large flint cross was dug up. The story is that it was placed on a cart drawn by twelve red and twelve white oxen, the intention being to take the cross to Glastonbury Abbey, but the oxen refused to go in that direction. Instead they made their own way across country until they came to Waltham, where they stopped by the church. Waltham therefore became the shrine of the cross,

Waltham Abbey church, where King Harold was buried after the Battle of Hastings.

known as the Holy Rood. In 1060 Harold consecrated a large new church in its honor, and miraculous cures and visions took place around it.

The Abbey Church of Waltham Holy Cross

Waltham became so rich from the pilgrims who flocked to the Holy Rood that about sixty years after King Harold consecrated it the church was rebuilt on a grand scale. It was over twice as long as the present building, which is merely the original nave. Harold founded a college of secular canons to serve in the church; by the end of the twelfth century it was occupied by Augustinian canons, and Waltham had become an abbey.

Waltham was the last of the abbeys to be dissolved by Henry VIII. Most of it was pulled down in 1540. Only the nave was left to serve as the parish church. The original tower to its east fell down in 1552, and a new one in checkered stone was built at the west end, supporting the rest of the building, which was in danger of collapse.

Inside the abbey one finds a splendid composition of Norman architecture, beautifully restored and maintained. Above the bulky pillars, decorated with zigzags and spirals, is a gallery and clerestory. Guidebooks are sold in the crypt below, and there is an exhibition of the abbey's history and details of excavations which took place in 1986: Foundations of earlier churches were uncovered beneath the abbey while central heating was being installed.

The fine state of the abbey interior is largely due to the Victorian architect and designer William Burges, who was in charge of restorations during the 1860s and 1870s. He rebuilt the east wall and added many fine furnishings, including the altar and reredos. Carvings around the windows were of his design. His marble pulpit has since been replaced by the old wooden one and is now exhibited in the Epping Forest District Museum in Sun Street.

Contributions were made by other leading Victorian artists. One of the first things one notices is the painted ceiling, executed to Burges's design in 1860 by Edward Poynter, who was later president of the Royal Academy. The paintings, done on canvas, show the four elements and the twelve signs of the zodiac, together with the activities—such as plowing and weaving—appropriate to each of the signs. A notice by the entrance states emphatically that these images have nothing to do with occultism or any such non-Christian practice!

In the center of Waltham Cross, about a mile west of the abbey, is a rare example of an Eleanor Cross (see pages 22–3), made in 1291 but since extensively damaged and restored.

WALTHAM ABBEY in Essex is about 16 miles north of London. Its nearest station is at Waltham Cross, one mile away, to which there are frequent trains from Liverpool Street Station in London. The journey takes half an hour.

The abbey is open daily.

Waltham Cross, one of the stone crosses erected in 1209 on the spot where the body of Queen Eleanor rested on its way to burial at Westminster Abbey.

THE CHILTERN HILLS

JORDANS: Relics of the Mayflower and the Woodland Shrine of William Penn

Jordans in Buckinghamshire, about 25 miles west of London and 2 miles south of Chalfont St. Giles, is a small village built around a green and set in the most delightful countryside. It is a favorite spot for walkers, and many footpaths wind through its gentle hills, by woods and meadows, to places of historic interest and pilgrimage. The entire area was once covered by an ancient beech forest; its most substantial remains are a few miles to the south where Burnham Beeches, a public beauty spot, is a famous resort of artists.

Americans and Quakers are naturally attracted to Jordans, for there, in the simple burying ground beside its seventeenth-century meeting house, lies William Penn, the founder of Pennsylvania, together with his two wives, ten of his sixteen children, and other notable early Quakers. Plain headstones mark all the graves. It is an enchanting place of wildflowers and birdsong. The old meeting house, with its original brick floor and wooden benches, is both a place of worship and a museum. Visitors are made welcome and are shown mementos of Penn and the early days of the Quaker movement.

From the burying ground a pathway leads up through an orchard to Old Jordans Farm, which is run by the Society of Friends as a public guest house; good accommodation and meals can be obtained there on reasonable terms. There is also a youth hostel nearby. A large old barn, one of the farm's

The Quaker meeting house and the burial place of William Penn, Jordans.

original outbuildings, is made of massive timbers which are reputed to have been taken from the *Mayflower* when she was broken up at Ipswich in 1624. On one of its beams are carved the letters R HAR I, possibly part of the original legend, MayfloweR HARwIch. Other relics of the *Mayflower* and the Quakers are exhibited in Old Jordans.

This medieval yeoman's farmhouse was almost derelict in 1911 when the Society of Friends acquired it. Since then it has been carefully restored and added to. Nothing is known of its early history or of the Farmer Jordan who presumably once owned it. In 1659 it belonged to William Russell, a Quaker sympathizer, who held meetings there which were attended by such early Friends as George Fox, James Naylor, Isaac and Mary Penington, and William Penn. Following the restoration of the monarchy under Charles II and the banning of noncomformist religious gatherings, the meetings were often broken up by the police and the Quakers imprisoned, but in 1688 the Declaration of Indulgence allowed freedom of worship, and in that year the present meeting house was built.

JORDANS is less than a mile from the nearest station, at Seer Green, to which there are frequent trains from Marylebone Station in London (forty minutes' journey). It is open every day from 10 to 1 and 2 to 6, except Monday afternoon and all day Tuesday. During the winter months it closes at dusk. Admission is free. Meetings take place on Sunday mornings at 10:30.

MILTON'S COTTAGE

About a mile north of Jordans, on the right side of the road as it enters Chalfont St. Giles, is the quaint old cottage that since 1887 has been the public shrine of John Milton, England's great Puritan poet. Of all the houses he lived in, only this one survives. In 1665, totally blind and out of favor with the restored monarchist government, Milton with his third wife and one of his daughters took refuge here from the plague that was then raging in London. Thomas Ellwood, one of the Old Jordans Quakers, took the cottage on his behalf. *Paradise Lost,* begun in 1642, was completed here (Milton earned no more than £5 for it), and Ellwood then inspired him to undertake *Paradise Regained.* The poet's habit was to rise early in the morning, at about four o'clock, and prepare his mind for the day's work in the quiet hours before his family awoke. A year or two later, after the plague had died down, he returned to London.

The two downstairs rooms of the cottage, its kitchen and living room, are crammed with local curiosities and a collection of Milton's works in early and foreign editions. The atmosphere is simple and informal. Colonel and Mrs. Clark, the curators, live upstairs and greet visitors kindly, explaining the exhibits (many of which have no connection with

Milton or his times but are agreeable nonetheless) and displaying the pretty garden, which they tend. In it is a mulberry tree grown from a cutting from the ancient tree at Christ's College, Cambridge, which Milton knew.

After seeing the cottage, one can prolong the peaceful mood it instills by strolling into the village for lunch or tea. A charming old church there has curious wall paintings and flights of angels adorning its roof.

THE NEAREST STATION to Milton's cottage is at Seer Green; another is at Gerrards Cross, about 3 miles away, from which there are buses to Chalfont St. Giles. Marylebone Station is the London terminus for both. Other nearby stations, served by London Transport from Baker Street, are at Amersham and Chalfont & Latimer. There is free parking near the cottage in the forecourt of a restaurant.

Milton's cottage is open from March 1 to the end of October, every day except Monday, 10 to 1 and 2 to 6. Admission £1.

STOKE POGES: A Poet's Country Churchyard

One of the most famous and best loved English poems is Thomas Gray's "Elegy Written in a Country Churchyard." He composed it during the 1740s beneath the ancient yew tree opposite the porch of St. Giles's Church, Stoke Poges, in Buckinghamshire. The village church stands only just beyond the northeastern outskirts of industrial Slough, the town which the late poet laureate Sir John Betjeman once cursed for its ugliness; but Gray's poem has sanctified the churchyard, and there today one can sometimes feel as he did, "Far from the madding crowd's ignoble strife." Fame,

The path to Stoke Poges church through the garden graveyard.

however, has its drawbacks: The place is much frequented by summer visitors, and in those circumstances it is not always easy to invoke the atmosphere of poetic melancholy as promised by the "Elegy."

To the extent that it has not been built upon, the land surrounding the churchyard is still unspoiled. Opposite the entrance is a field preserved by the National Trust, who have shown good taste by planting trees that screen a pompous monument designed by the architect James Wyatt at the end of the eighteenth century in honor of Thomas Gray. It consists of a huge stone box, inscribed with the poet's verses and topped with a sarcophagus. The monument was commissioned by John Penn, a grandson of Pennsylvania's founder, whose family home was the old Manor House that still stands just to the north of the church. He later employed Wyatt to build a vast and hideous Italian-style mansion nearby. In front of it, bordering the southern edge of the churchyard, is an elaborately designed garden of remembrance that covers some thirty acres.

The poet's burial place is a modest brick tomb a few feet to the east of the church. His mother and her sister had been buried there before him, and a tablet on the church wall opposite records his wish to be "laid in the same tomb upon which he has so feelingly inscribed his grief at the loss of a beloved parent."

St. Giles's Church

The church is built in a mixture of styles and materials. Parts of a Saxon chapel remain in one of the walls and windows of the chancel, which was rebuilt shortly after the Norman Conquest. Also Norman are the stout pillars of the nave, which survived a major reconstruction in 1220. Of that century are the masonry of the aisles and the great oak timbers of the porch. The older parts of the church are of chalk and flint, and a red-brick building, the Hastings Chapel, was added south of the chancel in Tudor times as the oratory of an almshouse which stood nearby. The thirteenth-century tower where, in Gray's poem, "The moping owl does to the moon complain" is no longer "ivy-mantled" because the ivy, thought to be harmful to the structure, was stripped off some years ago.

Inside the church are several interesting relics and memorials, including three fifteenth-century brasses in front of the altar. One of them is to Edmund Hampdyn and his family, kinsmen of the staunch patriot John Hampden, who is mentioned in the "Elegy." The heraldic stained glass in the Hastings Chapel was removed there from the manor house. Strangest of all is a small piece of glass now inserted in the west window as part of a memorial to victims of World War II. It shows a nude male figure blowing a trumpet and pushing himself along on what looks like a wheeled hobby-horse, a precursor of the bicycle. Its meaning has long been

Stoke Poges church with "ivy-mantled tower," as Gray knew it.

disputed by the learned, but it remains known by its popular name, the Bicycle Window. This too came from the old manor.

Before its decay and modern restoration, Stoke Poges Manor House was the seat of the Earls of Huntingdon and of Sir Christopher Hatton, a favorite of Elizabeth I. The Penns owned it up to Queen Victoria's time. A private entrance through a cloister gave access from their park into the north side of the church, wherein can be seen their family vault, pew, memorial plaque, and several heraldic hatchments. Others of the family, including the famous William Penn, are buried 5 miles to the north in the Quaker burial ground at Jordans.

Further notes on the Stoke Poges church and its famous poet can be found in the handbooks sold there, one of which contains the "Elegy" printed in full for the benefit of those who wish to read it in the place where it was written.

Thomas Gray

Thomas Gray was born in London in 1716, the only one of his parents' twelve children to survive infancy. He hated his father, a bullying businessman and wife beater, and clung to his long-suffering mother, who cherished her one remaining child and sent him at the early age of nine to Eton College, about 3 miles from Stoke Poges. Thomas was happy at Eton, but when he went on to Cambridge University his retiring, scholarly character caused him to be persecuted by his fellow students, who thought him effeminate and called him Miss Gray. He left Cambridge at the age of twenty-two,

The figure in the Bicycle Window at Stoke Poges.

intending to practice as a lawyer, but one of his old Eton friends, Horace Walpole, invited him on a tour of the Continent in search of classical antiquities. Traveling and studying among Roman relics was delightful to the young poet, but Walpole was more interested in society, and the two parted company, Gray returning to London just in time to celebrate the death of his father. Soon afterward his happily widowed mother retired with her sisters to Stoke Poges, to West End Farm (now Stoke Court), about a mile from the church.

Thomas found rooms in Peterhouse College, Cambridge, and so applied himself to his studies that he gained a reputation as one of the most learned men in Europe. His greatest delight was visiting his mother and aunt, and in the peaceful beauty of rural Buckinghamshire his poetic genius flowered. The years up to 1753, when Mrs. Gray died, were his finest period. Four years later he refused the post of poet laureate, and in later life poetry became detestable to him. As a professor of modern history he continued to live at Cambridge until his death in 1771 at the age of fifty-four. The first request in his will was that he be buried with his mother and aunt at Stoke Poges.

STONOR PARK: The Refuge of a Catholic Martyr

Stonor Park in Oxfordshire, about 5 miles north of Henley-on-Thames, is a beautiful spot with a long-accumulated air of sanctity. The great house lies sheltered in a fold of the Chiltern Hills, surrounded by a deer park and groves of beech trees. For eight hundred years it has been the home of the Stonor family, whose present head, Lord Camoys, lives there today. The Stonors have always been Catholics. Throughout the Protestant Reformation and the persecution of Catholics under Elizabeth I they remained true to the old faith, and in the chapel adjoining the house mass has been celebrated without a break since the twelfth century. Stonor is a unique sanctuary and place of pilgrimage for English Catholics. One of the rooms in the house is dedicated to the memory of Edmund Campion, the Jesuit missionary and martyr, who took refuge there before his arrest and execution in 1581.

The Stone Circle and Chapel

The first thing one sees on a visit to Stonor, just beside the car park, is a prehistoric stone circle—or so it appears. In fact it was built in 1980 to the design of the artist Edward Piper. However, it has some claim to antiquity: A stone circle at or near the site, and another on the hill behind the house, are mentioned in the charter of King Offa in the eighth century. They were later destroyed, but many of the old stones lay scattered nearby, and they were used to construct the modern circle. The present monument may not be genuine, but it is attractive, and it serves to emphasize the ancient sanctity of the Stonor valley.

Other large old stones are to be seen in the foundations of the nearby chapel, which dates from the twelfth century and is on the site of an even earlier building. Its eighteenth-century Gothic interior was splendidly restored in 1960. In and around it are buried members of the Stonor family, and a tablet commemorates one of its benefactors, the poet Edith Sitwell.

The House and Its Secret Printing Press

The house consists of a remarkable collection of buildings of different ages, concealed and united by an outer skin of mellow brickwork. At its core is the original thirteenth-century hall to which, over the centuries, numerous additions have been made. The conglomeration of old buildings in timber and flint was transformed in the sixteenth century into an E-shaped Tudor mansion. That is basically its form today, though it has been much modified by classical and Gothic features added in the eighteenth century.

Only in the last few years has Stonor been open to the public, and it still retains the intimate atmosphere of an old family house. Many of its fine pictures, tapestries, and pieces of furniture have been donated for exhibition by loyal members of the family. Everywhere are records of the Stonors' staunch adherence to Catholicism. In the great library, running the width of the house, are many rare Catholic books, including several which were actually printed at Stonor on a secret printing press during the time of persecution.

The press was operated in a hidden recess behind the chimney of a small upper room, known as Mount Pleasant, that was situated in a gable above the main entrance to the house. Edmund Campion and his collaborators were also hidden there during their visits to Stonor, and there Campion wrote his book *Decem Rationes* (*Ten Reasons for Being a Catholic*). In 1581, soon after Campion's arrest, Stonor Park was raided by the law, the press and literature were seized, and members of the family and other inmates were hauled off to prison.

Mount Pleasant and its secret hiding place are now shown to visitors. On the walls is an exhibit of the life and martyrdom of Edmund Campion.

The Story of Edmund Campion

During the reign of "Bloody" Mary (1553–1558), hundreds of good Christians were tortured and burned to death for being Protestants, and in the succeeding reign of Elizabeth I, Catholic Christians were cruelly executed at Tyburn (near the present Marble Arch in London). The most famous of the Catholic martyrs was Edmund Campion.

His story is a tragic but inspiring one. Born in 1540, the son of a London bookseller, he became a precocious scholar who at Oxford University so distinguished himself that he gained the friendship and patronage of Queen Elizabeth. Persuaded by her and other important admirers, he briefly became a Protestant and was ordained into the Church of England, but he soon reverted to his native Catholicism. On leaving Oxford he went to Ireland, where orders were given for his arrest as a papist. Disguised as a servant, he returned to England and proceeded to the college at Douai in France, where he formally reasserted his Catholic faith.

On a pilgrimage to Rome in 1572 Campion became a Jesuit, and eight years later he was chosen to undertake the dangerous mission to England. Upon landing at Dover he was at once arrested, but the mayor released him and he traveled on to London, where his preachings at private meetings of Catholics caused such excitement that the government decided to imprison him. However, he proved a difficult man to catch. In Catholic houses throughout the country, as at Stonor, secret rooms had been constructed for the concealment of fugitive priests, and many an old Catholic family preserved a "priest hole" where, according to legend, Father Campion himself took refuge during his elusive period. Finally he was betrayed and captured at Lyford Grange, a house in Berkshire not far from Stonor.

Even under arrest Campion remained a serious embarrassment to the government. He still had powerful friends who had admired him at Oxford, including the Earls of Leicester and Bedford, and they arranged a private meeting with him at which Queen Elizabeth was also present. Campion affirmed his loyalty to her, but he refused to give up his Catholic faith, even though it should cost him his life. He was sent to the Tower of London and twice tortured upon the rack. An attempt was made to discredit him by making him debate in public with leading Protestant divines, but Campion put his case with such modesty, reason, and good humor that his opponents were discomfited and several of his listeners were converted to Catholicism. After further torture he was tried on a trumped-up charge of treason, and on December 1, 1581, he was hanged, drawn, and quartered on the scaffold at Tyburn.

HENLEY-ON-THAMES can be reached by train from Paddington Station in London, but there are no regular buses from the town to Stonor, so the alternatives are a taxi or a pleasant 5-mile walk. The journey by car takes about an hour from London, the quickest way being by the M4 motorway, the exit to Henley, and the B480 road north of the town. Another approach is by the M40 (Oxford) motorway and the B480 to Stonor through Watlington.

Stonor Park is open to the public from April to September on Wednesday, Thursday, Sunday (and Saturday in August), 2 to 5:30. Admission £1.80. There is a gift shop, and homemade teas are served in the cafeteria.

WINCHESTER

Winchester claims to be the oldest cathedral city in England, and it is certainly one of the loveliest and most interesting. Its center has not been sacrificed to industry and traffic, as has happened to many other English cities, and even its few graceless modern buildings are absorbed by the harmony of its medieval streets and alleys. Winchester takes pride in its history and thus remains peaceful and prosperous, a good place to live and a pleasure to visit.

The origins of Winchester are traced to its legendary foundation in the ninth century B.C. by King Hudibras, the ninth ruler of Britain after Brutus. His name for it, Caer Gwent, the White City, may refer to the local chalk blocks of which the first town was built. A later king, Molmutius, the great road-builder, enlarged it. Several prehistoric tracks and roads either made or repaved by the Romans point toward Winchester, and the fact that they go to different centers in the city indicates that it was a large place in very early times.

Another legendary king, Lucius, is said to have built in the second century A.D. the first Christian church at Winchester during the time when it was an important Roman city. A Saxon cathedral was established in the middle of the seventh century. Kings were crowned and buried there, and Winchester became the capital of Wessex and the administrative center of all England. King Alfred (871–901), whose statue looks down the High Street from the top of the Broadway, made it the center of learning. That tradition is maintained to this day by Winchester College, the most select of English boys' schools, located south of the cathedral. Winchester was the capital of King Canute and the early Norman kings. In wealth and commerce, however, it could not rival London, which gradually usurped its administrative functions. The Black Death in the fourteenth century decimated the population and its wool trade declined, but Winchester did not so much decay as stand still. Though now a provincial city, it retains the dignity and grace which befits a former capital.

WINCHESTER CATHEDRAL

Low-towered, gray-green with age, the cathedral stretches across a lawn surrounded by the old houses of the close. Its 545-foot length makes it the longest in England. The present fourteenth-century building encases the stones of its Norman predecessor, a magnificent church begun by the first Norman bishop, Walkelin, in 1079. Before that the site was occupied by the Saxon cathedral dedicated to St. Swithun, which had replaced earlier churches going back to Roman times. A pagan temple stood there as well as an unknown form of prehistoric shrine, possibly a stone circle. Some old stones, said to have been part of a megalithic monument, were to be seen in the cathedral close up to the nineteenth century. In the crypt below the cathedral is its oldest sacred relic, a prehistoric "Druidical" holy well.

The plainness of the cathedral's exterior leaves one unprepared for the magnificence within. Here is Gothic architecture at its most effective and otherworldly. Vistas between

pillars and noble arches are punctuated with intervals of clear and dim light, creating an abstract, idealized landscape of woodland paradise. Herein are fulfilled the purposes of a great church, to attract sacred influences and to invoke the divine element in human imagination.

More great and noble people lie buried in Winchester Cathedral than anywhere else in England outside Westminster Abbey and St. Paul's. Their monuments were broken up or damaged during the Civil War when Cromwellian troops looted the cathedral and hurled the bones of Saxon kings through the stained glass windows. The only one of Winchester's renowned chantry chapels which escaped harm was that of a fourteenth-century bishop, William of Wykeham. He was also a rich businessman and founded Winchester College, whose alumni call themselves Old Wykehamists. When the sol-

Effigy of William of Wykeham on his chantry, Winchester cathedral.

diers burst into the cathedral, one of their officers, an Old Wykehamist, stood before the founder's chapel in the south aisle and defended it with drawn sword.

The damage to other chantries (small, ornate chapels where bishops and great men were entombed and masses sung for their souls) has been made good by skillful restoration. One of the finest, in the aisle south of the choir, is the chantry of Bishop Richard Fox, who built it himself before his death in 1528. To remind visitors of their own mortality, he commissioned a gruesome statue of a decaying corpse and placed it on the front of his chantry. A similar figure adorns the chantry of Bishop Gardiner, which is opposite Bishop Fox's, on the north aisle of the choir.

Most impressive of the more recent monuments is that of Bishop Samuel Wilberforce, who died in 1873, famous for his last-ditch stand against Darwin's theory of evolution. His effigy lies on top of a magnificent Gothic composition by Gilbert Scott in the south transept. Nearby in an adjoining chapel is a grave which draws many pilgrims, that of Izaak Walton, author of the fisherman's bible, *The Compleat Angler*. He died in 1683. A slab in the floor marks the grave, and above it is the Angler's Window, put up in 1914 and subscribed to by freshwater fishermen throughout the world. Sportsmen fishing for trout in the Itchen, Test, and other chalk streams near Winchester are naturally inclined to visit Walton's grave.

The cathedral's most popular attraction is the grave of Jane Austen in the north aisle of the nave. In later life she lived at Chawton near Alton, 15 miles east of Winchester, and her house there has been restored as a museum of her relics. The gravestone on the floor enumerates her many virtues ("the benevolence of her heart, the sweetness of her temperament, the extraordinary endowments of her mind," etc.) but says nothing of her literary achievements. Those achievements are referred to on a brass plaque on the wall beside the grave, and in the window above it.

Also in the north aisle of the nave is the black marble font,

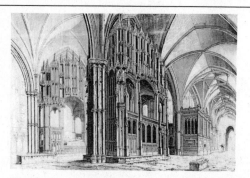

Some of the magnificent chantry chapels of Winchester cathedral. Waynflete's chantry is in the foreground.

Winchester cathedral: One of the rich geometrical ceilings to the chantries. This example is on the theme of the binary numbers 4, 8, 16, 32.

a unique furnishing from the old Norman cathedral. It is carved with scenes from the life of St. Nicholas (Santa Claus), who gave presents to poor children and performed miracles on their behalf. Illustrated is one of his feats; restoring to life some boys who had been chopped up and salted into barrels by a butcher.

A great national treasure, the twelfth-century illuminated Winchester Bible, is kept in the cathedral library, which is approached by steps off the south transept. Lodged in ancient chambers from the Norman cathedral, this is one of the oldest surviving libraries, and it has a famous collection of manuscripts.

The Crypt Behind a door in the north transept are stairs that lead down to the Norman crypt in which are preserved the shape and masonry of Bishop Walkelin's eleventh-century cathedral. The extension at the east end below the present Lady Chapel was made in 1200. Directly below the high altar is the holy well of traditional Druidic sanctity, around which the cathedral and the whole city of Winchester grew up. A second well is in an alcove nearby. Modern brickwork in the walls of the crypt was added during the great work of restoration that lasted six years, to 1912. The cathedral had

*The font of Winchester cathedral with scenes from the life
of St. Nicholas.*

been found to be sinking, and inspection showed that its
foundations rested on rafts of beech trees laid over watery
ground. Underpinning them with concrete required the use
of a diver; some of the beech timbers he brought to the
surface can be seen within the crypt.

St. Swithun the Rainmaker

In a place of honor on the central axis of the cathedral, at the
east end between two chantries, is a curious structure
resembling a metal bedstead with a triangular top. It covers
an inscribed stone which proclaims that the shrine of St.
Swithun which stood there has been destroyed but that
"none can destroy his glory."

St. Swithun, who died in 862, was a bishop of Winchester
noted for his humility. He used to walk everywhere, and he
traveled at night to avoid being seen. He loved the poor and
helped them by building a bridge across the Itchen. When a
market woman dropped some eggs on the bridge, Bishop
Swithun performed the humble but impressive miracle of
making them whole again. When he died, his request was
not to be enshrined with the grand folks in the cathedral but
to be buried outside it, under the eaves to the north, where
the rainwater would drip onto his grave.

This was done, but by popular demand Swithun was
canonized, and in 971 it was decided to move his bones into
the cathedral. This was attempted on the saint's feast day,
July 15, but as the monks began to dig up the grave, they
were driven indoors by a violent rainstorm which lasted forty
days. This accounts for the popular belief (which occurs in
various forms in the folklore of many countries) that if it
rains on St. Swithun's Day, it will go on raining for the next
forty days. On July 15 English country people keep a close
eye on the weather.

Nevertheless St. Swithun's bones were taken into the
cathedral, which had just been rebuilt. His grave had gained
a reputation as a place of healing, and St. Swithun's shrine
in the cathedral became the scene of mass cures. With every
healing miracle the monks were required to chant in gratitude, and they were kept so busy that they complained,

whereupon St. Swithun appeared in a vision and rebuked them.

In 1093 Bishop Walkelin had St. Swithun's relics exhibited before enshrining them within his new cathedral. There they remained until 1538, when in the spirit of the Reformation the shrine was demolished. Two years later Henry VIII ordered that the cathedral, which up to 980 had been dedicated to Saints Peter and Paul and after that to St. Swithin (or Swithun) be rededicated to the Holy Trinity.

A surviving portion of St. Swithun's shrine is the pair of iron gates at the top of the steps leading eastward from the south transept. They are part of a railing which protected the shrine in Norman times, and they are thought to be the oldest pieces of wrought ironwork in England. The original grave, outside the cathedral north of the nave, is now covered by a stone slab presented by Stavanger Cathedral in Norway, which was also dedicated to St. Swithun. In the crypt is a large stone coffin, hewn from a single block and furnished with a headrest, in which Swithun is supposed to have been buried.

The Strange Death and Burial of the Red King

A plain slab beneath the tower in the very center of the cathedral marks the burial place of King William II, known as William Rufus because of his red face and sandy hair. He was the favorite son of William the Conqueror and succeeded him in 1087. A deep mystery surrounds this monarch and the manner of his death and burial.

Rufus was a tyrant, cruel and grasping, but the extreme loathing in which he was held by some of his court, clergy, and those who knew him best was caused by something other than his style of rule. Attributed to him were certain unmentionable vices at which chroniclers of his time barely hint. On August 2, 1100, while hunting in the New Forest, he was killed by an arrow shot by one of his companions. Nothing more is recorded of the incident. The unknown regicide fled the scene, and later the body was found by some peasants who put it on a farm cart and carried it to Winchester. The very next day it was buried without ceremony beneath the cathedral tower.

No reigning king in Christendom has ever had such a humiliating burial. No mass was said, no bell was tolled, and even the late king's family were prevented by the priests from laying offerings on his tomb.

There has been much speculation about the nature of the Red King's abominable vices. Pederasty has been suggested, but no such predilection would explain why the Church refused him a proper Christian burial and only buried him at all out of respect for his rank. Dr. Margaret Murray was probably on the right track with her theory that William Rufus was a member of some occult order and thus put himself beyond the pale of Christianity. She points to certain features in the account of his death which hint at a ritual, witchcraft murder or sacrifice. The arrow that pierced his heart was apparently never removed and was buried with him, as though he had been a vampire or a black magician. Its shaft was found among the bones when his coffin was opened in 1868.

Seven years after Rufus's burial the central tower of the cathedral fell down onto his tomb. This was seen as the cathedral's protest against the evil spirit interred within it.

In the New Forest near the village of Minstead, 18 miles southwest of Winchester, stands the Rufus Stone, marking the traditional place of his death. The legend told there is that a courtier, Sir Walter Tyrrel, shot at a deer and the arrow, rebounding off an oak tree, struck the king. This is the version of the episode which has passed into popular history, but the truth of the matter remains unknown.

King Arthur's Round Table at Winchester

Winchester has many Arthurian associations; early chroniclers identified it with Camelot, King Arthur's capital, where he held ritual assemblies of his knightly Round Table order. This was accepted by Henry VII when in 1486 he chose Winchester Cathedral as the place of baptism for his first-born son, whom he named Arthur. His intention was to establish a link between his Welsh dynasty of Tudor and the Celtic lineage of Arthur—and for his son to reign as Arthur II. Thus the prophecy of Arthur's return would be fulfilled. However, Prince Arthur died young and the throne passed to his brother, Henry VIII.

Much valued by the Tudor kings was Arthur's Round Table, a relic which Winchester still preserves. Deprived of its original twelve legs, it is exhibited on a wall in the great

King Arthur's Round Table.

hall of the castle, opposite Westgate, at the end of High Street. It is made of oak, measures eighteen feet in diameter, and weights 1.25 tons. It is painted in segments, alternately green and white, with a rim bearing the names of Celtic nobles. A Tudor rose is at the center, and at the top, creating a twenty-fifth division, is painted an enthroned king. This table, so it appears, was designed to accommodate King Arthur and twenty-four knights—or twelve knights and their ladies.

In fact the painting is no earlier than 1522, and it was done for Henry VIII when he used the table for entertaining a visiting emperor, Charles V. The kingly figure is a portrait of Henry himself. The table, however, is considerably older. Radiocarbon tests indicate a thirteenth-century date, possibly in the reign of Henry III (1220–1272). It was more likely to have been made for his successor, Edward I, who modeled himself on the ideal of King Arthur and in 1278 went down to Glastonbury with Queen Eleanor to watch the opening of Arthur's tomb.

By 1450, when the table was first mentioned in literature, it was old enough to be considered a genuine relic of about 500 A.D., when the legendary King Arthur and his knights defended Britain from Saxon invaders. Even though it is probably much more recent, it was no doubt conceived in the Arthurian spirit by an English king who wished to revive the chivalric institution of the Round Table. That was achieved in the middle of the fourteenth century, when Edward III founded the Order of the Garter in imitation of King Arthur's circle of knights.

The Mizmaze on St. Catherine's Hill

A mile south of the cathedral, on the far side of the main A33 road bypassing the city on its way to Southampton, is Winchester's sacred hill, where formerly stood a chapel dedicated to St. Catherine. The foundations of the chapel are hidden in a clump of trees, to the east of which is the figure of a labyrinth cut into the turf. Its local name is the mizmaze.

When William of Wykeham founded Winchester College in 1382, he ordained that the scholars should walk twice daily to the summit of St. Catherine's Hill. This was probably in continuation of an earlier monkish procession. A college festival known as Hilles took place on St. Catherine's. From south of Winchester College a path leads to the top of the hill.

The low hill is surrounded by rings of an earthwork thought to be of about 500 B.C. Both the date and the ritual purpose of the mizmaze are unknown; estimates of its age vary from three hundred to more than a thousand years. Treading the maze, by walking the furrows between its raised banks, is a mystical and therapeutic experience. It may be that in following the spiral patterns of natural growth and energy, one orders the mind and attunes oneself to nature's rhythms. The labyrinths which sometimes occur on

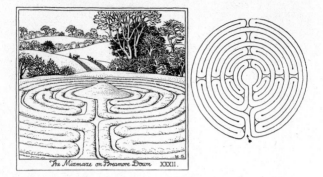

The mizmaze at Breamore, a sister to the maze on St.
Catherine's Hill above Winchester.

the pavings of medieval churches traditionally represent the pilgrim's journey to Zion.

Another mizmaze is found 23 miles to the west at Breamore (pronounced Bremmer), south of Salisbury. The lovely Elizabethan manor house there is open to the public, and beside it is a rare little Saxon church. From the church a path goes northwest across beautiful, wooded downland country for about a mile to the mizmaze, which is hidden within a wood. It is also cut into the chalk turf and has no known history.

The association between St. Catherine and the labyrinth symbol is discussed at Abbotsbury in Dorset (page 121), where the St. Catherine's hill has features similar to that of Winchester.

Looking north from the mizmaze on St. Catherine's Hill, one can see Winchester cathedral, and the line of sight is close to the line of the old processional pathway to the hilltop. Beyond the cathedral the line continues through the medieval Hyde Gate and the site of Hyde Abbey (where King Alfred was originally buried), through the twelfth-century Church of St. Bartholomew, and over a plowed-down long barrow at South Wonston, 3 miles beyond the city. Another 3 miles further on, the line strikes the center of a prehistoric earthwork, Tidbury Ring, where the remains of a Roman station or temple have been found. During the research for their book *The Ley Hunter's Companion*, Paul Devereux and Ian Thompson walked this line, and they consider it to be a deliberately planned alignment of sacred sites from prehistoric times.

WINCHESTER is in Hampshire, 65 miles southwest of London, off the M3 motorway. There are regular trains from Waterloo Station (journey of about eighty minutes).

The cathedral is open daily, 7:30 (before morning prayer) to 6:30 (after choral evensong). The crypt is open only during the summer because it floods in winter. The times and details of guided tours are given at the bookstall near the west-end entrance. The library is open during the summer months, 10:30 to 12:30 and 2 to 4, and on Wednesday and Saturday in winter. Entrance 30p.

King Arthur's Round Table in the great hall of the castle can be seen daily, 10 to 5. Admission free at time of writing.

CANTERBURY: *The Pilgrims' Way to the Shrine of the Holy Blissful Martyr*

All roads in the southeast of England lead to Canterbury. From London the ancient British trackway, Watling Street, paved by the Romans, was the route taken by Chaucer's Canterbury pilgrims to the shrine of St. Thomas à Becket. From Canterbury it continues in a direct line to the sea near Dover, 14 miles away. Another old road, made up from stretches of prehistoric tracks, ran mostly on hill ridges from Old Sarum, near Stonehenge in Wiltshire, past Winchester and thence to Canterbury. Sections of it are marked on Ordnance Survey maps as "Pilgrims' Way."

Along the Pilgrims' Way were hostelries and chapels, and ferrymen plied their trade at the river crossings. Modern pilgrims to Canterbury, driving on the M2 motorway or on the old A2 road (Watling Street), can visit one of their predecessors' resting places at Maison Dieu, Ospringe, on the western outskirts of Faversham in Kent. Those with leisure to explore a short section of the old route east of Winchester can make the 30-mile journey from London to Guildford, where the pilgrims were guided by two sacred

Maison Dieu, the old pilgrims' shelter at Ospringe near Faversham, Kent.

St. Catherine's hilltop chapel near Guildford.

landmarks, both set on high hills, the Chapel of St. Catherine and St. Martha's Church.

St. Catherine's Chapel, Guildford

Guildford, an old town with some fine buildings, is now almost a suburb of London. Its huge modern cathedral, founded in 1936 and finished in 1961, towers over the town from a nearby hilltop. Less than a mile from the town center, on the road to Godalming, a small turning to the left leads to the foot of St. Catherine's Hill. There is a car park from which one can walk to the ruined chapel on the summit.

This is a lovely spot. On the east side of the hill, just beyond the railway that cuts into its base, is the silvery River Wey, its valley bordered by wooded hills, on one of which, due east, is St. Catherine's sister church, St. Martha. St. Catherine's Chapel, of which only the walls are standing, was built early in the fourteenth century, but the hilltop was a sacred place before that time. Its position suggests that a pagan temple stood there, a shrine to the goddess of the River Wey. A traditional fair which took place there on October 2, the Feast of the Guardian Angels, was abolished many years ago because of riotous conduct.

In the Middle Ages the chapel is thought to have held sacred relics and to have been visited by travelers on the Pilgrims' Way, which borders the hill on its north side. This is one of a chain of St. Catherine hilltop chapels, the chain running westward to Winchester, Milton Abbas, and Abbotsbury. (See those entries for further discussion of the legend of St. Catherine and her function as patron saint of spinsters and voyagers.)

At the foot of the hill is the site of a religious establishment which vanished so long ago that no one knows whether it was a priory or a nunnery. The stretch of Pilgrims' Way which passes it goes between charming old cottages to the river, where the pilgrims' ferry has now been replaced by a footbridge. On the right of the path, just before it reaches the river, a spring wells up from a bank. This is the holy spring of the Virgin Mary that refreshed every pilgrim on the way to Canterbury. Its waters are clear and refreshing today.

St. Martha's Church
One can walk the 2-mile stretch of Pilgrims' Way from St. Catherine's Hill to St. Martha's Church, which passes through the outskirts of modern Guildford. The drive to St. Martha is by the A246 road to the east of the town. A half-mile from the town center, turning to the right, is the road to Albury. To the left of it, just past Tyting Farm, is a car park from which one can walk to St. Martha.

The walk of about five hundred yards lies along a sandy ridge and offers wide views of the Surrey countryside. The church has one of the finest hilltop positions in the country. It seems astonishing that a parish church should be placed on such a high, isolated spot; however, this is not merely a local church but a former chapel for pilgrims on their way to Canterbury's martyr shrine. Nor were they the first who resorted to this hilltop; in prehistoric times it was a beacon hill, where fires blazed to guide pilgrims of an earlier age traveling between the ancient British sanctuaries.

St. Martha's Church was originally the Chapel of Martyrs on the hill, of which the present name is supposed to be a corruption. In the Lives of the Saints, however, St. Martha, like St. Michael, is a dragon killer, and the legend of such exploits is attached to many of the high sanctuaries in Europe; it echoes some forgotten ritual once performed at these places. But St. Martha gives no further clues, for there are no other churches dedicated to her in England.

A stone circle and other megalithic remains were once to be found near the church, but no trace of them is visible today.

The lovely hilltop church of St. Martha on the Pilgrims' Way.

By the nineteenth century the church had fallen out of use and become a ruin. It was rebuilt in 1848, and now there are services on Sunday at 11 a.m. Trees have grown up around it, affecting its intervisibility with St. Catherine's Chapel, but there is an obvious spiritual link between the two hills. It is recognized in local folklore, which says that St. Martha and St. Catherine were built by two sisters.

FROM APRIL 1 through October St. Martha is open Saturday and Sunday, 10 to 6; Wednesday, Thursday, and Friday, 2 to 6. In other months it is open Sunday, 10 to dusk, and Wednesday and Saturday, 2 to dusk. One can walk to the hilltop and along the Pilgrims' Way at any time.

MURDER IN THE CATHEDRAL

From the time he was canonized, in 1173, to the extirpation of his cult by Henry VIII in 1538, St. Thomas à Becket's shrine at Canterbury was the most popular place of resort in England and was visited by pilgrims from distant parts of Europe. It was covered by plates of gold that were scarcely visible beneath the mass of precious stones which adorned it. Around the shrine was a forest of crutches left by cripples whom the saint had miraculously cured. Thomas Cromwell, the king's chancellor who supervised its destruction, needed twenty-six carts to carry away its gold, jewels, silken canopies, miters, rings, and other furnishings.

The story of St. Thomas' martyrdom is well known. Thomas à Becket was born in 1118 of undistinguished Norman parents living in London. His brilliance and energy gained him rapid advancement, and he became a close friend of Henry II, who made him his chancellor and the effectual administrator of the kingdom. He engaged in a successful war in France and paid for it by a tax levied on Church property. By exploiting his position he became extremely rich, and the magnificence of his household outshone even that of the royal court.

The Church at that time was a great power in the realm. The king's laws were not binding upon priests; if they committed crimes, they were subject only to ecclesiastical discipline. This state of affairs was intolerable to King Henry, and when the Archbishop of Canterbury died in 1162, he appointed Becket as his successor, hoping through him to remove the anomalous privileges of the clergy. Becket, however, took his new position seriously and refused to implement any reform which favored the temporal authorities at the expense of his church. On many occasions he quarreled furiously with the king, and in 1164 he was forced into exile in France. With the support of the pope, he returned to England six years later and was met at the coast by an enthusiastic crowd who escorted him to Canterbury, where he was triumphantly reinstalled in his cathedral. His provocative first act was to suspend from office the Archbishop of York and to excommunicate the bishops who had

Canterbury cathedral: The martyrdom transept where, at the bottom of the steps, Becket fell.

sided against him in his dispute with the king. This provoked King Henry to utter the fatal words which have gone down in history as, "Who will rid me of this turbulent priest?"

Four of the king's knights rode off immediately for Canterbury. They arrived on the evening of December 29, 1170, while the archbishop was at dinner. Forcing their way into the hall, they confronted him with the demand that he absolve the bishops whom he had excommunicated. That, said Becket, was impossible until they had done penance. The knights retired to don armor, and Becket was forced by his monks into the sanctuary of the cathedral, where vespers were being sung. Attended by three monks, Becket stood in the north aisle before the altar of the Virgin. The armed men burst into the cathedral and strode up to him, shouting out their demands, to which Becket replied that rather than comply he would die a martyr to the Church. An attempt was made to drag him from the sanctuary, and when he resisted, swords were brought into play. The archbishop was cut down and killed, and the murderers rode hastily away. The body was buried in the crypt below the scene of the crime.

Throughout and beyond England shock and hysteria followed upon the news of this sacrilegious act. Canterbury cathedral was closed for a full year to allow for its ritual purification. The pope refused to admit any Englishman into his presence. King Henry was horrified at what had happened and feared for his own position. At Canterbury he performed a humiliating public penance. After walking barefoot with bleeding feet through the city, dressed in a simple woolen shift, he prostrated himself weeping over the spot where Becket fell, and he was then led into the crypt where, before the martyr's tomb, he was whipped five times

A medieval drawing of Becket's shrine, Canterbury cathedral, once gloriously decked in gold plate and jewels.

by each of the bishops and abbots present and three times by each of the monks.

The first of the miracle cures at Becket's tomb took place a few days after his death, and for 360 years Canterbury was one of the great pilgrimage centers in Christendom. The phenomenal growth of the cult is not easy to understand; Becket was no humble saint but a haughty and arrogant person. It seems that he deliberately courted martyrdom, and he was certainly prepared for it, for on the evening before his death he drank deeply, telling his companions at dinner that he who must lose much blood should drink much wine. (For this remark he was made patron saint of the London Company of Brewers.) Yet his obstinacy was rooted in a firm belief in the Day of Judgment, of which he was more frightened than of any mortal vengeance. After he died it was found that he had long been wearing an agonizing hair shirt that was stinking and crawling with lice.

It was not simply because of the martyr's personal qualities that pilgrims flocked to his shrine. Every year people took to the roads, as we do now on summer vacations, in search of fresh air, fresh company, and foreign scenery. In visiting the "holy blissful martyr" at Canterbury, one acquired virtue along with pleasure. A further inducement was that, by joining the free spirits roaming the highways, one defied the authorities, who always prefer that their subjects remain quietly at home.

The City

As the Canterbury pilgrims of old neared the end of their journey, they would see from afar the white stone cathedral with its spire topped by a golden angel. This steeple was replaced in 1498 by the Bell Harry Tower, which rises from the center of the cathedral. To its north are extensive remains of monastic buildings and fine old houses of the cathedral close. To the south are the streets and alleys of the medieval town converging on Christ Church Gate, which gives access to the lawns surrounding the cathedral. The gatehouse, built in 1517, is ornamented with winged angels bearing shields.

Many of the streets are on Roman foundations, for the Romans took Canterbury soon after invading England in 43 B.C. and made it their first regional city. The remains of one of their town houses, centrally heated and with a magnificent mosaic floor, can be seen on Butchery Lane, and the foundations of their city wall lie beneath the fortifications that a later invader, William the Conqueror, raised upon them.

Much of the old city was destroyed by German bombing in 1942, and more damage was done afterward when Canterbury was reshaped by the city planners. Yet most of its churches and sacred monuments, and above all the cathedral, have survived unscathed. With these and its many museums and historic buildings, Canterbury is a place to explore over several days.

St. Augustine's Mission

The Celtic church was established in Canterbury during the Roman occupation, but in the fifth century, when the Romans departed and the heathen Jutes and Saxons succeeded them as rulers of southeast England, Christianity was extinguished in the city.

In about 580 the local king, Ethelbert, married Bertha, a French Christian princess. She brought a chaplain with her to Canterbury, and Ethelbert, though keeping to his own pagan religion, allowed her to repair an ancient Christian church to the east of the city and hold services there. The church, St. Martin, is still there and claims to be the oldest in England.

In England at that time, Celtic Christianity and Nordic paganism existed side by side without animosity. Rival kings were constantly at war with each other, but not for religious reasons. Both religions, Christian and pagan, were mystical; they acknowledged the local deities of the countryside, and they were influenced by the native tradition of Druidism. In some ways the Celtic Church had more in common with contemporary English paganism than with the Church of Rome.

Roman policy was to unify the Church under the pope and to destroy the influence of paganism in northern Europe. To that end Pope Gregory in 597 sent Augustine to England. The unlikely legend is that he had never heard of the country until he saw some towheaded Anglo-Saxon boys for sale in the Roman slave market, exclaimed, "They are not Angles but angels!" and decided to convert their countrymen. Augustine was rebuffed by the Celtic bishops, but he established Roman authority at Canterbury, and by the end of the seventh century the Roman authority prevailed throughout Britain.

On his arrival in Canterbury Augustine was welcomed by Queen Bertha and her fellow Christians. King Ethelbert was baptized in the church of St. Martin, and Augustine's influence was complete. He built an abbey to the east of the city wall, around Ethelbert's pagan temple, which became the Church of St. Pancras. Another old sacred building, a former Celtic Christian church, was reshaped as a cathedral. When Augustine died, he was buried in his abbey. Since the year of his arrival Canterbury has been a cathedral city; Augustine was its first archbishop, and there have now been more than a hundred of them. Canterbury's archbishop is England's senior clergyman and the leader of the Anglican Church worldwide.

CANTERBURY CATHEDRAL

Before the Time of Becket

The ancient Celtic church, dating from Roman times, which Augustine adapted as his cathedral, was in the form of a basilica with columns and a rounded east end. A unique feature of the present cathedral, forming its eastern termination, is a circular tower known as Becket's Crown. Tradition says it is on the site of the earliest church, and there has been speculation that its plan repeats the dimensions of a prehistoric stone temple which had existed there.

The old cathedral was rebuilt and expanded by successive archbishops up to the time of the thirty-third, Stigand, in 1067, when it was destroyed by fire. With it perished many

Canterbury cathedral from the northwest.

precious relics which had survived catastrophe in 1012, when Danish raiders sacked the cathedral and martyred its archbishop, St. Alphege. Stigand's Norman successor, Archbishop Lanfranc, began a new cathedral in 1070; that building has since been so altered that little of it remains apart from the crypt. This crypt is one of the most fascinating parts of the building, quite different from the rest of it in spirit, with strange Celtic or Saxon carvings on its ancient pillars. On the north side of the crypt is the site of St. Thomas à Becket's original tomb, where Henry II knelt in penitence and was scourged by monks.

After Becket
In 1174, four years after Becket's martyrdom, the cathedral caught fire and was gutted. The reconstruction was directed by a French master mason, William of Sens. When he was disabled by falling from scaffolding near the roof of the cathedral, the work was completed by his English pupil, also named William. The magnificent new building was a tribute to St. Thomas, whose bones were removed from the crypt in 1220 and placed with great ceremony in a new shrine, constructed at vast expense, in the Trinity Chapel east of the high altar.

For more than three hundred years the streets of Canterbury were crowded with visitors from every Christian nation who were drawn to the miracle-working shrine of St. Thomas. Kings and emperors were among them, and great wealth was accumulated by the city traders and innkeepers as well as by the cathedral authorities. When Henry VIII proclaimed Becket to have been a traitor and put an end to pilgrimage, Canterbury's trade was ruined. There were those who defied the ban by making summer trips to the city, but almost everything they wanted to see was gone. The saint's shrine had been destroyed and all his relics dispersed. Yet after all the efforts of the Protestant reformers and the Cromwellian Puritans to remove the evidence of Becket's cult, there are still many references to it throughout the cathedral. His legend unfolds as one walks around the interior in a clockwise direction, following the route taken by the Canterbury pilgrims.

Miracles in Glass
One enters the cathedral through the southwest porch, on which are statues of the founding patrons, King Ethelbert and Queen Bertha. Inside to the left is the great west window, glorious with the colors of stained glass from the twelfth to fifteenth centuries. Some of it was originally in other parts of the cathedral. The figures depicted are kings and patriarchs, and in the center of the base is Adam digging his garden.

At the end of the nave's north aisle, steps lead upward to the martyrdom transept, where the place of Becket's death is marked on the floor at the foot of the steps to the aisle of the choir. Along this aisle is a series of magnificent windows, beginning with two known as the Poor Man's Bible because of the scriptural and allegorical scenes they illustrate. One window shows the martyrdom of St. Alphege, the archbishop whom the Danes stoned to death in the eleventh century, whose shrine stood opposite.

The beautiful Trinity Chapel, to which one ascends by a further flight of steps, was designed as the most sacred part of the cathedral, for here was St. Thomas's shrine. A mosaic on the floor marks its former site. To enter this place was for many pilgrims the greatest experience of their lives. The light in the chapel comes through twelve stained glass windows, three of which are modern, the rest thirteenth century. At the top of the fifth window, Becket's shrine is depicted as it was in 1220, a golden, jewel-encrusted object of barbaric splendor. The spirit of Becket has emerged from it and is speaking to some sleeping monks in their dreams. The twelve miracle windows are filled with many hundreds of figures enacting scenes from the saint's legend, the cures and wonders performed at his shrine. In these and the other early windows Canterbury has the finest collection of stained glass in England.

One can spend hours in this noble building with its tombs, monuments, beautiful little chapels, and masterpieces of craftsmanship in stone, wood, glass, and metalwork. There are monuments to royalty, beginning with a statue of Ethelbert in the wonderful stone screen west of the choir. Around him are later kings, some of their portraits made from their death masks. One of the kings is Henry IV, whose tomb is on the north side of the Trinity Chapel. His chantry chapel, the most beautiful in the cathedral, is opposite, and on the other side of the Trinity Chapel is the tomb of Edward, the Black Prince, topped with his bronze effigy. Above both these tombs are painted panels of wood depicting the murder of Thomas à Becket.

On the south side of Canterbury choir is a carving based on the "bent hexagon," a theme of Islamic and other traditional schools of geometry.

After the Reformation all known portraits of Becket were destroyed, but one may still survive in the cathedral. At the base of a window in the north wall, opposite the site of the shrine, is a bearded figure whose features are thought to be those of Canterbury's martyr.

When the Canterbury pilgrims had said their prayers at Becket's shrine and rendered up their offerings, they would pass along the south aisle of the choir and down into the crypt to see where the martyr's body was first laid. This too was a place of miracles, as was the well in which his clothes were washed. The clothes themselves—even Becket's soiled handkerchief and toilet rags—were shown to pilgrims for a fee. Only the rich could afford to see the most precious relics, such as Becket's pastoral staff and pieces of his scalp. None of these things survived the Reformation. By the sixteenth century many people were disgusted by their exploitation and the superstitions they fostered. With their destruction the spirit of the cathedral was purified, and modern visitors experience its intensity without the aid of St. Thomas.

St. Augustine and Pagan Sites
At least two of Canterbury's churches, as well as the cathedral, are on sites which were sacred in Roman times. And this is probably true of most old churches throughout the country, for it was always Christian policy to take over and reconsecrate the pagan sanctuaries.

Before Augustine came to England he was instructed by Pope Gregory to continue this practice. Heathen temples, said the pope, were not to be destroyed but made into Christian churches. Festivals were to be held on the accustomed days, and the oxen that used to be sacrificed to the gods were now to be slaughtered for a church feast. The markets and the merrymaking of pagan feast days were thus continued under the patronage of a Christian saint, and pilgrims to Christian shrines still took the traditional routes which had been used from prehistoric times.

St. Pancras and Augustine's Abbey
The street south of the cathedral, Burgate, leads eastward to Longport, on the north side of which are gardens and the entrance to St. Augustine's Abbey. The abbey church, founded in 598, was replaced after the Norman Conquest by a more splendid building to serve the largest Benedictine community in England. It is now a sad ruin. At the Reformation it was seized for the Crown and the church demolished. The abbot's house became a royal lodging, where monarchs up to the time of Charles II stopped on their way to Dover. By the eighteenth century it was also a ruin.

To the east of the church is the most interesting building on the site, the mysterious Chapel of St. Pancras. Its eastern end, formerly a semicircular apse, was rebuilt in the fourteenth century; the rest of it is thought to be of St. Augustine's time. Its materials, however, are Roman, and tradition says that this chapel was originally King Ethelbert's pagan temple.

Another legend of St. Pancras's chapel concerns its dedication. St. Pancras was a Roman boy of fourteen who was martyred early in the fourth century. Because of his age he became a guardian saint of children, and it is said that St. Augustine gave his name to the old pagan temple in memory of Pope Gregory's encounter with the blond Anglo-Saxon boys that prompted the mission to England.

St. Martin's Church

North Holmes Road is the first turning to the left off Longport, east of the entrance to St. Augustine's Abbey. Entering it, one sees ahead a lych-gate to an old-fashioned country churchyard. Beyond the gate the path ascends a knobbly green hill on which is set the little Church of St. Martin.

This hidden sanctuary is the most ancient of Canterbury's, and possibly England's, Christian sites. Here was the old Celtic church which Queen Bertha found and repaired, where she and her chaplain held Christian services while her husband was still a pagan. The Venerable Bede recorded that "it was built of old while the Romans were still inhabiting Britain." The tower through which one enters is made of flint and chalk blocks and was added in the fourteenth century, but from the west wall, which contains bits of Roman windows, to the east end, the structure is largely of Roman bricks. There is no certainty as to its actual date. The eastern part, where some of the wall has been exposed to show the ancient building blocks, is supposed to be the original church which Bertha repaired, and it may previously have been a pagan temple. The nave is thought to have been rebuilt in St. Augustine's time.

A treasure in this church is the Saxon stone font, carved with interlinked circles. Its legend, which may well be true, is that in this font King Ethelbert was baptized by St. Augustine, thus initiating the establishment of Roman Christianity in England.

Outside the entrance, looking west through the yew trees which surround the hill of St. Martin, one can see over housetops the towers of the cathedral.

CANTERBURY, Kent, is 60 miles southeast of London, off the M2 motorway. The journey by train from Waterloo Station in London takes about one hour.

The cathedral is open daily, 8 to 8 (or dusk), except during services.

St. Augustine's Abbey and St. Pancras's Chapel can be visited between March 15 and October 15, daily, 9:30 to 6:30, Sunday, 2 to 6:30; for the rest of the year, daily, 9:30 to 4, Sunday, 2 to 4. Admission 75p.

The Tourist Information Centre is at 13 Longmarket. Telephone: Canterbury (0227) 455490 or 66567.

4

THE SOUTHWEST

WILTSHIRE, DORSET, SOMERSET

AVEBURY: *An Ancient Sacred Landscape*

Avebury, the greatest stone circle in the British Isles, is a wonderful monument, both in itself and in its setting. It stands in the center of a prehistoric sacred landscape, of which every feature—springs, streams, hills, stones—had its particular symbolism. To this landscape were added temples and related structures in the form of stone circles and avenues, long barrows with inner stone chambers, earth enclosures, and the largest artificial mound in Europe, Silbury Hill. The traditional sanctity of the area is commemorated in the local legend, like that of holy Ireland, which says that no snakes are ever found here, and that if any are brought in, they soon die.

The importance of Avebury as a central temple in Stone Age times is evident both from its immensity and from its central position in the ancient trackway system. The prehistoric Ridgeway from East Anglia to the Dorset coast passes by it, and the Old Bath Road from London to the west ran right through it. It can be seen on a map that Avebury is virtually at the center of southern England, near the midpoint of a line drawn from the east coast to the western tip of Land's End. This line marks the alignment of St. Michael's shrines through Glastonbury (see page 137), and touches the southern entrance to the Avebury circle.

THE STONE CIRCLES

The approach to Avebury from the east is through the attractive market town of Marlborough and along the northern bank of the River Kennet. Five miles beyond the town a line of dome-shaped mounds stands along the Ridgeway to the right, and straight ahead one sees the enormous bulk of Silbury Hill. Before it is reached, a signpost indicates a turn to the right into Avebury village a mile further on.

As one turns off the main road, stones begin to appear, first in the hedges and then striding in two rows across the field to the left. This is West Kennet Avenue, which leads to the southern entrance of the temple.

One enters Avebury through a gap in the huge embankment and trench, about a quarter of a mile in diameter, that surround it. All around are great, bulky stones, many of them worked into fantastic shapes by time and the elements, and among them are low concrete pillars marking the spots where other stones once stood. Many stones have been destroyed, and some of their fragments have been used to build the pretty cottages of Avebury which lie within and beyond the circle. In the center of the monument is a crossroads where the village inn is located, and a road to the left goes toward the village church, a beautiful old manor house, and the museum. The scene is delightful, a complete contrast to Stonehenge with its security barriers and vulgar tourist facilities. At Avebury one can wander freely among the stones and explore the village at one's own pleasure.

The site is so large and broken up that it is difficult at first to see its pattern. Basically it consists of three stone circles, two of them contained by the third. The two inner circles are thought to have been built first, in about 2600 B.C. They stood side by side, both 340 feet in diameter, with other stone structures in their centers. The northern ring consisted of two concentric circles, the inner of twelve stones and the outer of twenty-seven, of which only two stones remain. The two other stones at the site survive from a trio of monstrous size which formed a cove at the center. The southern circle contained other stones, including the tall obelisk, which is no longer standing (a concrete pillar marks its site).

The pretty village of Avebury is built partly within the stone circle, broken stones from which have been used in some of its houses.

Avebury: A section of the bank, ditch, and outer stone circle with the remains of the two inner circles beyond.

These circles are surrounded by a ring, formerly of about a hundred stones, geometrically designed in a series of arcs. It stands within the circular earthwork, through which there are four entrances—roughly, north, south, east, and west. They are still used by the modern roads, and the greatest stones of the circle are placed beside them. The approximate date of the outer stone circle and the earthworks is 2500 B.C.

The Discovery of Avebury and the Great Serpent

As recently as the eighteenth century the temple at Avebury was virtually intact. Stagecoaches passed right through it on the Old Bath Road, but—almost incredibly—it seems that no one noticed that the huge boulders around the village were other than naturally placed objects until, on a winter's evening in 1648, the antiquarian John Aubrey saw them. Riding home from a day's hunting and passing through Avebury, he recognized the great stones and earthworks as forming an ancient temple, which he attributed to the Druids.

In the 1720s the great Druidic revivalist William Stukeley spent several seasons at Avebury, drawing and charting the stone circles and neighboring monuments. As he did so, the stones were disappearing. Local farmers, greedy for a few more square yards of land, had discovered a technique for clearing away the stones by digging pits at their base and heating them with bonfires, after which they could be smashed by dashes of cold water and hammer blows. Stukeley was powerless to intervene; he could only record, and many features of old Avebury are known only through his drawings. In 1743 he published his book on Avebury, with wonderful illustrations and an interpretation of its meaning that greatly excited his contemporaries.

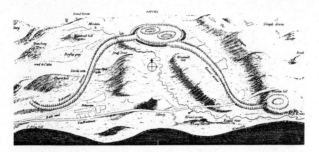

Eighteenth-century plan of the stones at Avebury by Wil-liam Stukeley. He interpreted the avenues as the body of a serpent passing through a circle and thus forming a tradi-tional alchemical symbol.

Stukeley's famous diagram shows the original plan of Avebury as representing a serpent passing through a ring. The front part of its body, formed by West Kennet Avenue, ends in a concentric stone circle which makes the head. This circle, the Sanctuary, has been entirely destroyed, but the positions of its stones have been marked on the site, which can be reached by a path on the south side of the A4 road.

As Stukeley saw it, this figure proved that the Druid priests who made it had anticipated the doctrines of Christianity, for the circle is a symbol of the Godhead, and the serpent represents the Son proceeding from the Father. Stukeley proclaimed that the Druids had inscribed a whole

Avebury: Two of the large stones within the northern inner circle suggest by their contrasting shapes a male and fe-male symbolism.

landscape with a divine pattern so as to invoke the blessings of Providence.

The stones of Beckhampton Avenue, forming the serpent's tail, were destroyed so long ago that archaeologists at one time doubted that Stukeley actually saw them. However, by removing the topsoil to reveal stone holes in the underlying chalk, excavators proved him right. One solitary stone in the serpent's tail remains standing in a field to the north of Beckington. It is one of a pair called Adam and Eve; Adam, upright and pointed, is the avenue stone, and the massive, squat Eve is the relic of a three-sided cove structure.

THE SILBURY TREASURE

An integral part of Avebury is Silbury Hill, situated on the north side of the main road 1500 yards south of the village. It is an artificial mound, cone-shaped, with a flat top. Its circumference at the base measures 1640 feet, and it is 130 feet high.

In the local folklore, Silbury was the tomb of a King Zel who was buried there on horseback. Stukeley reported that the top of the hill was dug into in 1723 and some bones were discovered together with an antique bridle. The idea that some rich royal burial chamber lies deep within the heart of the mound was cherished by archaeologists for many years. The Duke of Northumberland had a shaft drilled from the top to the bottom in 1776, and in 1849 Dean Merewether tunneled horizontally for 300 feet to beyond the center of the hill. Neither of these efforts produced finds. In 1967, Professor Richard Atkinson, the doyen of Stonehenge archaeologists, made a determined search for the Silbury treasure. Attracted by the prospect of discovering an ancient royal British tomb, the BBC agreed to finance and publicize his expedition. Tunnels were driven into Silbury at ground level, linking up with and extending those made by Merewether, and the core of the mound was thoroughly explored, but again nothing was found. Silbury, it seems, was not built as a tomb.

Though he recovered no treasure, Atkinson learned some interesting things about Silbury's construction. Radiocarbon analysis showed that the date of its foundation was around 2660 B.C. The actual year could not be determined, but the season of the year when the work at Silbury began was established to within a few days by the remains of plants and insects found on the original surface beneath the primary mound. Silbury was founded during the first week in August, at the feast of Lammas at the start of the harvest season.

The most remarkable fact about Silbury is that it is not a mere pile of earth, that it has an elaborate internal structure. At its core is a primary mound, 120 feet in diameter, built up in layers of clay, flints, chalk, gravel, and turf. On and around it the main bulk of the hill has been constructed from radial and concentric walls made of chalk blocks, and filled in with rubble. When finished, the hill took the form of a seven-stepped pyramid and was glistening white. Earth was then piled onto its terraces, and the whole structure was buried and grassed over. Being built up in this way, Silbury Hill has retained its original shape and size for more than 4500 years.

The Goddess of Silbury

The theory of Silbury Hill as a burial mound was finally discredited in the 1960s, leaving the question of its original purpose totally unexplained. Its possible uses for signaling, observing the heavens, and time-keeping have been suggested, but the most comprehensive interpretation of Silbury in relation to the entire Avebury complex was produced by an antiquarian artist, Michael Dames. In two learned and perceptive works, beginning with *The Silbury Treasure* in 1976, he identified Silbury Hill as a symbolic effigy of the Great Mother presiding over the fertility rituals which marked the course of the year. The mound itself is her pregnant womb, and her outline is traced by trenches in the flat ground surrounding it. At Lammas in August, when Silbury Hill was founded, the festival of the first fruits of harvest was celebrated; at that festival the Silbury goddess began to give birth.

A possible survival of the ancient round of festivals centered on Silbury Hill was the traditional fair held at Silbury on Palm Sunday, which died out many years ago. According to Stukeley, local people used to have a merry picnic on top of the hill and drink water from the Swallowhead spring.

That spring, which rises five hundred yards south of Silbury, is the source of the river now politely called the Kennet, formerly the Cunnit. The name relates to the

Silbury Hill from the west.

goddess mound and hints at ancient rituals beside the spring, where the spirit of the waters bestowed health and fertility.

The Church and the Dragon Font
St. James's Church at Avebury, set in a quiet country churchyard, is beautiful inside and out and of great age. Its earliest masonry is Saxon. It stands beyond the earthworks of the prehistoric temple, but the sarsen stones in its fabric may come from a megalithic monument formerly on the site.

On the primitive Norman or Saxon font at the west end of the church is an interesting carving that may be a symbolic illustration of the coming of Christianity to Avebury. It shows a bishop holding a book and piercing the head of a dragon with his crozier. It may refer to St. Michael, the dragon killer, or to some forgotten legend of Avebury's ancient serpent temple and how it was supplanted by the church.

The Museum
The Avebury Museum, discreetly hidden behind the church, is small and intimate, but its contents make it one of the leading archaeological museums in Britain. It was founded by Alexander Keiller to house the ancient objects he discovered during his excavations at Avebury and Windmill Hill between 1934 and 1939. Material from West Kennet, Silbury, and other sites in the district has since been added to the collection.

In the course of his Avebury work, Keiller, who lived in the lovely Elizabethan manor house beside the church, did much to restore the stone circles, digging up stones which had become buried, reerecting them in their original holes, and marking the sites of those which had vanished. While raising up one of the great fallen stones, he found beneath it the skeleton of a man who had been crushed by its fall. From a pair of scissors and other objects found with him, he was tentatively identified as a fourteenth-century traveling barber. His relics are in the museum.

SOME MONUMENTS AROUND AVEBURY

Windmill Hill For at least a thousand years before Silbury and the Avebury circles were built, people came from afar to attend festivals in the area. Plentiful remains of these gatherings have been found on Windmill Hill, a mile to the northwest of Avebury, which can be approached through Avebury Trusloe by a road that ends as a rough track. From one of the barrows on its flat summit the visitor can view the main features of the district, including Avebury and Silbury with the ridge of the West Kennet long barrow behind it.

There is evidence of temporary dwellings on Windmill Hill as early as 3700 B.C. About five centuries later the hilltop was enclosed by three concentric circles of banks and ditches, which have now been plowed under. Sheeps, pigs, and goats were brought to the festivals, together with agricultural produce and flint implements, all of which were doubtless marketed there.

The West Kennet Long Barrow This impressive monument can be reached by a footpath running south from the main road, a quarter of a mile east of Silbury Hill. It is one of the finest of long barrows, 330 feet in length, oriented east-west. Its date is about 3250 B.C.

It is entered at the east end through a portal of great stones from which there is a passage into the interior. Off the passage are five quite large side chambers. When excavated in the nineteenth century, it was found to contain the bones of forty-six people, twelve of them children. Two hundred years earlier the barrow had been plundered by a Marlborough doctor who took away bones to grind up for medicine.

A similar type of monument, the East Kennet long barrow, stands on private land a mile to the southeast.

The Grey Wethers All the stones of Avebury and the larger ones at Stonehenge came from local Wiltshire valleys where, in primeval times, large sandstone blocks called sarsens were strewn across the chalk soil. Part of one such valley can be seen from the main road, 2.5 miles east of Silbury, on the north side. It is covered with the stones John Aubrey called the Grey Wethers because in the evening light they look like a huge flock of sheep.

A mile east of the Grey Wethers, in Clatford Bottom, a fine dolmen called the Devil's Den stands in a cornfield.

AVEBURY is on the A361 road, 9 miles south of Swindon and the M4 motorway. Swindon has the nearest railway station.

There is free public access to Avebury, West Kennet Avenue, the Sanctuary, West Kennet long barrow, Windmill Hill, and Silbury Hill, all of which are in the care of English Heritage. About nine hundred acres of land around Avebury belongs to the National Trust, but many of the lesser monuments in the area are on private land.

The Avebury Museum is open daily, 9:30 to 6:30, in the summer, and 9:30 to 4 (Sunday, 2 to 4), in the winter. Admission 75p. Telephone: Avebury (06723) 250.

STONEHENGE

Stonehenge is an ancient ruined temple. It is the most remarkable prehistoric structure in Europe, and there is nothing like it anywhere. It stands on the upland turf of Salisbury Plain, 8 miles north of Salisbury in Wiltshire, in an open landscape which is thickly strewn with burial mounds, earthworks, and many other prehistoric monuments. The whole area is imprinted with the marks of ancient sanctity.

At the beginning of this century Stonehenge stood isolated on the open plain. Sheep grazed among its stones, which were freely accessible to visitors. At midsummer, on the day when the sun rises at its northernmost limit in line with the axis of the temple, a festive crowd would gather at Stonehenge to witness the dawn. Beginning in 1905, they were joined by a party of white-robed Druids, members of an order founded in the eighteenth century, who performed the rituals appropriate to sunrise in imitation of their ancient Druid predecessors.

The situation today is very different. In 1901 the owner of the land put a fence around the stones and levied a small fee for entry. On his death in 1915 Stonehenge was sold at public auction for £6,600, and three years later the benevolent purchaser gave it to the nation. Conditions attached to his gift stipulated free public access to the monument and prohibited the erection of further buildings or barriers in its vicinity. These conditions have all been ignored. Opposite Stonehenge is a large car park with shops and tourist facilities, from which the monument is approached by a concrete tunnel that passes beneath the formidable security fence that surrounds the monument. Since 1984 the public has been forbidden to assemble at Stonehenge at midsummer dawn, and the Druids are banned from performing their ceremony. An area of thousands of acres north of Stonehenge is occupied by the military, who have ruined many of the ancient monuments on the plain, while others have been plowed under by farmers or destroyed by roadmaking and other modern processes.

No doubt in years to come more suitable arrangements will be made and Stonehenge will be restored to a setting more worthy of it, but for the present visitors are warned that Stonehenge is no longer as it was in the days when such artists as Constable and Turner delighted in the loneliness of the site and the strange light and atmosphere that pervade it.

THE CONSTRUCTION OF STONEHENGE

Stonehenge in its present form was erected about four thousand years ago, according to radiocarbon dating. The technique was refined in the mid-1960s when its results were recalibrated by reference to the ancient Californian bristlecone pine, and this led to a discovery that shattered contemporary theories about the origin of prehistoric monuments in Britain. It had previously been assumed that the culture of the Stonehenge builders had originated in the Mediterranean, but the new datings showed that the stone monuments of northwestern Europe were in fact older than their supposed Mycenaean prototypes. The earliest period of building on the site of Stonehenge was found to have been around 3000 B.C.

The oldest parts of the monument, made in that period, are the ditch enclosing a circular earth bank, of about 320 feet in diameter, which surrounds the present temple, and a circle of pits called the Aubrey holes (fifty-six in all), which play an important part in modern astronomical theories. Their positions inside the earth bank are marked by a ring of white circles. The bank was originally six feet high, but it is now so worn away that it is scarcely noticeable. An entrance through the bank and ditch was left to the northeast, in the direction of midsummer sunrise, through which was visible a large, rough sarsen block called the Heel Stone, which stands a few feet from the road passing the monument.

A thousand years after the first works had been completed, between about 2150 and 2000 B.C., a new temple was built in the center of the circular earthwork. The sequence of events is not clearly established, but there is some evidence that the first new additions were the four "station" stones (of which two now remain) placed on the circle of Aubrey holes to form a rectangle in symmetry with the temple's axis. The main parts of the temple were then built, consisting of a circle of thirty upright pillars of local sarsen stone, supporting thirty lintel stones that were jointed together to form an unbroken ring. Within this circle were raised five enormous "trilithons" (two stones capped by a third), placed in a U-shaped formation.

At about the same time, a new kind of stone appeared at Stonehenge. Geologists have identified its source in the mountains of southwest Wales. It was evidently believed to have some special quality, for specimens of it that are much older than Stonehenge have been found in barrows on Salisbury Plain. Pillars of this Welsh "bluestone" form two of the features in the temple: a circle containing originally

Stonehenge restored.

View of Stonehenge from the northeast showing the surviving sequence of three lintels above the entrance and axis line.

some sixty stones, standing within the sarsen circle, and a U-shape of nineteen stones within the trilithon formation. Another "foreign" stone, a sixteen-foot slab of greenish sandstone, now lies across the axis of the temple, near the center. Its traditional name is the Altar Stone because it was once believed to have served for Druid sacrifices, but archaeologists now think that it once stood upright.

It is not known when Stonehenge was abandoned, but its ruin seems to have been gradual rather than one caused by a deliberate act of destruction. Over the centuries stones have been removed for roads or buildings and others have fallen, making it difficult at first to identify all the original features of the temple. Three of the five trilithons still stand; so does one pillar of each of the two others. The tallest, belonging to the trilithon which stood across the axis, measures twenty-two feet above ground and eight feet below, making it the longest ancient standing stone in Britain. The outer sarsen circle is best preserved toward the northeast, where a sequence of eleven pillars and three adjacent lintels are still in place, including the linteled archway framing the midsummer sunrise.

The Carvings

Earlier in this century Stonehenge was subjected to extensive excavations—which archaeologists now regret because little was learned from them while evidence was destroyed that might have been of value in the future. The most exciting discovery of recent years came not from excavation but from an observant eye. In July 1953 Professor Richard Atkinson was engaged in a photographic survey of the monument. The evening sun, casting an oblique light on the face of one of the trilithon pillars, revealed an ancient, eroded carving of a dagger. Beside it were the shapes of four axes.

Later that summer several more ax carvings were detected on the same stone and on two of the pillars in the sarsen circle.

The dagger was recognized as a unique type known only from Mycenaean burials, and its depiction at Stonehenge seemed to be evidence of a link with Mediterranean culture. The axes, on the other hand, were of a prehistoric Irish type. The date of the carvings was suggested on stylistic grounds to be around 1500 B.C.

Visitors are no longer allowed to walk among the stones, so the carvings can be inspected only with special permission from the caretakers of the monument, English Heritage.

The Sunrise Axis
The firmest structural clue to the meaning of Stonehenge is provided by its axis. It is marked by a line of sight between several pairs of stones within the temple, and it passes just to the left of the Heel Stone. In 1979 a large hole was discovered in the chalk on the other side of the axis from the Heel Stone, and this probably once contained its pair. The two stones would have framed the rising sun on the day it entered the temple at the midsummer solstice. Beyond the Heel Stone the axis continues its path toward the sun between the parallel earthworks of Stonehenge Avenue, which runs for about five hundred yards from the entrance in the bank surrounding the temple. The avenue has been dated to 2150 B.C. and is so eroded that it is now barely visible. It emphasizes the importance of the axis and the temple's solar orientation.

STONEHENGE ASTRONOMY

The alignment of the axis with midsummer sunrise in one direction and midwinter sunset in the other is the one undisputed astronomical feature of Stonehenge. Stonehenge is beyond doubt a solar temple, and it is apparently related to the orbit of the moon as well. This was first demonstrated in 1965 by an astronomer, Gerald Hawkins, in *Stonehenge Decoded*. The title was unfortunate, for the mystery of Stonehenge is far deeper than the single question of its astronomy, but Hawkins's claims attracted wide interest. He had studied archaeologists' plans of the early periods at Stonehenge, before the great stones were erected, and noted the positions of holes in the chalk that may have held stones or posts. Between these and existing features, such as the station stones, he discovered numerous alignments that pointed toward the extreme positions of the sun and moon on the horizon. In the course of a year the sun completes a round trip between its northernmost and southernmost rising and setting points. The moon has a more complicated cycle, involving two northern and two southern extremes, which it completes over a period of 18.6 years. Thus there are four extreme solar positions, rising or setting, and eight lunar positions—twelve in all. Every one of these positions was found to be indicated by an alignment within Stonehenge.

When the new Stonehenge temple was built some four thousand years ago, several of the old astronomical alignments were preserved and others were added. From between the pillars of the five trilithons, narrow sighting corridors through the archways of the outer sarsen circle lead the eye toward extreme sun or moon positions over distant hills. It was then discovered that several of the positions are marked on the horizon by ancient earthworks. This was noted by Professor Alexander Thom in the course of his astronomical survey of Stonehenge and district during the 1970s. Thus the implication is that Stonehenge is at the hub of an astronomical pattern which has determined the positioning of other monuments within its sphere of influence.

All these conclusions have since been challenged. Statistical analysis of Hawkins's alignments has proved that many of them are imprecise or could occur by chance. Several of Thom's long-distance markers have been shown to be much later than Stonehenge itself, ruling out the theory of their relationship to ancient Stonehenge astronomy. There is also radical dispute among theorists about the nature and purpose of the astronomical features in Stonehenge. The fashion in the 1960s was to claim it as a scientific observatory and computer of astronomical cycles. It was pointed out, for example, that the fifty-six Aubrey holes could have been used to record the fifty-six-year lunar eclipse cycle. On the other hand, the archaeological evidence is that the holes were filled in shortly after they were dug. The modern tendency is to dismiss the claims for Stonehenge as a scientific instrument and to regard it as a cosmic temple which, like all ancient temples, was designed with regard to the heavenly bodies whose light, penetrating into the temple at certain seasons, provided a focus for the ceremonies performed on those occasions.

One has only to witness the huge orange harvest moon rising above Stonehenge to feel the effect it must have produced on our prehistoric ancestors and to be assured of the important part it must have played in their religious observances.

THE STONEHENGE BUILDERS

The first literary reference to Stonehenge occurred in a work by the clerical historian Henry of Huntingdon, written in Latin in 1130. "No one," he remarked, "can conceive how such great stones have been so raised aloft, or why they were built there."

The two questions are still part of the Stonehenge mystery, and a third concerns who built it. Shortly after Henry's book was completed, another chronicler, Geoffrey of Monmouth, offered answers to all three questions. Stonehenge, he said, was built as a memorial to British chiefs who had been treacherously slain by Saxons during a peace conference nearby. The British king, Aurelius Ambrosius, having avenged the massacre by routing the Saxons in battle, consulted the wise man Merlin about a suitable monument. Merlin told him of a stone building in Ireland called the Giants' Round: Each of its stones had medicinal properties, but the stones were so huge that no modern man could move them. (They had originally been brought to Ireland from Africa by giants.) The Britons sent an expedition to Ireland, defeated the natives, and began trying to dismantle the stone ring; but, as Merlin had warned, they were unable to lift the stones. Merlin intervened and by his mysterious art moved the Giant's Round from Ireland to England and set it up on Salisbury Plain, where it became a burial place for kings.

This strange tale has a grain of truth in that some of the stones of Stonehenge (though not the tall pillars with lintels) were brought to the site from afar. The rest of the story is incredible, though no more so than many of the later theories of Stonehenge. In the vast literature on the subject the erection of the stones has variously been attributed to Phoenicians, Danes, Saxons, Romans, Druids, Brahmins, Egyptians, Chaldeans, and even American Indians. Other suggestions have included giants, dwarfs, Atlanteans, and extraterrestrials. Among all these claimants the Druids have had the strongest backing. The first writer to propose the Druids as the builders of Stonehenge was John Aubrey in the seventeenth century. In the following century some of the astronomical properties of the structure were noticed, and for many years thereafter the orthodox theory of Stonehenge was that it was built by the Druids as a temple to the heavenly bodies.

By the beginning of this century, theories of Stonehenge in relation to Druids or astronomy had fallen into disfavor. In archaeological publications the Stonehenge builders were depicted as primitive Ancient Britons, waving clubs and clad in animal skins. The Celtic Druids, it was said, did not appear in Britain before 600 B.C., long after Stonehenge was completed. However, that date is disputed by modern scholars, who find evidence of Celtic influence in Britain as early as 2000 B.C., coinciding with the most important period of building at Stonehenge. This implies that the Druids may well have been responsible for the present form of the temple, and their claim is strengthened by its astronomical features, for, according to ancient writers, the Druids' mystical philosophy was based on their knowledge of astronomy and other sciences. Everything about the design and construction of Stonehenge proclaims its builders to have been skilled in science and engineering and to have lived in an ordered society controlled by a professional priesthood. The evidence of astronomical features in other European megalithic monuments, many of them considerably older than Stonehenge, indicates an ancient native tradition of sacred science that the Celtic Druids no doubt inherited. In recent years fashion has come full circle, and it is no longer thought inappropriate to refer to Stonehenge once more as a temple of the Druids.

The Measurements of the Sarsen Circle

The most remarkable feature of Stonehenge is the circle of thirty sarsen pillars capped by the ring of thirty lintels. Only seventeen of the uprights and six lintels are still in place, but it has been found possible to establish the dimensions of the original circle to within a fraction of an inch. In its original state the lintel ring must have been one of the most exact and symmetrical works of architecture ever created. Each lintel is curved on its inner and outer rim to form arcs of two circles whose radii differ by a lintel's width. They are jointed together by tongues and grooves, and holes have been cut into their undersides to receive projecting tenons on the tops of the supporting pillars (see illustration). Their upper sides are perfectly leveled about sixteen feet above the ground. From outside the circle the pillars look rough and irregular, but their inner faces have been dressed and polished, and the centers of these faces are tangent to a circle whose measured diameter is 97.32 feet. That is also the diameter of the inner rims of the lintels, whose width, about 3.5 feet, makes the circle of their outer rims some 104.3 feet in diameter.

Modern researches in ancient metrology have made it possible to establish the precise lengths of the units of measure by which architects in prehistoric times designed sacred buildings. One of these units, first identified by Sir Isaac Newton through his study of the temple at Jerusalem, was the "sacred rod," equal to a six-millionth part of the earth's polar radius. This unit has been discovered also in the dimensions of the Mexican pyramids at Teotihuacan. Its exact value is 3.4757485 feet (1.0594071 meters). Measured by the sacred rod, the dimensions of the Stonehenge sarsen circle are:

inner diameter = 28 sacred rods = 97.32096 feet
outer diameter = 30 sacred rods = 104.272455 feet
width of lintel = 1 sacred rod = 3.4757485 feet

Thus the width of the stone ring made up of thirty lintel stones, being equal to one sacred rod, is one six-millionth part of the earth's polar radius.

The Traditional Pattern of the Cosmic Temple

The use of geodetic or earth-measuring units in the Stonehenge sarsen circle makes it a symbolic image of the terrestrial globe. Further conclusions can be drawn from the fact that the mean diameter of the circle, measured between the centers of the lintels, is 100.8 feet, making its circumference equal to 316.8 feet or a hundredth part of 6 miles. A circle of those dimensions is known to students of esoteric science as the New Jerusalem circle because it is the central feature in the traditional scheme of cosmological geometry which St. John in Revelation described as the groundplan of the ideal Holy City. The illustration shows the New Jerusalem diagram, its astronomical correspondence in the dimensions of the earth and moon, and how the Stonehenge plan conforms to it.

The basic figure of symbolic geometry in the design of Stonehenge is the "squared circle," consisting of a square and a circle of equal perimeters. It represents the combination of the heavenly, spiritual world (the circle) with the material world (the square). The circle of the heavens is formed by the mean circumference of the lintel ring, measuring 316.8 feet. A square of 316.8 feet round its four sides contains a circle of diameter 79.2 feet, which is the diameter of the Stonehenge circle of bluestones. Within that circle a hexagram contains the circle at the base of the central bluestone formation.

The meaning of Stonehenge is implied by the symbolism of this scheme of geometry.

THE MEANING OF STONEHENGE

A temple is a place for invocation, and every temple in the ancient world was designed for invoking the particular god or gods to whom it was dedicated. The understanding

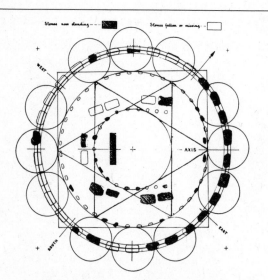

The ground plan of Stonehenge overlaid by the "New Jerusalem" diagram. The square containing the bluestone circle has the same perimeter as the circle passing through the center of the outer sarsen ring, 316.8 feet, or a hundredth part of 6 miles.

behind ancient sacred science was that "like attracts like." Each god had a corresponding planet, number, shape, sound, color, and other attributes, and the technique for attracting a god to inhabit a shrine or temple was to display the appropriate symbols in its structure and furnishings.

The solar orientation of Stonehenge, together with its lunar orientations, identify it as a temple to the sun and moon. These luminaries were not worshiped as gods in their own right but as symbols of the two great principles in nature, the male and female archetypes. The heat and splendor of the sun make it a natural emblem of positively charged energy, while the moon with its pale, watery light represents the negative pole. In traditional metaphysics the sun and moon are related as heaven to earth, the first being seen as active and fertilizing, the second as receptive and fruitful. All phenomena are produced by the interactions of the two opposite forces. Disturbances in nature reflect their violent encounters, while peace and harmony ensue when they are brought into amicable union—a process known esoterically as the sacred marriage.

Through its dual dedication to the all-encompassing solar and lunar principles, Stonehenge can be claimed as the oldest example of the cosmic temple, others of which are located at Jerusalem, Hieropolis, and sacred centers throughout the ancient world. The main characteristic of the cosmic temple was completeness. As a symbolic model of the universe, it contained all the numbers, shapes, and harmonies in the original blueprint of creation. Stonehenge is a synthesis of geometric types and proportions, an acknowledgment of all the gods in nature, designed to attract and harmonize the forces of the cosmos for the benefit of life on earth.

The learned priests who built Stonehenge were concerned above all with keeping the lives of their people in tune with the seasons and rhythms of nature. Stonehenge was their instrument for that purpose. Activated by the rituals which marked the stages in the farmers' and hunters' year, its influence reached far across the countryside. It was said of the temple at Jerusalem that when it was destroyed the world fell into chaos, and the ruin of Stonehenge was no doubt followed by a corresponding decline in the social order. Yet even now, in its sadly ruined, desecrated state, it exerts a certain power. For many different reasons, from curiosity to reverence, people flock to Stonehenge, and whatever ideas are brought to it, it somehow reflects them back. Theories about Stonehenge are legion, and each of them finds some support in the features of that remarkable structure. That is one reason for identifying it as a cosmic temple, an image of the created universe and its microcosm, the human mind. It is also a symbol of reconciliation. In recent years, reflecting the troubles in the world at large, Stonehenge has been the scene of angry confrontations between its Druids and festivalgoers and the police, local landowners, tourist operators, and others who lay claim to it. Yet Stonehenge is capable of accommodating all interests, for that was its original function. One day peace and concord will be restored there, exemplifying that future state which is a necessity for human survival, harmony among nations.

STONEHENGE is 8 miles north of Salisbury in Wiltshire, which has the nearest railway station. Buses from Salisbury go to Amesbury, 2.5 miles east of Stonehenge. The journey from London by car is about 80 miles by way of the M3 and A303.

The monument is open daily, 9:30 to 6:30, in the summer, and 9:30 to 4 in the winter (October 16 to March 14). Admission £1.30.

OLD SARUM: *From Cathedral City to Rotten Borough*

The high, earth-walled eminence called Old Sarum, two miles north of New Sarum or Salisbury, is widely visible from Salisbury Plain. Its outer ramparts are prehistoric, and its occupants have included Iron Age Britons, Romans, Saxons, and Normans. Several old Roman roads, stretches of which were built on earlier foundations, converge upon Old Sarum, testifying to its former greatness. It has been an important religious, administrative, and military center; now it is totally abandoned and ruined.

William the Conqueror acknowledged the national importance of Sarum by holding his victory parade there in 1070. Fifteen years later, in accordance with his policy of centralized power, he summoned England's principal landholders to Sarum and made them swear allegiance to him rather than to their local overlords. Meanwhile the Norman administration had moved the bishop's see from Sherborne to Sarum, where a new cathedral was built. The Conqueror's nephew, Osmund, became its second bishop; later he was made a saint. Five days after Osmund's cathedral was consecrated it blew down in a storm. It was rebuilt under the next bishop, Roger the Norman, and at the center of the old earthworks a moated mound was erected, bearing a castle keep. A picturesque medieval town grew up around it.

Things did not go well at Old Sarum. Howling winds drowned the music in the cathedral and eroded its fabric; there was not enough water; the priests quarreled with the military in the castle. Early in the thirteenth century it was decided that the cathedral should be rebuilt on lower ground. Two legends, both implying divination, tell how the new site was chosen. In one version Bishop Poore dreamed of a spot near the confluence of rivers. Another says that the site was chosen by the fall of an arrow shot from Old Sarum. The matter is discussed further below.

The old cathedral was demolished to provide materials for the new, and the old upland town gradually declined. By the beginning of the nineteenth century only ten voters re-

The ground plan of the former cathedral at Old Sarum seen from above.

mained in the borough, yet they retained their right to elect two members of Parliament. Thus Old Sarum achieved a last moment of fame as one of the "rotten boroughs" cited by advocates of the Reform Bill of 1832.

An Ancient Alignment of Sanctity
From Stonehenge the spire of Salisbury cathedral, the successor to Old Sarum, can just be seen in the distance. Precisely in line between the two places is the central citadel of Old Sarum. When one stands at the center of Old Sarum and looks south beyond Salisbury's spire, one sees the line continue to a corner of the wooded Iron Age earthworks of Clearbury Ring.

This alignment was first noticed about a hundred years ago, and it was also found that the intervals in the line from Stonehenge to Old Sarum, and from there to Salisbury cathedral, are of exactly 6 miles and 2 miles.

The various legends telling of the determination of the site of Salisbury cathedral, either by a bishop's dream or by the fall of an arrow, may be allegories of a system of divination by which sacred sites were traditionally chosen. Geomancy was the name of the science by which the proper sites for temples were located. Its methods are better known in eastern countries than in Europe, where such ancient practices were reserved as trade secrets by the powerful masonic guilds. Their business included selecting the auspicious site for a new church, and it was probably one of their order who placed the new cathedral at Salisbury in direct line with the old temple of Stonehenge and the center of Old Sarum.

TWO MILES NORTH of Salisbury, almost opposite the Old Castle Inn on the A345 road, is the turning on the left for Old Sarum. Cars are parked below the earthworks. Old Sarum is open daily, 9:30 to 6:30 (to 4 in winter); Sunday, 2 to 6:30 (to 4 in winter). Admission 75p.

SALISBURY: *A Thirteenth-Century New Town*

When the cathedral at Old Sarum was abandoned, the site chosen for the new cathedral was a beautiful spot on a meadow just north of the River Avon, where it is joined by four of its tributaries. The town that grew up around its close was planned, like a Roman city, on a rectangular, checkerboard pattern.

The location and planning of New Sarum were evidently successful, for from its very beginning Salisbury (as it became commonly named) has been a happy, prosperous city. A number of annual fairs were held there, and it still has a flourishing market in its central square. During one of the fairs a carnival figure, the Salisbury Giant—twelve feet tall, armed with a club and a sword, and smoking a clay pipe— was paraded through the streets by the guild of tailors. The Giant is now in retirement in the Salisbury Museum.

Salisbury is full of pleasant old streets and buildings, and the modern additions have generally (with some glaring exceptions) been well adapted to the old pattern. Among the fine houses in the cathedral close is Mompesson House, built early in the eighteenth century for a rich merchant and displaying some rare craftsmanship in its interior. It now belongs to the National Trust and is open to the public. The oldest church is St. Martin to the southeast, a venerable-looking building with a massive, low tower. Religious processions were made there by the priests of Old Sarum.

On a summer's evening there is no finer view in England than of Salisbury's lofty spire, seen from the south across streams and water meadows. There is a sacred quality to the light there which many artists, most successfully John Constable, have tried to capture.

SALISBURY CATHEDRAL

King Henry III laid the foundation stone, and betwen 1220 and 1266 the cathedral was built, much as it stands today, except for the spire, the cloisters, and the chapter house, which were added in the following century. The spire, 404 feet high, is the tallest in England. Steeplejacks tell of the magnificent view from its summit.

The Reformation caused little damage at Salisbury, but a

Salisbury cathedral: The tallest spire in England, 404 feet high.

great deal was done by James Wyatt, sometimes called England's worst architect, at the end of the eighteenth century. In the course of his "restoration" he destroyed many original features, including screens, chapels, tombs, a detached bell tower, and much medieval stained glass. The monuments he arranged in neat rows in the nave. As a result of his work, however, the inside of the cathedral looks awesomely vast and cavernous.

One feature Wyatt spared is the beautiful thirteenth-century painting on the roof of the choir. He merely covered it up, and it has since been restored. Also untouched is the octagonal chapter house, set around with fine sculptures and with a stone vaulted roof springing from a single pillar. The cathedral library, with its ancient manuscripts and printed books, is an antiquarian's dream.

A curious monument in the nave is a stone figure of a half-sized bishop in robes and miter, lying on his back. This is said to be the effigy of a "boy bishop" who died in office. It was the custom in all cathedrals and many parish churches for the choirboys to elect one of their number to serve as bishop for a period between the feasts of St. Nicholas and the Holy Innocents (December 6–28). St. Nicholas's Day was thus celebrated because of his miracle of restoring to life some children who had been butchered and pickled by an innkeeper. During his reign the boy bishop performed all the functions of the actual bishop except for saying mass, and he and the other choirboys took precedence over the dean and

The effigy of the boy bishop, Salisbury cathedral.

priests. This amiable custom was frowned upon by Henry VIII, revived under Mary, and finally suppressed by Elizabeth I.

Another unique item, displayed in the north transept, is the oldest clock in England, made in 1386. It was discovered a few years ago in the cathedral tower.

The gravestones in the close were swept away under James Wyatt's influence, and the cathedral is now surrounded by lawns and trees, providing a valuable precinct for resting, playing, or picnicking.

The Museum

Facing the close, opposite the west end of the cathedral, an old building, the King's House, is occupied by the Salisbury and South Wiltshire Museum. One of its rooms is devoted to Stonehenge, and there are models of Old Sarum that show the stages of its construction. There is a full display of prehistoric objects, based on the famous Pitt Rivers collection, which is now permanently housed in the museum. In the 1880s General Pitt Rivers inherited a large estate in East Dorset, to the southwest of Salisbury; a tract of it, Cranborne Chase, a former royal hunting park, was full of prehistoric earthworks and burial mounds, largely untouched. Pitt Rivers devoted his retirement to excavating them and removing their rich contents to his private museum. In the process he destroyed many ancient monuments, but he was careful in making records of his excavations. His collection, disposed of by his heirs, has mostly been reassembled at Salisbury.

Among the interesting local exhibits in the museum is the reconstructed surgery and waiting room, complete with model figures, of an old Salisbury doctor. By the entrance to the museum is a stuffed great bustard, a bird that used to nest on Salisbury Plain but has been extinct in England for about 150 years.

Another good local museum is that of the Wiltshire Archaeological and Natural History Society at Devizes, 20 miles north-northwest of Salisbury. It has good sections on Stonehenge, antiquities, and local curiosities. There are also a picture gallery, a delightful stained glass window by John Piper illustrating prehistoric Wessex, and an old library to which scholars are allowed access.

SALISBURY is on the main railway line from London's Waterloo Station; the journey takes about ninety minutes. There is a railway line from Salisbury to Bath and Bristol, and coaches and buses go to all parts of the country. The road from London is the M3 motorway.

The cathedral is open daily, early morning to dusk. Guided tours, including a trip to the roof, are available every day but Sunday throughout the summer, leaving at 10:30, noon, 2:30, and 6:30. The charge is 70p.

The museum is open daily, except Sunday, 10 to 5 in summer and 10 to 4 in winter; it is open Sunday in July. Admission £1.25.

The Devizes Museum, 41 Long Street, Devizes, is open Tuesday through Saturday, 10 to 1 and 2 to 5.

Salisbury's Tourist Information Office is on Fish Row. Telephone: Salisbury (0722) 334956.

KNOWLTON: *A Church Within a Stone Age Sanctuary*

The early Christian practice of building churches on ancient sacred sites is well illustrated at Knowlton, where the crumbling ruins of a Norman church, unused since 1647, stand in the center of a prehistoric henge or sacred enclosure. It is a lonely spot, far from any village, with a sinister reputation as a haunt of demons. The local belief is that covens of witches still use it for rituals.

Until a few years ago the church was surrounded by thorn bushes and ancient yews, but the site has been cleared, and the circular chalk bank of the henge is now a refuge for wildflowers. The floor of the church has been neatly covered with yellow gravel. Even so, the atmosphere of the place remains as it has long been, quiet and melancholy on summer afternoons and ghostly at sunset.

Two large mounds just outside the henge to the northeast and northwest are concealed by clumps of bushes.

KNOWLTON, 15 miles southwest of Salisbury, is reached by a turning to the right off the B3078 road 3 miles south of Cranborne.

WIMBORNE MINSTER

At a sacred spot where two rivers flow together the Romans made or took over a settlement, and in the eighth century a Saxon town grew up around a religious foundation. The old minster still dominates the town, which has preserved much of its medieval street plan and has been likened to a miniature cathedral city. Despite the intrusions of traffic it is a happy, intimate place, with all the proper amenities of a country town: a great church, a museum, an antiquarian

The ruined church within the prehistoric earth ring at Knowlton.

bookshop, quaint buildings, alleys, teashops, old inns, and beautiful surrounding countryside.

The minster at the heart of Wimborne is a friendly old building of curiously checkered appearance, being made of two kinds of stone, one blood-red and the other dove-gray. It has a great central tower and another at the west end, on the north outside face of which stands a wooden soldier who beats out the quarter hours on a pair of bells.

Two saintly princesses, Cuthberga (to whom the minster is dedicated) and Quinberga, sisters of King Ina of Wessex, founded a nunnery at Wimborne between 705 and 720. Cuthberga married the king of Northumbria but soon divorced him and took to a convent. She was canonized as a virgin.

In 871 Ethelred I was killed fighting the Danes and was buried at Wimborne by his successor, King Alfred. He is commemorated by a brass effigy and inscription in the presbytery. The Danes overran this part of Wessex, and St. Cuthberga's foundation was destroyed. Edward the Confessor restored it as a place of education with a great church, some of which survives in the piers and columns of the central tower and nave of the minster. On this tower there was once a lofty spire which was said to rival Salisbury's, but it was brought down by an electrical storm in 1600.

The interior of the minster has many curious features and memorials that have accumulated from Norman to Victorian times. Of the latter period is the fine painted roof to the nave. The twelve apostles are depicted in the window of the west tower, wherein is a precious Norman font of Purbeck marble that was quarried nearby. Its rich ornamentation was stripped away at the Reformation. On a wall above it is a remarkable orrery or clockwork model of the heavens, show-

Wimborne Minster church from the north.

ing the sun, moon, and stars in relation to the earth at the center. Constructed in 1320 by Peter Lightfoot, a Glastonbury monk, it is still in working order and gives the phase of the moon and its distance from the sun.

The choir and presbytery are raised above the level of the nave, and below is the crypt or Lady Chapel, the spiritual center for prayer and meditation. It can be entered from the Holy Trinity Chapel to the south, in which there is a monument to the strange whim of a seventeenth-century citizen, Anthony Ettricke. He swore that he would be buried neither in the church nor in the churchyard, so when he died his coffin was placed within a wall. Ettricke's other claim to fame is that he was the first magistrate to examine the Duke of Monmouth, who was found hiding in a ditch near Wimborne and was arrested as a fugitive after the failure of his rebellion at the Battle of Sedgemoor.

The great antiquarian treasure of the minster is its chained library, lodged in an upper room opposite the organ. It was founded in 1686 by local clergy and gentry who contributed their books to make a free library for the people of Wimborne. Thefts were frustrated by attaching the spines of the books to chains ending in metal rings that can be slid along a rod. Among the 340 volumes are some rare classical and theological works and three Breeches Bibles of about 1595, so called because they describe Adam and Eve as wearing breeches rather than (as in the Authorized Version) aprons.

The Museum

On the street east of the minster is the medieval Priest's House, now a museum. It is worth visiting for its agreeable miscellany of objects, ranging from prehistoric relics to old-fashioned illustrations of local history. Behind the mu-

Wimborne Minster: The view to the west from the raised sanctuary.

seum is a charming old walled garden, usually open to visitors, at the end of which is a shed with a collection of old farming implements.

WIMBORNE MINSTER is 5 miles northwest of Bournemouth and the main line railway, from which there are regular buses.

The minster is open daily, 9 to 5:30. Tours of the building and visits to the chained library are available upon request. The library is shown to visitors for a small charge, Monday through Friday, 10 to 4 (with a break for lunch).

The Priest's House Museum is open from Easter through September, daily except Sunday, 10:30 to 12:30 and 2 to 4:30. Admission 30p.

Tourist information: The Cornmarket, Wimborne, Dorset, Telephone: Wimborne (0202) 886116.

The chained library of Wimborne Minster.

MILTON ABBAS: *A Landlord's Dream Village*

Milton Abbas is unique among Dorset villages because it was all built in one period, during the 1780s, by a rich, autocratic landlord. The estate owned by Joseph Damer, Lord Milton (and afterward Earl of Dorchester) included the market town of Milton Abbas together with its old abbey. Beside the abbey he built a splendid Gothic mansion, and around it he planned a classical landscape with valleys and wooded hills. The old Dorset town was thought to ruin his view, so, despite the bitter protests of its citizens, he pulled it down. For those whom he rehoused Damer built a picturesque model village along a sloping street out of sight of his mansion. It consisted of two rows of identical thatched cottages, built in pairs with chestnut trees between them. A new church and some old almshouses rebuilt on the site completed the village.

This orderly array of simple dwellings was a rationalized image of the perfect English village, and Damer's anticipation of modern council planning was not unsuccessful. His own life took a tragic turn when his sons ran heavily into debt and the eldest committed suicide on that account, but the new Milton Abbas took root. Today, apart from the welcome addition of a village pub, it is much the same as when it was built. The pretty cottages are backed by woodlands, and green meadows in front of them border the village street.

The Lonely Abbey

A right turn at the end of the village street leads to the abbey a half-mile further on. In its beautiful, lonely setting, sheltered by hills and woods, it is an impressive sight. Next to the abbey is the great mansion, aesthetically designed in light mauve stone and flint with Gothic pinnacles by the eccentric architect Sir William Chambers in 1771. It is on the site of old monastic buildings, and it incorporates a medieval great hall. A boys' school now occupies it, and parts of the interior can be inspected by courtesy of the headmaster.

King Athelstan founded a monastery at Milton in 938, and in 964 King Edgar made it into a Benedictine abbey. A program of rebuilding during the fourteenth and fifteenth centuries was to have made it into one of the greatest abbeys in England, but before the nave could be added it was seized by Henry VIII. He sold it together with its rich estates for a nominal sum to his divorce lawyer, Sir John Tregonwell, to whom he owed a favor for arranging his separation from Catherine of Aragon.

Inside the abbey is Tregonwell's altar tomb, and outside, to the north, is a notice recording the remarkable adventure of his descendant, another John Tregonwell, in 1663. At the age of five, while playing on the abbey roof, he fell off it. Because he was dressed in a pantaloon shirt which caught the air, forming a kind of parachute, the boy was deposited unharmed on the turf below. He continued playing, and his frantic keepers found him happily picking daisies.

The abbey is now used as a chapel by the neighboring school, and it is often filled with music and choral song. It is a place of towering arches and pure, clear light. The religious ideals to which it has been adapted are those of high-minded Protestantism. Spirits of the surrounding landscape seem to be residing there. Also present is the spirit of Joseph Damer, who set the abbey in romantic isolation while depriving it of its town. A beautiful white marble sculpture by Carlini in 1775 depicts him reclining on one elbow beside his dead wife.

St. Catherine's Chapel

A few hundred yards east of the abbey, on the line of its axis, a flight of turf steps cut in a hillside mounts a steep slope to a simple old chapel. From the chapel there is a fine elevated prospect of the abbey in its sanctified surroundings. St. Catherine's Chapel is traditionally the mother of the abbey, for it stands on the site where its founder had a vision. King Athelstan, encamped there one night with his army while on his way north to suppress a rising of the Danes and Scots, was divinely assured of victory. His expedition was duly successful, and on his return south he is said to have built the chapel before founding his monastery on the meadow below. The chapel became a place of pilgrimage; an indulgence of 120 days was the reward for those who resorted to St. Catherine's shrine.

At one time it was also a place where country girls used to go in secret and whisper a prayer. The same was done at other shrines of St. Catherine in Dorset, including the saint's chapel on Cat-and-Chapel Hill near Cerne Abbas and her beacon chapel on the coast at Abbotsbury. This was the prayer:

> Sweet St. Catherine, send me a husband,
> A good one, I pray.
> But any a one is better than never a one.
> Oh, St. Catherine, lend me thine aid
> And grant that I may never die an old maid.

The present chapel contains no trace of Athelstan's work, its earliest masonry being of the twelfth century. Its religious use had lapsed by the nineteenth century, and it served in turn as a pigeon house, a laborer's cottage, a workshop, and a lumber store before being reconsecrated in 1901. Occasional services are still held there.

The chapel is usually open, but the turf steps and concealed bridge leading to it are closed to avoid wear. It can be reached by paths through the woods around it.

MILTON ABBAS is 12 miles west of Wimborne Minster and 6 miles southwest of Blandford Forum. A turning to the right at Winterborne Whitchurch off the A354 road from Blandford to Dorchester leads to the village 2.5 miles further on. A mile beyond it is the abbey. There is free parking behind the mansion, now Milton Abbas School, and the abbey and grounds are open to visitors during daylight hours.

DORCHESTER: *Thomas Hardy's Casterbridge*

The first known settlement at Dorset's county town was by the Romans, who fortified it and had their regional capital there. Roman regularity is still apparent in the layout of its streets. It is a dignified place, with fine Georgian houses and hotels. In the country around it are several stone circles and many other prehistoric antiquities, notably the vast hilltop enclosure, Maiden Castle.

Thomas Hardy was born nearby and lived at the eastern end of the town in his house, Max Gate. His novel *The Mayor of Casterbridge* is set in Dorchester.

There are many old New England families with roots in this district, for a party of emigrants set out from Dorchester in 1628 to found a community, New Dorchester, in the American colonies. In St. Peter's Church there is a monument to one of the founding fathers of Massachusetts.

South of Dorchester is Osmington, where John Constable stayed, and the beautiful coastal scenery he painted. A few miles to the west is Lulworth Cove with its sandy beach and curious rock formations. Fossils occur in the rocks along this coast.

The Museum

On the north side of High West Street, near its center, is a distinguished Victorian Gothic building of 1883 that houses the collection of the Dorset Natural History and Archaeological Society. This is one of the most enjoyable of England's provincial museums. The collection, built up since 1846, illustrates all features of Dorset life and the countryside. Its archaeological section is particularly well displayed. There are models of ancient sites and of stages in the rise and fall of Maiden Castle, together with prehistoric sacred artifacts. The Roman section is unique. Rustic musical instruments are among the fascinating objects of local culture, some of which are referred to in Thomas Hardy's books. At the center of an exhibit of Hardy's relics and mementos is a reproduction of his study, complete with furniture and books exactly as though he had just left it. His statue by Eric Kennington stands at the crossroads west of the museum.

St. Peter's Church

St. Peter, beside the museum in High West Street, is the only one of Dorchester's medieval churches to have escaped the fires which devastated the old town in the seventeenth and eighteenth centuries. It was restored in 1856, but it is mostly of the fifteenth century. Older features include the Norman doorway inside the porch.

Below the porch rests a former rector, John White, one of

the local Puritans who founded the colony of Massachusetts. He probably preached from the fine old pulpit in the church.

One of the grand memorials in St. Peter is a statue of Lord Holles in the garb of a Roman senator. He was Dorchester's member of Parliament before the Civil War, and he became famous in 1629 as one of two members who held the Speaker in his chair by force, thereby allowing the Commons to continue in session in defiance of the king's wishes. He fought on the parliamentary side in the Civil War but constantly strove for a reconciliation with the monarchy. At the Restoration his honest principles were recognized, and he became a privy councillor under Charles II.

As a young architect, Thomas Hardy worked in this church during its restoration in 1856. One of the plans he made at the age of sixteen is exhibited in the south aisle.

Outside the church is a statue of the Dorset poet and clergyman William Barnes, of whom it is said that every word he wrote was inspired by love of nature and humanity. His quaint, thatched rectory at Winterborne Came, 1.5 miles southeast of the town, stands near his little church in a park among oak trees. It is not open to the public but can be seen from the road.

St. George on a Roman Hilltop
Fordington, the eastern quarter of Dorchester, has its parish church of St. George on a hilltop with views over the country in all directions. It is one of the most interesting of church sites, with a record of sacred occupation which goes back to Roman times at the latest. To the northeast of Dorchester a straight 12-mile stretch of the Roman road to Old Sarum is aligned upon St. George's Church, where a Roman temple once stood. Parts of its stone pillars were found beneath the church porch during restorations at the beginning of this century, and they are to be seen near the entrance. A memorial or altar slab from the site, inscribed with the names of a Roman citizen and his family, is also displayed. Many of the straight trackways which the Romans paved were laid out in much earlier times, and St. George's Church may well be on the site of a megalithic shrine or mark stone toward which the original line of trackway was directed.

The importance of the site is acknowledged in the tradition that the church was the first in England to be dedicated to St. George. A large block of stone to the right of the entrance is not of local origin; it is said to have been brought there by crusaders from St. George's tomb at Lydda in Asia Minor.

Fordington became a royal manor when William the Conqueror gave it to his nephew, who became the first Bishop of Salisbury and was canonized as St. Osmund. He rebuilt the church and gave its rectors special privileges at his cathedral of Old Sarum. A relic of his time is the tympanum in the church porch, carved with figures in the style of the Bayeux tapestry to represent St. George's inter-

vention on behalf of the crusaders at a battle fought near
Antioch in 1098. Armed with a spear, the saint on his horse
is riding down a group of Saracens.

Maiden Castle and Other Antiquities

On the southern edge of Dorchester is a grassy enclosure,
ringed with high earthen banks, called Maumbury Rings. It
has always been a notable spot locally. In neolithic times a
stone circle stood there. The Romans replaced this with an
amphitheater, and in subsequent ages the site was used for
prayer meetings, games, such rustic amusements as cock-
fighting and bear-baiting, and (until 1767) public executions.

Two miles further south the road leads up toward Maiden
Castle, whose gigantic earth ramparts are visible from a
distance. In the late 1980s it is in the process of being
excavated, and visitors are invited to see the archaeologists
at work. Later an exhibition center will be established there.

This was a sacred hilltop in Stone Age times, and for more
than three thousand years it was protected by earthworks of
ever-increasing size. Just before the coming of the Romans,
a Celtic tribe strengthened the previous works and added
outer ramparts, enclosing some forty-five acres. The entrance was a labyrinthine structure, stoutly defended. Nevertheless, as excavation has proved, the Roman legions,
probably commanded by Vespasian in 44 A.D., stormed and
captured it. The hill was evidently reoccupied later, for the
foundations of a fourth-century temple have been found
within its walls.

A glance at the Ordnance Survey map for the Dorchester
region shows the dense cluster of prehistoric mounds and
stones in the country around Maiden Castle. To the west, on
Hampton Down above the village of Portesham, is an
attractive stone circle. Another, more accessible, called the
Nine Stones, is 3 miles to the north of it on the south side of
the A35 road; it is on the edge of a wood a quarter of a mile
west of Winterbourne Abbas. Wild garlic, the traditional
antidote to witchcraft, grows around it, and one of the stones
has been engulfed by the roots of a huge beech tree that has
invaded the site. The magic of this little prehistoric shrine
survives even its proximity to the main road.

DORCHESTER is approached by railway from all directions. The main line
from London's Waterloo Station goes through it by way of Bournemouth to
Weymouth, which has ferries to the Continent. Another line goes north to
Yeovil and beyond.

The museum is open daily except Sunday, 10 to 5. Admission 75p.

There is a car park below Maiden Castle, and one may climb the hill at
any time. Leave Dorchester on the A354 road to Weymouth, take the third
turning on the right after the railway bridge, and the car park is 2 miles
further on.

Tourist Information: Acland Road, Dorchester. Telephone: Dorchester
(0305) 67992.

ABBOTSBURY: *A Sanctuary of the Ancient Britons*

Abbotsbury is a village near the sea 9 miles southwest of Dorchester on the B3157 road between Weymouth and Bridport. The charm of its thatched, golden-stone cottages is somewhat marred by the main road which passes between them, but it is still a delightful village, and the country around it is magnificent. It lies low among rolling green hills, and above it, dominating the view as one approaches the village, stands a hilltop chapel which is one of England's most attractive places of pilgrimage. It is dedicated to St. Catherine, the friend of all women and patron saint to spinsters. To be seen before climbing the hill are the relics of the abbey which gave the village its name.

The parish church of Abbotsbury is built on a prominent green knoll in the village. Beside it to the south is the former site of a huge abbey which was almost completely destroyed after its suppression in 1539. Only a small piece of masonry remains of the abbey church of St. Peter, but the wealth of the old monastery is evidenced by a building visible from the site, a great stone tithe barn built in about 1400 to hold the produce of the abbey estates. This is a masterpiece of medieval construction, 270 feet long and 30 feet wide, and it is still in agricultural use.

Another relic of monastic times is Abbotsbury's famous swannery, which has existed at least since the fourteenth century. Apart from its large colony of swans, it provides a sanctuary for many varieties of geese, ducks, and seabirds.

In the parish church, which is dedicated to St. Nicholas, is displayed a plan and drawings of how the abbey must have appeared in its prime. There is also a note on the early origins of Abbotsbury as a Christian sanctuary. "In the very infancy of Christianity among the ancient Britons," a priest named Bertulfus had a vision of St. Peter, who authorized him to found a church in his honor. This implies that Abbotsbury was a Celtic sanctuary, and its beautiful secluded setting amid a cluster of prehistoric monuments suggests that it was once a center of Druidism and ancient pagan religion.

The recorded history of St. Peter's Abbey goes back to 1023, when it received a charter from King Canute.

The Hill Chapel of St. Catherine

A path from behind the village inn gives the easiest approach to the chapel atop St. Catherine's Hill. Though not so steep and conical as Glastonbury Tor, this hill plays a similarly dramatic part in the composition of its landscape. A smooth inclined plane which leads to its summit passes through the seven rings of a spiral earthwork etched into its sides. These have been explained as the terraces of a medieval cultivation system, and they may well have been used by the monks for orchards and vineyards. Their origin, however, could be

Massive stone walls preserve St. Catherine's Chapel from the sea gales.

much older. The more famous hillside spiral on Glastonbury Tor, which also has seven levels, is now thought to have provided a labyrinthine pathway for pilgrims and religious processions on their way to the sacred summit. No doubt St. Catherine was a sacred hill long before the fifteenth century when the present chapel was placed there by the Abbotsbury monks.

The chapel, raised high upon an earth platform, is a remarkable building, tall and sturdy with walls up to four feet thick. It is made entirely of stone and its stone barrel-vaulted ceiling is unique in England. Steps in a turret lead to the roof, from which there are sweeping views out to sea and down the coastline from Portland Bill in the east to the cliffs of Devon. A light was once maintained here for the guidance of shipping, for St. Catherine is also the patron saint of mariners.

The legend of St. Catherine is that she was a lady of royal birth who became a Christian in Alexandria early in the fourth century. She disputed with the learned and converted several pagan philosophers. This caused her to be persecuted by the Emperor Maxentius, who ordered her to be torn to pieces on a machine made of spiked wheels. A providential stroke of lightning smashed the wheels, after which St. Catherine was beheaded. Her first shrine was on Mount Sinai.

The holy places of St. Catherine are often found on beacon hilltops and sometimes, as at St. Catherine's Hill, Winchester, in association with a spiral labyrinth. Thus in landscape symbolism are reflected her attributes, as an example of female wisdom (the labyrinth), a protector of women (the rounded, maternal hill), and a guide to sailors at the mercy of the tides (the beacon). These attributes were inherited from a pagan deity whose cult flourishes widely in the orient. The Chinese goddess of mercy, Kwan Yin, likewise protects women and sailors, and she too was martyred, after which she arose from the ocean upon a lotus. She and St. Catherine represent an aspect of divinity—the wise, merciful female whose shrines have a traditional appeal to many types of pilgrims.

The particular cause of pilgrimages in modern times to St. Catherine's Chapel has been the reputation of the saint for procuring a husband or children for women who pray at her shrine. The most favorable season is around the saint's feast day on November 25. The humble words country girls at St. Catherine's Chapel, Milton Abbas, used when asking the saint to give them a man ("any a one is better than never a one") were made more demanding at Abbotsbury, where according to tradition the request was for a husband who was kind, rich, and handsome.

ST. CATHERINE'S HILL is on the coastal path along southern England and is accessible at any time. The chapel was restored in the 1960s, and its interior (though not the steps to the roof) is open daily except Sunday, 9:30 to 7 (May through September); 9:30 to 4 (November through February); and 9:30 to 5:30 (March, April, and October). On Sunday the opening hour is 2.

The abbey site can be freely visited, but the tithe barn is not open to the public.

CERNE ABBAS: *God of Fertility on the Hillside*

Eight miles north of Dorchester on the A352 road toward Sherborne, an astonishing sight appears on the right-hand side of the road: Carved on the side of a hill is the outline of a huge naked male figure, emphatically virile, brandishing a rustic club and standing 180 feet high within a coffin-shaped enclosure.

A turning to the right leads to Cerne Abbas at the foot of the Giant's hill. This is a large village, once a town, of exceptional beauty and interest, with medieval streets, fine old inns, and thatched yellowstone houses. It is a place of small streams and secluded pathways. The ruins of an abbey lie behind its ancient abbey farm. In the abbey churchyard is a holy well associated with St. Augustine. The "goddess" dedication of the village church of St. Mary balances the rampant god on the hill above. Here are symbols of the two opposite poles in nature, combining to produce a sacred landscape and generating the fine spirit which pervades the village. It is a place of quiet merriment; children skip in the streets, and on many summer evenings there is music and morris dancing in front of an inn.

The Giant

A public footpath through and beyond the graveyard at the end of Abbey Street leads up the hill to the Giant effigy. Its

The Cerne giant.

outlines are formed by trenches cut through the turf to expose the white chalk beneath. If they were not regularly scoured, these trenches would soon silt over and the figure would be lost. The most remarkable thing about the Giant is that, ever since he was first made, the people of Cerne Abbas have cherished him through every generation, ritually renewing him every five years. No doubt many other ancient hill figures have disappeared over the ages through neglect, but the Giant was never neglected. His phallic symbolism reflects his practical function as a trysting place for young couples and his symbolic function as a bestower of children on brides who resort to the appropriate spot on his anatomy. The phallus is longer now than it was originally because at some period the navel above it became merged with its tip.

On the summit of the hill above the Giant is a rectangular earthwork called the Trendle, which may have been the site of a temple to the god on the hillside. A maypole used to be erected there.

The date and original identity of the Giant are both unknown. On stylistic grounds the figure is ascribed to about the first century A.D. and is thought to represent Hercules. This theory is supported by recent archaeological research which has shown that beneath the giant's outstretched right arm is the buried outline of what might be a lion's skin. Hercules is represented thus, with club and lion's skin, in Celtic statuettes of Roman times.

The Giant's ancient name is given in a record of the thirteenth century which says that Cerne is in the pagan district of Dorset where the god Helith was once worshiped. Later he is referred to as Helis and Heil. Similar names adhere to such ancient monuments as the Hell Stone to the west of Dorchester and the Heel Stone at Stonehenge. Opinions differ as to their meaning, but a plausible derivation is from the Celtic word for the Sun. That accords with the apparent nature of the Cerne Abbas Giant as a masculine solar deity.

The land where the Giant stands now belongs to the National Trust, which has taken the responsibility for scouring his outline.

St. Augustine's Holy Well

In a sheltered spot near the center of the cemetery that lies behind the town pond on Abbey Street is a holy well. Beside it there once stood a chapel of St. Augustine. According to legend, that saint, the first Archbishop of Canterbury in 601, was on a missionary visit to Dorset when he was spitefully treated by some people near Cerne, who tied fishtails to his back and drove him and his party out of their village. Taking refuge at a spot in Cerne Abbas, he struck the ground with his staff and a spring of clear water welled up. The sanctity of the well attracted pilgrims to the abbey and also supplied its drinking water.

The Abbey

There was once a great abbey at Cerne; it was utterly destroyed by agents of Henry VIII in 1539, and only some outbuildings remain. It covered the eastern end of the cemetery and part of the field beyond, which is now a peaceful spot for contemplating nature and the past.

This spot had probably been sacred long before a monastery was built there in the ninth century. It became a Benedictine house, and periods of building in the tenth and twelfth centuries reflected its wealth and importance.

The abbey farm at the end of Abbey Street is on the site of the abbey's southern gateway, and many stones from the old buildings are in its walls. To the right of it a path leads onto private land (entrance 25p) where stand two picturesque relics of the old establishment. Behind the farm is a fifteenth-century building with an oriel window, once used as the abbey guest house, and just beyond it is Cerne's finest building, the towering porch to the abbot's hall. Three stories high and built of the golden stone from Ham Hill, it is ornamented with heraldic carvings. It dates from 1509; its fine oriel window was added in 1840.

All over the town can be found stones from the abbey that have been built into old houses. Some ruins of the abbey mill are still to be seen on the east bank of the River Cerne, and the abbey tithe barn, reduced from its former size, stands southwest of the town, off a street called The Folly.

St. Mary's Church

The parish church on Abbey Street was built by the monks of the abbey in about 1300. It was enlarged in the following century, and the tower was added in 1500. On it is a fine statue of the Virgin and Child which survived the Reformation. Grotesque heads carved on the facade of the church are thought to represent the Cerne Giant; one of them has arms and a club.

The light inside is clear and refreshing. There is a Jacobean pulpit, and on each side of the chancel are some fourteenth-century wall paintings. These, together with painted texts of a later date, are well preserved and restored.

SHERBORNE

Sherborne is a charming, neat, prosperous old country town, full of medieval and other interesting buildings. Villages in the countryside around it have thatched cottages built in a honey-colored stone which is quarried nearby at Ham Hill. One lovely example is the village of Sandford Orcas, 3 miles north of the town on the road to King Arthur's castle at South Cadbury. Sherborne and its abbey were also built of Ham stone; under evening sunlight the town has a mellow, golden glow.

Traces of Roman and earlier occupations have been found at Sherborne, but its history begins in the seventh century with the Saxons. On the edge of a small stream they built a church that in 705 became a cathedral. Its bishopric, created by dividing the see of Winchester, included Dorset, Somerset, Devon, and Cornwall. King Ine of Wessex appointed a kinsman, the scholarly St. Aldhelm, as the first Bishop of Sherborne.

From its earliest days to the present Sherborne has been a center of education. North of the church, where the present Sherborne Boys' School stands among old monastic buildings, is the site of the old school which King Alfred the Great is said to have attended. Two of his three brothers, Ethelbald and Ethelbert, who preceded him on the throne, were buried in the Saxon cathedral in the ninth century.

Sherborne Abbey
St. Aldhelm was succeeded by a line of twenty-six Saxon bishops that came to an end in 1075, following the Norman Conquest, when a new cathedral was built at Old Sarum and the bishop's seat relocated there. Sherborne became an abbey, served by Benedictine monks who had settled there in 998.

The abbey was rebuilt in the twelfth century, and in the fourteenth a parish church, All Hallows, was added on to its west end. Its parishioners used the abbey font for baptisms until 1437, when a quarrel broke out between the people and the monks. The abbey authorities moved their font and narrowed a doorway connecting the south aisle with the parish church. The intention may have been to obstruct some traditional procession of which the monks disapproved. When a new font was set up in All Hallows, the monks smashed it. A riot broke out, and it is said that a priest of All Hallows shot a flaming bolt toward the abbey, which was then being rebuilt. It caught fire and was largely destroyed.

The work of reconstruction started immediately, and the abbey in its present form, although retaining Saxon and Norman features, is essentially a creation of the fifteenth century.

By the time of the Reformation, Sherborne had become a backwater and the number of its monks had dwindled to sixteen. They were expelled in 1539, and the abbey passed into the hands of a local businessman who prepared to demolish it for the sale of its materials. These were valued at £326 plus a few shillings, and at that price they were bought by the people of Sherborne in order that the abbey might become their parish church. To recover part of the cost, they pulled down All Hallows and sold off its stones. Thus the abbey was saved to become the finest parish church in Dorset.

Victorian and recent restorations have left the abbey in excellent condition. Its historic and architectural features are of great interest, yet it is obviously a living church—not merely a showplace—and a center of local interests and activities. For more than a thousand years it has dominated its community, physically and spiritually, and so it continues today. Quiet old Sherborne offers more satisfaction to the discerning traveler than many of the grander places that are more popular with tourists.

A quaint Norman porch of about 1180 gives entrance to the abbey on its southern side. Within, immediately on the left, is the notorious doorway whose narrowing was the cause of the riot of 1437. Balancing it, on the north side of the west wall, is a more ancient doorway, a relic of Saxon times. Much of the masonry in this part of the building is of the same early period.

Side chapels on each side of the nave and choir and at the east end contain many fine old monuments. The glory of the abbey is its wonderful vaulted stone roof of fifteenth-century craftsmanship. It is a joyful expression in masonic geometry of the patterns of Creation. Ribs spring out like branches from the trunks of the pillars and generate a central geometric scheme which includes many symbolic designs, such as the cabalistic Tree of Life formed by stone bosses at the intersections of the ribs. Carved on the bosses (and probably once painted in colors) are little masterpieces of medieval art; some are of flowers and foliage, others are heraldic, and over the southeast bay of the nave is a long-haired mermaid holding a comb.

A boss in the choir vault shows the flaming arrow, shot by the clergyman of All Hallows, which caused the burning of the abbey. The monks of the time must have had great tolerance and humor to allow this event to be commemorated so soon after it had happened.

The vaulted roof with its fascinating design and symbolism

The beautiful ceiling of Sherborne Abbey: An engraving made when the interior was restored in 1858.

can be studied in comfort through horizontal mirrors installed in the nave and choir. The electric lighting, which brings out its details, can be turned on by a switch on the pier at the southeast end of the nave.

A strange event is recorded on a slate tablet in the south aisle. Christian churches were normally built on previously sacred sites, and the first church at Sherborne (from Scireburne, meaning "clear stream") is likely to have been built over the pagan shrine of the water spirit on the banks of the stream. On May 16, 1709, the spirit rose up. A storm with huge hailstones blocked the stream and diverted its waters through the church, where they flowed almost three feet high and ripped up most of the paving stones.

The Almshouses and Chapel of St. John

One of the attractive things about Sherborne Abbey is that it retains much of its medieval setting. The fifteenth-century almshouses bordering the road to its south are gems—the more so because they still fulfill the function of sheltering old people in the heart of their community. Founded in 1406 by a local parson, the institution was built up in 1438 and a chapel was added. The Victorians preserved the old structures and built further, making the whole extremely picturesque in Gothic style.

The chapel, dedicated to the saints John the Baptist and John the Evangelist, is a fine old building containing a rare treasure. In front of the east window is a fifteenth-century triptych depicting in glowing colors five miracles. The centerpiece shows the raising of Lazarus. The work is said to be Flemish or German. Somehow it survived the Reformation, hidden away and neglected until the nineteenth century, its images concealed under coats of heavy varnish.

A screen divides the chapel from the paneled hall, where some curious old items are exhibited, including some of the abbey pewter and a strange letter written to the almshouses by Sir Walter Raleigh.

Just beyond the town to the east is a towering ruin called the Old Castle, built in the twelfth century. It was smashed during the Civil War and is now in the care of the Department of the Environment. Sir Walter Raleigh acquired it and tried to restore it but gave up and built the New Castle nearby in 1594. It is a fantastic building, made more so by later additions. Today it is a stately home with fine furniture and surroundings.

SHERBORNE is on the A30 road between Shaftesbury and Yeovil. It has a railway station with trains from Salisbury.

The abbey is open weekdays, 9 to 6, and between services on Sunday. The almshouses are open daily, 2 to 4, except Monday and Wednesday. Entrance 40p.

The Museum in Church Lane, east of the abbey, exhibits a collection of local historic items and contains the Sherborne Doll's House. It is open weekdays (except Monday), 10:30 to 12:30 and 2:30 to 4:30; Sunday, 2:30 to 4:30. Admission 25p.

The New Castle is open Thursday, Saturday, and Sunday, 2 to 6, from Easter Sunday through September. Teas available.

The Sherborne Tourist Information Centre is on Hound Street. Telephone: Sherborne (0935) 815341.

GLASTONBURY: *England's Jerusalem*

Ynis Witrin, the Glassy Isle, was the old British name for Glastonbury, and in earlier times it was indeed an island, rising dramatically above an inland sea which has since given way to the marshes and flat meadows of Somerset. The landscape is dominated by Glastonbury's conical hill, the Tor, surmounted by a church tower. Pilgrims are drawn toward it from afar, and as one approaches one becomes aware of a peculiar change in the atmosphere: The light intensifies and takes on a quality unique to Glastonbury. It can scarcely be described, but the experience is unforgettable. Glastonbury is a famous sanctuary, a place of magic and legend, and the cause of its reputation is soon apparent to visitors. There is a natural enchantment to the place that has affected people in all ages and makes it appropriate for Glastonbury to be called the English Jerusalem.

Modern Glastonbury is a small country town, population 7000, brick built and architecturally undistinguished. Its ancient treasures are well hidden. One can drive through Glastonbury in a few minutes without being aware that behind its long, straggling High Street lie the ruins of a great

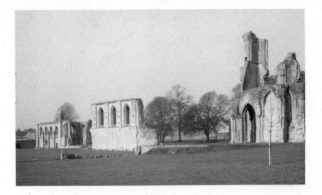

A view of Glastonbury Abbey ruins from the northeast. The St. Mary Chapel is on the left.

abbey built upon "the holiest ground in England." It is the resting place of saints, the first Christian shrine in England, and the center of a network of sanctity that links prehistoric sites far across the countryside. Here is Avalon, island of the blessed dead, gateway to the spirit realm. Legends of all ages have their settings in the surrounding landscape, where secluded spots by streams, groves, and hills are haunted by the memories of ancient saints and heroes. Every generation adds to the stock of Glastonbury lore, for the spirit of the place links past with present, and its mystical attractions are as powerful today as they have always been. Thus the legends of pagan gods, Christian visionaries, and Arthurian knights, for which Glastonbury has long been famous, are constantly augmented by fresh experiences and discoveries relating to the mysteries of Avalon.

The longer one spends at Glastonbury and the deeper one's reading about it, the more fascinating it becomes. There are stories of people who have gone there for brief visits and stayed on for the rest of their lives!

GLASTONBURY ABBEY: *Joseph of Arimathea in England*

A medieval gateway on Magdalen Street leads to a green meadow that is the heart of Glastonbury. There stand the gray stone ruins of what was once the greatest religious house in England. It is a charming spot even to those who do not know its history, but its supreme importance as a place of pilgrimage is due to its unique foundation legend which, if literally true, makes Glastonbury the site of the world's first Christian church.

The locus of that legend is the delicately sculptured, late twelfth-century building at the west end of the abbey, the Chapel of St. Mary. It is also called the St. Joseph Chapel because it is on the spot where St. Joseph of Arimathea, the

*The St. Mary or St. Joseph Chapel,
the site of the original church at
Glastonbury, before its modern
restoration.*

uncle of Jesus, is said to have built a church of wood and
wattles shortly after the Crucifixion.

The story of St. Joseph is that he was a tin merchant who
traded with the Cornish miners, and on one of his visits to
western Britain he was accompanied by his Nephew. That is
an old belief among the Cornish, immortalized in William
Blake's poem, ("And did those feet in ancient time/Walk
upon England's mountains green?"). Later St. Joseph returned to England as a Christian missionary, leading a party
of twelve from the Holy Land. Navigating the Somerset
waterways, he landed at Pilton, a few miles east of Glastonbury (where a modern banner in the church commemorates
the event). He then proceeded to Wearyall Hill, overlooking
the site of the abbey, where he planted his staff—which
miraculously burst into leaf and became the sacred Glastonbury thorn tree. The local king, Aviragus, made him a grant
of land, and there the missionaries settled, dwelling in
circular cells in a ring around the wattle church.

Whatever the truth of the matter, there is no doubt that in
very early times, long before the Roman Church was known
in England, the paramount sanctity of the Celtic Christian
shrine at Glastonbury was generally acknowledged. Before
the fire that destroyed the abbey in 1184, the library at
Glastonbury contained documents with reference to its
foundation. These were inspected in about 1130 by a scholarly monk, William of Malmesbury, and incorporated in his
work *On the Antiquity of the Church of Glastonbury*. Later
chroniclers added to it, but the original text bears witness to
the unique history of the place. Citing ancient records,
William stated that "the church at Glastonbury did none
other men's hands make, but actual disciples of Christ built
it." Further, he wrote:

The church of which we speak is commonly called by the Saxons the
Old Church on account of its antiquity. It was the first formed of

wattles, and from the beginning breathed and was redolent of a mysterious divine sanctity which spread throughout the country. The actual building was insignificant but it was so holy. Waves of common people thronging thither flooded every path; rich men laid aside their state to gather there, and men of learning and piety assembled there in great numbers. . . . The resting place of so many saints is deservedly called a heavenly sanctuary on earth.

At medieval church councils, where the question of precedence was important and was keenly disputed, the Abbot of Glastonbury was allowed priority over all other delegates on account of the antiquity of his church's foundation. Nor did he have to rely upon the legend of St. Joseph; documentary evidence, referred to by William of Malmesbury, proved that the Old Church had been rededicated in the year 166, at the behest of King Lucius, by legates of Eleutherias, the thirteenth pope after St. Peter.

Glastonbury and Her Saints

St. Patrick, patron saint of Ireland, by tradition responsible for converting the Irish to Christianity, ended his days as Abbot of Glastonbury. When he died at the age of 111, his holy relics became Glastonbury's greatest asset. They attracted many pilgrims from Ireland, including St. Bridget, who settled not far from the abbey at Beckery, and priestly scholars and philosophers from throughout Celtic Christendom. St. David of Wales arrived in Glastonbury with a retinue of bishops, intending to reconsecrate the church, but he was warned in a vision that the site had already been dedicated by Jesus Christ Himself to His Virgin Mother, so St. David fulfilled his mission by building an oratory to the east of the Old Church.

Undisturbed by Viking raiders, the Glastonbury monks accumulated an awesome collection of saintly bones and mementos, causing their shrine to flourish as a popular place of pilgrimage. Saxon governments followed the British in respecting its sanctity, and the shrine continued to prosper under Norman rule. The autonomy of Glastonbury, as a place too sacred to be subject to secular control or taxation, was confirmed in the Domesday Book. By that time the abbey estates had expanded far beyond the original twelve hides of land (1440 acres) granted by Aviragus to St. Joseph, but the land surrounding the abbey was still known as the Twelve Hides, and within its boundaries the abbot enjoyed absolute sovereignty. His Church of St. Peter and St. Paul had grown from St. David's oratory east of the Old Church to become the largest and most richly endowed in England.

Destruction by Fire and the Finding of King Arthur

The most precious of Glastonbury's relics were the remains of St. Joseph's original wattle church. In the seventh century the old structure was preserved within a timber building roofed with lead. Its interior was filled with sacred objects and, according to William of Malmesbury, it was held in such religious awe that no one dared keep watch there at night or commit an unseemly act in its vicinity.

On the night of May 25, 1184, the glory of Glastonbury suddenly departed. A fire swept through the abbey and spread to the Old Church, which was reduced to ashes. Efforts were made to locate some of the most important relics, such as the bones of St. Patrick and St. Dunstan, and the present Chapel of St. Mary was built on the sacred foundations of its predecessor. Architecturally, the abbey soon regained its splendor, but its reputation as a place of pilgrimage was much diminished. Then it was restored a few years after the fire by the dramatic discovery, sixteen feet below the surface of the burial ground to the south of the abbey, of two ancient oak coffins containing the bones of a large man and a woman with strands of golden hair still attached to her skull. Also found was an inscribed leaden cross, identifying the bodies as those of King Arthur, whose traditional place of burial was Avalon, or Glastonbury, and Queen Guinevere. The place of honor where they were later reburied, at the center of the abbey church, is marked today by an inscription.

The Fall of Glastonbury Abbey
From the twelfth century to the sixteenth century each successive abbot added to the magnificent range of abbey buildings. Still intact is the octagonal Abbot's Kitchen, built early in the fourteenth century, which stands in the abbey grounds and is now a museum. Beyond it, at the corner of Chilkwell Street and Bere Lane, is the abbey's tithe barn, built in about 1420, where produce from the abbey estates was garnered. This splendid, well-preserved timber and carved-stone building in the ecclesiastical style is open to the

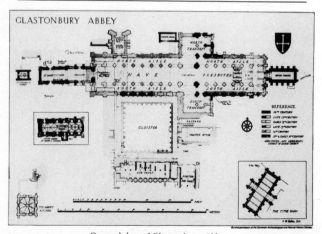

Groundplan of Glastonbury Abbey.

The abbot's kitchen in the abbey grounds of Glastonbury.

public as a museum of rural life. Its nobly worked fabric testifies to the medieval wealth of the abbey.

With the growing tendency toward centralized government in England, the independent power of the Church began to be seen as an anomaly. Areas of economic independence, such as Glastonbury under its abbots, were no longer tolerated. In 1539 the last Abbot of Glastonbury, Richard Whiting, was visited by agents of Henry VIII, who sought an excuse for confiscating his possessions. Nothing serious could be found against him, but he was accused of concealing abbey treasures, arrested, and brought to trial. His sentence was to be hanged, drawn, and quartered, and on November 15 Whiting and two of his monks were taken to the summit of the Tor, where their bodies were suspended on gallows in full view of the countryside. Parts of the abbot's body were distributed for exhibition in various cities as a warning against disobedience to the authorities.

Lost Treasures of Glastonbury and the Restoration Prophecy
The seizure of its assets and the dispersal of its monks reduced the abbey to an empty shell, and it soon fell into ruin. Its stones were sold off in cartloads for local construction purposes; many of them can still be found in buildings in and around Glastonbury. More completely lost are the manuscripts, reliquaries, and other treasures which Abbot Whiting was accused of hiding. No doubt he actually did so. Glastonbury underground is honeycombed with tunnels and crevasses, mostly sealed up and uninvestigated. Monks are notoriously fond of secret hiding places, and it may well be that objects of great intrinsic and historic value are awaiting their future revelation in Glastonbury's hidden recesses.

The Glastonbury cross, which marked the burial place of King Arthur, passed into private hands at the Reformation and was then lost. In 1981 it made a tantalizingly brief reappearance. Council workmen excavating a site near Waltham Abbey in Essex dug it from the ground and, not knowing what it was, gave it to a local man with an interest in antiquities. He took it for identification to the British Museum but refused to leave it there. When ordered by the courts to return it to the owner of the land where it had been found, he chose to go to prison rather than comply. After a few months he was released, still retaining the secret of the whereabouts of the Glastonbury cross.

Surpassing all other hidden treasures at Glastonbury is the sacramental vessel that St. Joseph was said to have brought with him from the Holy Land. It was the cup used at the Last Supper, and it had held the blood of Christ that dripped from the cross. This most sacred of objects, the Holy Grail, is said to have been buried at Glastonbury with the body of St. Joseph on Chalice Hill, which lies between the abbey and the Tor. It is traditionally believed that one day the Grail will be rediscovered, and then will follow the fulfillment of ancient prophecies that identify Glastonbury as the place of a spiritual and cultural renaissance. The power of those prophecies gives the country around Glastonbury its special character as the Holy Land of England.

The Stonehenge Connection

In one of the traditional Welsh bardic verses, the Triads, Glastonbury is named as one of the old perpetual choirs of Britain. "The choir of Ambrosius," or Stonehenge, was another, and a third was at the place now called Llantwit Major in South Wales. At these sites choirs of holy men maintained a constant liturgical chant which varied over the seasons and cycles. This was in times long before Christianity, when an archaic priesthood sanctified its society by keeping human activities in tune with the rhythms of the cosmos. Thus the traditional sanctity of Glastonbury goes far back into pagan times.

Another ancient link with Stonehenge is demonstrated in the planning of Glastonbury's religious buildings. St. Benedict's Church, on Benedict Street, two hundred yards west of the abbey, has the same orientation as the abbey and lies on the extension of its axis. The same axis line, continued eastward, passes through the archway to the abbey house and along a road called Dod Lane that becomes a footpath over the flank of Chalice Hill. Sixteen miles further east the line goes over a hilltop church, St. Michael at Gare Hill, and thence toward Stonehenge.

Dod Lane, which falls on the line and was a straight trackway up to a few years ago, is a form of Dead Man's Lane. Its name suggests that it was part of an ancient spirit path by which the souls of the dead passed from the old temple westward to Avalon and the other world.

Glastonbury's foundation myth provides another link with Stonehenge. After the fire of 1184, the monks rebuilt the Chapel of St. Mary on the foundations of the previous building, which contained, and preserved the dimensions of, St. Joseph's wattle church. From that clue, together with the legendary grant of twelve hides of land made to St. Joseph's party, one can reconstruct the original foundation plan of Glastonbury.

The figure shows the plan of the St. Mary Chapel and the scheme of geometry which develops from it. The width of the chapel, 39.6 feet, means that the side of the outer square is 79.2 feet in length, and the area contained by that square is equal to one ten-thousandth part of 1440 acres. There are 120 acres in one hide of land, so 1440 acres is the area of the twelve hides of Glastonbury. In this diagram the twelve hides are represented on a scale of 1:10,000.

Comparison of this diagram with the plan of Stonehenge (page 104) shows that the two are essentially the same. Here once more the Stonehenge–Glastonbury link is hinted at. Its meaning can only be surmised, but it prompts the suggestion that Glastonbury Abbey was once the site of a temple, similar to Stonehenge and of much the same period, about 2000 B.C. It is recognized that many Christian legends are restate-

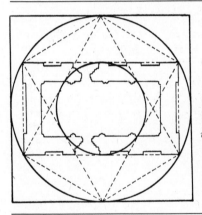

Groundplan of the St. Mary Chapel, Glastonbury, showing its hexagonal proportions. A circle drawn around it is contained in a square whose area, 0.144 acres, is one ten-thousandth part of the twelve hides, or 1440 acres, granted to St. Joseph and his missionaries.

ments of earlier pagan traditions, and it may be that the legend of St. Joseph's settlement at Glastonbury echoes a previous tale of Glastonbury's foundation by Druidic saints or divinities.

The Tor and its Labyrinth

The summit of Glastonbury Tor, the highest spot on the Isle of Avalon, is reached by the Pilgrim's Path along its spine. It offers a magnificent view of the countryside for miles around; on a clear day one can see the mountains of South Wales. Other landmarks are indicated on a plaque by the ruined tower which crowns the Tor.

The tower is all that remains of the Church of St. Michael, which in the fourteenth century replaced an earlier church on the site. Excavation in the 1960s exposed the foundations of an extensive monastic settlement alongside the church. In the early days of Christianity, when the Tor was covered

Glastonbury Tor with its ruined tower is visible for many miles around.

with trees and undergrowth, Celtic hermits occupied cells on its summit and slopes. Traces of prehistoric settlement have also been found, and the survival of a few ancient stones on and around the Tor indicates the sanctity of the place in the age of the megalith builders. As an object of pilgrimage, the Tor is as popular today as it has been for thousands of years.

In certain lights it can be seen plainly that artificial terraces have been carved around the sides of the Tor. It has recently been shown that these terraces form a huge labyrinth that encircles the hill and leads to its summit. The date of this work is unknown, but it is certainly prehistoric, and the symbolism of the labyrinth suggests that it was designed as a ritual pathway related to the ancient religious mysteries.

In walking a labyrinth, an initiate prepares to enter another world, and the discovery of the figure on the Tor recalls old legends of a hidden entrance to the hollow interior of the hill. Over the centuries many stories have been told of people who have found the entrance and gained access to the Tor's inner chambers, where the ancient mysteries were once celebrated. A former abbot of Glastonbury, St. Collen in the seventh century, is said to have retired to a hermit's cell at the foot of the Tor, where his contemplations were several times disturbed by a strange visitor who demanded that he ascend the hill and pass through a tunnel within it to meet the king of the underworld. Finally he agreed. Armed with a flask of holy water, the saint followed his guide into the bowels of the Tor and confronted Gwynn ap Nudd, the Celtic Lord of Hades, in the midst of his demonic court. A few words were exchanged, then St. Collen produced the holy water and dashed it over the king and his demons, who promptly vanished—whereupon the saint found himself alone in the hillside.

The inside of the Tor does indeed contain passages and chambers, formed by the underground waters which well up beneath it. Sacred springs once issued from its flanks, and today it conceals a reservoir that supplies the district with water.

The St. Michael Pilgrimage Path
The establishment of a Christian church on the Tor is attributed in the annals of Glastonbury to the founders of the abbey and to St. Patrick. Its dedication is to St. Michael—more properly, the Archangel Michael—who is depicted in a carving on the tower weighing the souls of the dead. Beside it, representing the female principle, is a carving of St. Bridget milking her cow.

As the leader of the heavenly hosts, the bearer of light, the slayer of the dragon, the revealer of mysteries, and the guide to the other world, Michael is the Christian successor to pagan deities with similar functions, such as Hermes, messenger of the gods, and the Celtic light giver, Lugh.

A fourteenth-century carving on the tower of St. Michael on the Tor is thought to represent St. Bridget, who was a milkmaid before she came to Glastonbury from Ireland.

St. Michael's shrines are commonly set on high places, where beacon fires once blazed on the days of festival. At such places the electric forces of the atmosphere make contact with the magnetic powers of the earth, producing strange effects whose causes are unexplained by modern science. Balls of light emanating from the Tor are often seen hovering above it, giving rise to legends which vary with the times, from tales of fairies and demons to modern reports of unidentified flying objects. Thus the reputation of the Tor as a place of magic and enchantment is not a matter of convention but has its roots in human experience and the mysteries of nature.

St. Michael on the Tor is one of the stations in an alignment of Michael shrines that extends along the spine of southwest England to its western extremity by the Land's End in Cornwall. It corresponds to the path by which, according to legend, Christ once proceeded from Cornwall to Glastonbury, and which his avatar will one day tread again; on which account the country people were careful to be hospitable to unknown travelers. In very ancient times the path appears to have provided a pilgrimage route from the

One of the most magical places in Somerset, the Mump or King Alfred's fort at Burrowbridge, crowned with a ruined St. Michael's Church.

west to the great temple at Avebury. Eleven miles southwest of Glastonbury, the road to Taunton skirts another prominent St. Michael's Hill, also topped by a ruined church, known as "the Mump" at Burrowbridge. From the church on the Mump, Glastonbury Tor is visible behind intervening hills. That alignment, from Mump to Tor, extends eastward precisely to the southern entrance of the Avebury ring, touching two of the enormous stones of the main circle. It continues on for a few miles to the church at Ogbourne St. George, dedicated to another dragon-killing saint who is said to represent the earthly aspect of St. Michael.

Close to the Glastonbury Tor–Avebury line stand the churches of Stoke St. Michael and St. Michael, Buckland Dinham; westward from Glastonbury, also near the line, is St. Michael's Church at Othery. Traveling further west, one's eye is drawn to the high rock on the western edge of Dartmoor, where the church of St. Michael, Brentor, offers a distant landmark to ships off the coast. Near the terminus of the line, slightly to the south of it, is the famous island rock of St. Michael's Mount (page 185).

The ancient rockpile on Bodmin Moor called the Cheese-wring marks the direct course of the St. Michael line.

Stretches of old trackway near Avebury and the Pilgrim's Path along the axis of the Tor fall onto the line, as does the axis of Burrowbridge Mump. Indications are that this alignment of pilgrimage stations, dedicated to an archaic deity whose attributes were assumed by St. Michael, was planned in remote antiquity, in times long preceding the age of the megalith builders. Today it provides a useful guide to modern pilgrims, leading them to the sacred high places and many of the obscure shrines of southwest England.

The Chalice Well and Garden Sanctuary
In the valley between the high eminence of the Tor and the gently rounded Chalice Hill—natural symbols of the male and female in nature—lies the most beautiful of Glastonbury's goddess shrines, where the indwelling spirit of the place can be experienced in tranquillity. At its center is an ancient holy well, fed by a spring of pure chalybeate water

from the depths of nearby hills. Long ago, in its natural state, the spring issued from the ground to form a stream that washed away the silt of the valley. A well house was built over it in the Middle Ages, but soil accumulated around it and it became buried. An excavation was made through its roof to form the present well shaft that leads to a stone chamber. The water never fails. Flowing at a rate of some thousand gallons an hour, its overflow comes to the surface below the well and passes through stone channels before disappearing again underground. Much valued for its sacred and healing properties, its fame has long drawn pilgrims to Glastonbury. The patina it leaves on the stone is a rich gold, and its blood-tinged color associates it with the lunar waters of the goddess.

Around the well is a simple country garden, set among the apple orchards of Avalon and sheltered by the ancient yew, the tree which flourishes at sacred spots. Daily access is afforded by the Chalice Well Trust, founded in 1958 by the Glastonbury mystic Wellesley Tudor Pole, who gave relief to many sufferers during World War II by his institution of the daily silent minute. Another such, Frederick Bligh Bond, designed the present well cover with its symbol of the *vesica piscis,* two interlinked circles that represent the merging of the worlds of spirit and matter.

At the entrance to the garden is Little St. Michael's House, belonging to the Trust, wherein is the Upper Room, a sanctuary furnished with objects of Glastonbury craftsmanship. A turning off Chilkwell Street gives access to the garden. At the gate is a small building for the reception of visitors and the sale of booklets relating to Glastonbury; the garden beyond is always peaceful and refreshing, intended as a resting place for pilgrims, especially those visiting the St. Michael shrines to the west.

Gog and Magog, the Oaks of Avalon

Certain trees, as they grow large and old, attract legends and veneration. Several of various species in the Glastonbury area are of impressive age, rooted in pre-Christian days of the Druid religion. Their sites may be even older, for it was an ancient practice to replace sacred trees in decay with saplings of their own seed.

Gog and Magog were ancient giants of Britain in the time of Brutus the Trojan, and their names have somehow attached themselves to a pair of great oak trees which are a feature of Glastonbury's legendary landscape. The trees are said to be more than two thousand years old, and in their gnarled and twisted limbs the mystic's eye descries faces and figures and simulacra of all the forms in nature. Once there were more of them, but their venerable companions were massacred by a farmer early in the present century. They formed part of an avenue leading toward the Tor, and legend has extended it even further: A local belief holds that an avenue of contemporary oaks once lined a causeway from the Tor to King Arthur's castle at South Cadbury. An old Glastonbury record says that King Arthur laid siege to the Tor, where a rival chieftain had his stronghold in about 500 A.D. If so, he would have marched there along the legendary causeway, shaded by the companions of old Gog and Magog.

As well as being worthy objects of contemplation, these trees are worth visiting for the sake of the walk, which leads by a National Trust footpath through beautiful scenery from Wick Hollow, across the vale called Paradise, to the foot of Stonedown, where stand Gog and Magog.

The Lake Villages and the Tribunal Museum

In the great days of Glastonbury Abbey, travel in the district was mostly by water. The abbot possessed an ornate barge from which he could inspect his estates, navigating the rivers and artificial watercourses that intersect the flat country around the Isle of Avalon. Much of it was formerly covered by a shallow lake, from which rose island hills. At Meare, 3 miles northwest of Glastonbury, the Abbey Fish House, built early in the 1300s, stands on the former banks of a large pool, now drained, which provided the abbey with fish. Local legend identifies it as the place where King Arthur's sword, Excalibur, was offered to him by the Lady of the Lake.

In prehistoric times this area was inhabited by numerous village communities, dwelling on the islands or in houses raised on timber piles from the bed of the lake. The villages were linked by wooded causeways, stretches of which have been preserved by the peaty soil of the district and are now being investigated by archaeologists. Current researches are illustrated at the small museum south of West Hay near the Sweet Track, a causeway over a mile long which is dated to about 3800 B.C. and is thus recognized as the oldest stretch of road in the world. The lake dwellers are found to have enjoyed a rich and varied diet through hunting, fishing, and agriculture. They were also masters of many crafts, including carpentry, bone carving, pottery, weaving, and metal work. Their houses were of wood and wattles in the same style as St. Joseph's original church. Avalon, one of their sacred isles, was where they buried their dead. Another, at Godney, is sanctified today by a small, simple church. The road there from Glastonbury, a turning off the road to Meare, passes the site of one of the lake villages.

Many of the objects found beneath the causeways and villages of the lake people are exhibited in the ancient Tribunal on Glastonbury's High Street, a picturesque fifteenth-century building which was the courthouse and administrative center of the Twelve Hides. Information is available there on current excavations and where to see them. In summer, when wild roses are growing among the willows which line the waterways of Glastonbury's moors, this beautiful, historic landscape invites exploration.

The Tribunal, Glastonbury.

SOME SACRED FEATURES IN THE GLASTONBURY LANDSCAPE

The Glastonbury Zodiac In 1929 a young artist, Kathryn Maltwood, was lodging in Glastonbury, engaged in illustrating *The High History of the Holy Graal*, which describes the adventures of King Arthur and his knights. The origin of this romance was said to have been an old Latin manuscript discovered in the library of Glastonbury Abbey. Walking the countryside after reading the book, Kathryn Maltwood recognized many of the landmarks around Glastonbury as the scenes of episodes in the Arthurian legends. The key to their understanding, she felt, was in the landscape itself.

One summer evening, gazing from a Glastonbury hill toward the legendary site of King Arthur's castle on Cadbury Hill, she noticed in the shadows moving across the landscape the outlines of gigantic effigy figures. It suddenly occurred to her that the tales of King Arthur were based on an astrological pattern, formed by natural and ancient artificial features in the local countryside. Working from maps and aerial photographs she commissioned, she identified a circle of astrological effigies and other figures which seemed to be referred to in local folklore and place names. Their outlines were marked by streams, tracks, contour lines, and boundaries, and their relative positions were in accordance with a map of the constellations.

Kathryn Maltwood's idea was that the zodiacal figures were roughly sketched by nature and had been given more precise form thousands of years ago by the ancient Sumer people of Somerset. No proof is attached to her thesis, but its poetic, visionary quality appeals to many, and it provides a useful synthesis of the various mythological themes which have settled upon the Glastonbury landscape.

Guidebooks with descriptions and maps of the Maltwood zodiac can be obtained at Glastonbury bookshops, and guided tours are offered throughout the summer.

The Great Yew of Dundon Five miles south of Glastonbury, off the road through the village of Street toward Somerton, is Dundon's wooded hilltop, surrounded by the earth ramparts of an ancient British settlement. To students of the Glastonbury zodiac it forms the head of the Gemini figure. Below it, on a grassy knoll, stands the village church. The church dates from the thirteenth century, and over the years it has gained some interesting memorials, but the main attraction is its atmosphere of peace and sanctity. The site is naturally adapted for worship and contemplation, and its qualities were no doubt recognized in Celtic times. Testifying to its early religious significance is the huge and venerable yew tree in front of the church porch. The yew is thought to have stood for more than a thousand years and is therefore older than the present church. Encircled by a wooden bench, the Dundon yew is a natural place of council for village elders.

Jan Christiaan Smuts, the South African leader, lived nearby after his defeat in the Boer War. In 1949 he returned to Dundon on a visit to his daughter, Mrs. Clark, whose house was in Street. Once more he walked through the churchyard, and his comment is recorded in a framed text on the west wall of the church: "As an old man I am glad to have had again this glimpse of Paradise."

St. Andrew at Dundon is one of the quiet corners where the ancient enchantment over the Glastonbury landscape can still be experienced.

King Arthur's Camelot Standing on Glastonbury Tor and gazing across the wide landscape, one grows aware of the natural kinship between the Tor and other hilltops of the district. This is reflected in the local mythology; Arthurian associations adhere to many of the prominent landmarks visible from the Tor. The King Arthur to whom the legends refer lived in about 500 A.D., but the legends themselves are rooted in far earlier times. Behind the Arthurian tales of battles and alliances between the hilltops of Somerset can be heard an echo from primeval times, when the hills were seen as elemental forces engaged in a mythological drama throughout the course of the year.

One obvious natural relationship is between the Tor and the high plateau 11 miles to the southeast, called on maps Cadbury Castle. Its proper name is Camelot, for that was what the locals called it when questioned by John Leland in 1542. On top of it, they said, was King Arthur's palace, and in a cave below the hill he still lies sleeping, awaiting the call to save his kingdom in time of peril. On certain winter nights the king and his retinue are supposed to ride across Camelot and down an old track to drink at a spring beside Sutton Montis church. At other times a band of ghostly knights is seen below the hill on the lost causeway to Glastonbury Tor.

The evidence of excavations at Cadbury Castle in the 1960s was in accordance with the legends. The four great

ridges of earthworks surrounding the hilltop were found to
have been heaped up over many periods from prehistoric
times. A town within the ramparts had apparently been
stormed by the Romans and for a time abandoned. Ancient
wells around the hill and evidence of a central shrine hint at
its occupation by hermits and holy men. Then, at about the
time King Arthur flourished, a great timber hall was erected
on the hilltop. The ramparts were heightened and capped
with stone, wooden walls were added to them, and strong
gatehouses were built. Cadbury Castle at that time could
lodge and protect an army. No other such stronghold of
Arthurian times is known in southern England. Its traditional identification as Camelot could hardly be a mere
coincidence; here, surely, is the site of King Arthur's court.

Camelot Today Its steep earth ramparts covered with dense
woods and undergrowth make Cadbury Castle as impregna-
ble today as ever. The only way up to it is by a steep and (in
winter) muddy path, which joins the south end of South
Cadbury village street just past the church, opposite the inn.

On a fine day the ascent of Cadbury is well worth the
effort. Antiquarian explorers and family picnic parties are
sometimes to be encountered, but one is mostly there alone.
The upland meadow and its surrounding woods shelter
many types of flower, bird, and animal life, and the view
from the site of King Arthur's palace is endlessly delightful.
Small villages with churches, set in wooded parkland, cluster
around the foot of the hill, while Glastonbury Tor beckons in
the distance. At Camelot one is at the center of the legendary
landscape of the quest for the Holy Grail.

THE RAILWAY STATION nearest to Glastonbury is at Castle Cary, 12 miles to
the south, but there is no direct bus from there to the town. Regular buses
from Bath and Bristol go to Wells, from which there is a bus to Glastonbury.
There are several car parks near the town center.

The abbey grounds are open daily, 9 to 7:30 in summer, and 9:30 to 5 in
winter. Admission 80p.

The chalice well is open daily, 10 to 6 in summer, and 1 to 4 in winter.
Admission 30p.

The Abbey Barn and Somerset Rural Life Museum are open daily, 10 to
5; weekends, 2 to 6:30 in summer, and 2:30 to 5 in winter.

The hours of the Tribunal and its museum are the same as those of the
Abbey Barn.

Books and booklets about Glastonbury can be obtained at bookshops at
the west end of High Street. Guided tours to Glastonbury's sacred places
and other sacred and legendary sites in southern England are offered at the
Gothic Image Bookshop, 7 High Street.

Further information from the Tourist Information Centre, 7 Northlode
Street, Glastonbury. Telephone: Glastonbury 32954.

WELLS: *The City on Sacred Waters*

Wells is the smallest of English cathedral cities, yet its Cathedral of St. Andrew is one of the most beautiful. The reason for the city's foundation is told in its name. Springs of clear water well up to the surface south of the cathedral, filling the moat around the bishop's palace and flowing down Market Place and High Street in an open conduit. The source of the waters is in the Mendip Hills, which shelter the city to the north. Medieval pilgrims were drawn to Wells because of the spiritual and healing qualities of its springs. It is a naturally therapeutic center, a shrine to the goddess in nature. Its sleepy, dreamy atmosphere is utterly different from the intense spirit of Glastonbury, whose Tor is visible 5 miles to the south. For this natural reason Wells and Glastonbury have always been rivals.

Anthony Trollope's cathedral city of Barchester is a fair representation of old-fashioned Wells, a backwater city animated principally by its ecclesiastical life. Nothing much has ever happened here. Three minor events are highlights in its history. In 1685 the Duke of Monmouth's rebel army quartered itself in Wells; his men stabled horses in the cathedral, smashed its monuments, melted lead from the roof to make bullets, and shot at the statues on the west front. Ten years later a lesser disturbance was caused by William Penn addressing a crowd of three thousand from a window in the medieval Crown Hotel, which still stands in Market Place. Penn was arrested but soon released on the intercession of the Bishop of Wells. A later bishop, Kidder, met a sudden death during the great storm of November 27, 1703, which sunk half of England's navy and destroyed the Eddystone

Wells cathedral from the southeast.

lighthouse; a chimney fell through the palace roof and crushed the bishop and his wife in their bed.

The Cathedral Precinct and West Front

Wells has a labyrinthine one-way traffic system, and visitors by car have to find a car park, the most central one being in Market Place alongside the cathedral. There stands a fountain in the symbolic form of a sacred spring with water trickling over a rock. On the east side of Market Place is the Bishop's Eye, a gateway to the grounds of the episcopal palace. Another sixteenth-century gatehouse, in the northeast corner, is called Penniless Porch because it was a haunt of medieval beggars. A narrow passage goes through it and onto the lawn in front of the cathedral's west end.

Here is a magnificent prospect. The cathedral green is bordered on three sides by rows of old buildings and terminated by the greatest sculptural composition in England. The west front of the cathedral, 150 feet wide, is ornamented with about six hundred sculptured figures, many of them life-size or larger, standing in niches. The whole work is a unity, a statement of theological cosmology with Christ in Glory at its apex.

The west front of Wells cathedral.

The identities of the figures on the west front and the symbolic interpretation of the design as a whole were a masonic secret. Since the completion of the west front in about 1236, the secret has been lost. Many of the figures are so worn and damaged that it is impossible to say whom they represent. Certain of them form tableaux illustrating biblical episodes, the Last Judgment and the Resurrection. Other figures are of angels, saints, prophets, kings, queens, and ecclesiastics. Shafts of blue-gray Kilkenny marble support the canopies over the figures and contribute to the geometrical design that underlies this great work.

The central upper part of the west front of Wells cathedral.

During the 1970s several of the most eroded figures on the west front were replaced with new sculptures, but it became apparent that modern work, however well executed, cannot capture the spirit of the medieval artists, and the program of restoration was suspended.

A leisurely way of viewing the west front is by sitting at a tea table on the lawn of the hotel at the opposite end of the cathedral green. To the left, on the north side, is the old Gothic deanery, and beside it the museum. Beyond is a great stone bridge called the Chain Gate, springing from the north side of the cathedral. It was built in the fifteenth century to give access to the Vicars' Close, where the young priests of the cathedral were lodged. The Vicars' Close consists of two rows of tiny houses with a chapel and dining hall, and externally it is so little altered that it has been called the oldest original street in Europe. The bridge enabled the priests to pass from their close to the cathedral without being exposed to the temptations of the city.

WELLS CATHEDRAL

As one enters the cathedral by a door in the west front, the cheerful daylight outside is suddenly replaced by the grave, awesome atmosphere within. This has been a hallowed place of Christianity since about 705, when Ine, king of Wessex, built a church beside the sacred springs where pagans had previously invoked the healing spirit of the waters. Two hundred years later Wells had its first bishop, and the present cathedral was mostly built in about sixty years after 1172. In 1321 the central tower was added, but it was soon found to be unstable and was ingeniously supported by interior cruciform arches. This accounts for the X-shaped stone structure which terminates the nave to the east; it is the form of cross appropriate to St. Andrew, and it forms the initial of the Greek word *Christos*.

Among the great memorials in the cathedral are many weird or humorous little carvings, hidden amid foliage on the tops of columns or beneath the wooden seats in the quire (as the choir is always spelled at Wells). Some of them refer to

Wells cathedral: The view eastward down the nave terminates at the curious arch added in the fourteenth century to support the tottering tower. With two "eyes" and a gaping "mouth," it resembles a leviathan or devouring beast.

contemporary jokes or sayings, others to masonic arcana. On a pillar to the west of the south transept a rustic carved figure suffers from toothache; it was made in about 1190 and commemorates the ancient reputation of Wells as a place of healing. Soothing aches was evidently one of its early specialties, and even after the Reformation people came to Wells for relief from pain, particularly toothache. The cure became located at the tomb of Bishop Button, who died in 1274, renowned for his saintly life and excellent set of teeth which, when his tomb was opened, were found perfect and undecayed.

The glorious quire is made subtly colorful by diffused light through the Jesse or Golden Window above the high altar to the east. Made in about 1339, it shows the genealogy of Jesus (in the center of the window) linked in a family tree, represented by a sinuous vine, to King David and the rest of his ancestry. The colors are predominantly gold and green. On the south side of the quire is the magnificent tomb of Bishop Beckington, who died in 1465. It is in the form of two stone slabs, one above the other. On top lies the bishop in the full glory of his earthly rank; on the lower slab is a sculpture of his decaying corpse.

Wells cathedral: A carved figure suffering toothache looks down upon Bishop Button's healing tomb in the south quire aisle. Another figure, carved on a capital above a pillar, is perhaps a pilgrim to Wells taking a thorn from his foot.

In the south transept is the famous fourteenth-century astronomical clock, in the same tradition as the one in Wimborne Minster and possibly made by the same master craftsman, Peter Lightfoot of Glastonbury. It gives the time of day and the phase of the moon, and at each quarter of an hour a little tournament takes place below it: Four clockwork knights charge each other in battle, leaving one of them dead. On the wall above, a figure called Jack Blandifer kicks his heels against a bell, strikes another with a hammer, and nods his head with the hours.

Northward from the transept a passage leads past the tomb of the unfortunate storm victims, Bishop Kidder and his wife, toward the noble staircase into the chapter house, the meeting place of the cathedral's administrators. It is a place that lifts the heart. In the center of the chapter house a stout column like the World Tree of Norse mythology throws off delicate stone branches which meet other branches that spring from columns around the octagonal walls. Here, as among the forestlike columns in the quire, one senses the love of idyllic nature which inspired the masonic builders. The chapter house was completed by 1306.

Another lovely spot is the Lady Chapel, dedicated to the Virgin Mary, at the far east of the cathedral. It is shaped as five sides of an octagon, and each wall has a window of stained glass placed there in 1326. The glass was damaged at the Reformation and by Monmouth's men, but much of it has been restored, and the light which filters through its colors is sublime and mystical.

The central pillar in the octagonal chapter house of Wells cathedral.

The oldest monuments in the cathedral are the tombs of early Saxon bishops to the north of the quire. Many other memorials were removed from the cathedral in the nineteenth century and placed in the cloisters to the south. Enclosed and made peaceful by the cloisters is the grassy burial ground with an old cedar tree in the middle.

A chained library in the cathedral, the entrance to which is behind the Saxon font in the south transept, has manuscripts that date from the tenth century.

The Bishop's Palace and the Sacred Wells

The cathedral cloisters give onto the grounds of the palace, but public access is through the Bishop's Eye gatehouse on Market Place. The rectangular moated palace was begun in the thirteenth century and made increasingly magnificent over two hundred years. Hard times came in 1550 when the lead was sold from the roof of the great hall, which became a picturesque ruin. The bishop still inhabits part of the palace, and croquet parties of Anglican divines can sometimes be glimpsed upon his lawns.

In the moat surrounding the palace spring water can be seen bubbling up to the surface. The sacred wells are to the north of it. A great attraction on the moat has long been a pair of swans which pull a bellcord on the palace wall when they want feeding. In 1986 one of them wandered into the town and was killed by a car, but the authorities succeeded in finding a new mate for the survivor (swans normally mate for life).

The Museum

In an ancient house a few yards north of the cathedral's west front, the local museum offers a delightfully mixed collection of objects, some of them of rare interest. Local geology and natural history are properly represented. There are old-fashioned domestic objects and a distinguished collection of samplers. Near Wells are the prehistoric lead mines of the Mendip Hills, below which are the remarkable Cheddar Caves, inhabited by wild animals and later by native tribesmen. The caves were excavated by H. E. Balch, who founded Wells Museum in 1893 and endowed it with his archaeological finds. An old inhabitant of one of the caves is called the Witch of Wookey Hole; her skeleton and magic crystal are shown in the museum.

One exhibit is a small model of a former Wells antique shop, complete with tiny antiques. It was a favorite of Queen Mary, the grandmother of Elizabeth II, who liked to see it whenever she was in the city.

St. Cuthbert's Church

The parish church west of the cathedral is the largest in Somerset, and its fifteenth-century tower is one of the most splendid. It is a fine church with a beautiful carved and painted roof adorned with angels. On the east wall of the St. Catherine's Chapel south of the nave is a most interesting but heavily mutilated carved reredos in the form of a Jesse Tree. From the organ of the recumbent ancestor of Jesus rises a tree, in the branches of which are placed colored figures of saints. It was systematically destroyed at the Reformation and the pieces hidden; they were rediscovered in 1848, and further restoration is planned.

ANCIENT AND SACRED SITES AROUND WELLS

Wookey Hole Two miles northwest of Wells is a spectacular cavern with stalactites and a subterranean river. On one of the rock pillars is shown the natural likeness of the Witch of Wookey, whose skeleton is in Wells Museum. The cave was a shelter and probably a shrine for prehistoric nomads. Nearby is a museum, a paper-making mill, and an outcrop of tourist attractions. The surroundings have been commercialized, but the cave retains dignity and awe.

Cheddar Seven miles northwest of Wells on the A371 road, Cheddar has been even more heavily commercialized, but behind the ephemeral clutter of cafés and souvenir shops are deep and wonderful caverns. The flint and bone implements found in them give evidence of human occupation as early as 14000 B.C. A skeleton in the Gough's Cave Museum has been dated to 7130 B.C.

The road northward through Cheddar passes between the extraordinary towering cliffs of the Cheddar Gorge.

The withered face and hooked nose of the Witch of Wookey is figured by a rock pillar in the cave.

The Rock of Ages A few miles north of Cheddar, on the other side of the Mendips, is another rocky ravine called Burrington Combe. The B3134 road runs through it and, traveling north, about a mile from the junction with the A368, one sees a cleft rock to the left of the road. A car park opposite serves this popular object of pilgrimage. It is supposed to be the rock in which the Reverend Augustus M. Toplady, an evangelical Calvinist who was a curate at nearby Blagdon between 1762 and 1764, took shelter from a storm and afterward wrote the famous hymn, "Rock of Ages cleft for me."

Priddy A village high on the Mendip Hills 5 miles northwest of Wells, Priddy was a center of prehistoric mining and religious activity. Many ancient monuments surround it, including the Priddy Nine Barrows and three mysterious great earth circles, each two hundred yards in diameter, aligned and pointing to a fourth. A local legend, recorded by Glastonbury antiquarians, said that Jesus Christ came to Priddy with his metal-trading uncle, St. Joseph, on their way to the Isle of Avalon. The place has a strange, wild atmosphere.

Stanton Drew Stone Circles About 12 miles north of Wells, off the B3130 road south of Bristol, is a little village called Stanton Drew. John Wood, the eighteenth-century builder of Bath, derived its name from Stonetown Druid and identified it as the site of an old Druid university because of the great stone circles there. They are far less well known and visited than Avebury, although some of the stones are comparable in size. They stand in fields near the Chew River on the east side of the pretty village. Near its inn, the Druid Arms, is the church, and beside it is a group of stones called the Cove. The three circles, a few hundred yards away, called the Northeast and Southwest circles and the Great Circle. Most of the stones have fallen, and so has the isolated stone known as Hauteville's Quoit, which lies beside the road to the north. It is named for Sir John Hauteville, reputed to have been a person of gigantic strength, whose effigy, with a lion at its feet, is in Chew Magna church, 1.5 miles west of Stanton Drew. The circles have not been scientifically dated, but they are supposed to be from about 2000 B.C. The local story is that they represent a wedding party turned to stone. An early antiquarian reported that every time he tried to measure them it started to pour with rain.

By the gate into the field containing the Great and Northeast circles is Court Farm (small charge for entry).

THERE IS NO longer a railway in Wells; buses go there from Bristol, 16 miles to the north, and from Bath.

The cathedral is open daily, 7:30 a.m. to 8:30 p.m. Conducted tours are offered at 11 and 2. The chained library can be seen Monday through Thursday, 2:30 to 4. Admission 20p.

The museum is open daily, 11 to 5. Admission 50p.

The Bishop's Palace is open Sunday and Thursday from Easter to October 31, and every afternoon in August.

Both Wookey Hole and the Cheddar Caves are open throughout the year. Separate admission charges are made at the caves, museums, and other attractions (details at the Tourist Information Office).

At Wells the Tourist Information Office is in the Town Hall, Market Place. Telephone: Wells (0749) 72552.

BATH: *Seat of the Goddess*

The best way of approaching Bath is by train from the east. As the train nears Bath Spa Station, it runs through beautifully landscaped parkland and allows glimpses of the city's famous architecture. Up to World War II Bath was an almost perfect Georgian city. Some of it was bombed during the war, but a great deal more was destroyed during the 1960s and 1970s, when buildings of inappropriate modern design were allowed to replace old stone houses. Nevertheless Bath is a gem among cities. Built over natural hot springs, it was in ancient times dedicated to the goddess, whose influence is apparent in its misty atmosphere, placid character, and hospitality to visitors.

Bath's modern prosperity began early in the eighteenth century when Richard "Beau" Nash, whose peculiar genius was for giving parties, made it the pleasure center of England. It had become the custom after the debaucheries

Interior of the elegant Pump Room, Bath. The spring is on the right.

of the London season for socialites to retire for a spell to Bath and restore their constitutions by sipping the medicinal waters. Under Nash's direction the quiet Bath season became a full-blown extension of London's. As master of ceremonies for more than fifty years, he refined and elaborated Bath's entertainments and attracted the most glamorous and aristocratic members of society to enjoy them. The demand for lodgings in Bath became overwhelming, and to satisfy it the first of Bath's graceful squares and crescents were constructed. Their architect was the mystical scholar John Wood the Elder, whose works include Queen Square (1736), the Circus (1754), and the design of the Royal Crescent, executed by his son, John Wood the Younger, also a prolific Bath architect.

After Nash's death and into the nineteenth century, Bath's architectural grandeur continued to increase. Then fashion turned against it: Sea bathing and seaside resorts such as Brighton became all the rage, and Bath reverted to its previous quiet, provincial character as a refuge for retired people.

The ebbing of the tide of fashion left Bath strewn with splendid public and domestic buildings, museums, art galleries, and formal parks. Details of all the interesting places in the city and its neighborhood can be had from the information office in the abbey churchyard. Our concern here, however, is not so much with Beau Nash's Bath as with the real source of its attraction in all periods, the hot mineral waters. Their history, and the sanctity of Bath, begins with King Bladud of the old Trojan dynasty, the tenth ruler of Britain in the days of the Druids.

Bath's Founder, the King Who Flew

The story of Bladud given in the twelfth century by Geoffrey of Monmouth, who repeated it from earlier chroniclers, is that he was sent by his father, King Hudibras, to study philosophy in Athens. While he was there his father died, and Bladud returned home in 873 B.C. to claim his throne, bringing with him some learned Greeks with whom he founded a university at Stamford in Lincolnshire. It flourished until the coming of St. Augustine, when Celtic learning was suppressed in favor of Catholic doctrines.

Bladud was skilled in magic. He conjured up the hot springs at Bath and built a temple to Minerva over them, in which he placed devices he had invented for producing a perpetual flame. He also invented a means of flying with artificial wings. With his wings he flew to London but crashed into the Temple of Apollo and was killed after reigning twenty years.

A legend which was current in the Bath district from early times adds details to the story. It says that during his father's reign Bladud caught leprosy and was banished from court. He wandered into Somerset and at Swainswick (swine's hollow) near Bath was given a job herding pigs. There was a certain spot where the pigs liked to wallow, and Bladud noticed that those of them with skin blemishes were cured by the mud. He tried the same treatment on himself and was likewise cured. When he became king he built the city of Bath and its temple on the healing spot, and that was the beginning of Bath's medicinal hot springs.

Bladud's flying exploit is similar to that of Simon Magus, who challenged the power of Christianity in the person of St. Peter and crashed onto the site of the cathedral in Rome. The same fate was met by the mythical Icarus, whose wings melted when he flew too near the sun. Scholars have suggested that the story of Bladud goes back to times when the hot springs were a Celtic religious center, the seat of the goddess Sul, for whom the Romans named the city Aquae Sulis. Her consort was the sun god, whose carved face, bristling with flames, was found during excavations beneath the present Pump Room. The story of Bladud's flight may derive from a former solar myth featuring this deity. It may also commemorate an actual event in times when Druids and shamans claimed the power of levitation.

Roman Bath

The center of Bath is the abbey churchyard, a paved area to the south and west of the abbey church. On its south side is the Pump Room, a grand classical building of 1795 Its face is inscribed with Greek letters meaning "Water is best." The same legend is repeated in English on a fountain outside the northwest corner of the abbey. Bath's water, which tastes rather bitter, can be sampled within the Pump Room. There in magnificent surroundings one can take morning coffee or afternoon tea, listen to a string quartet, and observe through the windows the steaming waters of the King's Bath. In a niche above the bath is an ancient statue of Bladud.

Below the Pump Room and all around it are the founda-

The Roman baths at Bath.

tions of Aquae Sulis, the Roman metropolis. The excavations that have been going on since 1755, when the first of the Roman baths was discovered, are gradually revealing its former greatness. The Roman baths covered a large area and were of different designs and uses. Turkish baths and saunas were heated by hypocausts. All were fed by a powerful hot spring from which the water was channeled in culverts and disposed of by ingenious systems of plumbing. For over three centuries, until the withdrawal of the legions, this great bathhouse must have been the solace of Roman administrators and their families forced to endure the British climate.

The entrance to the Roman baths is on Stall Street at the west end of the abbey churchyard, just around the corner from the Pump Room. Within is the natural shrine of the goddess around which Bath was built. It is a cavern or grotto, the source of the steamy waters. Votive offerings from Roman times have been recovered from it and are now displayed, together with many other Roman relics, in the adjacent museum. Its collection of mosaics, monuments, carvings, and objects of sacred and domestic use illustrate the wealth of the place in Roman times. The most precious object in the museum is a gilt-bronze head of Minerva from her former temple nearby.

The Abbey Church
When the Romans left Bath and Britain early in the fifth century, the city and its temples and baths swiftly fell into ruin. Those must have been desolate times, with the great country houses in the valleys around Bath lying abandoned, heir vineyards overgrown and the quarries where the Romans had cut the fine Bath stone fallen into disuse. The baths silted up and disappeared. Only the springs remained, and beside them, on the site of the fallen temple of Minerva, a humble shrine to the goddess perpetuated her worship. On

that same site in the seventh century a Saxon nunnery was said to have been founded. More certain is that in about 775 King Offa founded a church and college there which later became a Benedictine abbey. By 973 it was important enough for King Edgar, the first Saxon king of the whole of England, to hold his coronation in Bath Abbey.

In 1088 the Norman king, William Rufus, appointed a Frenchman as Bishop of Wells and gave him the whole city of Bath. No doubt in that time, as today, there was more society in Bath than in sleepy Wells, and the bishop moved his residence to the livelier city. (The see is now called Bath and Wells.) He set about building a grand new cathedral on the site of the old abbey. It extended far to the east of the present church, which is built on its nave.

A later Bishop of Bath and Wells found the Norman church so ruinous that he decided to rebuild it. His resolution was confirmed by a vision in which he saw the Holy Trinity and a ladder to Heaven with angels climbing up and down it. At the foot of the ladder was an olive tree with a crown in it, which he took to be a rebus or punning image of his own name, Oliver King. The church he began in 1500 is the present elegant structure. It is in the Perpendicular Gothic style with many large windows, giving the greatest possible amount of light with the least possible amount of stonework. The vaulted ceiling with fan tracery which is one of the glories of the abbey was completed during the nineteenth century.

The west front of Bath Abbey Church, with angels climbing ladders on the turrets in commemoration of Oliver King's vision.

The front of the abbey, seen from the churchyard, is designed to commemorate Oliver King's vision; on either side of the west window are stone ladders with angels climbing up and down them.

So many people of fame or wealth have retired to Bath and died there that the abbey walls are densely covered with monumental inscriptions and sculptures, some of them fantastically elaborate. Beau Nash and the actor Quin were buried there, and so was Thomas Malthus, who became famous through his theory that human population would soon outstrip food resources and the world would starve to death. Many of the others commemorated are admirals, generals, doctors, clergymen, and authors renowned in their times and since forgotten.

Some Sacred Spots Around Bath

Bath lies low in a valley through which flows the River Avon. Around it are seven hills that may have reminded the Romans of the seven hills of their city. They shelter many quiet old churches and burial places, several of which have been neglected and have reverted to nature sanctuaries. Pilgrims and those who seek places with a spiritual atmosphere will not be disappointed in the following sites.

Church of St. Thomas à Becket, Widcombe This is the oldest and most charming of Bath churches, situated in an adjoining village a half-mile from the city center. One can walk to Widcombe through the tunnel beneath the railway station and over the footbridge crossing the river. To the left is Widcombe High Street, and a road to the right at the end of it leads to the church.

The church stands at the meeting place of two lanes that shape its triangular churchyard. The porch is shaded by an old yew. Opposite the raised churchyard is a beautiful Georgian manor house with fountains in its gardens, and beyond it is a green valley and hills. Here one feels on sacred ground, and the impression is confirmed when one enters the church, which has the veiled, religious light of an old Celtic shrine. Walter Savage Landor, the poet who lived in Bath until he was driven from it by his alienated wife, loved this spot and wished to be buried here; his fate was to die in exile in 1864 and to be buried in Florence.

Langridge Church The church lies 3 miles north of Bath on the far side of Lansdowne Hill. From the road along the ridge of the hill, past Beckford's Tower and opposite the race-course, a small road to the right dips down to the church, which is on a ledge above a valley. The trickling of underground waters can be heard as one enters the churchyard between yew trees. As at Widcombe, the feeling here is of an old Celtic sanctuary. Around the simple country church are some curious gravestones, one of which reminds us of a melancholy truth: "As I am now, you soon will be." Appropriate to this natural sanctuary is the female dedication of the church, to St. Mary Magdalene.

St. Catherine's Valley Two miles east of Bath, in Batheaston, a turning to the left off the A4 road is signposted North End and St. Catherine's. This narrow road winds into an enchanting valley along the side of hills above St. Catherine's Brook. The church is 2 miles along it to the left of the road, raised on a knoll overlooking the valley. It is an appropriate shrine to the native spirit of this lovely spot. Next to the church is a great house, St. Catherine's Court, in whose grounds it stands, but there is a right of public access to the church at any time.

Just before one reaches the house and church, on the right, is the entrance to an old Bath institution, the Mead Tea Gardens. There for the last sixty years Bathonians have gone on summer afternoons for an open-air tea beside the brook. A nature trail from the gardens offers sights of wild orchids and other local plants.

By continuing on through St. Catherine's Valley and turning left at the end of it, one returns to Bath.

Bradford-on-Avon: The Mislaid Church Five miles east of Bath, with its railway station on the line from Bath to Salisbury, is one of the loveliest small towns in England. It once had many industries and was famed in the Middle Ages for its clothmaking and dying. Its prosperity vanished in the eighteenth century, leaving it much as it is now. Its steep, narrow streets are lined with attractive buildings, from groups of cottages to splendid Bath-stone mansions. There is also a huge fourteenth-century tithe barn and an ancient arched bridge over the River Avon. On the bridge is a tiny domed building which was once a chapel for pilgrims and later became the town jail. The parish church has some

St. Catherine's Church. She is the patron saint of Bath.

The Saxon Church of St. Laurence, Bradford-on-Avon, lost for many years until its rediscovery in the nineteenth century.

curious old monuments and medieval wall paintings, but its immediate charm is its site, a sacred spot beside the river in a grove of yew trees.

Up to the nineteenth century it was thought that nothing at all remained of Bradford's religious buildings from Saxon times. They included a monastery of which St. Aldhelm, later Bishop of Sherborne, was abbot in the early eighth century. It was recorded that he built a church in Bradford, dedicated to St. Laurence; but nothing was heard of the monastery after the Norman Conquest, and it was assumed that the church had vanished. In 1856 the local vicar happened to be looking down over a jumble of old buildings behind the town streets and noticed a stone cross on one of them. It proved to be the lost Church of St. Laurence. Authorities on Saxon architecture have called it the most perfect surviving church of its kind in England, if not in Europe.

BATH is about 100 miles west of London off the M4 motorway. Trains from London's Paddington Station go there about every hour. Journey time, seventy-five minutes. There is also a train to Bath from Salisbury.

The Pump Room, Roman baths, and museum are open daily, 9 to 6, from March through October, and 9 to 5 the rest of the year. In August they are also open evenings, 8:30 to 10. Admission £1.75. Entrance to the Pump Room for those taking tea there is free.

The Tourist Information Centre is in the abbey churchyard. Telephone: Bath (0225) 62831 for enquiries on museums and places of interest; (0225) 60521 for details of accommodation.

There is a Tourist Information Centre in Silver Street, Bradford-on-Avon, Wiltshire. Telephone: Bradford (02216) 2495. There, on leaving a returnable £5 deposit, one can borrow the key to the bridge chapel-jail. The tithe barn and Saxon church are open daily free of charge. There is ample free parking at Bradford-on-Avon.

5

THE WESTERN PENINSULA

DEVON AND CORNWALL

EXETER

Whether one travels by road or by rail, the main entrance to the western counties of Devon and Cornwall is through Exeter. It is an ancient town with a castle on a great prehistoric mound and a history of occupation by the Romans, who called it Isca. A later Saxon name was Monketon, implying that it was a place of anchorites. Exeter has often been involved in wars and rebellions, but until World War II its pattern of medieval streets was largely intact. Then in 1942 it was bombed in revenge for attacks on German cathedral cities. Exeter cathedral lost some glass but was otherwise little damaged; the town around it suffered badly. Exeter still contains many attractive old buildings, but much of the center has been rebuilt in a utilitarian modern style which is particularly depressing around the west front of the cathedral.

There is no record or legend of when the first Christian church was founded at Exeter, nor is anything known of the pagan temple which, in accordance with custom, it probably replaced. A large church stood there in Saxon times, endowed with many holy relics. In the tenth century King Athelstan presented it with some highly revered objects of dubious character, including a piece of the candle that the angel lit in Christ's tomb and a fragment of the Burning Bush in which God spoke to Moses. With such possessions the church attracted pilgrims, and by 1050 it had become so important that it was made the cathedral of a bishop's see which embraced Devon and Cornwall.

EXETER CATHEDRAL: A Gallery of Sacred Sculpture

Although not large by cathedral standards, St. Peter, Exeter, has great appeal to painters and sculptors because of its wonderful medieval carvings in stone and wood. Its interior is said to be the best example of the Decorated Gothic style in Europe. Apart from the two Norman towers which form

Some of the figures on the west front of Exeter cathedral.

the transepts north and south of the crossing, the present building is mostly a work of the late thirteenth and fourteenth centuries.

Unlike the six other medieval churches clustered around it, which are built of the local red stone, the cathedral is gray. The entrance is through a stone screen across the west front, on which are displayed a host of large statues carved in the late fourteenth century. Kings, saints, and angels, some of them in lifelike or humorous poses, jostle each other in lively fashion, each one a masterpiece of flowing sculpture. Time has eroded their details, and many were damaged by the annual bonfires that used to be lit in front of the cathedral. Several of the most severely affected have been replaced by modern carvings. These, though lovingly executed by experienced artists, lack the exuberant spirit of the originals and appear stiff and awkward by comparison. However, they serve a useful function as foils to the medieval statues, accentuating their now inimitable artistic qualities.

Inside the cathedral there is none of the gloom and mustiness which pervade many great religious buildings. This is no mere museum but a living church, beautifully lit by large windows and with a calm, devotional atmosphere. Along with its clear light, beloved by Protestants, it cherishes a great artistic heritage from pre-Reformation Catholic times. This happy combination of religious values makes Exeter one of the most pleasant of English cathedrals.

As one enters by the west door, the eye is drawn upward to the lovely vaulted roof which extends the entire length of the building. The central bosses are elaborately carved with foliage or religious scenes; one of them above the choir shows the murder of St. Thomas à Becket in Canterbury cathedral. The roof is supported by piers of blue-gray Pur-

One of the carved corbels in the nave of Exeter cathedral.

beck marble, gracefully molded into clusters of thin shafts. The corbels above them, which gather up the shafts of the vault, are carved into thickets of foliage among which appear occasional figures and faces. Here is depicted the beauty of nature as a creation of divinity.

These carvings have recently been repainted in the glowing colors they would have displayed in the Middle Ages. Also repainted is one of the glories of the cathedral, the fourteenth-century musicians' gallery. High up above an arch at the center of the north side of the nave, it is carved in front with figures of twelve angels playing twelve different musical instruments. They recall the days when the church was constantly filled with music. Another memento of those days is the organ, dated 1665, which stands above the magnificent carved screen at the west end of the choir. Its superb tone is unrivaled in Europe and makes Exeter a place of pilgrimage for musicologists. There is a record of a previous organ in the cathedral in the thirteenth century; such instruments were used in churches several centuries earlier than that.

The stalls and woodwork in the choir are mainly original, of the fourteenth century. Many of the carvings on the bench ends and the misericords beneath the seats are as sharply detailed as on the day they were chiseled. Faces peer from the luxuriant foliage, strange animals confront each other, an eagle attacks a heron. In such images, sculpted with unfailing delicacy and wit, one can sense the rich culture and imagination of the medieval artists. No finer example can be found in England of their work than in the Exeter choir stalls and the amazing bishop's throne, fifty-seven feet high, at the southeast end.

The orderliness of the cathedral extends to the side chapels and monuments, which are generally placed in

Strange battles on two of the misericords in the choir of Exeter cathedral.

symmetrical pairs on either side of the main axis. Some of the chapels seem to retain the sanctity of the relics they once held and the intensity of the faith which pilgrims once brought to them; others are now made to commemorate military glories. Former bishops lie opposite one another beneath their effigies in canopied tombs. Several monuments include a skull as memento mori, and in the north choir aisle is a remarkable full-length marble sculpture of a corpse in a state of putrefaction—the most durable of materials imitating the most transient.

The most beautiful spot in the cathedral is the center of the presbytery, east of the choir, lit by the glorious east window. Opposite it, the west window contains a circle with a rare geometrical design. Twelve circular roses with alternately four and five petals stand around the circumference, and in the center is a circle containing a pentagram. In this design are combined several different figures of esoteric or sacred geometry, as studied in the medieval lodges of masons. Each has its peculiar symbolism. The number five, here represented by the five-petaled roses and the central pentagram, is the number of humanity, referring among other things to the five extremities (legs, arms, and head) of the body. The number twelve stands for the framework of the cosmos (twelve gods, signs of the zodiac, months in a year, etc.). The number four signifies stability in relation to the four cardinal points, four seasons, and so on. On a simple level, the west window at Exeter can be seen as representing the perfected individual, placed in harmony with the universe.

EXETER is 170 miles west of London, off the M5 motorway and at the junction of the A30 and A38 roads into Cornwall. It has a railway station with trains from London (journey of two and a half hours), the north, and Cornwall to the west.

The cathedral is open daily, following matins at 7:30, to evensong at 5:30. During services the cathedral is closed to those not attending.

The Tourist Information Centre is in the Civic Centre, Paris Street. Telephone: Exeter (0392) 77888.

A LA RONDE: *A Temple of Ladies and the Conversion of the Jews*

A visit to A la Ronde provides a charming diversion from sacred sites of more solemn character. It is a quiet, domestic place but a highly eccentric one, and it has had a remarkable effect on modern religious and political history. It inspired the development in Victorian times of the Society for Promoting Christianity Among the Jews and thus contributed to the restoration of the Jews to their homeland in Palestine.

A la Ronde, overlooking the estuary near Exmouth, is a strange sixteen-sided house built in the last years of the eighteenth century by two unmarried ladies, Jane Parminter and her cousin Mary. They had just returned from a grand tour of Europe lasting ten years, during which they had been impressed by the sixth-century Byzantine basilica, San Vitale of Ravenna. They took it as the model for their house. In it they lived peacefully, occupying themselves with artistic works, until Jane died in 1811 at the age of sixty-four, followed by Mary thirty-eight years later.

Jane Parminter cherished a lifelong passion which she expressed by building a little nonconformist church a short distance behind the house. It was called Point-in-View, and the point which Jane had in view was that the Jews should be converted to Christianity and then led back to the Holy Land, where they would produce a new, Christian Messiah

The curious sixteen-sided house of A la Ronde, Exmouth.

in accordance with prophecy, leading to the millennium and the institution of divine rule on earth.

When Jane died (and was buried beneath the floor of Point-in-View) her money was bequeathed to form a trust whose object was to maintain Point-in-View and to provide accommodation nearby for four elderly spinsters and six little girls who were to be educated at a school in the church vestry. Christians of Jewish origin were to be preferred as applicants. The charity continues in an amended form to this day.

The Jews' Society and the Oaks of A la Ronde

Fine old oak trees grow all about A la Ronde, and Jane Parminter referred to them in a clause in her will: "These oaks shall remain standing and the hand of man shall not be raised against them, till Israel returns and is restored to the Land of Promise."

This clause had dramatic effects. In 1812 a rich tourist, Lewis Way, learned of it while visiting the neighborhood of A la Ronde and was so impressed that he devoted his fortune and the rest of his life to fostering the aims of the society for converting the Jews, commonly known as the Jews' Society.

From that time the society flourished. Under Queen Victoria it enjoyed royal patronage and the support of many powerful people, including the philanthropist Lord Shaftesbury, who persuaded his brother-in-law, Lord Palmerston, the prime minister, to incorporate its aims into British foreign policy. This was made formal by the Balfour Declaration of 1917, which committed subsequent British governments to allowing Jewish settlements in Palestine.

To that extent the aims of the Jews' Society were fulfilled, but the part of its program that promoted the conversion of the Jews to Christianity was almost a total failure. This was inevitable, for the society's missionaries, sent to Jewish colonies all over the world, found that any Jew they managed to convert was thereby cut off from his community and lost his livelihood. Of the very few Jews who were converted, the majority were rabbis, who could be found alternative employment as clergymen of the Church of England.

One can therefore make a link, however tenuous, between the oak grove of A la Ronde and the foundation of the state of Israel.

The House

A la Ronde is still owned and inhabited by descendants of the Parminter family, who show it to visitors. In its history of almost two hundred years it has always had a female owner, except for a period in the nineteenth century when it belonged to a clergyman who married into the family. He replaced the original thatched roof with tiles and put in dormer windows.

The inside remains much as the Parminter ladies designed and furnished it. In plan it consists of a central octagon from which eight doors lead to eight rectangular rooms, the spaces between them filled by triangular side chambers. The rooms are full of pictures and objects the ladies brought back from their grand tour. Many of them are crammed into an old-fashioned "cabinet of curiosities." The little library, drawing room, and dining room are still heavily under the spell of the nineteenth century. A gallery in the lantern turret high above the octagon, approached by narrow stairs, was transformed by the ladies into a shell grotto. Below are the kitchens where cream teas are now served to visitors.

Point-in-View Church

This must be one of the most eccentric churches in England, but its atmosphere and history are very moving, particularly to those who like simple forms of worship. The church is low, painted white, with a tiny central spire. Inside, a room has benches for a congregation of sixty-five and a remarkable organ with horizontal pipes which, when folded, becomes a pulpit. The vestry to one side, where the girls' school was once held, contains relics of the old days and a history of the place.

Jane Parminter's charity has been successfully adapted to modern times. There is no longer a school for girls, but additional accommodation has been built, and the community at Point-in-View now consists of six ladies (widows are admitted as well as spinsters), a retired minister and his wife, and the family of the present chaplain, who live in the manse. The little church at the center of their lives is always open, and visitors are made welcome.

A LA RONDE is a short distance along Summer Lane, a turning to the left off the A376 road from Exeter (9 miles) to Exmouth (one mile).

The house is open daily, 10 to 6 (Sunday, 2 to 7), from Easter through October. Guided tours are £1.50. Light lunches and teas are served in the kitchen.

Point-in-View Church, a quarter of a mile further up Summer Lane in a field to the right, is always open free of charge.

DARTMOOR: *Sacred Stones and Temples*

Most of southwest Devon, between Exeter and Plymouth, consists of Dartmoor, now a national park. It is a high, granite plateau, rising to over two thousand feet above sea level, about 20 to 25 miles long. The landscape on the moor is very different from the green pasture lands which surround it. Among the rocks and peat bogs grow heather, gorse, and bracken over which roam sheep and herds of wild ponies. In fine weather it is beautiful country, but mists and rainstorms may occur suddenly at any time, and there is no natural shelter. Unprepared walkers can easily become lost and wander into swamps.

An Ordnance Survey map is essential for excursions onto

the moor. It marks many of the prehistoric monuments and habitations which are to be found there. From very early times tin and other metals have been mined on the moor, and its surface is covered with the remains of ancient workings and the stone huts of the miners. Once there was a large population in this now desolate country. Five or six thousand years ago it was inhabited by the megalith builders who strewed it with a profusion of stone circles, standing stones, and alignments, creating a dense pattern of interrelated monuments and making Dartmoor a renowned center for students of the sacred megalithic science. The following is a sample of the more important and accessible places and antiquities.

Scorhill Stone Circle

The small, ancient hilltop town of Chagford on the eastern edge of the moor, 22 miles west of Exeter, 3 miles south of the A30 road, makes a good base for excursions onto Dartmoor; some notable monuments lie close to it.

The stone circle at Scorhill is 3 miles west of Chagford. It is signposted to the right at a corner of the lane from Berrydown to Scorhill Farm. From there it is an easy walk of less than a half-mile across moorland. The site is extremely lonely, with open moors in all directions. In certain kinds of weather it has a sinister appearance, and stories are told of odd things that have happened there: Cameras malfunction and horses sometimes refuse to pass through the circle. At other times it looks calmly impressive and dignified. Earlier writers claimed it as the most perfect Druidical shrine in Devonshire.

There were originally thirty-six stones in the circle, some of which are now missing. One of them is considerably taller than the others and may have been the centerpoint of the ancient ritual. The diameter of the ring is 86 feet.

A short distance south of the circle, in the rocky River Teign, lies a large boulder with a hole through it. This was once attributed to the Druids, and it may in former times have been the shrine of a spirit, although the hole is now thought to be natural. Near it is a prehistoric clapper bridge made of a single stone.

Several other stone circles lie within 2 or 3 miles of Scorhill. There are two ruined circles at Buttern Hill one mile to the northwest, and another mile farther on is the circle on White Moor Down. Two miles due south is the Fernworthy Circle. On a large-scale map one can see how these circles exactly align with each other and with other monuments and landmarks across the moor.

Kestor Rock and Alignments

Kestor Rock is 2.5 miles west of Chagford and can be seen from the town. It is a great, highly placed boulder, an unmistakable landmark for miles around. There are no ancient markings upon it, but it was clearly used by the

Bowerman's Nose, a natural outcrop which provides a familiar Dartmoor landmark and is said to represent a legendary hunter who roams the moors.

megalith builders as a point of reference in their mysterious system of alignments between stone circles and pillars. It features in two alignments:

I. Stone circle on White Moor Down (map reference: SX 634896); Scorhill stone circle (SX 655874); Kestor Rock (SX 665863); "hut circle" (SX 681847); Haytor. Another circle, the West Buttern (SX 643886), is not marked on the map but seems to lie on or close to the line.

II. Kestor Rock; tall standing stone at SX 660857; the northern of the two Grey Wethers circles at SX 638832.

The tall standing stone in alignment II is a half-mile southwest of Kestor Rock and can be approached from it. It is a fine granite pillar standing in a row of smaller stones. Long parallel rows of stones run northward from it and point directly to the Scorhill circle a mile away.

The Spinsters' Rock, Drewsteignton

This great dolmen, the only one of its kind in Devonshire, is all that remains of a large megalithic complex that was otherwise destroyed at the beginning of the nineteenth century. Early plans of it show that it must have been one of the most important megalithic sites in the country.

Two miles northeast of Chagford and 4 miles northward from Moretonhampstead on the A382 road, a small road to the right goes immediately over a bridge and on to Drewsteignton (Druid's Teign Town or Stone Town perhaps; the inn in the village used to be called the Druid's Arms). The small road winds uphill for almost a mile and passes a farm on the left, 2.5 miles west of Drewsteignton. The Spinsters' Rock is in the field opposite the farm. A notice at the gate tells its legend and permits free access.

The capstone, estimated to weigh over sixteen tons, is held up to eight feet high above the ground by three stone supporters. Two of them retain it on narrow tapered points, and the other has a ledge cut into its top on which the capstone rests. It may no longer be exactly as it was originally built, for the structure fell down in 1862 and was reerected.

The traditional local explanation is that the dolmen was put up one morning before breakfast by three spinsters. A writer in the eighteenth century identified it as an astronomical observatory. Others have connected it with Druidism. One aspect of its purpose is apparent at the site: It was meant to be seen over long distances. It stands on a ridge and, were it not for modern walls and plantations, would command views in all directions.

The avenues of standing stones that stood in fields due west of Spinsters' Rock on the far side of the road were said to have formed a great cross. One arm of the cross ran toward the dolmen. When the stones were pulled down they were tumbled against the steep bank below the road on its west side. There they lie today, a melancholy sight. The farmer who made this graveyard of megaliths was even more

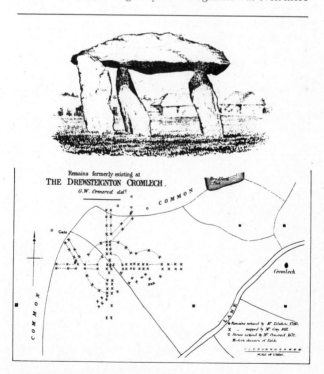

The Spinsters' Rock and a plan of the stone avenues which once led to it.

ruthless than the "stone killing" people of Avebury; nothing is left of the ancient avenues apart from useless heaps of stones.

Wistman's Wood, a Reputed Druidic Grove

One of the easiest and most delightful excursions on Dartmoor is by a path which goes north from Two Bridges along the West Dart River. To the right of the path, overlooking Two Bridges, is Crockern Tor, formerly a meeting place of the Old Stannery parliament which used to legislate for the affairs of Dartmoor and was particularly concerned with mining rights. A rock slab used as a table and chairs of moorland stone existed there up to the end of the eighteenth century, when they were removed for building blocks. On this exposed spot the traditional administrators of Dartmoor long preserved the Druid custom of holding solemn assemblies in the open air.

Just over a mile north of Two Bridges, along the path on the east side of the West Dart, can be seen a remarkable grove of trees which has long been celebrated as one of the wonders of Dartmoor. This is Wistman's Wood, a primeval tangle of gnarled, stunted oak trees, growing scarcely higher than a tall man can reach. Now it is a nature sanctuary, but it has never been replanted or trimmed and is in much the same state as in ancient times when, according to its legend, it was a sanctuary of the Druids, their sacred grove, and one of their last places of refuge in the west. The moor people believe that it is full of venomous adders, and one can easily imagine a tangle of snakes in the contorted roots of the little trees that cling sinuously to rocks and probe downward into the sparse soil. Mosses cover the ground and hang from the branches of the trees. This is a strangely quiet and at times sinister place. As well as sheltering the Druids, it has no doubt in its time provided refuge for escaped convicts from the prison at Princetown nearby. Absconding from prison was the lesser part of their problem; it was more difficult to elude the bogs of the shelterless moor and the bloodhounds of the warders.

St. Michael on Brentor

On the western edge of Dartmoor, 4 miles north of Tavistock on the road to Lydford, a high volcanic rock is visible for miles. On top of it is a little church, one of the smallest in the country, first built in about 1130 with a tower added in the fifteenth century. A scrambling climb, which in winter can be very unpleasant, is needed to gain the summit.

Inside the church is a window of St. Michael, to whom the church is dedicated. He is shown with the lance with which he transfixes the dragon. The legend that accounts for the lofty, inconvenient position of the building says it was originally founded at the foot of the hill but the devil kept carrying the stones to the top, where the church finally had to be built. The upper air is traditionally the realm of satanic

St. Michael's Church on the rock at Brentor.

forces, and St. Michael the Archangel, who vanquished Lucifer and commands the hosts of heaven, was made guardian of the high places against the powers of darkness.

Christianity emphasizes the fight against evil, but the earlier pagan religion was more concerned with transmuting forces and deriving benefit from all the elements in nature. It was based on the principles of alchemy and used its symbolism. Thus the pagan forerunner of St. Michael erected his spear on the high places, transfixing the head of the earth serpent beneath, by which was symbolized the attraction of positively charged cosmic energy into the veins of the earth current, negatively charged. Parallel with this image was one of the practices of ancient science, a form of "earth acupuncture" by which the land was made fertile and capable of supporting a large, settled population. The lance of St. Michael was not originally for slaying the serpent or dragon but for releasing the energies of the upper atmosphere in a productive way for the renewal of life on earth.

The remains of an ancient earthwork surrounding the upper part of the hill of Brentor indicate that it was a prehistoric sanctuary. The name means Burnt Tor, for on it once blazed a beacon fire, a guide to travelers across the moor and also to ships off the coast 18 miles away. One of the legends of the church is that it was built as a landmark for sailors by a grateful man who had been spared from a shipwreck. The beacon was probably tended, as at other elevated St. Michael shrines, by a hermit who made his cell in the rock.

Services are still held in the church during the summer months.

THERE ARE SEVEN National Park Information Centres around Dartmoor, at New Bridge, Okehampton, Parke, Princetown, Steps Bridge, Tavistock, and (the main one) Postbridge. The Postbridge Centre is in the middle of the moor on the B3212 road 9 miles southwest of Moretonhampstead and 3 miles northeast of Two Bridges. At this beautiful riverside spot there are places for picnics and other facilities. Lectures and guided walks on Dartmoor are offered. There is information on where to hire horses for riding on the moor and detailed maps and guides to ancient monuments.

From Two Bridges, 9 miles east of Tavistock, where the B3212 and the B3357 roads meet, is the walk to Wistman's Wood. Details of organized walks there can be had from one of the Information Centres. Telephone: Tavistock (0822) 88272.

CORNISH HOLY WELLS

As one crosses the River Tamar above Plymouth, traveling west, one enters a country which in spirit and culture is a foreign land. Politically, Cornwall has been part of England for more than a thousand years, which justifies its inclusion in this book. It is a Royal Duchy under the nominal rule of the Duke of Cornwall, who is Charles, the Prince of Wales. It remains, however, a Celtic country that once shared a common language with Wales to the north and Brittany to the south. At the time of the Roman invasion, the Cornish were in a confederacy with the Veneti of Brittany, whose navy was defeated by Caesar in 56 B.C. Thereafter the two countries grew slowly apart, and Cornish developed as a dialect of the old Breton tongue. Cornish has been moribund since the eighteenth century, though attempts are now being made to revive it.

Cornubia, as the Romans called it, was the western portion of the kingdom of Dumnonia, which included Devon and parts of Somerset. Its tribal rulers were united under a high king. From the fifth century to the ninth century it gradually lost its territories to the Saxons invading from the west. Legends tell of heroic resistance leaders and of battles won and lost. Early in the sixth century the western Britons, led by King Arthur, defeated the Saxons at the Battle of Mount Badon in Wessex. A few years later at the Battle of Camlan they were in turn routed and Arthur was slain. By the eighth century the Saxons had reached the River Tamar. For two hundred years more the Cornish preserved a diminishing independence until in 927 the last king of Cornwall, Howel, was forced to swear allegiance to King Athelstan the Saxon.

The Land of Saints

Cornwall is a rocky granite peninsula, full of minerals that in prehistoric and classical times were traded with merchants from the Mediterranean. From the inland mines tin was taken down to St. Michael's Mount on the south coast for export to the Continent.

With the traders came missionaries and scholars. Cornwall has always attracted mystics, and its ancient sanctity is proclaimed by the vast number of Stone Age temples and monuments which occur in all its higher regions. Among

them are curiously shaped rocks which Cornish antiquarians
used to identify as images of Druidic deities. Below, in the
wooded valleys, many natural shrines of the earth spirit
occur by streams and springs. Cornish folklore describes the
elemental forces in the landscape in terms of giants and
fairies.

The Celtic Druids invoked the spirits of nature in wild and
lonely spots, and the Celtic Church which sprang from them
inherited their sacred places. In the third century A.D. there
was a great religious revival in Cornwall. Local visionaries
were joined by missionary saints from Brittany, Wales, and
Ireland in raising the sacred spirit of the country. Quaint
legends commemorate the arrival of the Irish: St. Kea sailed
to Cornwall in a stone trough; St. Piran made the voyage on
a millstone; St. Patrick floated over on his altar. Such feats
are similar to those attributed to shamans and Taoist holy
men, whom the Celtic saints in many ways resembled. By
Cornish rocks and springs they communicated with spirit,
and at such places their names are still remembered. In the
words of Cornwall's greatest mystical poet, the Reverend
Robert Hawker, Vicar of Morwenstowe,

> They had their lodges in the wilderness,
> Or built them cells beside the shadowy sea,
> And there they dwelt with angels, like a dream . . .

THE HOLY WELLS

At Cornwall's holy wells, the most humble and natural of
shrines, the simple spirit of Celtic Christianity can still be
recalled. The old saints blessed and healed their communities with the waters of these wells, whose traditional virtues
were made use of locally for hundreds of years after the Age
of the Saints had passed. As late as the eighteenth century
there was still a rustic priestess in charge of the well near the
church at Gulval; her function was to assist visitors to
foresee their futures and fortunes in the movements of the
waters. Other wells were famous for curing certain disorders,
physical or psychological. They strengthened eyesight, cured
aches and rashes, and invigorated the old and children. They
were also a source of pure, healthy water to almost every
Cornish village. Drawn upon at their source at the appropriate season of the year, their natural medicinal virtues were
augmented by the blessings of their guardian spirit.

Almost two hundred wells are described in J. Meyrick's *A
Pilgrim's Guide to the Holy Wells of Cornwall* (1982). Many
of them can no longer be seen or are hard to find. A sample
of the more accessible of these most moving of ancient
shrines are described in the following pages, along with
other sacred monuments of their localities.

The Well and Monuments of St. Cleer
St. Cleer is a village 2 miles north of Liskeard, on the edge of
Bodwin Moor. The area around the village has been heavily

The holy well which cured lunatics at St. Cleer.

mined and quarried, yet it contains many ancient and sacred monuments. Near the center of the village, three hundred yards northeast of the church, is St. Cleer's holy well with a cross beside it. The fifteenth-century well house was restored in 1864 and remains in excellent condition. Its waters were once famous for healing, and the well was resorted to by the lame and the blind. In a pool nearby, fed by the well, lunatics were once treated. The method used at this and other wells was to shock the lunatic into near insensibility by immersing him suddenly and violently in the cold waters; then he was carried to the well chapel, where sacred chants were sung over him with the object of reconditioning his mind. This process is known in Cornwall as bowssening.

The Trevethy Quoit At the east end of the village stands a tall and impressive dolmen. Its great capstone, fourteen feet

The Trevethy Quoit.

long, is raised thirteen feet above the ground on a number of stone slabs. An odd feature of the capstone is that it is pierced with a hole, seemingly artificial. This has caused Trevethy to be compared with other holed dolmens, which occur widely—for example, in Spain, Portugal, and the Caucasus. The purpose of the holes could be to admit light at certain seasons of the year in order to mark a calendar or in connection with ritual.

The Hurlers and Rillaton Barrow Two miles from St. Cleer the road northward passes on the left three stone circles in line called the Hurlers because of the legend that they represent players of the Cornish game of hurling, turned to stone. Just before reaching the Hurlers, on the right of the road, is a tall standing stone which has been reshaped in the form of a cross. Beyond the Hurlers, to the northeast, is a large mound called Rillaton Barrow. The stone cross, the three circles, and the barrow stand together on a straight line and were no doubt connected in prehistoric rituals.

Stones in one of the Hurler circles.

The southernmost of the three Hurler circles is badly ruined. The others were restored in the 1930s, and concrete markers show the former positions of missing stones. Best preserved is the central circle. Of its original twenty-nine stones, all but one are either in position or marked. The circles are on open moorland, where larks sing overhead and relics of mines litter the landscape.

An old story told about Rillaton Barrow was that its guardian spirit would offer travelers a drink from an ever-flowing gold cup. This amiable custom came to an end when a guest snatched the cup and rode off with it—only to fall over a precipice. In 1837 the barrow was excavated and an exquisite gold beaker was found within it. It disappeared for a time and was later found on the dressing table of King George V, who was keeping his collar studs in it. The Rillaton cup is now in the British Museum.

The Cheesewring This extraordinary rock pile has attracted prolonged interest and controversy. It stands on the summit of Stowe's Hill, a mile north of the Hurlers, within a sacred Neolithic enclosure. It may have been the terminus of a processional path from the Hurlers by way of Rillaton Barrow. A barrow on the hill beside it yielded an urn full of flint spearheads, arrows, and a dagger.

Early antiquarians supposed that the Cheesewring was a Druidic idol to which sacrifices were made. Others have seen it as an astronomical marker intended to be observed from stone circles in the vicinity. It is also debated whether it is a natural or an ancient artificial structure. Whatever its origin, it was undoubtedly an important feature in the sacred, ritualized landscape surrounding it.

It is an easy walk across moorland from the Hurlers, past Rillaton Barrow, to the enigmatic Cheesewring. From there one can see far across Bodmin Moor. Standing by the Cheesewring, one is directly on the "St. Michael" line of sacred sites from Land's End through Glastonbury Tor to Avebury (see page 89). Was the Cheesewring constructed as a geodetic marker on the line? If it was, it must have been erected in an age long before that of the megalith builders, in the days of the legendary Cornish giants.

King Doniert's Stone The stone stands by the road a mile northwest of St. Cleer. Its ornamentation and inscription are probably of the ninth century. Faint letters spell out in Latin,

The Cheesewring.

St. Keyne's well before the disappearance of its famous three trees.

"Doniert asked for this on behalf of his soul." It is thought to be a monument to Doniert, king of Cornwall, who drowned in the River Fowey in 878.

St. Keyne's Well

Southward from Liskeard in East Cornwall runs the beautiful wooded valley of the River Looe. Alongside the river is a delightful little railway, nine miles long, from Liskeard to the harbor and resort of Looe. One of its small stations is St. Keyne, which serves the village about a mile to the west. Halfway between the station and the village church, on the left of the road, is the once famous well of St. Keyne. It is no longer as picturesque as it was in the nineteenth century when John T. Blight made his drawing; the nearby cottages and the trees which shaded it are no more. However, it is well restored and its waters are pure and refreshing.

The remarkable property of the well is to give to the first of any couple who drinks its water the upper hand in marriage. This belief was celebrated by the poet Robert Southey in verses about a newly wedded husband who, immediately after the marriage service, ran from the church so as to be the first to drink from St. Keyne's well—only to find out later that his bride had taken a bottle of the water to the church with her.

St. Keyne was a fifth-century champion of women's rights. She was extremely beautiful, and on her missionary and miracle-working journeys she was much harassed by amorous men. The "strength of her purity," however, preserved her from injury and insult. When she retired to a spot in the valley near her well, she endowed the water with its peculiar virtue in order to assist brides to prevail over their husbands.

This well was once one of the natural wonders of Cornwall because St. Keyne planted a tree root beside it, from which grew four sacred trees, an oak, an ash, an elm, and a willow. Three of them fell during a storm in 1703, and others were planted to replace them, but they no longer thrive.

Duloe's Stone Circle
The village of Duloe is 4 miles south of Liskeard and 2 miles beyond St. Keyne. Near the south end of its village street (the B3254 road), on the east side, a lane beside a house goes into a field where stands a most unusual stone circle. It consists of eight stones set close together in an oval formation, the tallest stone ten feet high. What makes it unusual—perhaps unique among megalithic monuments—is that all its stones are of white quartz crystal. This circle was not recorded until early in the nineteenth century, and it has preserved no particular legend.

St. Cuby's Well
Less than a half-mile southeast of the circle, on the right-hand side of the road to Looe, is St. Cuby's holy well. In front of it is an ancient chapel with stone seats and mossy walls. There was once a carved basin into which the spring water flowed, and local legends tell of the ill luck incurred by anyone who tried to remove the basin. Nevertheless it was moved to Trenant Park, a large house in the neighborhood, in the nineteenth century. The landowner who took it had to promise the workmen involved in the sacrilege that, if any of them dropped dead during the operation, he would give their widows a pension. The basin is now in the village church.

St. Cuby was of a Cornish royal house and heir to a kingdom; he renounced his inheritance for a life of scholarship, pilgrimage, and healing the sick. The waters of his well are clear and therapeutic though of no specific virtue.

The large stones of white quartz which make up the circle at Duloe.

St. Nun's piskie well, Pelynt.

St. Nun's Piskie Well, Pelynt

This is the most secluded and rustic of nature shrines, a place of pure spirit. It is not easy to find, but one's effort is rewarded by the peace and beauty of the spot. The well is situated on a steep slope to the west of the West Looe River, overlooking its valley, 1.5 miles southwest of Duloe. Halfway on the road between Sowden's Bridge and Machlarnick is the entrance to Hobb's Park. The easiest approach to the well is from the house at the end of the driveway, where it is best to ask permission to visit the well, which is on private land. It lies over the hedge to the right of the driveway.

The old well house is tucked away beneath the roots of three trees that overshadow it, an oak, an ash, and a thorn. Ivy, brambles, and wildflowers grow around it. Woodland butterflies frequent it. Within are rare ferns and mosses through which the water trickles.

St. Nun, or Ninny, the mother of St. David, gave her name to the well, but it has continued as the haunt of its more ancient guardians, the Cornish piskies or nature spirits who bring good luck to respectable visitors to their shrine and curse those who desecrate it. Local people used to propitiate the piskies by dropping pins into the stone basin within the well. As at Duloe, death and disaster are said to visit anyone who tries to remove it. The present basin, however, does not seem to be the original carved one illustrated in the nineteenth-century engraving; it shows the well house after its restoration about a hundred years ago. The chapel which was once behind the well has long since disappeared.

At. St. Nun's well the female element in nature is enshrined among the trees, ferns, and plants that are her particular symbols. The peace of mind which such places bestow can be acknowledged in the time-honored manner by leaving there some trifle, such as a pin or a small coin, as a thanks offering.

The well of St. Dominick, Dupath.

The Well of St. Dominick at Dupath, Callington

Callington is on the A390 road midway between Tavistock and Liskeard. A mile east-southeast of the town is a sign-posted path to the holy well. It is one of the most interesting and best preserved of such structures in Cornwall. Built in 1510, probably by the monks of St. Germans, it was restored in the nineteenth century by the rector of Callington. It is now cared for by the Department of the Environment.

When Blight made his illustration of the well in 1873, he said that it had "a deserted and neglected appearance; gloom and solitude hang over the place." Though no longer neglected, it retains its secluded air. The well chapel is built of granite blocks and roofed with stone slabs supported by an arch. The waters which run through it have been claimed as a cure for whooping cough. An old Cornish ballad makes it the scene of a duel between two Saxons for the love of a woman, which ended by each killing the other. In another version the survivor built a chapel on the spot.

Roche Rock, Hermitage, and Holy Well

On the A30 road 7 miles west of Bodmin is the Victoria Inn. There a turning to the left leads to the village of Roche and, a few hundred yards further on, to Roche Rock. It towers dramatically above a flat, barren landscape, rivaled only by refuse heaps of the china clay industry to the south.

Roche Rock is dedicated to St. Michael, guardian of high places. At its summit, built into the living rock, is a chapel with a hermit's cell beneath it. A succession of Celtic saints lived there, and it was occupied as a hermitage up to the fourteenth century. The chapel was added in 1409. Now it is a roofless ruin. A somewhat perilous route to the summit is given by steps cut into the rock. It was probably one of the duties of the old Roche hermits to keep a light burning on the rock for the guidance of travelers across the moors.

The hermitage chapel on Roche Rock.

The earliest hermit whose name is known was St. Conan, also called St. Roche, who became one of the first bishops of Cornwall. A later occupant of the cell was a leper whose daughter, St. Gundred, fetched him water from a nearby well. Among the holy wells of Roche parish, all but one of which have been lost, was a well at the foot of the rock which used to ebb and flow with the tides. This was either St. Conan's or St. Gundred's well, and both names are also attached to the existing holy well of Roche on the other side of the A30 road.

By going a quarter-mile to the west past the Victoria Inn and a similar distance up a lane to the right, crossing the railway line, one comes to Holy Well Cottage. A steep path down to the right leads to the holy well, where clear waters issue from beneath a ruined granite structure. This well of

The holy well near Roche.

St. Gundred (or St. Conan) supplied until recently the domestic needs of the neighborhood. It is also known for its medicinal properties, being visited for all kinds of ailments, especially children's eye diseases. Girls went there to divine their futures and used it as a wishing well, dropping bent pins into its waters as an offering to its spirit. The days when it was found most efficacious were Holy Thursday and the two following Thursdays, before sunrise.

There was once a chapel by the well of which nothing apparent remains.

MORWENSTOW: *The Parish of an Eccentric Reverend Poet*

On the wild northeast Cornish coast, 8 miles south of Hartland Point (and approached from there by a turning to the right off the A39 road) is the tiny village of Morwenstow. The cliffs hereabouts are spectacular and among the highest in Cornwall. Apart from the scenery, Morwenstow's attraction is that here, from 1834 to 1875, lived a saintly and most unconventional poet, the Reverend Robert S. Hawker.

The Reverend R. S. Hawker, Arthurian poet and saintly eccentric.

Hawker's eccentricity is apparent the moment one sees the Gothic vicarage he built in 1837. Its four chimneys are made in the shape of church towers, modeled on those of villages where he had previously lived. Nearby in a sheltered graveyard is the old church, full of curious Norman carvings whose symbolism delighted Hawker and was often referred to in his poems and mystical sermons. One of the church windows is Hawker's memorial. Below the graveyard a path down a cliff leads to Hawker's hut, where he contemplated the stormy sea and communicated with angels, sometimes with the aid of opium, to which he became addicted. There in 1848 Tennyson visited the celebrated Vicar of Morwenstow and was inspired by his host's poem "The Quest of the Sangraal" to undertake his own Arthurian *Idylls*.

Hawker's biography, *The Vicar of Morwenstow*, was written soon after his death by the Reverend Sabine Baring-Gould, the most prolific of Victorian writers, who is credited with over 150 books and innumerable hymns ("Onward, Christian Soldiers"), stories, sermons, and tracts. The book on Hawker, Gould's best-seller, is highly entertaining; it describes an unruly spirit, confined to a poor, lonely parish, alternating wild escapades with periods of deep religious melancholy and ecstatic vision. In company with the elemental spirits of the place, Morwenstow still seems haunted by the spirit of its former vicar.

The Holy Well of St. John the Baptist

Down a path behind the vicarage is a holy well that was one of Hawker's favorite resorts. Blight's drawing shows him and his dog beside it. On behalf of his church Hawker fought a successful lawsuit over the well with a local landowner who tried to appropriate it; he celebrated the victory by writing a poem to St. John's well.

The well is in good condition and gives clear, refreshing water which is still, as in Hawker's day, used for baptisms. Its dedication to John the Baptist is repeated in that of the south aisle of Morwenstow church.

Northwest of St. John's well is another, dedicated to St. Morwenna. She was one of twenty-six children of Brychan, a fifth-century Welsh king. (St. Keyne was another.) Most of them were girls, and all but one became saints. Hawker revered St. Morwenna, and in 1874 he repaired her well, but it is now overgrown and difficult to find. There is hope that it will soon be restored.

Hawker and his dog at St. John's holy well.

TINTAGEL: *King Arthur's Castle*

Its village is dreary and commercialized, but no imaginative visitor has ever been disappointed at Tintagel's high, rocky headland set in a raging sea, which is the legendary site of King Arthur's castle and birthplace. In the summer months a landrover bus goes there from the village; otherwise one scrambles down a ravine and up again to a bridge across a chasm. On the far side is the famous castle and sanctuary.

The fortifications, with a ruined hall and chapel through which one enters, are the remains of a castle built in the twelfth century. At that time writers were reviving old legends of King Arthur at Tintagel, and the castle was put there probably for a symbolic reason, to demonstrate Norman control of a place held sacred by the British.

Beyond the castle the island rock rises 250 feet above the Atlantic rollers which belabor its base. Excavations have shown that in the fifth century there was an important Celtic monastery with library, chapel, guest house, refectory, and sauna-type bathhouses. Fragments of Mediterranean pottery were found, indicating that oil, wine, and other luxuries were imported from abroad. The picture emerges of a Celtic center of culture and mystical learning, situated on a remote, sea-girt headland under the protection of a Cornish king. Thus archaeology supports the poet's image of King Arthur as a learned and noble-minded Celtic ruler who strove for the restoration of sacred order in Britain. The reason he chose to base himself at Tintagel can be appreciated only by one's going there.

On the shore below the headland is Merlin's Cave, which can be approached only at low tide. Other Arthurian names

Ruins of the medieval castle at Tintagel.

*In the valley of rocks below Tintagel's sacred headland a
rock face is carved with a traditional labyrinth pattern.
The date of the carving is unknown.*

in the district show how deep-rooted is the old Celtic
mythology in this heroic north Cornish landscape.

THE CASTLE AT TINTAGEL is open March 15 through October 15, daily 9:30
to 6:30 (Sunday, 2 to 6:30); for the rest of the year, daily, 9:30 to 4 (Sunday,
2 to 4). Entrance £1.

ST. MICHAEL'S MOUNT

Guarding the entrance to the Land's End district of Cornwall, off its southern coast, is a towering rocky fortress, like
a castle in a fairy tale, which at high tide is insulated by the
waters of Mount's Bay. Those who know Mont-Saint-Michel
off the opposite coast of Brittany are amazed, for here in
Cornwall is what appears to be a small replica of it. The
histories of the two places are closely related. On both sites,
visions of St. Michael were seen during the fifth century. At
St. Michael's Mount the archangel was observed one night
in 495 by fishermen in Mount's Bay, standing luminous on
a rock ledge, which is still shown to visitors.

In its earliest legend the Mount was the home of a giant
named Cormoran, who was slain by a Cornish Jack-the-
Giant-Killer. A holy well, drilled through rock halfway up the
Mount, is named for Cormoran, the Giant's well. Another
spring is said to have gushed forth when St. Keyne made her
pilgrimage to the Mount in 490. A memento of her visit is a
recess in the rock at the summit of a high precipice, called
St. Keyne's Chair. It had the same property as her well, that
whichever one of a couple first sat in it would be the
dominant partner. Visitors in the nineteenth century were
terrified at seeing young men and women risk a fatal fall by
climbing into and out of the chair. There is also St. Michael's
Chair, an old stone lantern on top of the church tower.
Pilgrims used to make the dangerous ascent of it.

The old name given to the Mount in the Cornish language

St. Michael's Mount.

means "the rock in the wood." This must date from the time when Mount's Bay was a forest, part of lost Lyonesse. Some writers have put the flooding of the Mount's Bay lands as late as the twelfth century, but if the Mount is Ictys, the offshore island where, according to Roman writers, British and foreign traders dealt in tin, it must have been insulated much earlier.

The Church
At low tide St. Michael's Mount is approached by a causeway from Marazion (a name meaning Market Jew), past Chapel Rock, where formerly was a shrine to the Virgin. From the little village and harbor a cobbled path ascends to the highest pinnacle, on which is built St. Michael's Church. It has developed from the Benedictine house founded there by Edward the Confessor in 1044. A cell containing a skeleton, discovered beneath the church in the eighteenth century, was probably occupied by a hermit. The priory on St. Michael's Mount was made subordinate to the abbey of Mont-Saint-Michel in recognition of the spiritual link between the two places.

Because of its remote location, the community on St. Michael's Mount remained small and old-fashioned, and it was almost extinguished by the Black Death in the fourteenth century. It was finally suppressed in 1425. The church, which had been rebuilt in its present form only a few years before, was put in the charge of a chaplain who encouraged the long tradition of pilgrimages to the Mount by constructing a pier. From that time until the seventeenth century St. Michael's Mount was predominantly a military stronghold.

The church stands on a high terrace. It has a magnificent north door and two rose windows that were added in the fifteenth century. Of the same period is its elaborate brass chandelier of Flemish design. Adjoining the church is the former Lady Chapel, which was converted into a pair of

On St. Michael's Mount, looking up to the church.

elegant drawing rooms, complete with contemporary furniture and portraits, in about 1750.

The Castle
St. Michael's Mount now belongs to the National Trust, but it is still inhabited by the St. Aubyn family, who have lived there peacefully for over three hundred years. Its history before their time was a stormy record of sieges, captures, and occupation by government troops and rebels in turn. Its strategic position allowed it to control shipping in Mount's Bay, and from the fourteenth century it was a strong fortress.

In 1473, during the Wars of the Roses, the Earl of Oxford sailed from France and, by disguising his men as pilgrims, was able to enter and seize the Mount on behalf of the Lancastrians. Edward IV ordered Sir John Arundell, Sheriff of Cornwall, to evict him. Arundell had long avoided the seacoast because a fortune-teller had warned him that he would be killed there; and so it transpired. The sheriff's army was repulsed and he was killed on the sands at Marazion. After another assault on Oxford failed, he was allowed to surrender on favorable terms.

In 1497 a pretender to the throne, Perkin Warbeck, landed in Cornwall, took the Mount, and lodged his wife there while he marched east. He was defeated and killed, whereupon Henry VII sent for his widow and generously granted her a pension and property.

Following the dissolution of the monasteries, the Mount was given by the Crown to another Arundell, Humphrey, who made it the base of his Catholic rebellion in 1549. On the defeat of his Cornish army, Arundell was executed.

Other episodes in the Mount's history include fights with privateers and marauding Frenchmen. During the Civil War its garrison held out for the king until the Royalist cause was defeated; the defenders were allowed to retire with honor to the Scilly Islands. Soon afterward the Mount was purchased by the St. Aubyn family. Piers St. Aubyn enlarged and rebuilt

the castle in the nineteenth century, giving it the picturesque appearance it has today.

THE LAND'S END: *Sacred Citadel of Lost Lyonesse*

West Penwith, the western extremity of the Cornish peninsula, was the last bastion of its independence and culture.
The Cornish language survived there until 1777, when it
died with its last native speaker, a fishwife of Mousehole
called Dolly Pentreath, who is commemorated by a monument outside Paul Church west of Penzance. In this small
area is the largest assembly of Stone Age monuments and
Celtic crosses to be found in England. Once it was part of a
larger country, Lyonesse; legends recorded by old chroniclers tell of rich lands which formerly existed to the west,
between the Land's End and the Scilly Islands. At some
unknown period Lyonesse was submerged, like Atlantis, by
the breaking in of the sea. Fishermen have reported drawing
up in their nets old doors and windows from the ocean bed,
and it is certain that Mount's Bay around St. Michael's
Mount was once a forest, for many old tree stumps have
been dredged up from beneath its waters. The memory of
lost Lyonesse is kept alive in the Arthurian romances and
has constant mystical appeal. Gazing out on a stormy day
from the cliffs at the Land's End, one can easily perceive a
phantom landscape in the mists and spray over the ocean
waves.

The Land's End district is a sacred country in miniature.
Its mild climate, clear light, and intensely spiritual atmosphere make it ever attractive to artists. Before them came the

*A fragment of lost Lyonesse: Rocks at Castle Treryn near
the Land's End.*

Celtic saints, whose relics are all over the district, as are those of their predecessors, the stone circle builders. Legends of an earlier race, the giants, are attached to many local rocks and tors.

Stone Circles in West Penwith

The stone circles at the western end of Cornwall have been called living monuments because of the effect they have on many people's subtle senses. Dowsers report strong reactions at their sites, and researchers with scientific instruments have found them to be centers of unexplained dynamic anomalies. From the circles were ranged alignments of standing stones and other stone monuments, creating a pattern of sanctity across the landscape.

Stone circles are generally dated to about 2500 B.C. There are several in this part of Cornwall, and others have been destroyed. These two are the most perfect and accessible.

Boscawen-un stone circle.

Boscawen-un Stone Circle Four miles west of Penzance the A30 road to the Land's End passes a wood to the left, immediately after which is a lane to Boscawen-un Farm. A ten-minute walk from there along a track, parts of which are probably ancient, takes one to the circle. A new, shorter path to it has recently been opened. It is signposted on the left of the A30 road, three fields past the farm entrance.

The site is one of the most beautiful of ancient places, carpeted with bluebells in spring and in summer surrounded by gorse and wildflowers with larks and the occasional buzzard overhead. St. Buryan church tower is visible to the south, and in the other direction a rocky outcrop has on it the mark of a huge foot, said to have been imprinted by one of the old Cornish giants. There are nineteen stones in the ring, one of which, to the southwest, is of pure quartz crystal. They surround a tall, leaning pillar near the center. Shadows cast by the rising sun early in May pick out faint carvings near its base.

In one of the old Welsh Triads (traditional bardic verses)

this circle is named as one of the three main Gorsedds—
assembly places of bards and augurs—in Britain. Modern
Cornish bards sometimes gather there. It is also the junction
of several alignments of standing stones. Unfortunately, the
last of the outlying stones formerly visible from the circle
was pulled down a few years ago. Other nearby stones
include one in the hedge on the right of the lane to the farm,
another in a field north of the track to the circle, and a fine,
tall granite slab called the Blind Fiddler on the north side of
the road from Boscawen-un eastward to Catchall.

The Merry Maidens and the Pipers At Boleigh, 5 miles along
the B3315 road southwest of Newlyn, is a well-preserved
circle of nineteen stones, 78 feet in diameter. It stands in a
grassy field near the road and is much visited. All around it
are other monuments: standing stones, barrows, stone
crosses, and holed stones. To the northeast on the far side of
the road are two of the largest standing stones in Cornwall,
the taller being fifteen feet high, called the Pipers. They
stand in line with the western rim of the circle and with
other stones in both directions.

The Pipers, a pair of tall stone pillars near the Merry Maidens.

The legend that the Pipers were set up to commemorate
King Athelstan's conquest of Cornwall in the tenth century
may refer to an actual event such as a peace treaty ritually
concluded there between the Saxon king and the last
independent Cornish ruler, Howel. Common legend says
that the Merry Maidens and the Pipers are revelers turned to
stone. This story was recalled by the archaeologist T. C.
Lethbridge, who investigated the stones with a dowsing
pendulum and felt them rocking and swaying and giving out
electrical impulses.

The Holy Wells of Sancreed and St. Euny
Most of the holy wells in the Land's End district are in need
of care and attention, but the well at Sancreed is perfect.

Sancreed Church with several ancient stone crosses in its circular graveyard, which was an old Celtic sanctuary.

Opposite Sancreed Church, 4 miles west of Penzance, is Glebe Farm, to the right of which a footpath leads to the well about three hundred yards away. It is a magical spot with a clump of trees, flowers, and ferns. Frequenters of holy wells have called it the most spiritual place in Cornwall; here is a corner of the old sacred landscape as the Celtic saints knew it. The surroundings of the well are now revered and tended by local inhabitants.

To drink the waters, one descends by stone steps into a small cavern wherein grows luminous green moss. Above the well are the foundations of a chapel and a modern Celtic cross.

The rounded churchyard at Sancreed has the air of being an ancient sanctuary, and five old stone crosses stand within it. The church and well are dedicated to St. Creed, or Credan, whose legend has been forgotten.

A mile west of Sancreed well is another holy well, dedi-

Medieval carvings on Sancreed's roodscreen.

cated to a sixth-century Irishman, St. Euny. The way to it is signposted from Carn Euny, the site of an ancient British village occupied from Neolithic times to the first century B.C. The village contains well-preserved houses and a "fogou," a mysterious type of subterranean structure unique to Cornwall. St. Euny's well is on the edge of moorland. Steps lead down to it, and on ledges above its vigorous waters are lodged coins and pieces of crystal. It once had a great reputation for curing all sorts of ills, including eye troubles and children's diseases. Divination was also practiced there.

One can go directly to Carn Euny by a signposted road to the right off the A30 at Lower Drift, 2 miles west of Penzance.

The Holy Well at Madron

Madron, the mother church of Penzance, lies a mile north of the town, from which a road passes through it. A few hundred yards past the village is a turning to the right, signposted to Madron well and chapel. A half-mile walk past an attractive old stone cross, where offerings are sometimes left, brings one into the wood which shelters one of the earliest sites of the Age of the Saints. The chapel and baptistry are well preserved, though roofless. Waters flow through them from the well just beyond, which has never recovered from being smashed by Puritan fanatics during the Civil War. Its waters, however, retained their reputation for healing and for giving mystical insight into the future. Sickly children were dipped in the well during the first three Sundays in May, at which season Cornish wells are traditionally at their most potent. The Wesleyans held services there during the nineteenth century, after which people would ask questions of the well spirit while dropping pins into the water. It was a favorite spot for baptisms. Those who were cured by the well customarily left a token offering nearby, often in the form of a rag tied to a bush. The practice continues, and evidence of stealthy visits to the well can be seen today in bits of cloth hanging around it.

On the moors north of Madron the Men-an-Tol, or holed stone, has the reputation of curing and invigorating people who pass through it.

CORNWALL is the most westerly county in England. Trains from London (Paddington) and all other stations go to Plymouth, then to the western terminus at Penzance. Among the many Cornish stations are those at Liskeard and Truro. The main road through Cornwall is the A30, which meets the A38 from Plymouth near Bodmin.

St. Michael's Mount is a half-mile south of the A394 at Marazion. It can be approached on foot only at low tides, but there is a regular ferry at high tides during the summer months. The opening hours are:

June 1 through October: Monday to Friday, 10:30 to 5:45 (last admissions, 4:45). There are no guided tours during this period; visitors may explore at will.

November 1 to March 26: Monday, Wednesday, and Friday by guided tour only, starting at 11, noon, 2, and 3 (weather and tide permitting).

March 28 through May: Monday, Tuesday, Wednesday, and Friday, 10:30 to 5:45. No guided tours.

Admission £2. A service is held in the church on Sunday at 11 a.m. A restaurant is open on the Mount during visiting hours from April 1 through October.

For visitors' information, telephone: Penzance (0736) 710507.

6

THE WELSH BORDER

GLOUCESTERSHIRE, WORCESTERSHIRE, HEREFORDSHIRE, CHESHIRE

The countryside along the border with South Wales has some of the loveliest scenery in England. It is a pastoral land of green hills and meadows watered by winding streams, with its natural center in the Malvern Hills of Worcestershire. They were the favorite haunt of a young musician who became England's greatest composer, Sir Edward Elgar, and in this district there is a great tradition of music and poetry. Every year in August a festival of sacred music is held in one of the three cathedrals—at Worcester, Gloucester, or Hereford—which form an equal-sided triangle around the Malvern Hills. The Three Choirs Festival, begun early in the eighteenth century, is the oldest of its kind in Europe.

The three cathedrals are the most prominent of the sacred places in Gloucestershire and the now combined counties of Worcester and Hereford. Everyone who travels this district in the spirit of pilgrimage will want to visit them and some of the other sacred sites which abound in their neighborhood. Among these are prehistoric long barrows of the Gloucestershire Cotswold Hills, the ubiquitous old parish churches, and places of Celtic, Roman, and Saxon sanctity.

GLOUCESTER

In Roman times Gloucester was Glevum, a fortified city on the River Severn commanding the approaches to Wales. The present cathedral stands on the northwest corner of the defenses, and the present street pattern closely follows that which the Roman surveyors laid down in about 48 A.D. Their central stone was at a point called the Cross, where a medieval high cross once stood at the convergence of Northgate, Southgate, Eastgate, and Westgate streets. Near the Cross were found pieces of a bronze equestrian statue of a Roman emperor and, in 1960, a hoard of fifteen thousand Roman coins. They are among a large collection of relics in the City Museum that includes much evidence of Roman religious life: allegorical mosaics, carved tombstones, and votive tablets from temples. One of the tablets shows Mercury with his Celtic consort, Rosmerta.

Before the Roman invasion Gloucester was a British port. Today its dock area is picturesque, with old ships (there is a quarter-sized replica of the *Mayflower*), huge warehouses, and a seamen's church. Commerce has ruined much of old Gloucester, bringing highways and ugly buildings close to its medieval center, but it is still a delightful place to explore for its fine houses, inns (especially the fifteenth-century galleried New Inn on Northgate Street), and odd corners. Down College Court off Westgate Street, one comes across the Beatrix Potter Museum in the house in which she illustrated her children's tale *The Tailor of Gloucester*. A walkway, the Via Sacra, leads from the cathedral along the Roman walls past many of the city's ancient buildings and the charming Quaker meeting house near the Church of St. Mary de Crypt on Southgate Street. In that church was baptized George Whitefield (1714–1770), the great preacher and gospel revivalist, whose voice was so powerful that it could be heard by thirty thousand people at one time. When he died in Massachusetts, it was estimated that ten million people had heard his sermons.

GLOUCESTER CATHEDRAL

Gloucester's abbey church of St. Peter was made a cathedral and rededicated to the Holy Trinity in 1541 after Henry VIII had suppressed the abbey and expelled the Benedictine monks. Its history began in 681 when Osric, the viceroy for

Gloucester cathedral from the southeast.

King Ethelred, founded a religious community for monks and nuns on the site of a Roman building, possibly a temple on the city wall. After several rebuildings the church was given to the Benedictines by King Canute in 1022. A more splendid church was built for them thirty-six years later. That church burned down in 1088, and the new Norman abbot began to construct the east end of the present building. It was finished by 1100, and the nave was completed in about 1160. The massive pillars of the nave create an effect which is more impressive than uplifting, as if to symbolize the military might of the Norman regime. In the following centuries efforts were made to lighten the construction. An early result was the remodeling in 1330 of the south transept in Perpendicular Gothic style, which seems to have been pioneered by the Gloucester Masons.

The Profitable Shrine of a Murdered King

At the east end of the cathedral, to the north of the presbytery, is the pinnacled tomb of Edward II with his

The effigy of Edward II from his monument, Gloucester cathedral.

recumbent effigy in alabaster. This was the source of the abbey's great wealth in the Middle Ages. Pilgrims thronged to the tomb because of its reputation for healing, and their gifts made possible the great building campaigns of the fourteenth and fifteenth centuries.

The cult of Edward II was certainly not based on his moral qualities. He was effeminate and frivolous, a drinker and a gambler, with a fatal weakness for the company of rough, lowborn youths. He was born in Caernarvon Castle in North Wales and, according to legend, was presented as a baby to the people of Wales by his father, Edward I, in fulfillment of his promise to give them a prince who spoke no word of English. The young prince was a disappointment to his father, who banished him from court for a spell because of his unsuitable friends; when his father died in 1307, he succeeded to the throne.

The reign of Edward II was troubled by unsuccessful wars

with the Scots and constant battles with the nobles of his own realm. Many of his most powerful subjects were disgusted by his style of living and his addiction to court favorites, particularly the dandified Piers Gaveston, to whom he gave precedence over senior officials. Gaveston was captured and executed by a group of nobles, and after many intrigues Edward was overwhelmed by his enemies and became a fugitive in South Wales. In 1327 he was deposed, seized, and imprisoned. One night in his prison chamber in Berkeley Castle, Gloucestershire, he was cruelly put to death, in a manner thought appropriate for sodomites, by means of a red-hot poker. The castle is said to be still haunted by his dying screams.

The body of the wretched monarch was spurned by each of three abbeys to which it was offered for burial. However, its potential value was recognized by the shrewd Abbot Thokey of Gloucester, who sent his own carriage to collect the corpse from Berkeley and arranged a grand procession to its burial place in the abbey church. The Welsh had always retained affection for Edward, and the story of his dreadful death, together with rumors that he had not died but had escaped to become a holy hermit, caused him to be acclaimed a saint.

The Builders of Gloucester
During the century following Edward's burial, the eastern part of the church where he lay was made glorious by a remarkable reconstruction. The heavy Norman architecture was overlaid with work in a totally different spirit, delicate, graceful, aspiring upward. The view eastward from the choir is reckoned one of the most beautiful in an English cathedral. Terminating it is the window which fills the entire east

A bracket in Gloucester cathedral gives a rare glimpse of the masons who built it. The old man with the leather bag, below, is thought to be the father of the climbing boy apprentice.

wall and is claimed as the largest in the world. It is in the form of a triptych with a central area over seventy feet high and two wings set at an angle. The subject is the coronation of the Virgin by her Son; around their figures at the top are grouped the apostles and seraphim, and below are arrayed saints, kings, abbots, and the heraldic shields of great people. The colors are enchanting, and so is the light that is shed on the interior. The window was erected in 1349 to commemorate the warriors who fought at the Battle of Crécy three years earlier.

Beyond the Crécy window is the Lady Chapel, added in the fifteenth century for services in honor of the Virgin Mary. Above its entrance a bridge connects the two parts of the elevated passage above the choir. Within it is the Whispering Gallery, so called for its strange acoustical properties.

The cloister north of the nave surrounds the monastic garden, where there is a well. The cloister was built by the same craftsmen who beautified the choir in the fourteenth century; its windows onto the garden and the fan tracery of its vaulted ceiling constitute one of the masterpieces of English architecture—and it is still in perfect condition. The masons who built it worked also at Wells cathedral and elsewhere in the West Country and are known to historians as the Severn School. Their achievements were based on a geometric tradition that was preserved and studied in their lodges; from it they derived insight into engineering princi-

The east window of Gloucester cathedral seen from the choir.

*Magnificent
fan vaulting covers
the broad cloisters of
Gloucester cathedral.*

ples and also their high standards of artistry. The model on which they based their work was the vault of heaven, conceived as a perfect, divine structure of true proportions and harmonies, as described in Plato's *Timaeus*. Plato's traditional cosmology was one of the main inspirations behind the Italian Renaissance, and its influence on masonic architects lasted throughout the Middle Ages. The universe was seen as a living organism whose parts were perfectly coordinated by the laws of geometry and the classical harmonies of music. In applying geometric proportion to their buildings, the masons were imitating the fabric of God's universal creation, thus making an ideal receptacle for the music and chants which constantly filled the medieval churches and were composed to reflect the music of the heavenly spheres. Architecture and music were derived from the same model, the ideal cosmos, and their effect in unison was to create a heavenly environment within the church, providing worshipers with a foretaste of paradise.

Together with the mathematical formalities of their science, the masons cultivated a love of nature. Apprentices were encouraged to study and delight in all created forms, and consequently their carefully proportioned works were decked with naturalistically carved animals and foliage. The humble, familiar creatures of the English countryside were depicted within Gloucester cathedral to make it a total celebration of God's handiwork. It is recognized as the earliest, most inspiring work of the Severn masons.

GLOUCESTER is 100 miles west of London, where trains leave from Paddington Station. The nearby motorway is the M5.

Three of the misericords in the choir of Gloucester cathedral, showing wrestlers, a leopard attacking a horse, and a giant-killing knight.

The cathedral is open daily until dark.

The City Museum and Art Gallery on Brunswick Road is open daily except Sunday, 10 to 5, without charge.

The Tourist Information Centre is in St. Michael's Tower at the Cross. Telephone: Gloucester (0452) 421188.

Guided tours on the Via Sacra walkway start at the Information Centre at 2:30 on Wednesday and Sunday during the summer.

COTSWOLD LONG BARROWS

The Gloucestershire hills are famous among archaeologists for their long barrows—chambered mounds of earth and stone from one hundred to three hundred feet long. They date to about 2500 B.C.; they are oriented generally to the east, they are mainly on hill crests, and evidence of human interment has been found in some of them. These monuments have accumulated much legend and folklore that makes them the haunts of spirits, repositories of treasure, and places of ancient magic which visit bad luck on those who disturb them. Their awesome reputation has preserved many such monuments intact into the present.

There are many theories about their uses. It is said that they are communal tribal tombs, chapels for preserving the relics of great people, initiatory lodges, astronomical temples, and much else. All that is commonly agreed is that they had some great and enduring religious significance to the people who built and maintained them, and that they were connected with a belief in the afterlife of the soul. Many who visit them say that the barrows retain a powerful atmosphere from the intensity of what was experienced there in the past.

Hetty Pegler's Tump Otherwise known as Uley Long Barrow, Hetty Pegler's Tump is on the B4066 road 3.5 miles northeast of Dursley, which is a village 13 miles south of Gloucester. The site is beautiful, on the edge of the Gloucestershire hills looking over the Severn valley to the distant hills of Wales. The entrance is through a stone portal between two walls in the shape of horns. Inside is a passage giving onto stone chambers. Behind a hole in the wall of one chamber is a small annex; it has been thought of as a passageway for spirits and as a hermit's food store, but the mystery remains.

One can explore this strange place freely at any time.

Belas Knap This long barrow is 2 miles south of Winchcombe, which is 5 miles northeast of Cheltenham, Gloucestershire. A small road off the A46 is signposted to Charlton Abbots, and the path to the monument is indicated to the right of it. It is open at all times.

This is a fascinating structure. The apparent entrance, between two convex dry stone walls which have been largely rebuilt in a modern restoration, is in fact false. There is no passage or chamber behind it. The accepted theory, for lack of anything more plausible, is that this was done to fool grave robbers. Three mound chambers are entered from the sides of the barrow. The best preserved is six feet wide and has a stone doorway nearly four feet wide. It is certainly a larger entrance than would be required for burial purposes. A ritual

Belas Knap: An aerial view shows the lobster claw shape and height position of the long barrow and the entrance to its northern chamber.

function is implied by six large stones that stand around the dry stone walls. This could have been a council chamber or a temple of magic ritual. Unlike the other chambers, which have been restored, it has its original roof.

CHEDWORTH: *A Villa of Early Roman Christians*

Cirencester, a market town 16 miles southeast of Gloucester, was a center of Roman life from the first century A.D. Ancient roads from several directions are aligned upon its magnificent church tower, which is on the site of a Roman temple. Its museum has an astonishing display of domestic and religious Roman relics excavated in the neighborhood. Within a radius of 10 miles from the town more than a dozen country houses or villas have been discovered, the residences of a provincial nobility who, though they may have been of British stock, adopted the fashions of Roman civilization. Their villas were large, virtually self-sufficient establishments with farms, craft workshops, and the elaborate heated baths which are the hallmark of Roman culture.

The villa at Chedworth, 7 miles north of Cirencester, is the best preserved example of a Roman-style country house in the area. It is beautifully situated in a hollow within the hills overlooking the valley of the little River Coln. It was built some time after 100 A.D. and lasted for about three hundred years, after which the Romans departed and their villas were abandoned to ruin. Its very existence was forgotten until 1864, when a gamekeeper noticed fragments of Roman mosaics in a rabbit's burrow. Excavations began that year, and the study and reconstruction of the buildings continue.

For students of Roman civilization, the attraction of Chedworth is its extensive range of Turkish and sauna baths, its apartments with underground and wall heating, and the fine

The villa at Chedworth reconstructed as in Roman times.

mosaic floors made up of naturally colored pieces of stone. The techniques of the Roman plumbers and heating engineers are wonderfully displayed; yet Chedworth is also interesting on a deeper level, as a place of religious ritual.

It is not at first obvious why the villa was built at this spot, for it faces east and is therefore cut off from the sun during most of the day. The reason for its position can be found at the northwest corner of the site. This is the place of the sacred spring, an infallible water source which wells up from the wooded hillside. A trackway approaches it from the nearby prehistoric Salt Way, indicating that it was a place of resort in times before the Roman invasion. The people of the villa heated its overflow for their bathhouses, and over the spring they erected a shrine, a nymphaeum dedicated to the local spirit of the waters. An octagonal pool, lined and rimmed with stone, is still to be seen at the center of the shrine. Around it was a paved area which was later renewed, the original stones being used elsewhere on the site. Two of them, discovered during excavations, are marked with the Chi-Rho symbol of early Christianity (the Greek letters *chi* and *rho* being the initial letters of *Christos*). The symbols at Chedworth, thought to have been carved in the second century, are among the oldest relics of Christianity in Britain.

In the middle of the site, blocking the view to the east, is a former hunting lodge which is now the custodian's house, and adjoining it is a small museum. Finds from the site are lodged there, including the Chi-Rho stones. Other exhibits relate to pagan worship. Four small altars are carved with figures of rustic deities, and from the site of a pagan temple a half-mile along the valley to the southeast came a stone carving of a huntsman's dog attended by a hound, a hare, and a stag. On the floor of the dining hall in the villa's west wing a fourth-century mosaic shows allegorical and classical pagan figures

On the mosaic floor of the dining room at Chedworth, winter is represented by a warmly dressed figure carrying a hare and a piece of firewood.

within a fine geometric design. It has been much damaged over the centuries by tree roots growing through it, and the central image can no longer be identified. (It was probably Bacchus surrounded by nymphs and satyrs.) The four seasons are represented at the corners by symbolic figures. A rare item in the museum, probably used to set out the design of the mosaics, is a pair of Roman dividers.

The wooded hills around the villa abound in wildlife, and its secluded hollow with the sacred spring is one of those spots which nature seems to have designated as a shrine of spirit. It is thus a natural center of pagan worship. Nearby are other Roman villas and temples, and with them are monuments some two thousand years older, signifying the prehistoric sanctity of the area. From one of them, a barrow to the north of the villa, was taken a funerary urn containing ashes from a cremation, which is now in the museum. No doubt there were several different forms of religion in Roman times, co-existing in the same valley: cults of local deities among the native British people, the worship of classical gods by the lord of the villa, and perhaps the new religion of the Chi-Rho symbol introduced by a Celtic Christian wife.

CHEDWORTH ROMAN VILLA is 10 miles southeast of Cheltenham in Glou-cestershire and one mile west of the A429 road south of its junction with the A40. Its custodians are the National Trust, and it is open from March 1 through October, daily (except Monday), 11 to 6. Admission £1.60.

DEERHURST: *A Celtic Sanctuary and a Saxon Chapel*

Seven miles north of Gloucester on the A38 road toward Tewkesbury a turning to the left (B4213) is signposted to Deerhurst 1.5 miles away. It is now a small village among orchards and meadows by the River Severn, but up to nine hundred years ago it was an important religious center. Traces of a Roman settlement have been found there, and it was the site of an early Celtic monastery. The ancient kingdom of Hwicce, consisting of what is now Gloucester-shire and Worcestershire, had its capital at Deerhurst; Christian and pagan kings ruled it at different periods until the late seventh century, when monks from Whitby in Yorkshire claimed Deerhurst for the Roman Church. After the Norman Conquest it lost its leading position locally and ultimately became a mere outpost of Tewkesbury Abbey 2 miles to the north.

The church at Tewkesbury is one of the most magnificent in England, but Deerhurst is much older and is almost unique in having two buildings, a church and a chapel, that go back to Saxon and probably earlier times. Their precise dates are a puzzle to antiquarians, and this adds to the air of mystery that pervades the village, which is in keeping with its ancient reputation as a place of unusual sanctity.

The Church of St. Mary

The Saxon tower through which one enters was added to a rectangular church attached to the Celtic monastery, which is the core of the present building. Other additions were made up to the tenth century, and the church has been altered and restored throughout its history, but its archaic features are still the most important. The heads of strange Celtic beasts are carved above and around its doorways and arches. The sculptures look primitive, but they were originally painted, and their details were added in color. On the

Deerhurst: The finest Saxon font in England.

outside of the church at the east end, which was once a seven-sided apse, can be seen the most famous of the Deerhurst carvings. A sign pointing upward reads, "To the Angel"; one looks up, and there, not in the sky but high on the church wall, is the angel, a unique ninth-century figure which has been compared by scholars with those illuminated in the Book of Kells.

The church once had an upper story that may have provided accommodation for monks, and there were upper chapels in the tower. High up on the inside of the west wall is a Saxon window to one of the chapels that is the finest example of its kind to be found in the country; some of its stones are thought to be Roman. (The only comparable example known to scholars is in a monastery in Ethiopia.) Equally celebrated is the stone font, covered with Celtic spirals, which was found in a local farmyard. A stained glass window in the church shows St. Alphege, who was a monk at Deerhurst before becoming Archbishop of Canterbury; he was martyred in 1012 by the Danes.

Unique and mysterious are two epithets commonly applied to Deerhurst. Some of its oldest features, dating from times before records, have been used in subsequent rebuildings, and their unusual artistry hints at the importance of the place in very early days. The Celtic monastery has long disappeared, but hillocks and hollows in the surrounding pastureland give evidence of extensive building work in the past. There may well be an unbroken religious tradition in this village from prehistory through Roman, Celtic, Saxon, and Norman times to the present day.

Odda's Chapel

A short distance past the church is Abbots Court, where in 1885 a local clergyman made a remarkable discovery: Beneath the medieval plasterwork of the house he found an almost complete Saxon chapel. It has now been restored and can be seen at any time.

In the chapel is a replica of an inscribed stone that was found in a nearby orchard in 1675 and is now in the Ashmolean Museum, Oxford. It records the building of the chapel in 1056 by Odda, Earl of Hwicce, as a memorial to his brother who had died near the spot. According to Edward Gilbert, the author of a scholarly guide to Deerhurst that is sold in the church, there are signs that the chapel may have been founded before Odda's time, implying that he repaired an existing building. There is evidence of a Roman building on or near the site.

WORCESTER

British chiefs and Roman generals ruled successive towns on the ridge above the River Severn, which is the heart of modern Worcester. A church that stood there in the seventh century was made into a cathedral, whose bishop ministered to the tribal kingdom of Hwicce. The first of Worcester's sainted bishops, Oswald, built a new cathedral in 983, which was replaced by the second bishop, Wulfstan, following the Norman Conquest.

St. Wulfstan was the only Saxon bishop to retain his see under the Normans. The reason traditionally given is that, when his resignation was demanded at a meeting in Westminster Abbey, he thrust his staff into the shrine of Edward the Confessor, from which it could not be moved. A more prosaic cause was that he gave support to William the Conqueror and aided the Norman dynasty against Welsh and English rebels. He was famous for asceticism and wisdom; the most impressive feat attributed to him was persuading the people of Bristol to give up their traditional trade of selling slaves to the Irish.

The cathedral Wulfstan built was on a grand scale, with an extensive Benedictine monastery to its south. The good bishop was evidently of two minds about the virtue of his enterprise, for while the demolition of the old building was proceeding, he was observed lamenting. In making these elaborate Norman churches, he said, "we are piling up stones to the neglect of souls."

Since Wulfstan's time the cathedral has been burned, violently assaulted, and so drastically stripped of its ancient features by reformers and restorers that little remains of the early Norman work apart from the fascinating crypt with its many pillars. The walls of the cloister are in part Norman, and a passage on its east side, the Slype, contains stones from St. Oswald's Saxon cathedral.

Worcester cathedral from the river.

A few incidents illustrate Worcester's checkered history.

1041: The city and cathedral burned by Danish raiders.

1113 and 1180: The cathedral badly damaged by accidental fires.

1139: A raiding party from Gloucester attacked the city; its citizens, with all their possessions, took refuge in the cathedral.

1175: The great tower collapsed.

1651: The city adopted the Royalist cause in the Civil War; after Charles I's defeat at the Battle of Worcester, six thousand of his followers were locked up in the cathedral, which was looted and stripped of furnishings and fittings and for some years lay derelict.

1756–1874: Successive restorers transformed the cathedral's interior according to their various tastes, incurring the wrath of subsequent architects who deplored the destruction of medieval carved stone and woodwork.

The city of Worcester itself has been similarly treated: Many of its old streets were demolished in the 1960s for commercial development. This is bitterly regretted by promoters of tourism; they can still point to fine old houses that survive—to College Green with its monastic buildings, thirteenth-century gateway, and views across the river, and to sixteenth-century Friar Street with its Tudor House Museum—but the old city exists today only in patches. It is now a less worthy setting for its great cathedral, which, despite all it has suffered, is still impressive by virtue of its great size and awesome atmosphere. The latter is augmented by the music of the choir for which Worcester is famous. A climax to its musical celebrations occurs every third year, when Worcester Cathedral is host to the Three Choirs Festival.

WORCESTER CATHEDRAL: Monument to a Failed Arthurian Revival

One of the most beautiful and moving parts of the cathedral is the chantry chapel to Prince Arthur, eldest son of Henry

Prince Arthur's chantry, Worcester cathedral.

VII, who died at Ludlow in 1502 at the age of fifteen and was buried at Worcester. With him were buried the hopes for the ideal kingdom which was to be established in England under his rule. The chantry is an expression of pious idealism, a creation of the age of chivalry. It is a noble, delicate structure, adorned with saints and Tudor symbols—the rose, the portcullis, and the garter.

Henry VII, like several other English monarchs, dreamed of fulfilling the old British prophecies which foretold the second coming of King Arthur and the restoration of a sacred, heroic order symbolized by the Round Table. His banner was the red dragon of Wales, and he claimed descent from the last Welsh king, Cadwallader, and from Brutus, the legendary first king of England. Scholars were encouraged to prove these claims and to establish the relationship of the Tudor dynasty to King Arthur. A pageant was arranged at Worcester, where the Tudor lineage from Arthur was to be celebrated in verse. It never actually took place, and Henry finally despaired of his playing the role of Arthur, but when his son was born he named him Arthur and had him christened at Winchester, one of the reputed sites of Camelot.

Prince Arthur was educated for his future position as a Christian philosopher-king; he was provided with a young bride, Catherine of Aragon, daughter of Ferdinand and Isabella of Spain, but the marriage was not consummated, and a few months later Arthur died. His magnificent funeral procession at Worcester was followed by a vast crowd of mourners. They soon had good cause to lament, for Arthur's brother succeeded to the throne as Henry VIII, married the widowed Catherine, and, in divorcing her, brought about the Protestant Reformation in England, which led to the destruction of sacred buildings throughout the realm and the abolition of traditional English rights and liberties.

Saints, Pilgrims, and a Black-hearted King

The relics of St. Oswald and St. Wulfstan, particularly the latter, were Worcester's great attraction for medieval pilgrims. To accommodate them, the Guesten Hall, whose ruins lie south of the cathedral, was built in 1320. By that time St. Wulfstan's reputation had brought great wealth to Worcester. He was canonized in 1203, and within a few years offerings from visitors to his shrine made possible an extensive program of building. The Lady Chapel was added to the east end of the cathedral in 1224, and the choir and other parts were lavishly remodeled. In the following century the cathedral was further enriched and extended. One of its glories today is the great west window, with stained glass showing the creation of the world and its creatures; on summer evenings the window is lit up by the sunset over the Severn.

In 1216 the ferocious, evil-living King John quarreled with the Worcester authorities and demanded of them such a heavy fine that the precious metals in St. Wulfstan's shrine had to be melted down to pay him. Remorse seized him a few months later on his deathbed, and he asked to be buried in Worcester between the shrines of St. Wulfstan and St. Oswald, where the devil would not dare to molest him. There, in the center of the cathedral, John's tomb was raised. Upon it is his effigy, said to be an accurate likeness. It is the earliest sepulchral effigy of an English king. When King John's tomb was opened in 1797, a monk's cowl was found on his skeleton. The exposure caused his bones to crumble into dust.

WORCESTER is 110 miles northwest of London, with trains from Paddington Station (journey time about two hours). It is off the M5 motorway.

The cathedral is open daily, following morning service at 7:45, to 7:30 in summer and 6 in winter.

The Tourist Information Centre is in the Guildhall on High Street. Telephone: Worcester (0905) 723471.

HEREFORD

Herefordshire is a dream county to lovers of English landscape. Its hills, plains, woods, and streams, all on an intimate scale, produce a variety of charming compositions which are often improved by their human elements. The small towns, villages, and farmsteads are so harmoniously adapted to their surroundings that one could imagine the entire landscape as the work of some great designer. Function, however, has been the guiding principle: The county is known for the wide variety of its produce. The distinctive red Hereford beef cattle graze the pastures, and the hills shelter some of the finest apple and pear orchards in England. It is a land of bee keepers and cider makers. Fields of hops supply Hereford's breweries, and cottage gardens satisfy most local needs. The tradition of a self-sufficient rural economy created the pattern of human settlement, the market towns and village craft centers, that delights the traveler today.

Many of the old farms and cottages are timber-framed and painted black and white, but the predominant colors in Herefordshire are brick red and emerald green. Red is the color of the soil and of Hereford city with its great red cathedral. The city provides a market for farmers from both sides of the Welsh border. Despite much modern redevelopment, it still has a peaceful, rustic air. With old streets and alleys converging on the cathedral close, it is one of the most pleasant of English cities.

ST. ETHELBERT'S CATHEDRAL

Hereford has a claim to being the oldest bishopric in England. It is not known when the first Bishop of Hereford was appointed, other than that it was in the days of the early British Church, some time before the sixth century. The first recorded church at Hereford was built in about 830. It was reconstructed two hundred years later, and in 1056 the new work was destroyed by Welsh invaders. A succession of Norman bishops from late in the eleventh century laid the groundwork of the present cathedral, which developed over the next four centuries, making it a virtual textbook of architectural styles.

In 1786 disaster occurred: The fall of the west tower brought down the Norman west front and demolished much of the nave. The work of restoration was entrusted to the foremost church architect of the time, James Wyatt. His

Hereford cathedral from the northeast corner of the close.

efforts have been criticized ever since, for ancient architecture was less respected then, and Wyatt was uninhibited in replacing Norman designs with his own. However, he was not responsible for the greatest act of vandalism, which had taken place thirty years earlier, when a perfect Saxon chapel beside the cathedral was pulled down by order of the bishop. Much of Wyatt's work was removed by Sir George Gilbert Scott in the middle of the nineteenth century, during his period of restoration. His most striking legacy is the elaborate, bejeweled metal screen illustrating the Ascension.

King Offa and St. Ethelbert
The story of the building of the first stone church at Hereford is that King Offa of Mercia commissioned it as an act of repentance to shelter the body of a man he had murdered. Offa is best known for the earthen barrier he built along his border with the Welsh; Offa's Dyke now forms a public footpath, passing 6 miles to the west of Hereford. At Sutton Walls, an ancient earthwork 3 miles north of the city, he held court, and there he was visited by King Ethelbert of East Anglia, who sought to marry his daughter. For some unrecorded reason Offa had the visiting king beheaded. On the day the victim was buried a pillar of light descended from the sky, and some days later a nobleman dreamed that Ethelbert was demanding burial elsewhere. He dug up the head and body and placed them in his carriage which, guided by another light, arrived at Hereford. During the journey the severed head cured a blind man, and further cures took place near the spot where the head and body were reburied at Hereford.

Offa sent two bishops to investigate, and when they reported that the miracles were genuine, the Mercian king raised a shrine over the relics and a church to contain it. He then went on a pilgrimage to Rome. The cult of St. Ethelbert flourished so vigorously during the next two centuries that the great Saxon church of 1030 was built to accommodate pilgrims.

There is a fourteenth-century effigy of St. Ethelbert in the choir of the cathedral.

The Shrine of a Grand Master
Though it is not mentioned by his official biographers, it is known in Hereford that Bishop Thomas de Cantelupe (1218–1282) was a former grand master for England of the Order of Knights Templar, the league of military monks who protected the pilgrimage routes to the Holy Land. Founded in the twelfth century, the order was suppressed in 1312, in part because its great wealth made it a rival to Church and State, in part because of the esoteric rituals practiced by its members. The evidence that Bishop Cantelupe was a grand master appears on his shrine in the north transept of the cathedral: The pedestal is carved with fifteen figures of Knights Templar.

The pedestal of the shrine of St. Thomas de Cantelupe, Hereford cathedral.

Cantelupe was a great man in his time, nobly born, extremely rich, a lawyer, theologian, and royal councillor. In 1275 he was appointed Bishop of Hereford. His reputation there was that of a stern disciplinarian, demanding high standards of conduct from his monks and clergy and upholding the rights of his office. At the same time, he was generous and charitable. His weak spot was his love of litigation; he was always invoking the law against powerful opponents, and finally he quarreled with the Archbishop of Canterbury, who excommunicated him. This took him to Rome to plead his cause with the pope, and there he died. His followers boiled down his bones before carrying them back to England. The archbishop tried to deny him a Christian burial, but he was a popular saint in Hereford, and his bones were enshrined there. The tomb became famous for healing animals. When any of Edward I's favorite hawks fell ill, he sent them to Hereford for a cure.

After a long inquiry in which Cantelupe's life and the miracles around his shrine were investigated by the papal authorities, he was canonized as St. Thomas de Cantelupe. The number of miracles increased, and at one time the cult of St. Thomas at Hereford was second only to that of St. Thomas à Becket at Canterbury.

The Mappa Mundi
Exhibited in the south choir aisle of the cathedral is Hereford's prize possession, a piece of vellum measuring 65 inches by 53 inches, on which is inscribed a map of the world. It was made in about 1314 by a Lincolnshire monk, Richard of Haldingham. The earth is shown flat, surrounded by oceans, with Jerusalem in the center; England and Ireland are placed on the outer edge. The details include famous cities, classical scenes, and episodes from the Bible: the Egyptian pyramids, the Cretan labyrinth, Mount Sinai,

*The Mappa Mundi,
Hereford cathedral.*

the journeyings of the tribes of Israel. Figures of men, beasts, birds, fishes, and mythological creatures are strewn across the surface. At the top of the map are images of paradise and the Day of Judgment.

Many of the figures on the map are from the natural history works of Herodotus, Pliny, and other ancient writers. The image of the earth centered on Jerusalem was probably derived from the writings of Cosmas, a sixth-century monk of Alexandria, whose *Christian Topography* was intended to refute the "false and heathen" notion that the earth is a sphere (as had been known in pagan times). It is, he said, a rectangular plane with Jerusalem at its center and the firmament surrounding it; the sun revolved around a north polar mountain, circling its peak in summer and its base in winter.

The object of Christian flat-earth cosmology was to discredit the scientific tradition passed down from ancient times, and to represent the Church, through its holy city of Jerusalem, as the central, dominant authority. This was held as an article of faith up to the sixteenth century, when Copernicus first questioned it. A generation later, Galileo braved the wrath of the Inquisition by confirming through experiments the ancient opinion that the earth is round.

The Hereford cathedral owns a rare collection of manuscripts and early printed books, which are kept above the east aisle in the largest chained library in the world. Another of Hereford's churches, All Saints on High Street, has a library in which the books are chained to their shelves to avoid theft. The oldest treasure in the cathedral library is a seventh-century commentary on the Gospel of St. Matthew.

HEREFORD is 135 miles from London; trains leave from Paddington Station. It is on the A49 road from Gloucester and the A4103 from Worcester.

The cathedral is open daily, 7:30 to 6:30; Sunday, 7:30 to 5.

Books in the chained library of Hereford cathedral.

The Tourist Information Centre is in Hereford Town Hall. Telephone: Hereford (0432) 268430.

Churches of the Knights Templar

For those interested in the mysterious Knights Templar, Herefordshire offers not only Bishop Cantelupe's tomb in the cathedral but also two churches built by the Templar order. The most interesting and beautifully situated is that of St. Michael and All Angels at Garway, 10 miles south of Hereford off the A466 road. The site was given to the Templars by King John in 1199. Like all Templar churches, it was built circular in imitation of the Holy Sepulchre at Jerusalem, but the original survives only in the chancel arch and foundations to the north of it. The tower, a strong building that served as a fortress against Welsh raiders, was detached from the church until the seventeenth century, when it was joined to it by a corridor. The place has a haunted atmosphere, and women visitors sometimes feel uneasy there, as if exposed to the ghostly glare of the celibate knights.

Six miles southwest of Garway, on the east side of the A466, is Welsh Newton, where St. Mary's Church was built as a chapel by the Knights Templar in the thirteen century.

Fantastic figures carved around the outside of Kilpeck church.

On the north side of its chancel is the Seat of Freedom, probably the official seat of the precentor who presided over Templar meetings. The Catholic martyr St. John Kemble, who was hanged at Hereford in 1679, is buried in front of the cross in the graveyard.

KILPECK

Almost every parish church in the Herefordshire villages is worth visiting, but Kilpeck is outstanding. The village is 7 miles southwest of Hereford, a mile to the south of the A465 road. The church was built in about 1140, soon after the foundation nearby of a Benedictine priory which has since disappeared. Kilpeck Castle once stood to the west of the church, which was within its walls, but that too has gone to ruin, leaving only the great mound and earthworks on which it was built.

The church is the most perfect Norman building in the British Isles. Apart from a gallery at the west end, added in the eighteenth century, it has hardly changed in 850 years. The carvings on it, inside and out, are quite astonishing. There was an earlier church on the site, and the Saxon masonry can be seen in the northeast corner of the nave; some of the carvings may have come from the earlier church. The tympanum over the south doorway, for example, is carved with an image of the Tree of Life, the Irminsul of Nordic mythology. This was the chief symbol of the pagan religion, as the cross is of Christianity; to find it above a church door is indeed unexpected, and Kilpeck has many more such surprises.

All around the outside of the church is a "corbel table" studded with carved figures. Grotesque heads of people, beasts, and monsters are mingled with pagan and Celtic mythological symbols, sometimes uncompromisingly sexual in imitation of the vital energies in nature. Some of them were defaced by nineteenth-century restorers who regarded them as obscene, but a few can still be made out. Among them are examples of a popular image in Celtic mystical art, that of an impish woman exposing herself. The pillars and arch of the south doorway are covered with intricate designs

of beasts and writhing dragons, inter-linked with intricate scrollwork that is still sharply detailed.

The inside of the church is also rich in archaic sculpture. The piers to the arch at the east end of the nave each show three Celtic monks standing on each other's heads. The top figures bear a book and a cross, the next a book and a key, and the lower a book and a water sprinkler. One can spend hours contemplating these curiously wrought, grave or humorous carvings and wondering at the nature of the religious doctrines which inspired them.

CHESTER: *A Work of Roman Augury*

Chester is on the edge of the lovely Welsh Border country, but only a few miles to the north is a huge area of industrial dereliction along the River Mersey. The city provides the bulwark against further desecration of the landscape. This is one of the most perfect of Europe's historic cities. Unlike many other English towns, it refrained from destroying its ancient center—as was the fashion for about twenty years from the 1950s—and thus it has retained its prosperity and serves as the cultural center of a wide region.

Deva, the Roman name for Chester, is the goddess of the River Dee, which loops around the city shortly before reaching the coast. Situated at the head of its estuary, Chester was an important Roman and medieval port. Many of its Roman features remain, including a large amphitheater, the foundations of the city wall (which makes a two-mile circuit of the old center), and above all the old Roman street plan. There is even a Roman look to the main streets, which are lined by the "rows," the pil-

Celtic bishops with symbolic objects stand each side of the arch to the east of the nave, Kilpeck.

lared galleries above the street-level shops that give access to the upper rows of shops. This traditional arrangement (it may well be an inheritance from Roman Deva) is perfectly adapted to modern conditions and creates a tranquil, high-quality shopping area which in recent times has been skillfully expanded by the city architects. In the middle of the city, where Eastgate Street meets Northgate Street, the old high cross that for years lay in a museum has been set up again. From this point the Roman augurs (surveyor priests) laid out the original streets and measured distances to outlying forts and stations. From there today the town crier shouts out Chester's midday news.

The Chester citizens of Victorian times respected the characteristic black-and-white, half-timbered architecture of their city and added buildings in the same style. Their most splendid monument is the Town Hall of 1869, west of the cathedral. Through its traditionalism the city has retained the good fortune which the Roman augurs planned to attract through their mystical science of orientation. In building the city wall, they made a barrier that was both practical and magical, repelling human foes and at the same time keeping out the disruptive energies and influences of the outside world. Alone among English cities, Chester has preserved an ancient wall around its entire perimeter. It has been rebuilt at various dates, but always on the Roman plan. One can walk on top of it and find towers and gates where they have always been. By thus maintaining its magical pattern and defenses, Chester has kept its enchanted atmosphere. Its constant attraction can be seen any day in the bustle of its streets and the crowds who are there for shopping or to visit the theaters and museums. There is a lesson here for modern city planners on the use of sacred principles to design communities which please visitors and bring prosperity to the inhabitants.

CHESTER CATHEDRAL: *St. Werburgh's Revival of a Dead Goose*

The Cathedral of Christ and the Virgin Mary was formerly the abbey church of St. Werburgh, founded for Benedictine monks by the local Norman lord, Hugh Lupus, in 1093. Only since 1541, when Henry VIII expelled the monks and gave their church its present dedication, has it been a cathedral. Before that time Chester cathedral was the Church of St. John the Baptist on Vicar's Lane east of the city wall.

On the site of the present cathedral there was a British church that was probably founded in Roman times and was dedicated to the saints Peter and Paul. It was followed by a Saxon church, built in about 900 over the relics of St. Werburgh, which were the glory of Chester and the foundation of its pilgrimage trade.

St. Werburgh was one of a remarkable group of saintly Saxon princesses who were friends or relations of St. Ethel-dreda, the founder of Ely. Her mother came from a long line of high-born Saxon saints, and her grandfather was Penda, the last pagan king of Mercia. She studied under St. Etheldreda, who was her great aunt. Nothing certain is known about her life, but judging from the number of churches across England which are dedicated to her, she must have been an active missionary. Her reputation for simple holiness is illustrated by a legend that is the subject of a carving in the cathedral.

Under one of the seats in the choir (the sixth from the west on the north side) the carver has created a three-part

The west end of Chester cathedral.

scene. On the left, the saint is driving wild geese into a pen to prevent their eating crops. One of her servants has stolen and killed a goose, and the other geese tell Werburgh what happened. On the right, the servant confesses his crime and is told to fetch the dead goose. The centerpiece shows the miracle: The goose is dipped in a font and restored to life, whereupon it flies up to join its companions, who look down from above. Behind this charming tale the carver hints at some deeper allegory; his group of three figures at the font are enacting an alchemical process, the union of spirit and matter in the lustral bath. Similar hints can be found in many other old church carvings. Designs which appear on the surface to represent simple, rustic subjects also display symbols of the mystical doctrine that was taught to initiated masons and craftsmen in their medieval lodges.

The Swallowing of St. Oswald's Church
The red sandstone cathedral was built up and adapted over many centuries from Norman times to the Victorian era, when it was largely remodeled by Sir Gilbert Scott's restoration. One enters from the south into the transept, which is considerably larger than the opposite transept to the north. When the building was an abbey church, the monks wanted to enlarge it, but they were unable to expand to the north because their cloister and domestic chambers were there. Therefore they extended the south transept by adding to it the adjoining parish church of St. Oswald. The parishioners evidently objected for they insisted up to 1880 on retaining the right to hold services within the area of their old church.

The Shrine, Carvings, and Saints in Glass
In the Lady Chapel behind the high altar are restored fragments of St. Werburgh's shrine, which was destroyed at the Reformation. Medieval pilgrims derived cures and blessings from it; today it has a neglected air. The shrines of old saints are not supposed to be centers of attraction in Protestant churches, but it is noticeable that in places where they are honored they become vibrant, concentrate spiritual energies, and heighten one's experience of visiting the churches that contain them.

To make up for the disappointment of the shrine are two magnificent works of pious artistry, one of the fourteenth century, the other of the twentieth century. The first is in the stalls and canopies of the choir. Despite their being moved and mutilated by nineteenth-century restorers, the stalls are generally in fine condition and display the full wonder of medieval carving. Because of their similarity to the choir stalls at Lincoln, made in about 1370, those of Chester are thought to be by the same team of master craftsmen ten years later.

The original purpose of the canopies above the choir stalls was to shelter the monks from drafts in the church during their hours of chanting. Their function was transcended by

The south transept of Chester cathedral.

the medieval carvers who made them in the image of heavenly thrones. The two tiers of the Chester canopies are of almost incredible delicacy, with needle-thin spires above a tracery of foliage, niches, and pierced parapets with battlements. On corbels below them, on the ends and armrests of benches, and around the misericords beneath the seats is a fascinating collection of legendary and allegorical figures. Very few of the subjects would today be considered of religious significance. Mostly they illustrate such popular legends as the miracle of St. Werburgh and apparently random incidents from everyday life. One of the misericords, in the center of the north side, shows a woman beating her husband. Others depict fights between mythical beasts, hunting scenes, the killing of a unicorn, and—among the jokes and satires—a fox in clerical garb deceiving his congregation.

Some of the misericords were removed by the Victorian restorers because their humor was considered too coarse; they were replaced by new, innocuous carvings. Still surviving, on an armrest on the south side, is a little head looking out from between a pair of legs. The virile member of Jesse, blossoming into a genealogical tree, is the subject of a carved bench end at the west of the south side. Seated in front of it is a little figure in fourteenth-century dress; he once held a staff and probably represents a pilgrim to St. Werburgh's shrine.

The hint of an esoteric reference in some of the carvings is sustained by a misericord on the south side which shows a figure rising from a shell and smiting dragons. This has been identified as a symbol from the Egyptian or Chaldean mystery religion.

The bishop's throne in the choir, the screen between choir and nave, and the stone organ loft were designed by Sir Gilbert Scott in imitation of the ancient work and are not unworthy of it.

The oldest parts of the cathedral, with masonry from Norman times, are the north transept and the monastic buildings leading off it. They are set around a cloister that was rebuilt in the sixteenth century and include the dormitory, parlor, cellar, and refectory. Refreshments are now served in the refectory, and near its entrance is the cathedral bookshop.

In the six years up to 1927 two stained glass artists, A. K. Nicholson and F. C. Eden, filled the windows of the cloisters with figures of the saints of the Church of England calendar. Below the saints are their feast days. This is a work of great beauty and interest, and several of the windows illustrate English cathedrals with their saints or founders; there are Ely with St. Etheldreda, Winchester with St. Swithun, and of course Chester cathedral with St. Werburgh.

CHESTER, the county town of Cheshire, on the border with North Wales, is 180 miles northwest of London. There are trains to it from all parts of England; from King's Cross Station in London the journey time is about three hours.

The cathedral is open daily, 7 to 7.

Chester Castle, with Agricola's tower, fortifications, and a twelfth-century chapel, is open March 15 to October 15, daily, 9:30 to 6:30 (Sunday, 2 to 6:30); during the rest of the year, daily, 9:30 to 4 (Sunday, 2 to 4). Access is from the Assize Court car park on Grosvenor Street.

The Roman amphitheater on Vicar's Lane has the same opening times as the castle.

The Chester Heritage Centre in St. Michael's Church, Bridge Street Row, offers an exhibition of Chester's religious and secular history. It is open daily (except Wednesday), 10 to 5 (Sunday, 2 to 5). Admission 50p.

The Grosvenor Museum, Grosvenor Street, has a large collection of Roman relics from Chester, including altars and inscriptions; it is open daily, 10:30 to 5 (Sunday, 2 to 5). Admission free.

Further information on Chester can be had from the Chester Visitor Centre, Vicar's Lane. Telephone: Chester (0244) 313126.

Tourist Information Centre, Town Hall. Telephone: Chester (0244) 318356.

ST. WINIFRED'S WELLS

Across the Welsh border at Holywell, 20 miles west of Chester, is the famous shrine and holy well of St. Winefride. It was almost unique among such places in surviving the Reformation, and it remains a popular place of pilgrimage to this day. Those who have followed this guide as far as Chester will no doubt want to visit it, but Wales is not within the territory here covered. However, there is another well of St. Winifred (as the name is spelled in England) 25 miles southwest of Chester, and it shares many of the charming qualities possessed by the better-known Welsh shrine.

Four miles southeast of Oswestry in Shropshire, in the small village of Woolston, an unpaved lane at a bend in the road leads a short distance to a farm and cottages. One can park there opposite a gate with a notice directing the way to St. Winifred's well. A grassy path, hollowed by the feet of pilgrims, leads to the well cottage, spring, and pools of healing water.

The water rises in a buried stone chamber within the foundations of the ancient half-timbered cottage above it. One can squeeze in and drink at the source; the traditional use of the water is for healing wounds, bruises, and fractured bones. It trickles from the spring into stone-lined pools which can be stopped up to make baths, then it passes into a nearby brook. This lonely spot was once of local importance, for the cottage was built about four hundred years ago as a courthouse. It replaced the well chapel for medieval pilgrims and was probably a stopping-place for those on their way to St. Winefride's well at Holywell. Today the well is little visited, and the peaceful spirit of nature reigns there undisturbed.

The legend of St. Winifred, which is supposed to have been enacted at Holywell and several other spots, is that she was a British princess who in about 660 was persecuted by a Welsh prince, Caradoc. When she resisted his advances, he cut off her head, and where the head rested there sprang up a holy well. Her uncle, St. Beuno, lived nearby and saw what had happened. He placed the head next to the body and prayed over them, whereupon they became united, leaving only a thin red line where they joined. Caradoc sank into the ground in shame. When St. Winifred died, her body was enshrined in the abbey at Shrewsbury.

7

THE NORTH

CUMBRIA, NORTHUMBERLAND, DURHAM

STONE CIRCLES OF CUMBRIA

The landscape of the Lake District in the southwest part of Cumbria is considered by those who like dramatic, elemental scenery to be the most beautiful in England. Every summer its roads are jammed with cars, and the local farmers and shepherds are outnumbered many times over by visitors. Yet away from its main roads and public attractions is an endless paradise for ramblers, artists, and lovers of the wild spirit in nature. The spirit of the place gave voice to the nineteenth-century Lake poets who opened the eyes of their Victorian contemporaries to the glory of the English countryside and its sacred places. The house of William and Dorothy Wordsworth can be seen at Rydal by the beautiful lake, Rydal Water; Samuel Taylor Coleridge, Thomas De Quincey, and other friends lived nearby. Many of the old abbeys and sanctified spots mentioned in this book were celebrated in the poems of Wordsworth and thus revived as places of pilgrimage. The most ancient of Wordsworth's haunts were the two great Cumbrian stone circles which have inspired poets and scholars ever since, Castle Rigg, near Keswick, and Long Meg and her Daughters, near Penrith, 20 miles to the northeast.

Castle Rigg Circle, Keswick

"A dismal cirque of Druid stones upon a forlorn moor" was John Keats's description of this circle. On a gloomy, wet evening it is very appropriate, but at other times the stones seem vibrant with life and spirit. Their site is perhaps the most beautiful of any stone circle. It is on the flat crown of a low, green hill, almost surrounded by mountain ridges. The stones are of local metamorphic slate and vary in size. The tallest, to the southeast, weighs about sixteen tons. Some thirty stones remain standing in the ring, and others are fallen. Within the ring on the eastern side is a rectangular stone arrangement which may be the relic of a cairn or shelter.

The winter view northward through Castle Rigg typifies the beauty of the site in relation to its surrounding landscape.

In 1967 Alexander Thom surveyed Castle Rigg in his *Megalithic Sites in Britain*, showing how the setting of the stones corresponds to features in the surrounding landscape and to seasonal positions of the sun and moon. Something of this occurs to many visitors at first sight, for there is an obvious harmony between the stones and the mountains around them. It is as if the circle forms the center of a gigantic work of art which makes a unity of all that is within sight. As a place of aesthetic development and mental readjustment this spot has no rival.

One feature Castle Rigg shares with many other stone circles is that it is near a river. The sinuous River Greta is a half-mile to the north and may preserve the name of a local goddess. Less obvious is the location of the circle on a traditional line of power between two mountain peaks, but this can be seen on a local map. The two highest mountains in the district, both over three thousand feet, are Skiddaw to the northwest of the circle and Helvellyn to the southeast. The distance between them is 10 miles exactly, and a straight line drawn from one peak to the other goes along the eastern rim of the circle, where the perimeter has been flattened slightly, as if to give passage to the line. The course of this line toward Skiddaw coincides with the shortest walk from the circle to the River Greta.

The Design and Astronomical Indicators Castle Rigg is not a true circle but exemplifies a megalithic construction which Thom refers to as Type A, where part of the perimeter is flattened so that the perimeter is equal to three times the length of the diameter.

The construction is shown on the diagram in dotted lines. The circle is divided geometrically into six segments, and four of them are enclosed by the regular circumference. Two

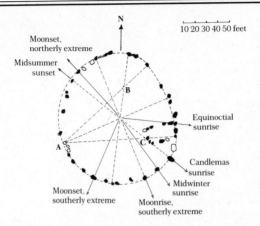

The ground plan of Castle Rigg, showing construction lines
and the astronomical positions of its stones in relation to
the surrounding landscape.

of the radii are bisected at B and C, and lines from the base
of the figure at A are drawn through those points. The small
side arcs have centers at B and C, and the perimeter is
completed by an arc centered on A. A simpler version of the
construction is shown below.

The striking thing about this interpretation of the Castle
Rigg geometry is that two of the construction lines are also
indicators of sun and moon positions. The transverse axis of
the figure points to the most southerly point the moon
reaches in the course of its 18.6-year cycle, and another line
points in one direction to the midsummer sunrise and in the
other toward the rising sun at Candlemas, one of the feast
days in the Celtic calendar.

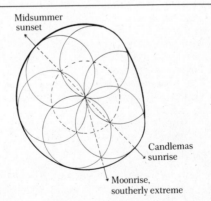

Underlying the design of the flattened circle of Castle Rigg
is a classic geometric figure formed by six equal circles, one
of which is omitted to produce the flattened effect.

Some years ago the artist John Glover, photographing the circle on midsummer evening, captured an extraordinary effect that is visible there every year at sunset. The sun goes down over a mound on Latrigg Hill to the northeast; as it sets it throws a shadow from the tallest stone in the southeast part of the circle, and because the ground falls away in that direction the shadow extends along the ground for about a half-mile, creating a visible line in the direction of Candlemas sunrise.

Other lines, sighted from the center of the circle over stones in the perimeter, point to spots on the horizon where the sun rises at the equinox and midwinter and to the most northern and most southern positions of the setting moon.

Age and Function Stone circles are conventionally dated to the second or third millennium B.C., and Castle Rigg is considered one of the earliest. Its positioning in relation to sun, moon, and landscape indicate that it was apparently designed as a temple or magical control center, one of its functions being to regulate the hunter's, farmer's, and herdsman's year in accordance with the seasons. It provided an accurate calendar for the solar year, and it marked the lunar cycles that are important to cultivators and cattle breeders.

None of this accounts for the symbolic features in its geometry and siting, which belong to the world of ritual magic. Mountains are traditionally a source of metaphysical power that energizes the paths between them, and the position of Castle Rigg on the line between the two tallest local peaks suggests that the energy which flows from the high places was of interest to its builders. Other landmarks of the district were symbolically linked to the design of the circle through their being indicated by the construction lines of its geometry. These arrangements imply a round of rituals at the circle, with climaxes at annual solar feast days and at longer lunar intervals. At such times the temple would receive light from one of the heavenly bodies, and shadow paths and other natural effects would be observed and incorporated in the rituals. One can imagine a sacred drama, endlessly maintained through the seasons and cycles, which reflected the movements and influences of the heavenly gods, activated their powers, and attuned human society to the moods of nature.

The old stones of Castle Rigg, so worn by wind and rain that they appear to have stood there forever, provide a passage into the ancient world; for the prospect there around one is the same now as it was in the time of the circle's builders, and at the spot where they placed their temple, one has a sense—as they must have had—of being at the center of a divinely ordered landscape.

CASTLE RIGG is 1.5 miles east of Keswick in Cumbria. On the outskirts of the town a turning to the right off the A594 road goes to the circle, which is on the right near the first road junction. Admission is free at any time.

Long Meg and Her Daughters, Penrith

This is the largest stone circle in the north of England, 360 feet in diameter. It stands among trees in a grass field, with a farm track running through it. There are about seventy stones in the ring, the largest weighing thirty tons. This big stone and another almost as large mark the cardinal points east and west and define the longer axis of the circle. Other large stones are clustered to form an entrance at the southwest.

Long Meg, a tall, thin, red sandstone pillar standing just outside the entrance to the circle, probably came from the bed of the River Eden a half-mile to the west. On its sides are prehistoric carvings that include a spiral, concentric circles, and indented cup marks. Their meaning has been much debated—but so far inconclusively. By analogy with such markings elsewhere, particularly on the great chambered mounds of Ireland, they may have had significance at certain days of the year, when picked out by shadows or sunlight. Some of the carvings on Long Meg are clearly visible only at sunset. In megalithic art the spiral seems to symbolize the turn of the year at midwinter, when the sun has reached its lowest point on the horizon and the days start to lengthen again. Its parallel meaning is the journey through death to new life. This is in accordance with the position of Long Meg, which from the center of the circle marks the point of midwinter sunset.

There are many legends about Long Meg. One that explains the name says that Long Meg was a witch and the other stones her hard-hearted daughters. In another version she was a beautiful woman who was saved from being raped by her seventy suitors through a merciful enchantment which petrified the entire group. There is testimony to the strange powers which are believed to focus on these circles in a nineteenth-century record of Long Meg: When a local landowner tried to clear the land by blasting away the stones,

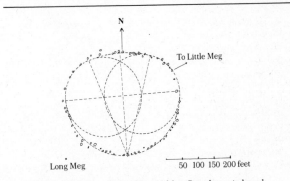

The ground plan of Long Meg and her Daughters is based on a figure of sacred geometry, the vesica piscis, *formed by two intersecting circles.*

a supernatural storm arose with such violent rain, hail, and thunder that the workmen fled for their lives.

A much smaller circle, Little Meg, stands to the northeast. There is believed once to have been another circle in a neighboring field. In the eighteenth century two mounds were visible within the Long Meg circle, and from one of them, it is recorded, the bones of a giant were taken.

The circle's geometry is an example of the form classified by Alexander Thom as Type B. It is a simpler version of Type A as displayed at Castle Rigg. The construction, as shown in the diagram, is based on the *vesica piscis*, the two inter-linked circles that provide the basic design of many ancient temples. On its northern rim the circle is flattened by means of an arc struck from the base of the figure.

LONG MEG and Her Daughters is 5.5 miles northeast of Penrith, Cumbria. The A686 road from Penrith goes to Langwathby, and from there a road to the left (north) leads through Little Salkeld to the circle. Admission is free at any time.

CARLISLE

An unforgettable approach to this grand old stone town in England's northwest corner is by railway from the south, which winds along the valley of the River Eden. The name of the Garden of Paradise is well applied to the landscape with its enchanting hill scenery. Carlisle is a walled city with a castle, a cathedral, and a long history of warfare, for it is not far from the Scottish border, and the Roman Wall erected against the tribes of the Picts and Scots is just to the north of it.

The ancient British city on the eminence where the castle now stands was called Caer Luel, from which comes the present name. The Romans under Agricola seized it in about 80 A.D. and made it their regional capital. Their name for it was Luguvallium. On several occasions the northern tribes swarmed over the Wall and sacked it, as did the Vikings in the ninth century, and even after William Rufus built the castle and walls in 1092, it continued to be fought over by the Scots and the English. No English town has a more enbattled history. All this is reflected in the modern character of Carlisle, which is still that of an outpost. There is no other large town near it, and for centuries Carlisle has had to look after its own interests and placate its neighbors. Thus it retains an independent air and a reputation for hospitality.

CARLISLE CATHEDRAL

The cathedral stands on the central hill of the city, a site previously occupied by early Christian, Roman, and Celtic buildings. The five ancient wells beneath it are probably the earliest features of the place. Nothing is recorded of the

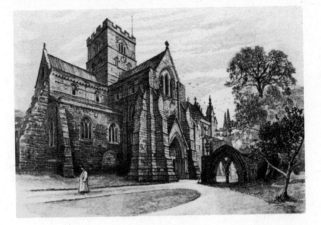

Carlisle cathedral, buttressed and stout as a fortress.

original pagan shrine or of the Christian church that replaced it, but a Christian community was flourishing there in 685 when St. Cuthbert of Lindisfarne visited the town. Carlisle was presented to him by King Egfrid of Northumbria, who rebuilt the church and the town walls in his honor. St. Cuthbert is much commemorated at Carlisle, in carvings and paintings in the cathedral and in the dedication of the neighboring civic church. There is still a school at Carlisle which claims to have originated in the church school St. Cuthbert founded.

When the Normans fortified the city in 1092 and made it their northern bastion, they also rebuilt the old Saxon church using stones from nearby Roman buildings. It was a large, plain edifice, strongly built to serve also as a fortress. In 1101 Henry I added a priory for Augustinian canons to its south side, and in 1133 it was made a cathedral, the only one in England belonging to the Augustinian order. The monks wore black habits and lived more strictly than the Benedictines, holding themselves aloof from the townspeople, worshiping in the choir of the cathedral, and partitioning it off from the nave, which was used as the parish church. Thus there were two churches under one roof. It was not until the nineteenth century that a new parish church was built, the partition removed, and the two parts of the cathedral united. By that time they no longer matched, for the Augustinians had rebuilt their part, the choir, in the thirteenth century and widened it by an extension to the north.

A fire that burned much of the town and all its old records in 1292 also destroyed the new choir. The work of reconstruction went on through much of the fourteenth century, by the end of which the cathedral was at its most magnificent and was considerably larger than it is now. Most of the nave was pulled down in 1646 when a Scottish army captured the city for the Parliamentarians after an eight-month siege and used the cathedral stones to repair the castle and walls. That is why the cathedral is now truncated and lacks a formal west front.

The Grandest Window in England

The greatest work of art in the cathedral is the east window, which has been called the finest in England or, according to some critics, in the world. It was constructed over five years from 1340 and fills most of the wall. From the nine lights at its base springs an elaborate geometric pattern of tracery containing fourteenth-century stained glass, that of the lower parts being modern. The whole is a representation of the Day of Judgment, with Christ the Judge at the summit, and below him are shapes like angels' wings, the blessed ascending to the heavenly Jerusalem and the damned sinking into the abyss.

Of the same period as the east window are the pillars supporting the arches of the choir. Their capitals are carved with figures engaged in appropriate occupations for each month of the year. Six of them are hidden by the canopies of the choir stalls. February, on the south side, is characterized by a familiar English winter scene, a man holding a wet boot over a fire. Less familiar in England today is the image for October on the north side: a man harvesting grapes. The November man is plowing, and in December he is killing an ox for Christmas. These scenes from rural life remind one that one of the original functions of a great church was to

The east window of Carlisle cathedral from the choir.

maintain a round of feasts and saints' days, thus marking the seasons in the farmer's and the countryman's year.

The choir stalls and canopies were made early in the fifteenth century and were originally painted, gilded, and ornamented with carved figures, most of which were destroyed by Puritans. The carvings which survive, however, are likely to be of more interest today than the controversial religious figures which were removed. Hidden on the misericords below the hinged choir seats, they show scenes from medieval life and imagination. Many of them were derived from bestiaries or books of combined natural history and fantasy. Subjects include a mermaid with a mirror, two dragons, a fox and a goose, and a pelican feeding her young. The rounded ceiling above the choir is painted blue with golden stars to represent the vault of heaven.

Painted on the backs of the choir stalls is a rare series of fifteenth-century illustrations showing the lives of the saints Cuthbert, Augustine, and Anthony and figures of the apostles. Above each picture a two-line verse describes what is shown. The technique is similar to that of a children's comic book. The sayings and adventures of the saints must have been as widely familiar in medieval times as are those of cartoon characters today.

In the course of its nine-hundred-year life the cathedral has suffered all kinds of damage. Subsidence at its foundations has twisted its pillars and arches, and it has been scarred by fires, wars, and fanaticism. Attempts at restoration from the seventeenth century to the early twentieth century have resulted in the loss of many ancient fittings. Yet the cathedral is still full of medieval treasures which enhance the natural sanctity of its site, making Carlisle a leading place of pilgrimage in the north of England.

ARTHURIAN CUMBRIA

Caer Luel, the Celtic town which preceded Carlisle, was located at a place of natural sanctity where three rivers meet, the Eden, the Calder, and the Petteril. Such places have a magical quality that tends to make them centers of legendary landscapes, and the beautiful country around Carlisle is full of local legends about a former kingdom which flourished there up to the seventh century. Its name was Rheged and its most famous ruler was King Arthur.

Arthurian landscapes occur in other parts of Britain—in Scotland, Wales, Somerset, and Cornwall—as well as in Brittany. The same man could hardly have performed the same heroic feats in all these places, and scholars have long disputed about which of his reputed kingdoms King Arthur actually ruled. That Carlisle has strong claims to having been the Arthurian capital of Camelot is implied in several of the earliest written versions of the legend. According to the *Morte d'Arthur* of Sir Thomas Malory, Carlisle was the city where King Arthur received a Roman delegation, and there is a record from Norman times of an ancient building called Arthur's Chamber, which stood near the cathedral and was believed to have been part of King Arthur's palace. In the neighborhood of Carlisle there are many spots with Arthurian names or associations.

Arthur's Well A holy well of this name existed near Greenhead in Northumberland on the Roman Wall 17 miles east of Carlisle. Its location is no longer known for certain, nor is its legend, but it probably marked an episode in the Arthurian myth and was ritually linked with places of similar name in the district.

Arthur's Chair On the northern side of Hadrian's Wall, 6 miles east of Greenhead, are the King's and Queen's Crags, two rocky outcrops a half-mile apart. Between them is a large boulder, said to have been hurled by King Arthur from a rock called Arthur's Chair on King's Crags. It was directed at Queen Guinevere, seated on Queen's Crags, with whom he was quarreling. It hit her comb and bounced off, and the marks of the comb can still be seen upon it. This was clearly not the Celtic Arthur who fought the Anglo-Saxon invaders, but one of the elemental giants of prehistoric legend.

Sewingshields: The Cavern Where He Sleeps South of the Crags a long, well-preserved stretch of the Wall runs northeastward from Housesteads Roman fort and passes over Sewingshields Crags. Just beyond them, on the north side of the Wall, is the site of Sewingshields Castle, which was demolished in the nineteenth century. A story from before that time tells of a local farmer who found his way through a crevice below the castle into an underground chamber where King Arthur with his queen, knights, and hounds lay sleeping. On a table were a stone sword and a horn. The man should have blown the horn to awaken the sleepers, but he failed to do so and thus missed the opportunity of ending the spell by which the heroes were imprisoned. The cavern has never since been rediscovered. A similar story is told at other places in Britain and Europe.

Housesteads Roman Fort The Roman fort at Housesteads is one of the many stations and temples on the 90-mile length of Wall which have been restored and opened to the public. It is a beautiful, lonely spot among magnificent scenery. The museum has Roman altars and other relics.

THE FORT stands on the B6318 road nearly 3 miles northeast of Bardon Mill. It is open March 15 to October 15, daily, 9:30 to 6:30 (Sunday, 9:30 to 6:30 from March 28 to September 30); for the rest of the year, daily, 9:30 to 4 (Sunday, 2 to 4). Admission £1.

Birdoswald Roman Fort, or Camboglanna East of Carlisle and 3 miles west of Greenhead, near Gilsland, a turning off the

Housesteads fort on the Roman Wall.

B6318 road leads to a Roman fort on the Wall. Its massive, ruined ramparts are on an attractive spot overlooking the River Irthing. Access to it is free at any time. Its old British name, Camboglanna, is equivalent in Welsh to Camlann, which is the name of the place where King Arthur fought his last, disastrous battle and was killed.

Arthur's Round Table The name Round Table occurs at five places in the British Isles. They are generally amphitheaters, circular earthworks, or henges, places of religious and ritual assembly from prehistoric times. The Cumbrian Round Table, known also as Mayburgh Henge, is by a river at the intersection of the A6 and A592 roads a mile south of Penrith, which is 18 miles southeast of Carlisle.

The Round Table is a flat, circular platform, about 160 feet in diameter, enclosed by a trench and an outer earth wall. Entrances are to the north and south. There may once have been a stone circle on the platform. The fact that the trench is inside the wall shows that the structure was not made for defense. It was evidently a ceremonial center for initiations, religious drama, or other purposes which can only be guessed at. The date of this Round Table is thought to be about 2000 B.C..

In the graveyard of St. Andrew's Church, Penrith, is a "giant's grave" marked by two tall stone pillars standing fifteen feet apart, which is supposed to be the height of the man buried there. Local folklore identifies him as Owein, a sixth-century king of Rheged who features in Arthurian romance as Yvain or Ewan. A further story is that the bones of an enormous man were found when the grave was opened about four hundred years ago.

Pendragon Castle From Kirkby Stephen, 40 miles southeast of Carlisle in the Eden valley, the B6259 road continues south for 4 miles to a spot where it approaches the river. Between the road and the river is an artificial mound topped by a small ruined castle among trees. The castle is of the twelfth century, but the mound is probably much older, and it is said to have been fortified by Arthur's father, Uther Pendragon. The story is that he tried to divert the waters of the Eden to form a moat around the mound. This may explain the traces of cuttings and earthworks which can be seen at its base.

King Arthur and the Ugly Woman: A Legend of Carlisle

A story from the days when King Arthur held court at Carlisle is related in a traditional border ballad. Outside the city walls Arthur was overpowered by a local knight who spared his life on the condition that within a year he would return with the answer to a puzzling question: What is it that women most desire? None of his court could produce a convincing answer, and Arthur was honor-bound to return to the knight at the end of the year and forfeit his life. On his way to the meeting he was approached by a hideously ugly woman who said that she would give him the answer provided he found her a husband. This was agreed, and the woman told him that the one thing women desire is to have their own way. The answer proved correct, Arthur's life was saved, and he appointed one of his knights, Sir Gawain, to be the ugly woman's husband.

Sir Gawain treated her with knightly courtesy, and the woman offered him a reward. She would become beautiful half the time, either by day or by night; the choice was his. Remembering the wise words she had imparted to King Arthur, Gawain told her that she could have her own way and make the choice herself. His response broke the spell under which the woman had been laid, and she immediately became beautiful by both day and night.

This story is not unique to Carlisle; it occurs with variations in other parts of Europe. Carlisle also has rivals in its claim to be the site of King Arthur's Camelot. (One of them is Cadbury Hill near Glastonbury in Somerset, page 141–3.) Yet it is remarkable how densely clustered in the old kingdom of Rheged are places and folklore items of Arthurian significance. Rheged extended from Carlisle down the Eden valley, along the Roman Wall, and north into Scotland, covering the main northern strongholds of the Arthurian legend. Here was once a complete cycle of Arthurian mythology, its various episodes linked to natural features in the landscape. It goes back to times before settlement and agriculture, when migratory tribes acted out a creation myth as they journeyed between the sacred places of their territory. In this myth the prototype of King Arthur must have played a leading part, probably as a planetary, solar, or stellar deity. Thus he has left his mark on an entire landscape.

The glorious, legendary countryside along the Roman Wall is typified by this view from the Roman station at Birdoswald.

Camelot can be identified with Carlisle, the fatal battle of Camlann may have been fought near the Roman fort at Birdoswald, and perhaps King Arthur's resting place is beneath Sewingshields Castle on the Roman Wall. But these legendary sites are not confined to the old kingdom of Rheged; they occur in Arthurian landscapes elsewhere. The events they commemorate are essentially mythological, and they are also archetypal, that is, they are reenacted by different heroes in different countries and at different historical periods. One looks in vain for a single historical Arthur, yet one observes in certain landscapes the qualities of light and natural harmony which makes them appropriate settings for the Arthurian myth cycle. The Arthurian associations in the countryside around Carlisle were not imparted to it by any individual hero; they arise from the beauty and natural sanctity of the landscape itself.

CARLISLE is in the northwest corner of England, 300 miles from London, and can be reached by train or by the M6 motorway.

The cathedral is open daily during the daylight hours.

Details of Roman and Arthurian sites in and around Carlisle can be obtained from the Tourist Information Centre in the Old Town Hall. Telephone: Carlisle (0228) 25517. Further information about excursions along the Roman Wall and within Northumberland National Park is available from the Information Centre at Once Brewed (2 miles west of Bardon Mill on the B6318 road east of Carlisle). Telephone: Bardon Mill (04984) 396.

LINDISFARNE: *The Holy Island*

Off the Northumberland coast in the northeastern corner of England is an island 3 miles long with a village, a ruined

The silvery light of the Holy Island of Lindisfarne is captured in this view toward the castle.

priory, and a castle on a rock. It is not always an island because at low tide one can walk to it across the sands, and at certain times one can drive there along a causeway constructed in the 1950s. Rare birds, driven by storms, find refuge there, and it is a sanctuary for many other kinds of wildlife. Its 250 inhabitants include old, established families of fisherfolk with an admixture of artists, naturalists, mystics, and seekers of solitude. The clear light and pale, subtle colors of the island make a lasting impression on the thousands of pilgrims who go there each year. The Saxons called it Lindisfarne, and later it became known as Holy Island because from the seventh century it was the source and stronghold of Christianity in northern England. Today it is revered as the most remote and awesome of English pilgrimage places.

THE SAINTS OF LINDISFARNE

St. Aidan's Foundation The first half of the seventh century was a time of struggle between the forces of Christendom and the pagan kings of western England and Wales. For a time the pagans prevailed, and Oswald, the Anglo-Saxon king of Northumbria, succeeded his father while his family was in exile. Their refuge was Iona, the island off the west coast of Scotland where St. Columba of Ireland had established a center of Christian learning.

Young Oswald renewed the battle against the pagans and by 634 had regained his kingdom. However, many of his people remained true to their old pagan customs, and Oswald sent to Iona for a missionary teacher to convert them. The first who came proved unequal to the task and was replaced by a thirty-four-year-old Irish monk, Aidan. His method of promoting Christian culture was to exemplify a life of pure, spiritual simplicity. For the headquarters of his mission he chose lonely Lindisfarne. King Oswald, whose stronghold was Bamburgh Castle on the mainland opposite the island, appointed him Lindisfarne's first bishop. From their humble monastic settlement, on or near the site of the existing priory, Aidan and his companions traveled on foot far across the country, preaching the message of Christianity and encouraging promising young men and women to join them in their quiet, studious life on Lindisfarne.

During the lifetime of St. Aidan missionaries from Lindisfarne planted Christian communities across northern England and in Scotland. The rule in such places was one of self-denial and discipline. The novices, many of them from rich and powerful families, renounced their possessions and adopted a regime with long hours of prayer, little sleep, and a sparse diet. Their compensation was access to the best teachers and education of their time. At Lindisfarne and its dependent communities there was a renaissance of scholarship and the arts and crafts. The Celtic Church combined classical and native Druidic learning with Christian humanism, and the product was some of the most inspired works of art in England's history. The finest example is the Lindisfarne Gospels (now displayed in the British Museum), the wonderfully illuminated manuscript which was created in about 700 in the scriptorium on Holy Island.

St. Cuthbert On the night St. Aidan died in 651, a shepherd boy on the Scottish hills saw a great light in the sky, with

High cliffs of the Farne Islands, with nesting kittiwakes and other birds.

angels carrying heavenward a saintly soul. The boy, Cuthbert, went immediately to the monastery at Melrose and became a monk. His sweet nature and talent for learning distinguished him above his contemporaries, and he was soon given positions of responsibility, first at Melrose and later at the monastery in Ripon, where he was made guest master and received visitors. This post recognized Cuthbert's great personal charm and social abilities: He was said to have been the most diplomatic and gently persuasive person of his time.

Cuthbert's gifts were much needed in 664 when, at the Synod of Whitby, members of the Celtic Church were forced to accept the rites and orders of Rome. Many of the monks at Lindisfarne resisted the changes, and Cuthbert was sent there as prior to instruct them in the new ways. By tact, patience, and the example of his saintly, ascetic life he succeeded in the task. His wisdom, holiness, and healing powers attracted to him numerous followers. After twelve years on Holy Island, Cuthbert decided to withdraw to a hermit's cell.

The Farne Island Hermitage Six miles east of Holy Island is a group of rocky islets called the Farne Islands. They are surrounded by stormy, treacherous seas, and only seals and sea birds live there. Traditionally they are the haunt of demons. The largest of them has about sixteen acres with some grass and a clear water spring, and there St. Cuthbert made his hermitage. It consisted of a stone oratory and a cell with one window which gave a view only of the sky. A high surrounding wall perfected the hermit's seclusion. In it was a small opening through which he spoke with those visitors who braved the sea crossing in search of his blessing and with the monks who brought him provisions. A hut near the jetty gave accommodation to visitors compelled by the weather to stay overnight. In stormy seasons the island was inaccessible, and St. Cuthbert lived on the produce of a little garden he had planted. The periods of isolation allowed him to enjoy fully the life he had chosen, combating the Farne demons and communing with angels and elemental spirits. It was said that ravens nourished him and otters came out of the sea to warm his feet.

After he had spent nine years on the island St. Cuthbert was summoned back to duty by the Church. At first he refused to move; only after a deputation of high dignitaries, led by the king himself, had sailed to his hermitage to beseech his return did he consent to become Bishop of Lindisfarne. Back on Holy Island he worked energetically as a teacher and administrator and made long missionary journeys that exhausted his strength within two years. Feeling the approach of death, he demanded to be ferried back to the Farne Islands. There, in his cell, attended by Lindisfarne monks, he died two months later in 687.

The lighthouse tower and chapel on the island where St. Cuthbert had his hermitage. The site of his cell is near the chapel.

St. Cuthbert's body was returned to Lindisfarne and placed in a coffin beside the altar of the priory church. It was found to be still uncorrupted when the coffin was opened eleven years later, and it was seen again in the same perfect state in 1104. Meanwhile it had had an adventurous career. The story of how St. Cuthbert's remains were carried for many years around the north of England is told in the section on Durham cathedral, where his remains now rest (page 248).

Lindisfarne Priory

In 793 Viking raiders burned down St. Aidan's church and monastic buildings on Lindisfarne and killed many of the monks. The settlement was renewed, but in the following century it was destroyed again by the Danes. Holy Island was not safe from marauders until the eleventh century, when monks from Durham built a new priory there. Its ruins lie beside the village. On Holy Island the winds blow strong, and the red sandstone blocks of the old priory have been shaped and smoothed by the elements. Decorated Norman arches frame vistas of the harbor and, beyond it, the castle on a rock. At dawn or evening, under moody skies or pale sunlight, one can appreciate how the spiritual energies of this beautiful spot rewarded the old monks for their life of hardship.

At the entrance to the priory from the village is a small one-room museum with an interesting display of finds from the site and illustrations of the priory in its days of prosperity. There are also pictures of the curious relics found in St. Cuthbert's coffin when it was opened at Durham, in the nineteenth century. Among them were his portable altar, a crucifix, and a bishop's stole.

Ruins of the old priory and the castle on the rock at Lindisfarne overlooking the sea.

St. Mary's Parish Church

The parish church lies at the west end of the priory. It was built around 1140, but its foundations are those of an earlier Saxon building. It is a place of Anglican pilgrimage, with daily services, and it is always open during daylight hours. In it are exhibitions on the lives of St. Aidan, St. Cuthbert, and other Lindisfarne saints. Displayed in a glass case is a printed copy of the Lindisfarne Gospels, produced some thirteen hundred years ago on almost this very spot. Visitors to Lindisfarne may notice the beautiful colors of its illumination repeated in the island's natural scenery.

The church faces the sea, and opposite it is a tiny island, marked by a cross, where St. Cuthbert retired for prayer during his spells of duty at Lindisfarne.

The Castle

A short distance from the village, on the far side of the harbor, is a rocky eminence on which stands an imposing castle. For the old monks the site would have provided a natural hermitage, a lookout point, and a place for signaling to Bamburgh Castle on the opposite shore. Commanding the harbor and the sea lanes to Scotland, it is also a natural stronghold, and it was probably fortified by the fourteenth century. In the sixteenth century it was given a permanent garrison against foreign invasions. The Royalists held the castle at the start of the Civil War, but it fell to the Parliamentarians in 1642 and lapsed into ruin. A wealthy admirer of Holy Island purchased it at the beginning of the present century and commissioned Sir Edwin Lutyens to rebuild it in the romantic image of a seagirt castle on a rock. In this he succeeded admirably, but guests at the castle complained that it was the coldest, most uncomfortable house in England.

HOLY ISLAND lies off the coast 5 miles east of the A1 road at Beal, which is 6 miles south of Berwick-upon-Tweed, Northumberland, the nearest railway station.

One can drive to the island between periods of high tide, which last for about five hours. Information on the times of the tides can be obtained from the Post Office, Holy Island. Telephone: Berwick-upon-Tweed (0289) 89271. On file there also are details of accommodation, rentals, and visitors' facilities on the island.

Lindisfarne Priory and the museum are open March 15 to October 15, daily, 9:30 to 6:30 (Sunday, 2 to 6:30); October 16 to March 14, daily, 9:30 to 4 (Sunday, 2 to 4). Admission 75p.

The castle is open May 1 through September, daily except Friday, 11 to 5. Days of opening vary during the winter months. Entrance £1.50.

A trip to the Farne Islands and the site of St. Cuthbert's hermitage can be arranged with boatmen at Seahouses, 8 miles down the coast from Holy Island.

BAMBURGH

St. Oswald's Castle

From Holy Island the most prominent landmark visible on the mainland is the mighty castle at Bamburgh. On its site, at the top of a steep hill and a precipice to the sea, was the timber palace of King Oswald, St. Aidan's patron. Its original builder was King Ida in 547. Up to the ninth century it was the royal capital of Northumbria. The massive keep and ruined chapel date from its rebuilding as a castle in Norman times. It was often besieged, particularly during the Wars of the Roses, when it changed hands five times. In the eighteenth century the castle was owned by Lord Crewe, Bishop of Durham, who increased its size and magnificence. Since 1894 it has belonged to the family of its present occupant, Lord Armstrong.

On the upper terraces of the castle, cannons point out to sea and there is a wonderful view over the Farne Islands 4 miles away.

St. Aidan's Church and Deathbed

The road from the castle winds past a green lined by pretty stone houses, and on the right is the thirteenth-century Church of St. Aidan. In a shelter built against the wall of an earlier church on the site, St. Aidan died in 651. The spot is marked by a shrine with candles in the northwest corner of the chancel to the present church. A crypt below, rediscovered in the nineteenth century, probably held the saint's relics.

King Oswald, who became a saint, is also associated with Bamburgh church. At one time his right arm was kept there as a holy relic, for St. Aidan had prophesied that the hand which gave so generously to the poor would never perish. After he was killed in battle with the pagans his body was dismembered. The arm in its silver shrine was later stolen from Bamburgh by a monk and carried off to Peterborough.

The saints Aidan and Oswald stand together at the top of a finely carved nineteenth-century stone reredos at the east end of the chancel. Below them are other Lindisfarne saints, including St. Cuthbert, who holds the severed head of St. Oswald. (The head was placed in St. Cuthbert's coffin and went with it on its long journey to Durham.)

An interesting monument on the north side of the chancel, next to a suit of armor, is to a brave woman, Dorothy Forster. Her husband, a Northumberland squire who joined forces with "Bonnie Prince Charlie" during the 1715 rebellion, was captured and sent to Newgate prison in London to await trial. Dorothy and a servant rode south from Bamburgh and, by a clever stratagem, managed to free the prisoner and smuggle him to France.

Grace Darling, the Shrine of a Modern Saint

The greater part of Bamburgh's relics and memorials belong to a Victorian cult, that of Grace Darling. Her robed effigy, clutching an oar, lies above a canopied tomb in the graveyard. It replaced an earlier effigy in marble which is now preserved within the church. A stained glass window in the north transept commemorates her brave exploit. Opposite the church is her museum.

Grace Darling was cast in the image of sainthood, being small and pale and spending her entire life on the Farne Island rock which has the lighthouse. She was one of the nine children of William Darling, who had succeeded his father as the lighthouse keeper. In September 1838, when Grace was twenty-two, a passenger steamer, *The Forfar-shire*, struck a nearby rock and sank during a raging storm. The family in the lighthouse saw a group of nine survivors clinging to a rock over which the seas were breaking. Their little boat needed at least two people to row it, so Grace went with her father, and through heavy seas they reached the people on the rock. They took five of them, two of whom assisted William on a second trip to save the others.

Grace and William were rewarded for their heroism, and when the circumstances of Grace's life became known, she was elevated by popular acclaim to virtual sainthood. In addition to being brave, it was discovered, she was chaste and religious. William Darling had brought up his family to eschew frivolities and to study divine providence in works of scripture and natural history. Even at the height of her fame, when she had been made rich through public subscriptions, Grace continued to live on the lighthouse rock. Her glimpses of the world beyond it had disinclined her from marriage. She died of consumption in 1842 at the age of twenty-six.

The Grace Darling Museum in Bamburgh, run by the Royal National Lifeboat Institution, preserves relics of the heroine's life and the boat in which the rescue was made.

BAMBURGH is at the end of the B1341 road, a turning to the east off the A1 road and 12 miles north of Alnwick.

The castle is open daily, 1 to 6, in July and August; 1 to 5 in April, May, June, and September; and 1 to 4:30 in October. Admission £1.50.

WARKWORTH: *A Boat Trip to a Hermit's Cave*

Huddled in a bend of the River Coquet below the ruins of its castle, Warkworth was until recently entered by a fourteenth-century bridge through a gatehouse. This is now for pedestrians only, and cars go to the town center over a modern bridge. On the site of the parish church, renowned among antiquarians for its Norman fabric and rare stone spire, the remains have been found of a Saxon church founded in the eighth century by a king of Northumbria who became a monk.

The castle dominates the town and indeed the whole area. For a period of six hundred years from the fourteenth century it belonged to the Percys, the family name of the dukes of Northumberland, whose residence is now Alnwick Castle a few miles to the north. From the castle hill at Warkworth one can see far over the woods and meadows of the surrounding countryside and up the coast to the castles at Dunstanborough and Bamborough. Though stripped of its roof in the seventeenth century, Warkworth is the most magnificent of the many castles in Northumberland.

A path from the castle leads down to the riverside, along which one can walk a half-mile upstream to the hermitage and chapel. On weekends during the summer one can sail there by boat. Situated in a lonely spot shrouded by trees, the hermitage consists of three chambers cut in the rock with

The approach to the hermitage at Warkworth.

some masonry added. First is a narrow chapel, eighteen feet long, carved with architectural features, with an altar at the east end and a figure at prayer, possibly representing the original anchorite. A recumbent female figure is nearby. Leading from the chapel is a small apartment about five feet wide with another altar and a niche in the wall for the hermit's couch. The third and smallest chamber once had a gallery overlooking the river; it was long ago ruined by a cliff fall.

The hermitage is thought to have been constructed in the fourteenth century, but there is no record of who made it or first occupied it. At one time the Percy family maintained a chantry priest there. Its legend is that the rock chambers were hollowed out by a young man called Bertram who had murdered his brother and spent the rest of his life in solitary repentance.

WARKWORTH is 7.5 miles southeast of Alnwick in Northumberland on the A1068 road.

The castle is open March 15 to October 15, daily, 9:30 to 6:30 (Sunday, 2 to 6:30); for the rest of the year, daily, 9:30 to 4 (Sunday, 2 to 4). Between March 28 and September 30 the Sunday opening is at 9:30. Admission 75p.

The hermitage is open March 28 to September 30, Saturday and Sunday only, 9:30 to 6:30. During this period boats go there from the castle. Admission 50p. At other times access for parties to the hermitage can sometimes be arranged. Telephone: Alnwick (0665) 711423.

HEXHAM: A Sanctuary Amid Turbulence

Hexham is a small, secretive old town with narrow streets disappearing uphill from the central marketplace. It stands below hills on a bank of the broad River Tyne, which flows placidly in summer and in winter can become a raging torrent. The history of the place has a similar character; periods of calm under benign ecclesiastical rule have been interrupted by massacres and violent destruction. The position of the town near the Scottish border, just south of Hadrian's Roman Wall, exposed it to northern raiders, who on several occasions burned its houses and sacred buildings. It is not surprising, then, that Hexham's old abbey church has the look of a battered fortress.

St. Wilfrid and the Chaste Queen

The church at Hexham was founded in 674 by St. Wilfrid, the worldly cleric who founded Ripon (page 274). Its site and a large estate around it were given him by Queen Etheldreda of Northumbria, a lady of remarkable chastity who later became a saint. She was the daughter of a king of East Anglia who gave her in marriage to another local ruler. After her husband's death the king of Northumbria procured her as a bride for his son and heir, Egfrid. She was then thirty, her bridegroom fourteen.

Etheldreda was not interested in men or marriage but only .n the salvation of her soul. She soon fell under the spell of St. Wilfrid and made over to him the Hexham estates that she had acquired as part of her dowry. When he succeeded to the throne, Egfrid bestowed on Hexham the rights of sanctuary. He also begged St. Wilfrid to intercede on his behalf with the queen and urge her to perform her wifely duties by sharing his bed. This St. Wilfrid refused to do. Etheldreda, he said, had preserved her chastity through two marriages and was firmly dedicated to the religious life. The king made an attempt to seize her, but she eluded him and with St. Wilfrid's help fled south to Ely, where she built the first Christian church on the site of the present cathedral.

St. Wilfrid's Church, Crypt, and Sanctuary Chair
The church at Hexham which St. Wilfrid completed in 678 was one of the largest and most splendid in the country, richly furnished and filled with relics, manuscripts, and precious vessels. A few years later it became a cathedral with St. Wilfrid as its first bishop. Much of the stone used in the building came from a Roman fort nearby, and there are many Roman carvings in the church today, including three altars and a monument showing a centurion riding down a Briton armed with a dagger.

Scandinavian marauders destroyed the church and its contents and slaughtered the townspeople in the ninth century. In 1113 the church was rebuilt together with a priory, which was subsequently laid waste on several occasions by the Scots. Despite all these upheavals an important part of St. Wilfrid's Church survived intact. It was discovered in the eighteenth century and is now open as the crypt of the present church. St. Wilfrid's crypt is a unique Saxon relic,

St. Wilfrid's Church, Hexham, from the marketplace.

The Fridstool, St. Wilfrid's chair, Hexham.

larger and more impressive than the crypt at Ripon. All its stones are probably from the Roman fort at Corbridge, and one of them in the ceiling bears a Roman inscription. This deep, dark cellar was the goal of many a Saxon pilgrim, for in it were kept the miracle-working relics of the old saints. They could be viewed and perhaps touched within the small arched chamber at the heart of the crypt.

In the center of the east end of the church is its greatest historical relic, the Fridstool, or seat of peace, known also as St. Wilfrid's chair. It is a block of stone carved into a seat with scroll decoration on its arms. It is said to have been St. Wilfrid's episcopal throne, but a man of his dignity would scarcely have been content with a simple hollowed stone unless that stone were already a sacred object before his time. It is possible therefore that it was previously a coronation stone for the crowning of pagan rulers.

The Fridstool marked the centerpoint of Hexham's area of sanctuary, which extended for a mile around it. Those claiming sanctuary seated themselves upon the stool and were thereby made safe from arrest or molestation.

The Church After the Reformation

When Henry VIII's commissioners rode into Hexham in 1536 to organize the suppression of its abbey, the priests and citizens made a determined resistance. When finally they were made to surrender, the prior and several of his priests were taken to London and hanged at Tyburn. The abbey church later became the parish church, and up to the middle of the nineteenth century it was a treasurehouse of curious monuments and carvings from Roman, Saxon, and medieval times. It was then ruthlessly restored, and many of its ancient furnishings were ejected. Most of the old carved benches were sold off for firewood. Still remaining are some delightful misericords in the choir, rare painted panels, and a fine wooden screen. Stone carvings in the fifteenth-century chantry are of saintly and allegorical figures, with popular medieval jokes (such as a fox preaching to geese) and representations of human sins and graces.

HEXHAM in Northumberland is 22 miles west of Newcastle-on-Tyne on the A695 road and a mile south of the A69 between Newcastle and Carlisle. From those two towns there are trains and buses.

The church is normally open daily, 9 to dusk.

The Tourist Information Centre is at the Manor House on Hallgate. Telephone: Hexham (0435) 605225.

DURHAM

Durham is quite a small city, but with its university, museums, superb cathedral, and the natural beauty of its setting it is the cultural center of northeast England. Its charms are particularly appreciated in this area, which has so much mining and industry. Throughout the Middle Ages and after, it was also the power center of the region. Durham is still known as a County Palatine, meaning that it makes its own laws. Since 1836 all but the vestiges of its ancient privileges have been abolished, but in earlier times the Bishop of Durham reigned as a prince in his own realm, issuing his own coinage, levying taxes, and presiding over his courts. The source of these powers was the sanctity of Durham's greatest possession, the body of St. Cuthbert.

The heart of Durham is a tall hill around which the River Wear makes a hairpin bend, almost insulating it. Streets of old houses lead up to its summit, where stands the castle, built by William the Conqueror to keep down the northern rebels, and St. Cuthbert's shrine within the massive cathe-

One of the most striking sights in England, Durham cathedral perched high over the river.

dral. According to legend, its commanding site was chosen by the saint himself more than three hundred years after his death.

St. Cuthbert's Traveling Coffin

Anticipating a raid on their settlement from Scandinavia, the Lindisfarne monks abandoned their island in 875, taking with them their most precious relics, including St. Oswald's head and the bones of St. Aidan, which they packed into St. Cuthbert's coffin along with the saint's uncorrupted body. During their years of wandering, many miracles took place at the coffin. Wherever it rested a church to St. Cuthbert was founded. At Chester-le-Street, north of Durham, it remained for a hundred years, and the territory around it was declared a sanctuary in the saint's honor. In 995, fearing another Danish attack, the monks picked up the coffin and took to the road again.

As they approached Durham the coffin began to grow heavy, and one of the monks had a dream in which the saint named the spot where his body should be laid: Dunholme. None of the party knew where that was, but they heard a local woman ask another if she had seen her cow; the other said she had seen it on Dunholme. This proved to be a hill in a loop of the Wear, and there the coffin was placed. A rustic shrine of branches was erected over it. That was the beginning of Durham cathedral. Today, high up on its northern outside wall, one can see the carving of two women and a cow which commemorates its foundation.

DURHAM CATHEDRAL

The Sanctuary

One approaches the cathedral from the north across Palace Green and enters it by the north door. This is unusual, most cathedral entrances being at the west end, but at Durham the west end terminates in a drop to the River Wear. On the door is a grotesque face with a doorknocker in its mouth, a replica of the old sanctuary knocker by which fugitives from justice would signal their demand for refuge. At one time there were chambers over the door, in which monks kept constant watch for claimants to sanctuary. Most of those who came were murderers, but if they obeyed the rules—such as wearing special clothing—they were safe within the boundaries of the sanctuary, which were delineated by stone crosses. The right of sanctuary had been transferred to Durham from Chester-le-Street together with the body of St. Cuthbert.

After a certain period the refugees were made to leave the sanctuary. Dressed only in a coarse shift and carrying a cross, they were enjoined to make their way along the highroads to the nearest port. It must have been a humiliating journey: if they turned off the highways or broke any

*The sanctuary knocker
at the north entrance of
Durham cathedral.*

other conditions, every man's hand was against them and they could be killed with impunity.

The Building of the Cathedral

Durham cathedral is acclaimed by architectural students as the finest Norman building in Europe. After a series of Saxon churches had replaced the original shrine over St. Cuthbert's coffin, the foundations of the present cathedral were laid in 1093 at a ceremony attended by the king of Scotland. A Benedictine monastery adjoined it. Forty years later it was completed, much as it is now. The only major alteration took place in the thirteenth century, when the demand for oratories near St. Cuthbert's shrine caused the original apses at the east end to be replaced with the present Chapel of the Nine Altars.

In the Middle Ages the cathedral was richly ornamented and furnished. Then much of its splendor was stripped away by Puritan zealots, and in 1650 Cromwell used the cathedral to house three thousand Scottish prisoners of war, who smashed monuments and kept themselves warm by burning the carved stalls and other interior woodwork. At the end of the eighteenth century much further damage was done by James Wyatt, who also wreaked havoc at Salisbury cathedral (page 109) in the name of restoration. Disliking the ancient, weathered look of the outside walls, he had two or more inches of stone pared from their surfaces, thereby destroying the carvings. He also demolished the old chapter house, one of the glories of Norman architecture in Britain, bringing down its vaulted ceiling to crush the tombs of early bishops beneath. A partial restoration has been made since.

The Nave

Norman architecture is often thought of as heavy, but at Durham the sturdy piers and columns which support the roof are made graceful by their perfect proportions. Down the nave they consist alternately of clustered shafts and cylindrical pillars, carved with geometric patterns. Their height, 22 feet, is the same as their circumference. Their diameter is therefore 7 feet, and thus their masonic builders demonstrated the 22:7 relationship between the width of a circle and the measure around it. From the pillars spring pointed arches and vaulted ceilings, the earliest examples of

The nave of Durham cathedral with its massive, ornamented Norman pillars.

their kind. The Durham masons were pioneers of Gothic architecture. From strong foundations the masonry soars upward, making this the most solemn and noble interior in England.

In the center of the nave, toward the west end, is the font with its elaborately carved wooden cover which, like the choir stalls and other woodwork, was made in about 1660 during the replacement of the furnishings destroyed by the Scottish prisoners. In the paving in front of the font an inlaid strip of marble marks the eastern limit of the part of the church to which women were admitted in monastic times. St. Cuthbert was said to have become a misogynist in his old age and would have been upset by women approaching too near his shrine. According to his later biographers, this was a monkish fiction.

The Galilee Chapel and the Shrine of the Venerable Bede
Further evidence of St. Cuthbert's alleged aversion to women arises from the position of the Galilee Chapel, which was built on to the west end of the cathedral in 1175. It is so named because the priests used to process there in imitation of Jesus's return to Galilee. It was originally planned as a Lady Chapel and should therefore have been placed in the customary position toward the east end. That was the builders' intention; but when they started work, strong signs of disapproval emanated from St. Cuthbert's nearby shrine, producing falls of masonry. It was understood that the saint would not tolerate a Lady Chapel in his vicinity, so the

building was completed on the narrow ledge between the west end and the cliff above the river.

Two small doors lead in and out of the Galilee, which is built on a lower level than the main building. It is a work of breathtaking beauty, a perfect expression of medieval piety and vision. Delicately carved arches rest on slender marble columns. The quality of the light here is unique, quite different from the somber variety within the rest of the cathedral. On the wall above an altar to the northeast is a rare twelfth-century painting of the saints Cuthbert and Oswald.

Raised above the floor is a great stone slab inscribed in Latin, "In this tomb lie the bones of the Venerable Bede." This great saint and scholar (674–735) spent most of his life in the monastery at Jarrow, 15 miles northeast of Durham. There he chronicled the lives of Cuthbert and other saints and produced works on astronomy, arithmetic, and geography. He was so holy that even stones respected him. This was proved during his last missionary journey, when he was nearly blind and had to be guided by a young monk. They passed a stone circle in a field and Bede, mistaking the stones for a congregation, began preaching to them. The young companion was embarrassed on his account, but Bede never discovered his mistake because, when his sermon was over, the stones tactfully responded, "Amen, our venerable father."

Durham acquired Bede's bones by dishonesty and theft. One of its monks in the eleventh century was notorious for swindling or wheedling relics from other monasteries. At Jarrow he pretended such devotion to Bede's relics that he was left alone with them; he snatched them up and hastened back to Durham. There they were first hidden in St. Cuthbert's coffin, where Jarrow monks would never dare to search. It was not until three hundred years later, in 1370, when the hue and cry had died down, that the bones were transferred to a magnificent shrine above their present site. They were reburied after the shrine was destroyed at the Reformation.

One of Bede's prayers is displayed on an altar in front of his tomb.

St. Cuthbert's Shrine

For many years after the cathedral was completed St. Cuthbert's was its only tomb, no one else being thought worthy of sharing his place of burial. The first to be allowed entry, at the beginning of the fourteenth century, was Bishop Anthony Bek, whose resounding titles included Patriarch of Jerusalem and King of the Isle of Man. His tomb is below the north window, in the Chapel of the Nine Altars at the east end. Next to it is the tomb of Bishop van Mildert, the last bishop to reign as a prince over the County Palatine. He died in 1836. On the south side of the choir is the magnificent monument to a previous ruler, Bishop Hatfield.

He designed it during his own lifetime in the form of a grand episcopal throne, elevated above a chantry where his body was laid in 1381.

The inhibiting presence of St. Cuthbert and the destruction of tombs after the Reformation has left Durham with comparatively few monuments. Thus the cathedral is spared the clutter of marbles which afflicts other great churches and interferes with a full appreciation of their noble proportions.

The saintly shrine is raised on a platform above the Chapel of the Nine Altars. It lies behind the high altar and is separated from it by a fourteenth-century stone screen that once held many figures of saints and divinities. Up to the Reformation the shrine, now plain and simple, was colorfully decked with gilded carvings, marbles, and costly woods and hung around with bells. During the reign of Henry VIII all this was stripped away, the shrine was demolished, and the remains of the saint were buried beneath it. A stone slab now marks his resting place. Near it is a statue of St. Cuthbert holding St. Oswald's head.

The Cloisters and the Library

The beautiful Monks' Door at the southwest of the cathedral gives onto a green lawn surrounded by cloisters which were rebuilt in 1828. This is the area of the old monastic buildings. On the east side of the cloisters is the restored chapter house, and opposite it to the west is the old monks' dormitory, now the library. It is a magnificent hall, 194 feet long, roofed with the trunks of oak trees. There and in the treasury below

The bishop's throne, Durham cathedral.

By the shrine of St. Cuthbert, a statue of the saintly bishop holds his traditional emblem, the head of St. Oswald.

are many precious objects and relics, including one of the finest manuscript collections in England, Celtic sculptures, and the contents of St. Cuthbert's coffin, rifled in 1826. Interred with him were found his altar, cross, and robes and the skull of St. Oswald.

The crypt, which houses the treasury, also has a restaurant.

DURHAM CITY in County Durham is 15 miles south of Newcastle-upon-Tyne and 3 miles west of the A1 motorway. It has a mainline station with trains from London (King's Cross), a journey of about three hours.

The Cathedral of Christ and Blessed Mary the Virgin is open in summer (May through August) daily, 7:15 a.m. to 8 p.m.; in the other months, daily, 7:15 to 5:45. The treasury is open daily except Sunday, 10 to 4:30. The hours of the Undercroft Restaurant are daily, 10 to 5 (Sunday, 12:45 to 5).

8
YORKSHIRE

YORK

Since ancient times York has been the great sanctuary and stronghold in the north of England. Its legendary founder in 994 B.C. was King Ebrauc, the sixth king of Britain in the dynasty of Brutus the Trojan, who founded London. The Romans who captured it from the Brigantes tribe in 71 A.D. called it Eboracum and made it their northern headquarters. Substantial remains of their fortifications can be seen in Museum Gardens, the site of the Yorkshire Museum with its wonderful collection of Roman statues, paintings, and relics. Nearby is York Minster, the largest complete medieval church in Europe, on the spot formerly occupied by the Roman temple of Diana. Constantine the Great, said to have been a native of York, was installed there as Roman emperor in 306.

York Minster seen over the roofs of the medieval city.

On the ruins of the Roman temple the newly baptized Saxon king, Edwin, built the first Christian church in the north. The Danes burned the whole city in 867 and then rebuilt it as their English capital, which it remained for almost a hundred years. Their name for it was Jorvik. The way of life under their rule is well illustrated by an exhibition at the Jorvik Viking Centre on Coppergate.

The eminence of York as both a religious and a military center survived its destruction by the Normans in 1069. They extended its fortified walls, and Norman archbishops began reconstructing the old Saxon cathedral. The work continued through the fifteenth century, and as the cathedral or minster grew, so did the town. The Industrial Revolution largely passed it by, and modern York with its museums, art gallery, grand old buildings, and medieval streets and churches offers more attractions to the cultured visitor than any other English provincial city.

YORK MINSTER

King Edwin's Conversion

In the crypt below the high altar of York Minster is the spot where King Edwin was baptized in 627 and where later his severed head was buried. Here, at the sacred center of the building, can be seen remains of the Saxon church built with material from the earlier Roman temple. Finely ornamented pillars from Archbishop Roger's Norman church of 1171 support the ceiling.

Edwin was a pagan king of Northumbria who captured and made his capital at York and then married a Christian princess, Ethelberga of Kent. She brought with her to York her confessor, Paulinus, who had come to England with St. Augustine's mission. He set himself the task of winning the king over to Christianity. His rival was Coifi, the high priest of Woden. A grand debate was held between the two parties at Market Weighton 20 miles east of York. The record of what happened there gives valuable insight into the pagan mentality in Britain and illustrates the ease with which the old religion accepted the Christian revelation.

The most telling contribution to the debate came from an old pagan speaker who gave a poetic description of the king and his court seated at dinner in a great hall. From the stormy darkness outside a sparrow flies in through an upper window, crosses the warm, well-lit room, and flies out again by a window opposite. That, said the speaker, is a parable of human life; for a fleeting moment we pass through this world, coming from an unknown state of being and disappearing again into the darkness beyond. If the Christian doctrine is able to offer guidance on where we come from and where we go after death, it would be well to adopt it.

Coifi, the high priest, was either genuinely swayed by the arguments in favor of Christianity or thought it expedient to

The entrance to the holy well in the crypt of York Minster.

join the winning side. He demonstrated his conversion in dramatic style: Calling for a warhorse and a lance—and thus breaking his priestly oath against bearing arms—he charged at the temple of Woden nearby and smashed it to pieces. The site of that temple is where the Norman parish church of Goodmanham now stands, 1.5 miles northeast of Market Weighton. There Coifi was baptized by Paulinus. The baptism of King Edwin at York took place shortly afterward.

During the reign of good King Edwin it was said that a defenseless woman with a baby could travel across the kingdom without danger. The king repaired the roads and had drinking fountains placed at intervals along them for the comfort of travelers. In 633 he was killed in a battle against the pagan kings of Wales and Mercia, and his head was buried in the church where he had been baptized at York. Penda, the pagan king of Mercia, was so tolerant of Christianity that he did not desecrate the royal sanctuary. A succession of Saxon churches was later built there, followed by the great Norman minster.

York Versus Canterbury: A Medieval Rivalry

Although Canterbury, where there had been a Christian church long before the coming of St. Augustine, was the older foundation, the archbishops of York long strove to assert their priority. One basis for their claim was the wonderful collection of holy relics at York. It included the bones of five saints: Paulinus, Wilfrid, Chad the patron saint

of Lichfield, John of Beverley, and William, whose wonder-
working shrine stood behind the present altar. There was
also a bone of St. Peter, to whom the minster is dedicated,
and a part of his sandal, presented by Archbishop Roger in
the twelfth century.

An earlier archbishop, Gerard, caused a rumpus at a
council in Westminster in 1102 by kicking over his throne
because it was placed on a lower level than that prepared for
the Archbishop of Canterbury. At a later council Roger of
York caused an even more outrageous scene. On his arrival
he found that the Archbishop of Canterbury had forestalled
him and had taken his seat in the honored position on the
right side of the papal legate. Roger tried to push his way
between the legate and his rival, and when he was resisted
he thrust Canterbury back into his throne and sat down on
his lap. The followers of Canterbury seized him and beat
him, covering him with dirt and bruises. When he complained to the king he was merely laughed at.

The rivalry between York and Canterbury was tactfully
settled by the pope in 1353; he conferred upon York's
archbishop the title Primate of England while allowing
Canterbury's to be called Primate of All England.

Inside the Minster
It is difficult to appreciate the vast size of York Minster from
the narrow streets of the city which crowd upon it. The best
views are from atop the old city walls, where one can see it

*The west front
of York Minster.*

The stone screen across the west front with effigy portraits of
the first fifteen English kings after the Norman dynasty.
William the Conqueror is on the left, Henry VI on the far right.

across the roofs of houses. Externally its most celebrated
feature is the richly carved, scientifically proportioned west
front, flanked by two eight-pinnacled towers between which
is one of the most magnificent Gothic windows in the world.
Over the central door, giving an archiepiscopal blessing, is a
statue of Archbishop Melton, during whose time in about
1330 this part of the building was completed. Also notable is
the massive fifteenth-century central tower, almost two
hundred feet high, the largest in England yet made graceful
by its simple, carefully proportioned design.

The most impressive spot inside the minster is at the
crossing beneath the central tower. Here the full power of
the building is concentrated. The mystical light and atmosphere is the creation of medieval glaziers, for the minster
retains much of its original glass, dating from the early
thirteenth century to the fifteen century. The quality of the
old stained glass, which cannot be reproduced today, is that
it does not project areas of color but breaks up and diffuses
the external light to produce an otherwordly effect within.

Sacred light from four directions bears upon the center of
the building. The deeply toned western window faces the
kaleidoscope of color in the window at the east end, wherein
is depicted the entire biblical story from Creation to Apoca-
lypse. Opposite the rose window in the south transept is the
famous Five Sisters Window to the north. Its panels in pale,
subtle bands of color are said to have been designed by five
York spinsters who first made their patterns in needlework.
A range of old glass lights the nave and the choir, where two
great windows illustrate the lives of St. Cuthbert and St.

*The chapter house
of York Minster.*

William. The beautiful glass in the chapter house is slightly
later than the early thirteenth-century Five Sisters.

The octagonal chapter house off the north transept was
built over twenty years from 1290. By the entrance is carved
in Latin the proud masons' inscription, "As the rose is the
finest of flowers, so is this the finest of houses." The interior
of the chapter house seems to justify the boast; it is the most
luminous of medieval buildings, with lofty walls mostly of
stained glass and wonderful stone carvings. The roof has no
central pillar to support it and is made of timber.

A Fanatical Incendiary and an Ominous Fire

Like all great cathedrals, York Minster has suffered from
periodic outbreaks of fire. Two that have afflicted it in
modern times occurred in peculiar circumstances. The first
was in 1829 when Jonathan Martin, a religious maniac,
attempted to fulfill what he supposed to be God's purpose by
setting the building alight. Concealing himself in the minster until everyone had gone home for the night, he then
arrayed himself in episcopal robes and made a pile of other
vestments and hangings in the choir. These he burned and
the fire spread to the choir stalls and roof. Almost all the
woodwork east of the central tower was destroyed. Martin
escaped but was later arrested and confined to an asylum.

A fire of unknown cause began in the southwest tower
eleven years later; it reduced to ashes the woodwork in the
nave and melted the great bells.

The greatest sensation was caused by the fire of July 9,
1984. Three days before it happened, the new Bishop of

Wild men and beasts play together among oak leaves carved in the chapter house, and a "green man" peers from among foliage in the vestibule to the chapter house of York Minster.

Durham, David Jenkins, had been installed at the minster by the Archbishop of York. The service was interrupted by some Protestant fanatics whose shouting caused them to be ejected from the minster. Their complaint against Dr. Jenkins was that he had recently, on television and in the press, expressed disbelief in the literal interpretation of the story of Jesus's virgin birth and bodily resurrection. They were, he explained, types of spiritual allegories.

The outbreak of fire so soon after the installation of the controversial bishop gratified the fundamentalists who saw it as a token of God's wrath. It was indeed a strange happening. There were no local thunderstorms that night, but a small cloud appeared over the minster and from it came a bolt of lightning that set fire to the south transept. By the time the blaze was brought under control the fifteenth-century roof had collapsed and the floor was covered with wreckage and melted lead. The damage is still being made good.

The York Line of Sanctuaries

In the Middle Ages there were forty churches in York, most of which still survive. Several of them can be explored by following a straight line across the city from the minster through Clifford's Tower, the keep of the Norman castle. The sites along the line are in some cases of probable prehistoric origin, while others seem to be later. The York antiquarian Brian Larkman, who first noticed the alignment in 1984, suggests that the master masons who planned the medieval churches may have sited them on an esoteric line of sanctity out of respect for ancient tradition.

The southern terminus of the line is at the point of junction between the rivers Ouse and Foss. It is at the end of St. George's Field, which once belonged to the Knights Templar, and the site of their chapel, now entirely obliterated, was on the line about a hundred yards to the north. The other aligned sites in order are:

Clifford's Tower The present thirteenth-century building is on a high mound where William the Conqueror made his stronghold in 1070. His castle was burned by the York mob in 1190 during their merciless slaughter of the city's Jewish population. The mound may have been raised on the site of a Roman or earlier earthwork.

St. Mary's Church Now a heritage center, this church has an ancient crypt which was rediscovered only a few years ago. One of the persecuted Jews took refuge and was killed there.

All Saints Church This is one of the oldest of York's churches, with foundations from Saxon times. It is also one of the most interesting. It stands at the very center of the city beside the old market cross. Its octagonal lantern tower used to be lit up at night to provide a landmark for travelers in the neighboring countryside. Directly between this church and St. Mary is the archaeological excavation of the Viking settlement.

St. Samson's Church The fourteenth-century building is now a senior citizens' center.

York Minster The line passes through the center of the crossing beneath the great tower. This was the sanctuary of the original Saxon church. Nearby in the crypt is a holy well dedicated to St. Cuthbert that may be of prehistoric sanctity.

North of the minster the line strikes the thirteenth-century chapel in the Archbishop's Palace, now used as a library and not open to the public. All the sites in the line can be seen together from the central tower of the minster, to which the public would normally have access but which has been closed for repairs since the fire in 1984.

YORK is 210 miles north of London on the A64 road, 12 miles east of the A1. It is a railway center with trains from all parts of Britain (journey time from King's Cross, London, just over one hour), and its National Railway Museum is an attraction to transport enthusiasts.

The minster is open every day during daylight hours.

The Yorkshire Museum in Museum Gardens, near the minster, is open daily, 10 to 5 (Sunday, 1 to 5). Admission £1.50.

The Jorvik Viking Centre on Coppergate is open April 1 through October, daily, 9 to 7; during the rest of the year, daily, 9 to 5:30. Admission £2.50.

Clifford's Tower in Castle Street near the Castle Museum is open March 15 to October 15, daily, 9:30 to 6:30 (Sunday, 2 to 6:30); during the rest of the year, daily, 9:30 to 4 (Sunday, 2 to 4). Admission 75p.

RUINED ABBEYS OF YORKSHIRE

The Cistercians

The great ruined abbeys of northern England are generally secluded deep in the countryside in beautiful surroundings beside a stream in a valley. Many of them were founded by Cistercian monks, who sought to dwell in the loneliest spots, where the vanities of this world could be forgotten and angelic communion could be achieved through the medium of nature. The early Cistercians were kindred spirits with the Celtic saints and hermits and imitated them in many ways, except that they lived in communities for the sake of protection and convenience. Over the years their simple, primitive settlements grew into enormous churches surrounded by splendid buildings. Then, with the dissolution of the monasteries, they fell into ruin and became the refuge of owls, bats, and ferny plants as nature recolonized their sites. Thus arose the contrast between the soaring piles of medieval masonry and their wild, desolate settings which so affects the imagination.

The Cistercian movement began in 1098 when Stephen Harding, a native of Sherborne in Dorset, found fault with the laxity and worldly conduct prevailing in his Benedictine monastery near Dijon in France and led a group of monks to seek a sterner life in the wilderness. They settled at Citeaux in a remote corner of Burgundy, a place of stagnant marshes within almost impenetrable forests. Their example of asceticism became widely imitated, and colonies of white-robed Cistercians, deriving their name from Citeaux, began springing up throughout Europe. The great St. Bernard was one of their first abbots. The site of his monastery, later known as Clara Vallis, the Bright Valley, was described at first as a "savage, dreary solitude," haunted by robbers and named Valley of Wormwood. The district was so barren that for a time St. Bernard and his monks subsisted on beech leaves.

The Cistercians began as extreme puritans. Their first churches were wooden huts, and when they could afford stone buildings they kept them as plain as possible. Towers, turrets, and stained glass were forbidden, and so were all precious metals. The monks fasted and prayed while the practical work in the fields, gardens, and craft shops was performed by lay brothers. By the middle of the twelfth century there were almost five hundred Cistercian houses, including many in Britain. The holiness of the monks attracted gifts and patronage from rich donors anxious to ensure the salvation of their souls. Through the toil and skills of the lay brothers the former wildernesses became productive farmlands. Yet despite their need for ever larger churches, living accommodations, and administrative buildings, the Cistercian architects maintained the simple, classical ideals of their order. Their greatest buildings, such as those at Fountains, Rievaulx, and Tintern in Wales, were

The ruins of Fountains Abbey across the River Skell.

designed in the Gothic style to imitate natural patterns of growth. Thus they were attuned to their surroundings, and even in their present state of ruin they continue to ennoble the beautiful landscapes where the monks located them.

FOUNTAINS ABBEY AND STUDLEY ROYAL

The landscaped surroundings of Fountains Abbey make it one of the most beautiful sites in England, and it is acclaimed as the finest ecclesiastical ruin in Europe. Its monks were expelled by Henry VIII in 1539, and parts of the abbey's domestic buildings were demolished seventy-two years later to provide stone for nearby Fountain Hall, but its remote location and the eighteenth-century taste for picturesque ruins spared it much further damage. Parts of its fabric are still wonderfully intact.

Adjoining the abbey is the estate of Studley Royal, which in 1720 belonged to the Chancellor of the Exchequer, John Aislabie. In that year the "South Sea Bubble" burst, ruining thousands of families. The Bubble was the South Sea Company, backed by Aislabie, which invited public investment and was designed through its profits to pay off the national debt. Its shares were officially promoted and soared to great heights before suddenly collapsing. The company was found to have been run on fraudulent lines, and Aislabie was one of those blamed; he was arrested and sent to the Tower of London but was ultimately allowed to retire quietly to his Yorkshire estate.

To forget the fiasco of his political career Aislabie threw himself into gardening. At Studley Royal he created one of the landscape masterpieces of his age, a classical composition of hills, woods, and water studded with temples and monuments. In that setting the local nature spirits could be imagined as nymphs and dryads. Fountains Abbey was made the climactic feature of the design. Aislabie constructed an artificial hill to conceal it from those walking in the gardens until, at the extreme limit of the walk, the great ruins suddenly came into sight across a moon-shaped lake. That is how they can best be seen today; one can go directly to Fountains Abbey from the car park at the west end of the estate, but the most rewarding approach is from the east, by lakeside paths in the beautiful wooded valley of the River Skell. Therein are the delights of a classical landscape with its harmony of trees, water, and discreetly secluded temples. The mind is lulled by contemplation of peaceful nature, and in that state one has one's first dramatic glimpse of the Gothic abbey ruins.

The Gardens of Studley Royal

On the death of John Aislabie in 1742, his son William inherited the great house at Studley Royal and dutifully followed in his father's footsteps, both as member of Parliament for Ripon and in completing his design for the gardens. His heirs continued the work of beautifying the landscape into the nineteenth century. In 1768 William was able to fulfill his father's greatest ambition by purchasing Fountains Abbey and adding it to the Studley Royal estate.

William Burges's church at Studley Royal, aligned upon Ripon cathedral.

The approach to the gardens from Ripon is by way of a broad, straight avenue which is aligned upon Ripon cathedral 3 miles to the northeast. To terminate the vista at the other end of the avenue, William Aislabie erected a pyramid in memory of his father. It was replaced in 1805 by an obelisk that still stands but is hidden behind a church on a knoll. This is the

The tower of Fountains Abbey framed in an archway of Anne Boleyn's Seat.

church of St. Mary, built in the 1870s by William Burges, whose work at Waltham Abbey has been commented on in an earlier chapter. It is a masterpiece of Victorian craftsmanship, its interior made brilliant by the light through stained glass windows and enriched by carvings and rare marbles.

To the north of the church are the ruins of Studley Royal House, which burned down in 1946 and is now closed to the public. All around it is a deer park with ancient forest trees and herds of native red and fallow deer together with the little Sika deer from Manchuria. On the southern side of the avenue is the entrance to the car park and gardens.

Here one can spend any amount of time exploring the paths which wander by lakes, woods, and monuments. The most direct walk to Fountains Abbey takes about twenty minutes, but the most effective first view of it is from a little Gothic pavilion called Anne Boleyn's Seat, placed high in the woods above the half-moon pond at the end of the gardens. A path to the left opposite the pond leads up to it. The view of the ruins from this vantage point is surely one of the finest in England.

Robin Hood's Well Beside the path on the left bank of the River Skell, just before it reaches the abbey, is a stone wellhead set into a hillside. It looks rather neglected, but the water which springs up there is fresh and sweet. The well takes its name from a legendary encounter that took place nearby between the famous outlaw Robin Hood and a Cistercian monk of Fountains called Friar Tuck. The monk may actually have been a lay brother, for he served as the estate gamekeeper, guarding the deer in the forests and providing the abbey with venison.

Friar Tuck had a reputation as a man of great strength and was much feared by poachers. Robin Hood determined to poach his deer, and the two had a long battle whose many episodes, involving both wits and muscle, were celebrated in medieval ballads. Finally they called a truce and the monk went off with Robin Hood to join his merry band in the greenwood forest.

Fountains Abbey

In this once desolate spot, where springs of water gush from the banks above the River Skell, a party of twelve monks took shelter in the winter of 1132. They had walked there from a house at Ripon belonging to Archbishop Thurston of York, who had taken them in after they had left their monastery of St. Mary, York, in protest at the easygoing life there. Their first wooden building was constructed around the trunk of a great elm. During their first year they were so hungry that they were reduced, like St. Bernard, to eating leaves—those of the elm which sheltered them. Whatever little they had was offered to needy travelers, and the legend of their generosity brought them gifts from local people, followed by the patronage of the great and wealthy. Within a few years their rustic church, dedicated to Sancta Maria de Fontibus (Our Lady of the Fountains), had been replaced by a towering edifice of stone.

About ten years after it was built, in 1147, the abbey was sacked and burned by followers of the new Archbishop of York, whose appointment had been opposed by the Abbot of Fountains. The abbey was quickly rebuilt on a larger scale, and it continued to expand in size and wealth up to the beginning of the sixteenth century, the great central tower being added shortly before the dissolution. In its preserved

The cellarium of Fountains Abbey, with its slender pillars and noble arches.

state of ruin the abbey perfectly demonstrates the pattern of medieval monastic life. At the east end of the church is the magnificent Chapel of the Nine Altars, wherein each of the monks said mass every day. Its soaring Gothic architecture is one of the glories of England. To the south of the church are the cloisters, chapter house, refectory, and rooms for the monks' domestic uses, all of which are labeled on the site. From the south wall of the church, near its west end, a long building extends across the River Skell. It was the monastery storehouse and cellar and also the lay brothers' dormitory. Lavatories and washrooms were placed at its far end, where it crosses the river.

Beyond the abbey is a small museum and a grand Tudor mansion, Fountains Hall, built in 1611. It now belongs to the National Trust and houses an exhibition illustrating the history of the abbey and the Studley Royal estate. It stands at the western entrance to the grounds, near the car park closest to the abbey.

Fountains Abbey in North Yorkshire is 4 miles southwest of Ripon, which lies to the west of the A1 road on the B6265 road from Boroughbridge. The road continues through the town, and turnings to the left from it are signposted to Studley Royal and the abbey.

The abbey and gardens are open daily, 10 to 8 (July and August), 10 to 7 (April, May, June, September), and 10 to 4 (other months). £1.50. Car park 70p.

St. Mary's Church is open from March 29 through September, daily, 11 to 6. Fountains Hall has the same hours and is open at other times of the year, daily, 11 to 4. Admission free.

On Friday and Saturday evenings, July 18 to October 25, the abbey ruins are floodlit and remain open to 10:30. Concerts and other events are sometimes held there. Details from the National Trust officer. Telephone: Sawley (076586) 333.

RIEVAULX ABBEY

All Cistercian houses were dedicated to the Holy Virgin, representing the tranquil spirit of nature, and the site of Rievaulx Abbey (pronounced "Reevo") is an obvious shrine to that spirit. The twelve disciples of St. Bernard who came there in 1131 recognized it as the best possible place for their communal hermitage. They found a grassy meadow near the spot where two streams join the little River Rye, sheltered by steep, wooded hills beyond which are the wild Yorkshire moorlands. It was described as "a place of horror and lonely waste," but the monks prospered there and became so attached to the site that, even though its size and shape made it impossible to build a church with the usual orientation to the east, they preferred to align their building almost north-south rather than move elsewhere.

The beauty of Rievaulx has made it a popular subject for English landscape painters, and it has been much celebrated by poets. William Cowper wished he could spend his entire

Rievaulx: The abbey ruins viewed from the terrace above.

life in sight of the ruins, and Dorothy Wordsworth, who visited the abbey with her brother in 1802, recorded in her diary how they were spellbound by the atmosphere of the place. In the eighteenth century a local landowner, Thomas Duncombe, whose estate included the hills above Rievaulx, made the ruined abbey the focal point in his scheme of classical landscaping. On the ridge above it he laid out a terraced walk with temples at each end. Trees along it were so arranged that at certain intervals they frame picturesque views of the abbey below. There today one can stroll or picnic, enjoy one's first distant prospect of Rievaulx, and experience the enchanting spirit of the place which so attracted the old Cistercian monks that there they made their first settlement in the north of England.

The Abbey and Its Monks

The site of Rievaulx Abbey was granted to its founder monks by a Norman warrior lord called Walter l'Espec. He later joined their order and spent the last two years of his previously warlike career practicing humility in the Cistercian manner. By the time of his death in 1152 the community had become vast in size and wealth. Under their first abbot, William, whose shrine remains among the abbey ruins, the monks began building in stone, and the work continued through the time of their sainted abbot, Aelred, who died in 1167. His wisdom and holiness attracted so many people that the buildings at Rievaulx had to be extended to accommodate 600 lay brothers and 140 monks.

In the well-tended ruins of the abbey one can see the apartments in which the monks passed the narrow round of their daily lives. Adjoining the church are the library and cloisters, where they studied the scriptural writings allotted to them. Even in the summer one can imagine how cold they must have been with no artificial heating on a freezing winter's day. Afterward they had a spell of physical labor in the fields and gardens. Otherwise, with short breaks for eating their one vegetarian meal and sleeping, their days and nights were entirely devoted to praising God in prayer and chant. At midnight, and again at early dawn, they were aroused for two hours of chanting. There were long periods of fasting, solitude, and silence. Thus they achieved peace of mind, and their lives were so widely admired that those who were admitted as Cistercian novices were selected from a large number of applicants.

Those who lacked the education or other qualities necessary for becoming a monk could be admitted as lay brothers. As the monks gave up their lives to spirituality, so the lay brothers devoted theirs to practical affairs. They also lived under strict rule, sleeping in dormitories, eating communally, and spending almost all their waking hours in labor. Apart from being taught to read certain sacred inscriptions, they were not supposed to be literate. In these circumstances they became absolute masters of their various crafts. At Rievaulx the chief monument to their skills is the magnificent arched choir to the church, added in about 1225. The sandstone of which it is built was quarried from nearby hills and floated to the site on canals watered by the River Rye.

The Abbot of Rievaulx succumbed to the Black Death in 1349, and plague decimated the monastery. It never re-gained its former strength. The lay brothers were replaced by hired servants to work the abbey farms. Some of the old buildings fell into disuse and were pulled down. By the time of the dissolution the number of monks had fallen to twenty-two. Their abbot, Helmesly, stoutly resisted attempts by Henry VIII's commissioners to seize their property, but he was replaced by another, more amenable abbot who surren-dered the abbey to the Crown in 1539. The monks and servants were paid or pensioned off with monies raised by the sale of lead from the abbey roof. Some of the stones were carted away for building nearby houses, but a substantial part of the masonry remains intact.

The site today is no longer in the wild state it was in when the Wordsworths visited it. In government care, with paths, fences, and a site museum, it is a little too well kept for some tastes. However, it remains a place of beautiful light and scenery, one where the religious spirit of the old monks seems hauntingly present.

The Rievaulx Terrace At either end of the terrace lawn, with its great trees, is an eighteenth-century classical temple. The temples agreeably terminate this loveliest of walks. One of them is circular with pillars in the Tuscan style and is dedicated to the spirit of solitude. The other is rectangular

The Doric temple at Rievaulx.

and Ionic. Thomas Duncombe furnished it as a dining room for entertaining his neighbors to hunting suppers. Now restored to its former richly decorated state, it is shown to visitors. Below it in the basement is an interesting exhibition of landscape designs.

RIEVAULX ABBEY and village are 2.5 miles northwest of Helmsley in North Yorkshire. To the left of a road off the B1257 are two turnings within a few yards of each other; the first is signposted to the Rievaulx terrace, the second to the abbey.

The abbey is open May 15 to October 15, daily, 9:30 to 6:30 (Sunday, 2 to 6:30); during the rest of the year, daily, 9:30 to 4 (Sunday, 2 to 4). Admission £1.

The Rievaulx terrace is open Easter Saturday through October, daily, 10:30 to 6. Admission £1.20.

BYLAND ABBEY

A neighbor of Rievaulx, Byland, was another Cistercian abbey. It is a mile south of the A170 road, 4 miles west of Helmsley, on a side road signposted to Coxwold village. Opposite it is an inn, one of the few buildings in this lonely region.

The Byland monks were originally Benedictines, but in the middle of the twelfth century they accepted the Cistercian reformation and in 1177 they built a great church and monastery on land which they had reclaimed from a marshy swamp. As well as farmlands they owned extensive fisheries and iron mines. A succession of abbots administered the estates and supervised the peaceful round of prayers and chanting up to the time of the dissolution.

The abbey ruins in a green meadow are impressive and melancholy. From the west front of the once mighty church a lone turret points like a finger to the sky, and beside it is a large semicircle, all that remains of a rose window. Green and yellow glazed tiles forming geometric patterns once covered the floors of the nave and transept; many of them have survived. Other relics are displayed in the site museum.

THE OPENING HOURS of Byland Abbey are the same as those of Rievaulx (above). Admission 75p.

JERVAULX ABBEY

As an architectural monument, Jervaulx (pronounced "Yervo") cannot be compared with the greater Cistercian houses such as Fountains and Rievaulx, but to lovers of sacred ruins it has particular appeal because of its natural wild condition. It has not been tidied up and labeled—all the better for those who like to contemplate the past among tumbled, overgrown stones and wildflowers.

A lonely spot nearby was first settled in 1145 by a small band of monks from Savigny in France. They placed themselves under the protection of the Abbot of Byland, but even with his help the district proved too rough for them. Wolves ate their flocks and at times they nearly starved. A new beginning was made twelve years later on the present abbey site by the River Ure, from which Jervaulx derives its name.

The Abbot of Jervaulx, like his brother abbot at Rievaulx, was a victim of the Black Death in 1349, and the number of monks had dwindled by the time of the dissolution. The

The ruins of Byland Abbey with the broken rose window.

abbey at that time was briefly notorious as a center of northern resistance to Henry VIII's policy of seizing monastic lands. These lands, though nominally owned by the monks, were not worked for their benefit alone. Their expert husbandry produced a huge surplus of meat, grain, and other commodities that was shared by the whole district. Under monkish guidance the countryside became productive and populous. When the monasteries were suppressed and their estates were granted by the Crown to private landowners, the local people were deprived of many traditional rights and occupations, and rural populations declined. This was the reason for the Pilgrimage of Grace in 1537, a northern rebellion in which Catholics took a leading part.

During the uprising a party of rebels descended on Jervaulx to demand the abbot's leadership in their fight against the government. Abbot Sedbar, who was on the point of yielding up his properties to the Crown, was so confused by the rival demands upon him that he went into hiding. The rebels made it known that unless he returned they would burn down the abbey. Sedbar confronted them, only to be beaten and abused as a traitor. He escaped into hiding elsewhere; nevertheless he was rounded up with others accused of leading the rebellion, tried in London, and hanged at Tyburn. The abbey was systematically destroyed and has ever since been a place of solitude and past glories.

JERVAULX ABBEY in north Yorkshire stands on the right of the A6108 road from Masham northward toward Middleham. The splendid old castle at Middleham is about 2 miles from the abbey.

There is a car park opposite the site of the abbey ruins, which are made accessible without charge to the public by courtesy of their owner.

MOUNT GRACE PRIORY

The Carthusian monks had nine houses in Britain, of which Mount Grace was the most important. They were even more strict and ascetic than the Cistercians, living as hermits in separate dwellings around their church. The ruins of their simple, honey-colored church and cloisters at Mount Grace stand in a valley below the Cleveland Hills. In spring the lawns around the site are covered with daffodils, and at all times of the year it has a peaceful and secluded air appropriate to a place of religious retirement.

The Carthusians were founded by St. Bruno at La Grande Chartreuse in 1084. Their object was to withdraw as far as possible from the world of the senses in order to study and experience the essential world behind appearances. The monks wore hair shirts under their black cowls, ate mostly herbs, and spent much of their time in solitary cells. At assemblies in church they covered their faces, rarely spoke to each other, and left their cloister only for the purpose of taking a weekly walk together. There was no communal dining; each monk lived off the produce of his individual

Mount Grace priory church is in ruins, but its beautiful wooded setting is unimpaired.

garden plot. If a monk was sick he was attended to in his cell, where eventually he died.

This way of life is illustrated by the ruins of Mount Grace Priory, founded in 1398. The church stands between two cloisters consisting of the monks' and prior's apartments, twenty-four in all. They are spartan but surprisingly roomy. One that has been restored is twenty-seven feet square with two stories; on the lower floor are living room, bedroom, oratory, and lobby with a water tap, and above is a workshop. Only the prior's cell has a fireplace. Behind each cell is a little garden, but evidently the monks did not live entirely on what they grew, for in the wall of each cell is a partitioned opening that allowed the inmate to receive food without seeing the person who brought it.

Beyond the cloisters are remains of a guest house, stables, and farm buildings, parts of which were rebuilt as a private house in the seventeenth century.

MOUNT GRACE PRIORY is 7 miles northeast of Northallerton in north Yorkshire, signposted off the A19 road one mile north of Osmotherley. It is open March 15 to October 15, daily, 9:30 to 6:30 (Sunday, 2 to 6:30); during the rest of the year, daily, 9:30 to 4 (Sunday, 2 to 4).

RIPON

One of the smaller English cathedral cities, Ripon was once known for its lacemakers and is now locally important as a marketplace. It is a natural center from which to visit the abbeys and other sacred places of Yorkshire. Until the end of Elizabeth I's reign the town was governed by a wakeman who ran a system of property insurance for the townspeople. Every night at nine he sounded his horn, and from then until daybreak he was responsible for any losses the citizens

incurred through burglary. In return the householders each
paid him an annual fee. A ceremonial wakeman is still
appointed and blows his horn nightly beneath the market
cross. The cross now takes the form of a ninety-foot obelisk
with a gilded horn on top as weathervane. It was erected in
1781 as a memorial to William Aislabie, the creator with his
father of the Studley Royal gardens, who was for sixty years
Ripon's member of Parliament.

Opposite the cross is the town hall, bearing on its cornice
the biblical phrase, adapted for Ripon, "Except the Lord
keep the city the Wakeman waketh in vain." Near it is the
old Wakeman's House, a thirteenth-century building which
now houses a folk museum with some curious items of old
Ripon history; it also contains visitors' information office.

St. Wilfrid

Ripon's patron saint and the founder of its cathedral, Wilfrid
(634–709) was one of the worldiest of clerics, prefiguring the
princely bishops of the Middle Ages. He began his career at
the age of fourteen as a monk at Lindisfarne, where he was
educated by the great St. Aidan. The quiet, contemplative
life on the Holy Island was not at all to his taste, for Wilfrid
was ambitious, and as soon as he could he left the place
forever and made a journey to Rome. The pope favored him
and instructed him as a Roman missionary to subordinate
the Celtic Church. On his return to Britain he found a royal
patron who expelled some Scottish monks from a monastery
they had constructed at Ripon and gave the place over to
Wilfrid.

At the Synod of Whitby in 664 Wilfrid proposed and
carried the motion that the rites of the Celtic Church should
be replaced by those of Rome. Afterward he became Archbishop of York. He had made many enemies among the old
Celtic clergy, and his haughty, arrogant style so alienated
the royal court that on several occasions he was driven into
exile. Always he regained his position until finally even his
papal connections could not save him from being deposed.
Yet even though his qualitites were more political than
spiritual, Wilfrid's life was held up by the Church as an
example of saintliness, and his shrine at Ripon became an
attraction to pilgrims.

The Sanctuary

The west front of the cathedral, built magnificently in 1220,
faces the town. Around it was once an area of sanctuary
where, as at St. Cuthbert's shrine at Durham, criminals and
debtors were free from arrest. This privilege is said to have
been granted by King Athelstan out of respect for the shrine
of St. Wilfrid, but it may have descended from far older
times. At the heart of the cathedral is an ancient subterranean chamber, thought to have been the crypt to the church
St. Wilfrid built in 672. However, there was an earlier
church on the site that belonged to the Scottish monks

The west front of Ripon cathedral. Its towers were once topped by spires.

whom Wilfrid supplanted. The chamber and the right of sanctuary could have been of their time or of even earlier, pre-Christian origin.

The Building of the Cathedral

Ripon had a bishop for a few years in the seventh century, but it was not until 1836 that its church became a cathedral again. Wilfrid's church had been rebuilt at least once before Archbishop Roger laid the foundations of the present building in 1154. It was altered and added to in every subsequent century up to the sixteenth, giving its interior a somewhat eccentric look. The most obvious clash of styles is in the arch supporting the central tower at the east end of the nave. The low shaft to the left (north) is part of the original twelfth-century work, while opposite it is the taller Perpendicular shaft, one of those built to strengthen the tower in 1450 when it seemed in danger of collapse.

Originally the central and the two western towers were topped by spires, but near the end of the sixteenth century the central spire was struck by lightning and the other two were removed for safety.

Scarcely altered since Roger's day is a three-storied structure south of the choir. Above its crypt, once used as a bone house, is the chapter house with a stone roof supported by two pillars, each of a single stone block. The original Lady Chapel over the chapter house has been for many years the cathedral library; it contains some odd relics as well as a valuable collection of manuscripts and early printed books. Cathedral guides will open it to visitors upon request.

The Underground Chamber

Beneath the central tower is the chamber or crypt which was part of St. Wilfrid's church. It is approached by steps leading down from the nave and is now devoted to an exhibition of gold and silver vessels belonging to the cathedral and neighboring parishes. The cylindrically vaulted chamber has a narrow hole in one wall that gives on to a passage beyond. It is called St. Wilfrid's Needle, and nineteenth-century guides used to squeeze visitors through the hole for their good health and fortune.

Now restored and brightly illuminated, the crypt does not have the same air of mystery it had in the days before electricity, but its original function is a mystery still. One theory is that it was a repository for the holy relics St. Wilfrid brought from Rome. Pilgrims could have viewed them through the hole in the wall. The relics of St. Wilfrid himself, which disappeared at the Reformation, may have been shown there, and it has been suggested that they may one day be rediscovered hidden within the masonry of the crypt. Another belief is that the crypt was for a priest hearing confessions; it has also been identified as an initiation or vigil chamber.

The Preaching Fox and Other Carvings

The choir is separated from the church to the west by a delicately carved stone screen of the fifteenth century whose niches once held statues. Later in the same century the canopied stalls east of the screen were made. They were labeled with the ranks of the church dignitaries entitled to occupy them. Some of their finely carved woodwork was destroyed when the central spire fell through the roof in 1594, but the damage has since been made good. The hinged seats fold upward to show the misericords. Medieval

St. Wilfrid's Needle in the crypt of Ripon cathedral. The mysterious opening is between the passage (left) and the underground chamber.

Carvings on the choir stalls of Ripon cathedral include St. Cuthman wheeling his aged mother across Sussex in a barrow.

carvers would hide their most fanciful designs on the undersides of the seats, and those at Ripon are some of the strangest and most ingenious to be found anywhere.

Handwritten texts in the choir explain the misericords insofar as they can be interpreted. Many of them illustrate forgotten sayings and legends. There is a fox preaching to a gullible congregation of geese, a pig playing bagpipes to dancing piglets, a lion stalking a monkey, and there are figures of animals real and mythical that include a dragon catching rabbits, a mermaid with mirror, a pelican, a griffin, and an owl. Most remarkable is the figure of a man, seen from above, pushing another person in a wheelbarrow—a masterpiece of perspective. The man is thought to be St. Cuthman, whose legend is that he carted his aged mother in a wheelbarrow across Sussex. A carving on the bishop's throne, of an elephant standing on a turtle and supporting a castle on its back, is like a figure of Hindu cosmology. A battle is raging around the castle, and the elephant has seized one of the attackers in its trunk.

Ripon is on the A61 road, 12 miles north of Harrogate in north Yorkshire. It has no railway station, but there are stations at Harrogate and York from which there are buses to the town. An express bus service between Newcastle and London's Victoria Station passes through Ripon several times a day.

The cathedral is open daily, dawn to dusk.

The local history and folk museum in the Wakeman's House, Market Place, is open May 1 through September, daily, 10 to 5 (Sunday, 1 to 5). Also in the Wakeman's House is the local Tourist Information Office. Telephone: Ripon (0765) 4625. Another, serving a wider district, is at Harrogate. Telephone: (0423) 525666.

SACRED AND CURIOUS ROCKS

KNARESBOROUGH

Set high on a limestone cliff overlooking the River Nidd, Knaresborough is a small market town with some fine old buildings and curious antiquarian attractions. Among the former are the ruins of its fourteenth-century castle, built on earlier foundations, and its parish church, with interesting monuments in and around it. The oddities of Knaresborough include the oracular cave of England's most famous woman prophet, Mother Shipton; a "dropping well" whose waters turn to stone objects placed in them, a rock-cut hermitage and chapel, and a quaint cottage carved into a cliff face.

Mother Shipton's Cave and Petrifying Well

On the right of the A59 road from Harrogate, at the entrance to Knaresborough just before the bridge over the River Nidd, is the gateway to the popular shrine of Mother Shipton. A small museum by the gate has illustrations of her life and the history of the place and some peculiar petrified objects from her well.

Mother Shipton, born Ursula Sontheil in 1488, had the proper parents for a girl of supernatural powers, her mother being an outcast beggar woman and her father a local spirit or demon who haunted the forests outside Knaresborough. There they met, and Ursula was born in a forest cave. Soon afterward the mother retired to a convent, leaving her infant daughter in the care of the parish.

She is said to have been a hideous little creature, deformed, shriveled, and lame, with a huge twisted nose covered in pimples that were said to glow in the dark. Even so, she found a husband and became Mrs. Toby Shipton.

As compensation for her appearance, Mother Shipton had second sight and the gift of seeing into the future. Thus she became first locally and then nationally well known, and her fame lasted several centuries. The Great Fire of London in 1666 was recognized at the time as the fulfillment of one of her prophecies. The major triumph of her lifetime was over the powerful Cardinal Wolsey, who she had prophesied would never enter the city of York. Hearing this, Wolsey swore that not only would he enter York but he would go on to Knaresborough and burn Mother Shipton as a witch. He was at Cawood, 12 miles from York, when the king's officers arrested him on a charge of high treason. He died at Leicester on the way back to London.

Since they were first published in the seventeenth century, there have been many editions of Mother Shipton's prophecies. Some of her later editors have been shameless in adding spurious material. Thus she has been credited with couplets—such as, "Carriages shall without horses go, and accidents fill the world with woe"—which do not appear in the early editions. Perhaps the art of making posthumous prophecies is one of the hallmarks of a great sibyl!

A ten-minute walk through a pretty woodland belt beside the river leads to the head of the steps to the cave and well. Visitors are met there by guides and conducted further.

The dropping well is a strange sight indeed. A large rock basin is filled with water that drips down into it over a rounded rock face. Moss and grass around the basin have been petrified by the action of the waters, which are giving a lime coating to an assortment of objects suspended on a line below the rock face. People send treasured souvenirs to the proprietors of the well—baby shoes, dolls, toys, stuffed pets, hats, gloves—which are then suspended in the waters for a year or so and are thus made permanent in stone. This eccentric practice perpetuates a most ancient custom, that of adorning the shrine of a well or waterfall spirit with votive offerings.

Mother Shipton's cave, where she was born, lived, and gave oracles, is a few paces from the dropping well. Guides tell her legend in front of her eerily lit effigy. Her nutcracker profile can also be discerned in stone outcroppings around the well.

The Hermitage Chapel of St. Robert and the Cottage in the Rock

If instead of returning by the same path one continues on past Mother Shipton's well, one soon comes to the Low Bridge entrance to the estate, where stands the Mother Shipton Inn. Across the river to the right is Abbey Street, with a cliff to its left. About three hundred yards along it, just after the last cottage, a path winds upward to a door in the cliff face, beside which is carved a primitive figure of a giant wielding a sword. Inside is a chapel. To borrow the key to the door, one climbs further up the cliff path to another door in the cliff. There dwells the keyholder to the chapel below, who is also the owner of a curious house that she opens for visitors' inspection.

The house in the cliff is called Fort Montagu, from the family name of a former Duchess of Buccleuch. She was the

The entrance to St. Robert's rock-cut chapel, Knaresborough.

friend of a poor Knaresborough philosopher, Thomas Hill, who in about 1770 solved his housing problem by hollowing out a rock cell. The duchess encouraged him to go further, and utimately he completed three rooms in the rock, one above the other, linked by a staircase and warmed throughout by a chimney from a fireplace below. A fourth story on the level above the cliff has a street entrance. Inside Fort Montagu are two gifts the duchess bestowed on Thomas Hill: a fine portrait of himself, now blackened with age, and an ancient linen chest. The house is still inhabited by his direct descendants.

The rock-cut chapel below Fort Montagu has the intense atmosphere of a hermit's oratory, which it once was. Lit by a small window, it is about ten feet square and features an altar, two piscinas, and four odd little carved faces. The roof is shaped to imitate ribbing.

The chapel is now dedicated to Our Lady of the Crag, and Roman Catholics hold occasional services there. In about 1200 it was the chapel of a recluse, St. Robert, who inherited it from another hermit. Its earlier history is unknown. St. Robert, a former monk at Fountains Abbey, may have done the interior carving. It has also been attributed to a later occupant, John the Mason, in 1408.

St. Robert lodged in a cave a short distance farther along the road past his chapel. Later the cave became notorious as the scene of a murder which thrilled eighteenth-century England and was widely recounted in prose and verse. A young scholar of the town, Eugene Aram, together with an accomplice, lured his rival in love, Daniel Clark, to St. Robert's cave, where the two men killed him and buried him beneath the floor. The body was not discovered for fourteen years, and by then Aram was a respected schoolmaster in Norfolk. He was arrested in front of his class and taken back to Knaresborough to be hanged.

KNARESBOROUGH has a railway station and lies 4 miles west of the A1 motorway, 7 miles north of Wetherby in north Yorkshire.

Mother Shipton's estate, with the well and the cave, is open daily, March through October, 9:30 to 5:15. Admission £1.85. Telephone: Harrogate (0423) 864600.

Fort Montagu can be approached either from above, at 8 Crag Lane, or from Abbey Road below. It is generally open to visitors daily, 1 to 6, or at the convenience of its resident. Admission 70p. The key to the rock chapel can be borrowed there.

BRIMHAM ROCKS: *Natural Rock Sculptures and Druidic Images*

On a high plateau above Pateley Bridge is a marvelous collection of sculptured rocks that have been blasted over the centuries by wind and rain into a variety of suggestive shapes, many of which resemble living creatures or archetypal forms of creation. Such places—another occurs in the

Forest of Fontainebleau outside Paris—are called by the French *points d'amour*, implying that they reproduce the generative processes and patterns of nature. All kinds of speculative ideas are stirred by the sight of Brimham Rocks. Mystics and philosophers have a particular affinity with the spot, and it also appeals to antiquarians of the more imaginative sort, for some of the rocks are shaped like dolmens and other instruments of prehistoric religion. There is no direct evidence that Brimham was once a Druid sanctuary, as has often been suggested, but the magic of the place would certainly have affected the ancient priesthood in the same way it affects sightseers today.

From an old stone house among the rocks, now an information center, one can ramble over fifty acres of fantastic rock shapes. The stacks of millstone grit take on such forms as a turtle, a dancing bear, a baboon's head, a sphinx, and other natural shapes and symbols. Almost incredible is a huge goddess form, estimated to weigh two hundred tons, which stands upright on a pivot whose narrowest width is no more than ten inches.

Fresh air and fine prospects are among the further attractions of Brimham. One can picnic in the shelter of the rocks and gaze at Ripon cathedral 8 miles to the northeast. By ancient custom one of the Brimham rocks in sight of the cathedral was once regularly whitewashed and may thus have provided a landmark for astronomical sightings.

BRIMHAM ROCKS are to the south of the B6265 road, 8 miles southwest of Ripon and 2.5 miles east of Pateley Bridge. There is a car park, a shop, and a refreshment room. Admission free; cars 80p.

Two fantastically weathered rock forms at Brimham. Left, the "baboon's head"; right, a natural goddess idol, two hundred tons of rock supported by a pivot ten inches wide.

BOROUGHBRIDGE

The Devil's Arrows
Travelers passing Boroughbridge on the Great North Road to
Scotland (now the A1) catch sight of three enormous stone
pillars to the east of the road. To inspect them more closely,
one follows the signposts to Boroughbridge and the road
toward Roecliffe, by which they stand.

The southernmost pillar, alongside the road, is the tallest
at 22.5 feet; all three are of massive girth though elegantly
shaped. Two are in fields and are approached by a path along
a hedge. It is a pleasure to touch their venerable sides of
millstone grit, which have been deeply grooved by rainwater
trickling from the apex. The quarry from which they were
taken was probably at Knaresborough, 7 miles away. The
modern estimate of the date they were erected is around
2000 B.C. Once they had a fourth partner; it was removed in
the seventeenth century to make a bridge.

The traditional explanation of these stones is that they
were bolts shot by the Devil in an attempt to destroy the
neighboring town of Aldborough. Modern research has
shown how they feature in the system of alignments that
links many ancient sites in Britain. The three Devil's Arrows
are not precisely in line; from the southern stone, a narrow
sighting corridor separates the other two. One of the lines
through the stones runs 11 miles northwest, passing directly
over four henge monuments. Three of them, at the far end of
the line, are the Thornborough henges, consisting of circular
earthworks, each of about eight hundred feet in diameter.
Between them and the circle is the Nunwick henge. The
henges had a ceremonial function whose nature is unknown.
Other alignments passing through or between the stones
indicate the probable reason for their great height, that they
were designed to be seen over a long distance.

The Refuge of an Unworthy Saint
Boroughbridge is an attractive town with a cobbled marketplace that has a well covered by a cupola. There are many old
inns here, for this was once an important commercial center.
The church has fragments of Norman stonework from an
earlier building which was pulled down in the nineteenth
century. In 1322 Thomas, Earl of Lancaster, was dragged
from the church, where he had attempted to claim sanctuary, and carried off to execution at his own castle of
Pontefract.

Lancaster had become the sworn enemy of Edward II
because of his treatment of the king's favorite, the dandified
Piers Gaveston, ten years earlier. He had taken Gaveston
prisoner on a promise of safe conduct and then allowed him
to be murdered, ignoring the wretched man's entreaties. The
Battle of Boroughbridge, where he defeated and captured
Lancaster, was Edward's revenge.

Lancaster was described as a coarse, brutal, vicious individual, but something about him evidently appealed to the populace, for after his death he was treated as a saint. Miracles were said to have occurred at his tomb in Pontefract, and pilgrims from all over the country made it their sacred shrine. At one time it almost rivaled in popularity the shrine of Thomas à Becket at Canterbury. Behind both cults was the obvious purpose of annoying the authorities.

9

EASTERN ENGLAND

LINCOLNSHIRE, CAMBRIDGESHIRE, NORFOLK, SUFFOLK

LINCOLN

Large and lonely Lincolnshire in the eastern Midlands has as its county town one of England's most interesting cities. It is built around a hillside on the summit of which is the magnificent cathedral, the third largest in England after York Minster and St. Paul's. Lincoln was Lindun, an important British town, before its capture by the Romans, who renewed its fortifications and rebuilt it to their standards of civilization with baths and piped drinking water. Many relics of their time have survived, including parts of their town wall and a gateway, the Newport Arch, through which an ancient straight road, Ermine Street, enters the city to the north.

Because of its position on a fortified hilltop above the navigable River Witham, Lincoln remained an important military and trading center after the withdrawal of the Romans. Its colonnaded streets, heated baths, sewer system, and land drainage channels fell into decay, but Saxon and Danish rulers held court there and the walled city flourished until 1068, when William the Conqueror swept away the houses on the hilltop to make space for a huge, menacing castle, erected on the old British earthworks.

During the twelfth century Lincoln saw much warfare and the castle was several times besieged, but at the same time the city prospered as a center of finance. A colony of mercantile Jews occupied an area of the old town below the cathedral, where two of their houses can still be seen: the picturesque Jews' House at 15 The Strait, and Aaron's House on Steep Hill, said to be the oldest inhabited dwelling in England. Disaster struck in 1255 when the Jews fell victim to the recurrent medieval libel accusing them of ritual murder. A young boy, Hugh, was said to have been crucified at a secret ceremony. He was immediately proclaimed a martyr and buried in the cathedral, and mass hysteria ensued. More than a hundred Lincoln Jews were arrested and many of them executed. The cult of Little St. Hugh at

Lincoln was for years a focus of Christian anti-Semitism. It has long been suppressed.

LINCOLN CATHEDRAL

Lincoln had a Christian church in late Roman times and a bishop in the fourth century. In 628 Paulinus, the first Archbishop of York, introduced Roman Christianity in place of the former Celtic rites and built a new stone church. In troubled times, when the Danes were ravaging England, the bishopric was removed from Lincoln, but under firm Norman rule a new bishop was appointed. Bishop Remigius was a small man with great spirit. He began the construction of an enormous cathedral on the hilltop beside the castle. The two buildings, visible from afar, were ostentatious symbols of Norman supremacy and were bound therefore to stimulate local resentment. Remigius did much to reconcile people to the new order through tact and humility. He labored personally with the cathedral builders and gave generous alms to needy citizens. By 1092 the cathedral was ready to be consecrated, and Remigius invited all the dignitaries of the kingdom to attend the ceremony on May 6. The one notable absentee was the Bishop of Hereford, who had discovered by astrology that the date was unpropitious and that something would prevent Lincoln's bishop from being installed in his cathedral on that day. So it proved; three days before the ceremony, Remigius died.

The most conspicuous remaining part of the Norman

The west front of Lincoln cathedral.

The central Norman doorway of the west front of Lincoln cathedral.

cathedral is the central arch of the west front. Much was destroyed by a fire in 1141, and twenty-four years later the building was wrecked by an earthquake. It was reconstructed on a larger scale under Bishop Hugh of Avalon, an obscure French Carthusian monk who had been promoted by royal favor. This did not prevent his opposing the king in defense of popular rights, and his wisdom, courage, and saintly life earned him canonization after his death in 1200. His was one of four shrines in the cathedral which produced miracles and made Lincoln a place of pilgrimage in the Middle Ages. The other three were shrines of saints by popular acclaim who were never officially canonized, Little St. Hugh and Bishops Grosseteste and John of Dalderby.

Bishop Grosseteste built the great central tower of the cathedral in about 1237; he was also said to have been the indirect cause of its downfall. He was a mystical theologian of noble but cantankerous personality who quarreled with his own dean and chapter about the conditions under which he was entitled to enter the cathedral. The pope became involved in the dispute, which expanded into other areas of disagreement. Grosseteste denied certain rights claimed by the Vatican, and when the pope sent his own nephew to Lincoln to serve as a canon, the bishop refused to receive him. In the course of the long, complicated row the bishop excommunicated his opponents and was himself excommunicated by the pope. The fall of the tower shortly after it was built took place at the height of the quarrel between Grosseteste and the priests of his cathedral. One of the canons was denouncing the bishop to a congregation in the nave: "If we do not speak out," he said, "the very stones will cry out on our behalf"—whereupon the tower collapsed. The new tower was begun immediately and finished by John of

Dalderby in the following century. It is one of the finest in England, and its original spire, which was destroyed by lightning in 1548, was second only to that of old St. Paul's in height.

Throughout the thirteenth century the cathedral grew ever more vast and elaborate. The west front, through which one enters, extends 175 feet across two towers which once had spires. At its center the venerable Norman masonry is encased, as if in a reliquary, by an ornate structure of thirteenth-century carving. A pinnacle at the south end bears a statue of St. Hugh of Avalon, and on the corresponding northern pinnacle is figured the Swineherd of Stow, whose example in giving his humble life savings toward the cathedral's building was much quoted by ecclesiastical fund-raisers.

The Bishop's Eye and the Angel Choir

The interior of Lincoln cathedral is one of the richest in England. Its shrines were destroyed at the Reformation, and Puritans smashed many of its monuments, yet its most glorious features remain. They include some of the most beautiful medieval windows, stonework, and wood carving to be seen anywhere.

Almost the whole building, from the spacious nave to the angel choir raised over the shrine of St. Hugh of Avalon at the east end, is a work of the thirteenth century. Above the former site of the shrine, a flight of angels with extended wings, playing musical instruments, is the culminating feature of an intricate and delicate composition in carved

The angel choir of Lincoln cathedral.

*Tracery of the Bishop's Eye window in the south transept of
Lincoln cathedral. It is filled in with a mosaic of ancient glass.*

stone, designed to honor St. Hugh. The artists who sculpted
it expressed their reverence in no solemn spirit but with
exuberance and humor. That is made plain by the famous
Lincoln Imp, a grotesque little Puck-like figure who sits
cross-legged in the foliage atop one of the pillars to the north
of the angel choir.

Two fine rose windows can be seen from the crossing
beneath the central tower. The one at the end of the north
transept is called the Dean's Eye because it is the business
of the dean to protect the building from destructive forces,
which traditionally come from the north. The Bishop's Eye is
the window to the south, for in that direction lie the spiritual
influences which the bishop invokes. This window was
probably made in honor of John of Dalderby, the unofficial
saint whose healing shrine once stood below it.

East of the crossing, St. Hugh's choir has stalls and
canopies by a brilliant team of fourteenth-century wood-
carvers who also probably made the choir stalls at Chester.
The carvings at Lincoln are unsurpassed. Strange figures
and scenes from pagan mythology and popular legend
enrich the stonework on corbels, bosses, and the capitals and
bases of pillars, and the woodwork of the choir displays the
breadth of the medieval imagination. Beneath elaborate
canopies, three tiers of stalls have carved bench ends and
misericords below the seats. One can spend hours admiring
the curious details of this work. In the limited and defined
spaces at their disposal, the carvers consistently managed to
produce little masterpieces of anecdote and humor. "The
carvings are quaint and in some cases of a ludicrous
character," a nineteenth-century canon of Lincoln wrote,
"and they are not very suitable to a religious building." That
of course depends on one's concept of religion. The medieval
craftsman, having no notion of Victorian morality, accepted

every element in nature and the human mind as fit subjects for religious art.

One group of carvings, beginnning on the bench end of the precentor's stall, typifies the enigmatic charm of the whole. It tells a story, otherwise unknown, of a baboon who stole the monkeys' butter. On one side of the bench end two monkeys are churning butter from milk. On a second side the baboon who has stolen it hides among bushes. The third side shows the monkeys hanging the baboon, who is saying his prayers, and carved on the misericord of the seat below is the baboon's funeral. These scenes must illustrate some simple, once popular, now forgotten story that was probably also a parable. They provide a glimpse into the current of fable, folklore, and popular wisdom which in medieval times ran parallel to the mainstream of Christian doctrine.

LINCOLN is 140 miles north of London; it is reached by the A46 off the A1 near Newark 15 miles to the southwest. It has a railway station, and trains from King's Cross, London, take about two and a half hours.

The cathedral is open to visitors after morning service and before evening service, daily, 10 to 5 (Sunday, 1 to 3:30).

The City and County Museum, with exhibits of Roman Lincoln, is on Greyfriars Pathway off Broadgate. It is open daily, 10 to 5:30 (Sunday, 2:30 to 5).

Further details from the Tourist Information Centre. Telephone: Lincoln (0522) 28928.

THE ISLE OF ELY

From Cambridge northward for 40 miles up to the coast at the Wash is a flat country that in its primeval state was covered with water and marshes from which protruded a few islands of solid land. The Romans built canals and drained the area, but after their departure it reverted to its natural condition. The modern drainage system began in the seventeenth century when windmills were built for pumping the water off the land into channels. The land thus reclaimed has rich black soil and is ideal for agriculture and cattle raising. Its level has sunk considerably since it was drained, and the water is now pumped upward into embanked watercourses.

From times before Christianity the islands in the fens were sanctuaries for hermits, holy men, and outlaws. Ely, whose name means Island (some think it refers to the eels in the local waterways), is the greatest of them. It was once known as the Sacred Island of the English, a type of Avalon. Until a few years ago, when an unwelcome reform of local government abolished or remodeled many of the old counties, the Isle of Ely retained its own separate administration. In earlier times its bishops ruled it as virtual monarchs. Like many other cathedrals, Ely's was built over a holy well; the well is no longer visible, but the record of it is an indication of Ely's pre-Christian sanctity.

ELY CATHEDRAL

Under certain conditions Ely cathedral is the most hauntingly beautiful sight in England. The best views of it are from the east, the hill at Stuntney, a mile southeast of Ely, being the vantage point artists favor. From there at sunset, with mists rising about it from the fens, it can be seen in its original character as the towering citadel of a sacred island. Nowhere are landscape and architecture better combined.

The approach to the cathedral from the southeast is through steeply rising wooded meadows—a rare rustic setting for such a noble building. The little town around it still has the isolated feeling of an island in the fens. Some of it has been damaged in the interests of commerce and road building, but the medieval center north of the cathedral has some charming old streets and houses. To the south are substantial and picturesque remains of the former abbey buildings, mostly now occupied by a school. Opposite the west front, on Palace Green, is the grand old Bishop's Palace, and past it is an historic house where Oliver Cromwell once lived. The Puritanism he practiced still seems to linger at Ely. The manner of the town is plain and unpretentious, and so is the tone that prevails in the cathedral.

The Cathedral's Lady Founder
St. Etheldreda, who built the first church on the site of the cathedral in 673, was one of five daughters (all of them were canonized) of a local East Anglian king. She married in

The west tower and lantern of Ely cathedral from the meadows to the south.

Ely cathedral from across the river to the east.

succession two other kings; from the first she obtained the Isle of Ely as a dowry, and the second gave her lands in the north which she passed on to her spiritual mentor, St. Wilfrid (see page 244). To neither of her husbands, both of whom were much younger than herself, would she yield her virginity. When the second, Egfrid of Northumbria, grew insistent, she fled to Ely, a fastness inaccessible to all except those who knew the secret causeways through the fens.

St. Etheldreda's journey from the north was attended by many miracles. Once she was saved from her pursuing husband by the timely intervention of a flood, and on another occasion her staff blossomed into a tree. At Ely she was joined by St. Wilfrid, who helped her with the design of her church. Around it she built a nunnery and a college staffed by monks that became a famous center of education. St. Etheldreda and her entourage of chaste aristocratic ladies maintained a rule of high-minded austerity. Her death was caused by a swelling on the neck which, she said, was punishment for her vanity as a young girl in wearing a necklace. Some years after she was buried at Ely her coffin was reopened and her body was found uncorrupted. The wound on her neck, made by medical treatment of the swelling, had healed over.

The shrine of St. Etheldreda was Ely's great attraction to medieval pilgrims. Miraculous cures occurred there until 1541, when the Benedictine abbey at Ely was suppressed and relics were destroyed. The present King's School in the old abbey buildings was founded at that time by Henry VIII. One part of St. Etheldreda's body survived the Reformation. A reliquary containing her left hand was smuggled by an Ely monk to London and then hidden. It was found again in 1810 when a secret chamber for fugitive priests was discovered in a Surrey farmhouse. The small, withered hand is now preserved as a relic in St. Etheldreda's Roman Catholic Church on Egremont Street in Ely, where it may be seen on request.

Eight scenes from the life of St. Etheldreda are carved on top of the pillars in the Octagon in the center of the cathedral. Her local name was Audrey, and an annual St. Audrey's Fair used to be held on her feast day, October 29, near the cathedral. Colored ribbons and trinkets, sanctified by contact with the saint's shrine, were sold on those occasions, and thus from St. Audrey came the word "tawdry," applied to things cheap and flashy.

Ely's Camp of Refuge and the Anti-Norman Resistance

After William the Conqueror won the Battle of Hastings in 1066 he set about confiscating English lands and offices and granting them to his Norman lords. This was naturally opposed, and the Conqueror wreaked bloody vengeance on the north and other parts of the country that dared to rebel against his tyranny.

The sturdiest resistance he encountered was at Ely. It became the stronghold of Hereward the Wake, a Saxon warrior of whom little is known except that he had been made an outlaw at home and had spent several years adventuring on the Continent. His first recorded exploit, in 1069, was to sack the monastery at Peterborough in alliance with a party of Danes. He then repaired to Ely and made it the center of a campaign against the Normans. People of all ranks flocked to his standard, and Hereward became the symbol and last hope of the English resistance.

King William was so alarmed that he went to conduct the assault on Ely in person. The fens, however, were too much for him. It was impossible for an army to cross the watery wastes, and attempts at building a causeway were sabotaged by Hereward's guerrillas. The Conqueror had to retire, but the siege was finally ended in his favor. Hereward was betrayed by the monks of Ely, who showed the Normans the secret paths across the fens. The "Camp of Refuge" was overwhelmed, and the fate of Hereward is unknown. He is said to have escaped and, according to one account, to have entered a nearby house of religion.

The monks profited from their treachery, for they and their possessions were spared injury by the Normans, and it was several years before a Norman abbot was appointed over them.

The Tower and Lantern of Ely

Ely and St. Etheldreda's church were burnt by a Danish army in 870, but the raiders were apparently afraid to touch the saint's coffin, so the bodies of Etheldreda, her sister

Sexburga, and other saintly ladies went on attracting pilgrims. In 974 a new foundation at Ely was made by Benedictine monks. The first Norman abbot to be appointed after the defeat of Hereward's rebellion was Simeon, a cousin of the Conqueror. He was eighty-seven years old but immediately began an ambitious program of church building and lived to be one hundred. In 1109 Ely church became a cathedral.

From the time of Simeon to the end of the twelfth century the bulk of the present building was completed. Its great west tower, later crowned with a lantern, was flanked by pairs of magnificent Romanesque turrets. Those to the north of the tower fell down at some unknown date in the Middle Ages, giving the west front an unsymmetrical appearance. The porch in front of the tower was added early in the thirteenth century.

The height of the west tower is 230 feet, and one can pace out that same length by treading a marble labyrinth on the floor below it. This labyrinth is the work of Sir Gilbert Scott, who restored the cathedral in 1870. In making the length of its pathway equal to the height of the tower, Scott was following a practice of mystical masonry. Other cathedral labyrinths occur at Chartres and elsewhere in Europe; they have a wide range of symbolism and represent, among other things, the pilgrimage journey as a pathway to paradise.

The structure of the wooden framework of the lantern of Ely cathedral (right).

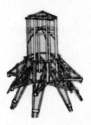

The octagonal lantern of Ely cathedral with its roof supported by eight massive oak beams.

Another great Norman tower originally stood over the crossing at the center of the cathedral. In 1322 it began tottering, and the monks dared not chant beneath it; eventually it fell with a mighty crash, demolishing the choir. In place of it the cathedral's master mason, Alan of Walsingham, executed one of the most amazing works of medieval architecture, the famous Ely lantern. As well as radiating light from the cathedral far across the fens, it creates a pool of light in the center of the building and lifts the hearts of all who behold it. Massive yet graceful, the lantern rises above a delicate structure of timber vaulting which seems far too slender to support it. The pattern of the work is octagonal. At its base are four tall, widely spaced arches with four walls set diagonally between them. The walls have arches below and tall windows above, and the more one gazes at this work the more wonderfully contrived it all appears. This nearly incredible feat of engineering—four hundred tons of timber and glass made to appear to be floating in space—betrays no sense of effort, almost as if it were a work of nature. The beauty of its proportions and detailing hide the stresses at work below the surface. Behind this structure is an initiate's knowledge of geometry as taught in the old masonic schools. By study and codification of the ratios of natural growth, and through their access to the ancient tradition of scientific proportion, the medieval masons were able to create harmonious works of structural audacity which, even with modern materials, could hardly be reproduced today.

To make the lantern as planned, it was necessary to find eight huge, straight trunks of oak, capable of forming beams sixty-three feet long and three feet square. The country was scoured for such timbers—today they would be sought in vain—and when they were found the work of transporting them to Ely was enormous. Roads had to be made and bridges strengthened. Cased in lead, the eight oak beams do not feature visibly in the structure; the part they play in the scheme and other details of the carpentry can be seen in the model displayed in the cathedral.

The Cathedral Interior
From the western entrance under the tower one can see down the full length of the cathedral, 517 feet. The long Norman nave with twelve bays once had painted walls and colored carvings. Now the only color is on the wooden ceiling, admirably painted by two local gentlemen in the nineteenth century. The light from the roof ahead draws one on to stand in the octagon beneath the central lantern, where the harmony and nobility of the whole building can best be appreciated. On the hammerbeam roofs of the transepts are carved and painted angels. To the east are the glorious fourteenth-century carved stalls, canopies, and misericords of the choir. High up on the south side of the choir, visible through the central arch, are two little imps sitting one above the other. They are typical of the curious faces and

forms which appear unexpectedly in odd corners of the cathedral.

At the eastern ends of the aisles are two highly elaborate chapels. The one to the north commemorates Bishop Alcock and was built in 1488. Its intricate web of sculpted stone was mutilated at the Reformation, when all the figures in it were smashed by Puritans. The same thing happened to Bishop West's chapel to the south. It was begun in 1534 and was still incomplete six years later when the iconoclasts broke down its sacred images. In the Lady Chapel, approached from the north transept, their work of destruction was even more thorough. It is a large hall with fine windows east and west, and its walls are covered all round with a most ingenious design of fourteenth-century stone carving, formerly colored. All but one of the statues enshrined in it have been smashed off or decapitated by hammers. Certain images with no Catholic significance were spared: Near the center of the south side can be seen the face of a "green man" with foliage growing out of his mouth. Another is figured on one of the carved roof bosses, and there is one in a strip of medieval wood carving over Steeple Gate on the north side of the close. Apparently the green man symbol represented the vital spirit of nature, which dies with the waning year and is reborn every spring. Its popular name in old England was John Barleycorn, a rustic god who was identified with the last sheaf of grain to be reaped at harvest time and in that form was ritually sacrificed.

The cloth on the high altar is worked with three crowns in memory of the first three royal abbesses: Etheldreda, queen of Northumbria, her sister Sexburga, queen of Kent, and her niece Ermenilda, queen of Mercia. A plaque on the floor marks the former site of St. Etheldreda's shrine, probably on the spot where she founded her church. A relic of her day is a Saxon cross, taken from a local village and placed on the south side of the nave, which is inscribed as a memorial to Ovin, Etheldreda's faithful steward, who looked after her Ely estates while she was in the north.

Near the southwest corner, entered by a round Norman arch, is a chapel to St. Catherine, now set aside for rest and prayer. Opposite it, at the west of the north aisle, bodily needs are catered to by a restaurant. In front of it is a bookstall that offers recordings of the famous Ely choir. One may be lucky enough on a visit to hear them sing; the experience helps one to understand why such a vast church was built on this isolated spot in such a thinly populated region. Not only did the sight of its towers and the sound of its bells sanctify the country for miles around, but in quieter days than now the chanting of its monks, amplified by the acoustics of the building, was audible far beyond it. There is a story that King Canute early in the eleventh century was charmed by the singing of the Ely monks, which he heard as he was being rowed toward the island in his royal barge. The almost perpetual chant that issued from the cathedral had the effect of a spell, instilling peace and order into the minds of all who lived or passed nearby. With the aid of recordings, the singing of the Ely choir has a similar and even wider influence today.

ELY is 70 miles north of London on the A10 road from Cambridge. There are trains from London through Cambridge, also from East Anglia and other parts of England.

The cathedral is open daily, 7:30 to 7 in summer, 7:30 to 6:30 in winter; Sunday, 7:30 to 5. Admission £1.70. (This is the only cathedral that levies an entrance charge for the entire building.)

In the Cathedral off the north transept is a stained glass museum which is open March 1 through October, daily, 11 to 4, Sunday, noon to 3. Admission 70p.

The Ely Museum in Sacrist's Gate, High Street, is open Saturday and Sunday (and Thursday during the summer), 2:15 to 5. Admission 20p.

The Tourist Information Centre is in the library on the north side of Palace Green opposite the cathedral. Telephone: Ely (0353) 2062.

PETERBOROUGH

A Flat-earth Experiment on the Fens

The train from Ely to Peterborough, 28 miles to the northeast, crosses the lonely plains of Fenland and goes over a waterway called the Old Bedford Level at a point where it runs dead straight for 6 miles. This stretch of water was the scene of a strange nineteenth-century experiment. It was conducted to settle a bet between Alfred Russel Wallace, Darwin's collaborator in stating the theory of evolution, who held the scientific view that the earth is round, and some die-hard members of the Flat Earth Society. Their objection to the earth as a globe was based on the Bible, but they were prepared to test the matter scientifically. The two parties met at a bridge on the Old Bedford Level and peered through a telescope along the waterline to another bridge 6 miles away. The question was whether they could see an object suspended from the far bridge near the water, as the flat-earthers thought they should, or whether it was hidden by the curvature of the earth. In the event there was disagreement as to what they saw, and the dispute ended in the law courts, where a wary judge avoided having to rule on whether the earth was round or flat and rejected the bet as invalid.

PETERBOROUGH CATHEDRAL

There is no legend to explain why Peterborough on the western edge of the fens should have been such an important early sanctuary. Its low-lying site has none of the natural qualities of Ely, but it has always been convenient for travelers, being on the road from London to the north and also on an old pilgrimage path to the shrine at Walsingham, 50 miles east. Roads and railways converge upon it today. The modern industrial town has few attractions for tourists, apart from the venerable cathedral. Its famous west front, built early in the thirteenth century, is one of the most stately works of architecture in England, and the old-fashioned cathedral close, entered through a medieval gateway, retains the atmosphere of days before railways when Peterborough was a sleepy provincial city.

The church at Medehamstede, the old name for Peterborough, was founded in about 660 by King Peada of Mercia, a converted pagan. A Celtic monastery was established there by monks from Lindisfarne and became a successful missionary center. The Danes who sacked Ely in 870 did the same at Medehamstede, but the rebuilt church was spared in 1069 when other Danes, in company with Hereward the Wake, raided the monastery.

In about ninety years from 1118, when the foundation stone was laid, the present Norman building was completed. The east end was extended at the end of the fifteenth century, but otherwise the history of the place has been one of gradual decay only recently arrested. The fabric of the building has never recovered from the treatment it received under the Commonwealth, when Cromwell's soldiers systematically smashed and burned the furniture, monuments, and carvings of its interior. In earlier times it was a treasure house of religious and historical relics.

The Peterborough monks in the Middle Ages were notorious for their dishonesty in the matter of relics and the ruthless way in which they acquired them. Their most valuable possession was the uncorrupted right arm of St. Oswald, which they stole from Bamburgh (page 241). They

The west front of Peterborough cathedral.

also preserved some of his ribs and a box of the miracle-working soil on which he was killed. A list of the relics at Peterborough, compiled in the twelfth century, makes fantastic reading. It includes pieces of the infant Jesus's swaddling clothes, of the manger where he was born, of his cross, of the five loaves with which he fed the multitude, of the Virgin Mary's cloak, of Aaron's rod, and of Lazarus's sepulcher. Among the relics of more than seventy saints were bones of Peter, Paul, Andrew, Bartholomew, Philip, and James. There was a shoulder blade from one of the Holy Innocents, a piece of the hair shirt of St. Wenceslas, a hand from St. Magnus the Martyr, an arm of St. George the Martyr, three finger joints of St. Adelard, two fragments of St. Cicily, the blood, bones, and clothes of St. Eutrophia, the hair of St. Athelwold, a tooth of St. Sexburga, an arm of St. Sebastian, and St. George's head. With such interesting objects on display, it is not surprising that medieval Peterborough attracted flocks of pilgrims.

In St. Oswald's Chapel to the east of the south transept are steps to the gallery where monks used to keep constant vigil over the saint's precious arm. A crypt below has masonry from the Saxon church.

The Shrine of Catherine of Aragon

High up on the west wall inside the cathedral is a large portrait of an elderly rustic with a spade. This is Robert Scarlett, who was born in 1496 and served through almost the entire sixteenth century as the cathedral gravedigger until his death at the age of ninety-eight. He buried several generations of Peterborough citizens and had the distinction of making graves in the cathedral for two queens. The second royal burial, which took place in the south choir aisle in 1587, was that of the unfortunate Mary Queen of Scots, a great-niece of Henry VIII and mother of James I, who later caused her body to be removed to Westminster Abbey. Opposite, in the north choir aisle, is the tomb of Henry VIII's first wife, Catherine of Aragon, who died in 1536. In the course of her tragic life she was made use of to bring about the Protestant Reformation.

Robert Scarlett, the gravedigger who buried two queens.

Catherine's tomb, like everything else within the cathedral, was wrecked by Cromwell's soldiers in 1643. In its place is now a plain marble slab, put there late in the nineteenth century and paid for by a public appeal to all women with the name Catherine. In front of it is an exhibition on the life of Queen Catherine.

Catherine was born in 1485, the daughter of Ferdinand and Isabella of Spain, who had united their two kingdoms and won great victories over the Moors. In the year she was born Henry VII fought his way to the throne of England, and when in the following year his eldest son Arthur was born, he immediately began negotiating with the Spanish court to secure Catherine as his daughter-in-law. At the age of fifteen she was brought to England and married to Prince Arthur. He died within a few months, and the king then married her to his second son, the future Henry VIII.

Catherine's misfortune was to fail in her duty of providing a male heir. Her only surviving offspring was a daughter, Mary, who later came to the throne and instituted a brief Catholic revival. Henry VIII grew tired of his wife and took up with other women. The queen found herself in a position of great embarrassment and danger. She refused to agree to a legal separation from her husband, and the pope, to whom Henry applied for a license to divorce her, was unable to oblige because he was in the power of her parents. Henry then broke with Rome, established the Church of England, and contracted a bigamous marriage with Anne Boleyn. Catherine was banished from court to a succession of dreary

The Norman nave of Peterborough cathedral.

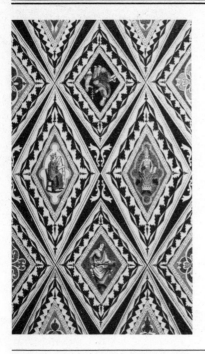

*Part of the painted
ceiling in the nave of
Peterborough
cathedral.*

country houses where her health declined; it was thought at
the time that she was being poisoned by the king's agents.
Her last letter to her husband, exhibited opposite her tomb,
shows great dignity and love and contains the words, "I vow
that mine eyes desire you above all things." It was said that
even the black-hearted Henry wept when he read it.

Catherine died in 1536 and was laid in her tomb at
Peterborough. Later it was claimed that miracles occurred
there. In a belated act of homage, Henry VIII gave the
church where she was buried the dignity of a cathedral and
appointed the first Bishop of Peterborough.

Because of Queen Catherine's tomb, St. Peter's Cathedral
was spared damage after the Reformation, but the assault
upon it in Cromwellian times so weakened its structure that
the authorities had to pull down the lovely Lady Chapel and
sell off its materials in order to pay for the restoration. For
many years the cathedral was almost a ruin, used for
workshops and other secular purposes. Over the last hundred years it has gradually been brought into repair. Still
intact are the wonderfully painted thirteenth-century
wooden ceiling to the nave and the fan-vaulted ceiling east of
the altar. The heavy Norman nave with its rounded arches
has the look of an ancient Roman building.

PETERBOROUGH is 90 miles north of London on the main line railway;
journey time from King's Cross, London, one hour. It is near the A1 road
from London to the North.

The cathedral is open daily, 7:30 to 6:30.

The Tourist Information Centre is in the Town Hall. Telephone: Peterborough (0733) 317336.

ISLAND SANCTUARIES OF FENLAND

The Angels of March

The old churches of Fenland have much to reward those with the time to explore them, and the little islands on which they stand are sanctified by legends of early English saints. March, formerly an island 6 miles long and a mile wide, midway between Ely and Peterborough, has a small town and a truly wonderful church. Up to the Reformation it was the shrine of the most beloved of Fenland saints, Wendreda, and the church is a tribute to her memory.

Wendreda was a childhood friend, perhaps a relative, of St. Etheldreda and her sisters; her father, King Anna, lived at Exening on the outskirts of Newmarket, 25 miles southeast of March. At Exening is a holy well consisting of three springs in a wood, now neglected and hard to find. It is dedicated to St. Wendreda, who was baptized there and later became its resident sibyl. She was adored by the local people and was much visited because of her healing powers and knowledge of herbal remedies. When King Anna was killed in battle by pagans, she moved to March and continued her mission. With other religious women she built a church, the first to be planted in that wild region. On her death she was enshrined therein. Some years later her bones were transferred to Ely.

Early in the eleventh century a Danish army invaded England, and the Saxons marched against them with the coffin of St. Wendreda, hoping it would bring them victory. Wendreda was not, however, a warlike saint. The Saxons were routed, but the coffin was the cause of a miracle more fruitful than victory in battle. The Danish leader, King Canute, had it brought to him, and when he heard the saint's legend he was so impressed that he became a convert to Christianity. He ordered St. Wendreda's body to be enshrined in Canterbury cathedral, where it rested for three centuries.

In the middle of the fourteenth century the remains of St. Wendreda were restored to March whence they had been taken six hundred years earlier. The old church was rebuilt in her honor, and over the years it was made increasingly glorious. Its lofty steeple is visible far over the fens. In about 1475 the most beautiful church roof of its kind to be found in England was raised over the shrine. It is a double hammerbeam, a masterpiece of craftsmanship, decked with flights of angels. Their wings are spread, and they are blowing trumpets or playing other musical instruments. Together with saints and martyrs, the number of figures in the roof is 136. Through this work can be felt the emotion which inspired it, not merely of piety but of intense love and reverence for the lady saint of March.

The Devils of Crowland

Toward the end of the sixth century one of the boatmen who plied the fens landed a solitary passenger on a desolate island 8 miles north of Medehamstede (now Peterborough). Secluded from the world, the man built a cell and began the life of a hermit. During the nineteenth century the hermitage of St. Guthlag was rediscovered at the western end of Crowland's ruined abbey church.

The legend of St. Guthlag says that he was a warrior and an expert swordsman. After a riotous youth he withdrew to a monastery, but because the communal life did not suit him he moved on to the island of Crowland. He found the island haunted by vicious demons who tormented him and dragged him through briars. To fight them off he made a whip, which became his symbol. When he died in 714, his friend King Ethelbald, who as Guthlag had prophesied had succeeded to the throne of Mercia, founded a Benedictine abbey at Crowland over his place of burial. During their incursion of 870 the Danes tortured the monks to make them give up the fabulous church treasures, but they had been hidden out of reach elsewhere, and so the brethren were slaughtered and their church burned.

By Norman times Crowland was again prosperous, and in 1076 it acquired a further asset in the body of Earl Waltheof, saint and martyr. He was an ally of Hereward the Wake who, according to one legend, was buried at Crowland with his Flemish wife. William the Conqueror evidently considered Waltheof the most dangerous of his enemies, for he was the only Saxon rebel whom he condemned to execution. This took place at Winchester, after which the body was taken to Crowland. The head was later placed with it in the coffin, and sixteen years later it was found that the two parts had joined together again, the only sign of their former separation being a thin red line around the neck. The sainted earl became known as the Healer because of the many cures which took place at his tomb. One of his descendants is Queen Elizabeth II.

Through an accidental fire in 1109 the church was destroyed; shortly afterward it was rebuilt on a grander scale. A relic of its former glory is the west front with its tiers of sculptured figures representing St. Guthlag with his whip (second tier, third figure from the left) and other saints. They date from the thirteenth century, when the original front was blown down by a storm. The tower to the northwest was built in the fifteenth century. Over the door to the nave are carvings of the legend of St. Guthlag.

After the Reformation the people of Crowland bought the north aisle of the building to use as a parish church, which it still is today. It contains some interesting monuments and

Crowland Abbey.

a curiosity: ninety-foot-long bell ropes that are said to be the longest in the world. Attached to them are Crowland's famous old bells; one of them, named Guthlag, had a reputation for curing headaches.

Most of the ruin which has overtaken the rest of the church was caused during the Civil War, when it was fortified by the Royalists and battered by the Roundhead artillery.

An antiquarian relic in the town is the thirteenth-century triangular bridge with a figure of Christ holding a global image of the world. It was formerly on the front of the church. When the bridge was built the streets of the town were waterways, two of which met there. They have long since vanished, and the bridge now passes over dry land.

CROWLAND is off the A1037 road between Spalding and Peterborough, from which there are buses.

Thorney Island

Thorney is the same name as the island on which Westminster Abbey was built. Some see in it a reference to the Norse god Thor, but the usual explanation is that the island was covered by thorn bushes.

Thorney today is a lovely village on the A47 road 5 miles east of Peterborough, not far from its medieval monastic rival, Crowland. The history of the two places is similar: a Christian foundation in the seventh century, destruction by the Danes, the Saxon church replaced by a huge Norman building with a Benedictine monastery in the eleventh century, and dissolution in 1539. Part of the church, as at Crowland, is used as the parish church today.

Three members of the Celtic church at Peterborough decided soon after its foundation that they would leave it for somewhere more solitary. They were two brothers, Tancred and Tortred, and their sister Tona—all three recognized as saints. They crossed the fens to little Thorney Island, and later they were joined there by other hermits. From their foundation grew the large, opulent abbey of medieval times. All that remains of it today are a few odd stones and part of the nave of the old church.

Thorney must always have been a lovely spot. The monks drained the marshes and grew crops among vineyards and orchards. The local population expanded and prospered through their skills in husbandry. Thorney was also a renowned center of scholarship; William of Malmesbury in the twelfth century described it as "a hostel of chastity, a tavern of honesty, a gymnasium of divine philosophy." It was, he said, a veritable paradise.

An eighteenth-century Duke of Bedford carried on the agricultural tradition of Thorney. His estate there was well managed and productive; the delightful cottages he built for his laborers are to be seen along the main road. Houses in the village, dating from the sixteenth and seventeenth centuries, stand peacefully among tall trees and greenery. In the center is the old church. Its low roof is supported by huge Norman pillars, once free-standing and now joined by the walls of the diminished church. The west front, viewed from the road, is the best of what remains. On it is a gallery of nine statues representing Thorney saints. One of them, the third from the right, is a portrait of Tatwin, the boatman who rowed St. Guthlag to Crowland and later followed him as a hermit.

A strange tradition that was observed on Thorney Island into monastic times prohibited women from approaching within 9 miles of it except as daytime pilgrims. This was surely a survival from prehistoric times, when Thorney was a tribal center of male initiation rites.

WALSINGHAM

A Vision of the Virgin Mary

Little Walsingham is a charming small town near the north coast of Norfolk, 46 miles northeast of Ely. The countryside around it is beautiful parkland with low, wooded hills. Visitors may observe that as they approach the district the light over the landscape takes on the dreamy quality which is associated with places of particular sanctity. Such a place is Walsingham. Throughout the Middle Ages it was one of Europe's most popular shrines of the Virgin Mary, and it is now the most powerful of the active pilgrimage centers in England.

The fame of Walsingham began with a vision in 1061. A local lady, Richeldis de Faverches, was visited by the Virgin Mary, who transported her to Nazareth, where she beheld the Holy House in which Joseph, Mary, and the infant Jesus had lived. She was instructed to note the appearance and dimensions of the building and to make an exact replica of it at Walsingham. The vision was repeated three times.

Richeldis drew up plans and assembled craftsmen, but she could not decide where the building should be placed. One night there fell a heavy dew, and in the morning two rectangular dry patches, about one hundred feet apart, were noticed in a meadow. This was taken as a sign from heaven; the patch which lay beside two holy wells was selected as the appropriate site. However, the size of the dry patch did not match the dimensions of the house, and the following morning it was found that the building materials had been moved miraculously to the other patch and fashioned into the shape of the Holy House. It was later enclosed within a stone church; in it was placed a statue of the Virgin and Child that became the source of many miracles.

Walsingham's Milky Way

From the eleventh century to the sixteenth century the remote, rustic shrine at Walsingham was rivaled only by Canterbury as England's leading place of pilgrimage. Augustinian canons built their priory church on the south side of the Holy House and Franciscan friars established themselves nearby. At Little Walsingham (considerably larger than Great Walsingham adjoining it) inns and hostelries sprang up to accommodate the pilgrims.

Roads led to Walsingham from all directions, and along them were shrines, chapels, and lodging houses. An inter-

The center of Walsingham and the town pump.

esting survival is the Red Mount Chapel 27 miles southwest of Walsingham at King's Lynn, where the pilgrim paths converged. Built in about 1485, it is octagonal and stands on a mound. A mile before their journey's end the pilgrims would leave their shoes in the Slipper Chapel at Houghton St. Giles, which is now a Roman Catholic church, and proceed barefoot.

One of Walsingham's holy relics was a finger of St. Peter. It was kept in the Chapel of St. Lawrence, which was built on the dry patch of ground first chosen as the site of the Holy House. Of far greater importance was a vial containing the Virgin Mary's milk. This wonderful liquid came from the grotto where Mary had nursed Jesus, and some said that it was not actually her milk but a mixture of clay from the floor where she had sat. It caught the public imagination, and the route from London to Walsingham became known as the Milky Way. As pilgrims passed along it, stopping at the holy places, their journey took on the nature of a trip to paradise. By the will of the Virgin Mary herself Nazareth had been established at Walsingham, which had thus become an image of the Holy Land. Because of Walsingham the land of England became known throughout Christendom as Mary's Dowry.

The last but one of the many kings who made pilgrimages to Walsingham was Henry VII. On his final visit, in 1505, he took with him the teenage son who later succeeded him as Henry VIII. The young Henry was pious and made more than one pilgrimage to Walsingham. After his marriage to Catherine of Aragon he walked there barefoot to pray for the health of their son. The boy died, and Henry VIII turned against the old religion. When it became known in 1537 that the Walsingham shrine was about to be dissolved, monks and local people banded together to form a resistance movement. Several of their leaders were executed, and the following year the monks were driven from Walsingham and the image of the Virgin in the shrine was taken to London to be burned.

The Modern Revival

After the shrine was destroyed in 1538, Walsingham's religious houses fell into ruin and its inns closed for lack of custom. All that remained was the oldest feature of the site, the pair of holy wells near the patch where the shrine was originally to have been built. Thousands of pilgrims, including Henry VIII, had knelt on the stone between them to invoke the healing spirit of their waters, which was good for headaches and stomach troubles. After the Reformation they became known as wishing wells; the procedure was to dip each hand in one of the wells and make a wish while drinking some of the water.

At the end of the nineteenth century pilgrimages to Walsingham began anew, and in 1921 a new vicar, the Reverend A. D. Hope Patter, placed in the parish church a

A solitary arch remains of Walsingham Abbey. Behind it are the twin holy wells.

new image of the Walsingham Virgin copied from a picture of the original on a monastic seal. Ten years later a new shrine was built. The choice of its site was seemingly inspired, for as workmen were preparing the foundations an ancient holy well was discovered, fed by the same spring as the other two. Modern pilgrims to Walsingham are blessed with water from this well. The shrine which houses it also contains the image of the Virgin, transferred from the church, and many other statues and religious offerings. An atmosphere of peace and intense devotion has accumulated there.

During the pilgrimage season, from Easter through September, more than 100,000 people annually visit the shrine of Our Lady of Walsingham. Once more the town is full of houses belonging to a variety of religious orders. There are a Greek Orthodox church, Roman Catholic and Anglican parish churches, and a Methodist chapel. The Church of England runs a hospice for pilgrims by the modern shrine of Our Lady. The Roman Catholic National Shrine of Our Lady is in the Slipper Chapel at the end of the Holy Mile.

A DIGRESSION TO NORWICH

Pilgrims to Walsingham may well pass through Norwich, where there are more medieval churches than in any other city in England. Beside one of them—St. Julian on King Street—is the restored cell of Mother Julian, whose saintly life ended in 1413. Her inspired, contemplative work, *Divine Love*, has made her one of the most beloved of Christian mystics. Other Norwich monuments include the birthplace of the famous Quaker philanthropist, Elizabeth Fry, on Magdalen Street, and the tomb of the First World War heroine, nurse Edith Cavell, in the cathedral.

Old Norwich, with its fine, tall-spired, Norman-Gothic
cathedral, is a lovely place to visit, but unfortunately it is one
of the many worthy places which, for lack of space, cannot
fully be described in this book. It was known in the Middle
Ages as a city of anchorites; later it was the center of the
famous Norwich school of landscape painters, Cotman and
Crome among them. Today in its old alleys and in the rural
countryside surrounding it one can experience the clear,
tranquil atmosphere which attracts saints and artists.

WALSINGHAM in north Norfolk is 27 miles from both nearest railway stations,
at Norwich and King's Lynn. Both places offer bus service to Fakenham, 5
miles from Walsingham, and a local bus from Fakenham completes the
journey.

The road from King's Lynn is the A148 to the outskirts of Fakenham,
where the B1105 is signposted to Walsingham. From Norwich the A1067
goes through Fakenham to the junction with the B1105.

A Pilgrim Taxi Service is on call day and night. Telephone: Walsingham
(032872) 483.

Information on pilgrimages, retreats, and accommodation from the Man-
ager, Pilgrim Bureau, Friday Market, Little Walsingham, NR22 6EG
(Roman Catholic); the Administrator, The College, Walsingham, Norfolk
(Anglican).

A Tourist Information Office with a small museum is on the Common
Place, Little Walsingham.

EAST DEREHAM: *The Theft of a Saint's Relics*

East Dereham, 18 miles west north west of Norwich, is a
small, pleasant market town. It would have been a place of
great importance, so its citizens claim, had it not been for a
disastrous loss which it suffered in the year 974, when it was
raided by the abbot of Ely. He and his men stole Dereham's
most valuable possession and the source of its prosperity at
the time, the body of St. Withburga. Deprived thereby of its
pilgrimage trade, Dereham was left in rural isolation, nursing
a grudge against the people of Ely which is maintained to the
present day.

There remains, however, St. Withburga's healing holy
well, on the site of Withburga's original grave. It is one of the
most attractive of the minor shrines in East Anglia. She was
the youngest of King Anna's five sainted children, of whom
St. Ethelburga of Ely is the most famous. Like many other
noble Saxon ladies of her time she grew weary of mundane
society, and withdrew with her chosen companions to found
a convent at East Dereham. There she was buried in 654,
and her body lay in the graveyard until after 870, when the
church at Dereham was burnt by the Danes. The new
church was designed to enshrine the relics of its founder,
and St. Withburga's grave was opened. Two miracles then
occurred. The body was found to be uncorrupt and a spring
of clear water welled up. A well chapel was built over it,

cures were reported there and at the saint's shrine, and visitors came in droves.

Great Ely grew jealous of little Dereham's success as a center of pilgrimage, and the abbot and his monks devised a plot to seize the remains of St. Withburga and place them with those of her sisters in Ely cathedral. It was an occasional right of the abbot to hold court at East Dereham, and this he exercised, taking with him a large party of monks and armed servants. They were entertained and feasted by the Dereham ecclesiastics, and when their hosts were asleep they entered the church, removed the saint's coffin from its shrine and hastened through the night to the river at Brandon, twenty miles away, where they had moored a barge. The Dereham people soon awoke to their loss and gave chase, but they were too late to prevent the robbers from getting to their boat and navigating down the center of the river towards Ely. They were followed almost to the outskirts of the city by the men of Dereham, who were running along the bank and hurling abuse and clods of earth.

The raiders were acclaimed at Ely as triumphant heroes, but Dereham has never given up, and at the time of writing (1987) an action is proceeding in the ecclesiastical courts to compel the Eliens (people of Ely) to make restitution for their crime of a thousand years ago.

The Healing Well

The most lasting monument to St. Withburga, which no one can steal from Dereham, is the holy well on the site of her tomb. Up to the Reformation it continued to be known as a source of healing, and its reputation was revived in the eighteenth century when a bathhouse was built beside it for the relief of invalids. This no longer exists, but the well, surrounded by the ruined walls of its chapel, is carefully tended and its waters are as clear, cool and full of virtue as ever. Over it is a notice sternly informing visitors about the theft of the saint's body by the abbot and monks of Ely. Every year on July 8, the anniversary of the theft, a service is held beside the well.

St. Withburga's well is in the graveyard outside the west end of East Dereham's lovely church of St. Nicholas where her shrine should properly be located. Visitors are likely to be impressed by the natural sanctity of the spot, and one can speculate about the antiquity of its reputation as a place of healing. It may have been that reputation which caused the saint and her nuns to settle at Dereham, near a spring whose waters were locally respected and could be used for baptisms and the making of potions.

BURY ST. EDMUNDS

This Suffolk market town on the River Lark gained its name and fame as the burial place in 903 of the East Anglian king

Ruins of the abbey church, Bury St. Edmunds.

St. Edmund the Martyr. His body lay in a jeweled shrine within an abbey church which from the eleventh century was one of the largest in England. It was a place of royal and popular pilgrimage until 1539, when Henry VIII expelled the monks from the abbey, confiscated their wealthy estates, and carted off their valuables, including St. Edmund's shrine. The abbot was pensioned off but died soon after of grief. The abbey fell into ruin and its stones were taken away for other buildings.

Little remains of Bury's once glorious abbey, but it is still a delightful place to visit. The houses of the town have Georgian and Victorian fronts concealing structures which in some cases date from Norman times. There is a charming Regency theater and a large church has been a cathedral since 1914. On the central square, Angel Hill, is the Angel Hotel, made famous by Dickens for being patronized by Samuel Pickwick. A more humble place of refreshment is The Nutshell, the smallest pub in England.

Opposite the Angel a grand fifteenth-century stone gate-house gives entry to the abbey ruins. A pleasant park going down to the River Lark and the old abbey bridge contains the foundations of the abbey, part of its west wall into which picturesque cottages have been built, and a tall Norman gatehouse.

The History and Legend of St. Edmund
In churches and cathedrals throughout England a certain image occurs repeatedly among the carvings: a wolf holding the head of a man or guarding it between its paws. This is a reference to the legend of St. Edmund.

Edmund was crowned king of East Anglia in the church at Beodricesworth, as Bury was then called, in 856. He became loved as an exemplary ruler, but the peace of his kingdom was broken by the bloodthirsty Danes, and Edmund led his Saxon army against their hordes. At the Battle of Thetford in

The Martyrdom of St. Edmund, a carving in Ely cathedral.
Edmund is tied to a tree and shot with arrows by Danes; on the
left is his severed head, on the right the wolf that guarded it.

869 the Saxons were routed, and Edmund took refuge at
Hoxne (pronounced "Hoxen"), 25 miles east of Bury. At that
time Hoxne was an important place with a cathedral; today
it is a pretty village with a street leading from the church on
a rise, through the village green to a bridge over the
Goldbrook. Beneath that bridge, it is said, Edmund hid from
his Danish pursuers, but a wedding party that was passing
saw sunlight glinting on the king's spurs and betrayed him.
It has since been a tradition that wedding parties never cross
that bridge on the way to Hoxne church.

The Danes bound Edmund to a tree and shot him dead
with arrows. Until 1848 this tree survived, known as St.
Edmund's Oak. When it fell, an arrow was found deep inside
it. Some of the tree and other relics of St. Edmund's time are
exhibited in Hoxne church. The former site of the tree, in a

Greensted's Saxon church, where the body of
St. Edmund rested.

field to the left of the road four hundred yards past the Goldbrook bridge, is marked by a concrete pillar.

The martyr's head was severed from his body, and those who came to bury him could not find it. They were directed by a voice calling, "Here, here!" It came from a wood, and there they found a wolf guarding St. Edmund's head. It willingly yielded up the head and later followed the funeral to the king's grave at Hoxne. Some years later the head and body were dug up and enshrined at Bury.

St. Edmund at Greensted

In 1010, when Scandinavian marauders were again on the warpath, the relics of St. Edmund were carried to London for safety. Three years later the danger had passed and St. Edmund returned once more to his abbey. The slow, ceremonial journey took several days, and at night the chest containing the relics was lodged in some holy place. One place where it rested survives today as one of the most remarkable buildings in England, Greensted church.

Greensted is just beyond the northern outskirts of London, one mile northwest of Ongar in Essex. The nave of the church is made of huge, upright oak logs. It is the only wooden Saxon church and the oldest wooden church in the world. It has been scientifically dated to 845, so it was already more than 160 years old when St. Edmund's relics found shelter in it. In the sixteenth century its thatched roof was replaced by tiles and the brick chancel was added.

The present location of St. Edmund's body is unknown. His shrine at Bury was so encrusted with gold plates and jeweled crosses in 1539 that the iconoclasts found it "very cumbrous to deface." Some said that the body had been smuggled away to France, but it is believed at Bury that the saint is still buried within the grounds of his abbey.

BURY ST. EDMUNDS is 60 miles northeast of London and 26 miles east of Cambridge. There are trains from London's Liverpool Street Station (journey time about two hours, fifteen minutes).

The abbey ruins are open free during daylight hours. Further details from the Tourist Information Centre. Telephone: Bury St. Edmunds (0284) 64667.

FURTHER
READING
AND
INDEX

FURTHER READING

In addition to the many useful supplementary guidebooks available at each sacred site, the following, more general works are particularly helpful.

Anderson, William. *Holy Places of the British Isles*, London: Ebury Press, 1983.

Ashe, Geoffrey, *A Guidebook to Arthurian Britain*. London: Longmans, 1980.

Bames, Michael. *The Avebury Cycle*. London: Thames and Hudson, 1977.

Bames, Michael. *The Silbury Treasure*. London: Thames and Hudson, 1976.

Berresford Ellis, Peter. *Celtic Inheritance*. London: Frederick Muller, 1985; Boston: Salem House, 1986.

Bevis, Trevor. *Fenland Saints, Shrines and Churches*. March, Cambs.: T. Bevis, 1986.

Blythe, Ronald. *Divine Landscapes*. London: Viking, 1986; New York: Harcourt Brace Jovanovich: 1986.

Bonney, T. G. (ed.) *Cathedrals and Abbeys of England and Wales*. London: Cassell, 1981.

Bord, Janet and Colin. *Sacred Waters: Holy Wells and Water Lore in Britain and Ireland*. London: Granada, 1985.

Boulter, B. C. *The Pilgrim Shrines of England*. London: Philip Allan, 1928.

Brennan, Martin. *The Stars and the Stones*. London, New York: Thames and Hudson, 1984.

Bryant, Arthur. *The Story of England*. London: Collins, 1961.

Butler, Albal. *Lives of the Saints*. London: Burns, Oates and Washbourne, 1938.

Chippindale, Christopher. *Stonehenge Complete: Archaeology, History, Heritage*. London: Thames and Hudson, 1983; Ithaca: Cornell University Press, 1983.

Crossley, F. H. *The English Abbey*. London: Batsford, 1935.

Devereux, Paul, and Thompson, Ian. *The Ley Hunter's Companion*. London: Thames and Hudson, 1979.

Gordon, E. O. *Prehistoric London: Its Mounds and Circles*. London: Covenant Publishing, 1905.

Graves, Tom. *Needles of Stone*. London: Granada, 1983; Chicago: Academy Chicago, 1984.

Hole, Christina. *English Shrines and Sanctuaries*. London: Batsford, 1974.

Jameson, Anna. *Sacred and Legendary Art*. London: Longmans, 1883; Michigan: Scholarly Press, 1972.

Meyrick, J. *A Pilgrim's Guide to the Holy Wells of Cornwall*. Falmouth: J. Meyrick, 1982.

Murray, John. *Handbook to the Cathedrals of England*. London: John Murray, 1861.

Thom, Alexander. *Megalithic Lunar Observatories*. London and New York: Oxford University Press, 1971.

Thom, Alexander. *Megalithic Sites in Britain*. London and New York: Oxford University Press, 1967.

Wall, J. C. *Shrines of British Saints*. London: Methuen, 1905.

INDEX

Abbotsbury, 116, 120–2, *illus*. 121
Adams, John Q., 5
Aelred, St., 268
Aidan, St., 236–7, 241–2, 274
Aislabie, John, 263–4, 274
A la Ronde, 164–6, *illus*. 164
Alban, St., 13, 53–5, *illus*. 55
Aldhelm, St., 125, 129
Alfred, King, 68, 76, 112, 125
Alphege, St., 85, 205
Anna, King, 301, 309
Apollo temples, 9, 19, 154
Aram, Eugene, 280
Arthur, King, 5, 16, 50, 74–5, 125,
    131–2, 140–3, 172, 184, 208
  in northern England, 231–5
  his round tables, 74–5, 233,
    illus. 74
Arthur, Prince, 74, 207–9, 299,
    illus. 208
artists' tombs, 29
Arundell family, 187
astronomical orientation, 7,
    100–1, 105, 176, 224–7
Athelstan, King, 115, 116, 160,
    172, 190, 274
Atkinson, Richard J. C., 93, 99
Atlantis, 8, 102
Aubrey, John, 91, 96
Audrey, St., 292
Augustine, St., 15, 83–4, 87–8,
    124, 154, 231
Austen, Jane, 70
Avalon, 129, 132, 134
Avebury, 89–96, 138, *illus*. 90,
    91, 92
  church, 95
  museum, 90, 95

Bacon, Sir Francis, 56
Bamburgh, 237, 240, 241–3, 297

Baring-Gould, Sabine, 183
Barnes, William, 168
Bath, 152–9, *illus*. 153, 155
  Abbey, 155–7, *illus*. 156
Beaker folk, 10
Becket, St. Thomas à, 80–2,
    85–7, 161, *illus*. 81, 82
Bede, Venerable, 88, 251
Belas Knap barrow, 201–2, *illus*.
    201
Belinus, King, 18
Bernard, St., 262, 266
Betjeman, Sir John, 42, 62
Black Death, 68, 186, 269, 271
Bladud, King, 18, 19, 153–4
Blake, William, 47, 130
Blight, John T., 177, 180, 183
Boadicea, 53
Bond, F. Bligh, 139
Boroughbridge, 282–3
Boscawen-un circle, 189–90
Bowerman's Nose, *illus*. 168
Bradford-on-Avon, 158–9, *illus*.
    159
Bran the Blessed, 13, 50
Breamore maze, 76 *and illus*.
Brennan, Martin, 7
Brentor, 138, 170–1 *and illus*.
Bridget, St., 38, 131, *illus*. 137
Brimham rocks, 280–1 *and illus*.
Bristol, 51, 206
Brittany, 7, 172, 173, 185
Brutus, King, 17, 27, 50, 68, 139,
    208, 254
Bunyan, John, 39, 47
Burges, William, 58–9, 265, *illus*.
    264
Burrowbridge Mump, 138 *and
    illus*.
Bury St. Edmunds, 309–12, *illus*.
    310

Button, Bishop, 147; *illus.* 148
Byland Abbey, 270–1 *and illus.*

Cadbury Castle, 142–3
Cade, Jack, 32
Caesar, Julius, 11, 12, 50, 53, 172
Cambridge, 51
Camden, William, 19
Camelot, 74, 142–3, 231, 234–5
Campion, Edmund, 65–7
Cantelupe, Thomas de, 212–13 *and illus.*
Canterbury, 77–88, 256
    Augustine's Abbey, 87
    cathedral, 84–7, *illus.* 81, 84, 86
    church of St. Martin, 83–4, 88
    church of St. Pancras, 84, 87–8
    pilgrimages, 77–80, *illus.* 77
Canute, King, 57, 68, 295, 301
Carlisle and cathedral, 16, 228–35, *illus.* 229, 230
Castle Rigg circle, 223–6, *illus.* 224, *plans* 225, 227
Catherine of Aragon, 208, 298–300, 306
Catherine, St., 75–6, 78–80, 116, 120–2, 158, *illus.* 78, 121, 158
Celtic Church, 13, 16, 83, 131, 154, 173, 236–8, 274
    culture, 10–13, 102–3, 184
    saints, 13, 173, 180–1, 189, 236–40
Cerne Abbas, 116, 122–5, *illus.* 123
Chambers, Sir William, 115
Charles II, 25, 26, 61
Chartres, 293
Cheddar Gorge, 150
Chedworth Roman villa, 202–4, *illus.* 202, 203
Cheesewring, 138, 176 *and illus.*
Chester and cathedral, 216–21, *illus.* 218, 220
Cistercians, 262, 267–72
Clearbury ring, 107
Collen, St., 136
Colman, Bishop, 15
Columba, St., 236
conservation, xii, 68, 217
Constable, John, 97, 117
Constantine the Great, 254
Coram, Thomas, 35
Cornwall, 135, 172–93
    language of, 188
Coronation stone, 23–4, *illus.* 23
Cotswold monuments, 200–4, *illus.* 201–3

Cowper, William, 267
Cromwell, Oliver, 23, 29, 69, 249, 297
Crowland, 302–3 *and illus.*
Crown Jewels, 50
Cuby, St., 178
Cuthberga, St., 112
Cuthbert, St., 15, 229, 231, 237–40, 247–53, 258, 274, *illus.* 253
Cuthman, St., 277 *and illus.*

Dalderby, John of, 286–8
Damer, Joseph, 115–16
Dames, Michael, 94
Danes, 46, 85, 102, 112, 239, 255, 285, 292, 297, 301, 302, 310
Darling, Grace, 242
Dartmoor, 166–72; *illus.* 168, 169, 171
Darwin, Charles, 11, 21, 70
David, St., 131, 179
Deerhurst, 204–6
Defoe, Daniel, 39
Delphi, 9
Devereux, Paul, 52, 76
Devil's Arrows, 282
Diana, temple of, 27, 41, 254
Doniert, King, 176
Donnelly, Ignatius, 56
Dorchester, 117–19
dowsing, 9, 189
dragons, 9, 79, 94
Druids, 10–14, 83, 92, 97, 99, 102–3, 135, 167, 170, 173, 176, 281, *illus.* 12
Duloe, 178 *and illus.*
Dundon, 142
Dunstan, St., 132
Dupath well, 180 *and illus.*
Durham and cathedral, 247–53, *illus.* 247, 249, 250, 252, 25

East Dereham, 308–9
Easter, 14
Edgar, King, 115, 156
Edmund, St., 38, 45, 309–12, *illus.* 311
Edward I, 22, 75, 196, 212
Edward II, 196–7, 282, *illus.* 19
Edward III, 23, 27, 75
Edward, the Black Prince, 86
Edward the Confessor, 19, 22, 112, 186, *illus.* 22
Edwin, King, 255–6
Eleanor of Castile, 22–3, 75, *illus.* 59
Elgar, Sir Edward, 21, 194

Elizabeth I, 25, 38, 49, 67, 110
Elizabeth II, 24, 302
Elizabeth of Bohemia, 25–6
Ellwood, Thomas, 61
Ely and cathedral, 289–96, *illus.*
    290, 291, 293
Epping Forest, 57
Essex, Earl of, 24
Ethelberga, 255
Ethelbert, St., 211
Ethelbert and Bertha, 83–8
Etheldreda, St., 48, 218, 244–5,
    290–2, 295
Ethelred I, 112
Ethelred the Unready, 28
Euny, St., 191–2
Exening, 301
Exeter and cathedral, 160–4,
    illus. 161, 162, 163

Fackenham, Abbot, 18
fairies, 175, 179
Farne Islands, 238, 242, *illus.*
    237, 239
festivals, 6, 78, 87, 94, 97
Fontainebleau, 281
Forbes, J. Foster, 4
Fountains Abbey, 263–7, *illus.*
    263, 265, 266
Fox, George, 61
Fulton, Missouri, 31

Galileo, 213
Garway, 214–15
Gaveston, Piers, 197, 282
geomancy, 107
George V, 176
George, St., 118–19, 138
giants, 122–4, 139, 185, 189,
    232, 233, *illus.* 123, 200
Gibbons, Grinling, 21, 42
Glastonbury, xv, 57, 75, 128–43,
    illus. 141
    Abbey, 129–35, *illus.* 129, 130,
      133, *plans* 132, 135
    lake villages, 140
    zodiac, 141
Glaver, John, 226
Gloucester and cathedral,
    194–200, *illus.* 195–200
Gog and Magog, 38, 139–40
Golden Age, 5
Gomme, Sir Lawrence, 32
Graves, Tom, 9
Gray, Thomas, 62–5
green man, 295
Greensted, 311–12, *illus.* 311
Gregory, Pope, 83, 87–8
Grimthorpe, Lord, 54

Grosseteste, Bishop, 286
Guinevere, Queen, 132, 232
Gulval, 173
Guthlag, St., 302–3, 304

Haakon VII of Norway, 44
Hadrian's Wall, 228, 232, 244
Hampden, John, 63
Harding, Stephen, 262
Hardy, Thomas, 117–18
Harold, King, 21, 57–8, *illus.* 58
Hatton, Sir Christopher, 49, 64
Hawker, Robert S., 173, 182–3,
    illus. 182, 183
Hawkins, Gerald, 100
Helmesly, Abbot, 269
Henry I, 229
Henry II, 80–2
Henry IV, 86
Henry VII, 25, 74, 208, 299, 306
Henry VIII, 18, 37, 54, 58, 73–5,
    85, 110, 115, 124, 195, 208,
    269, 272, 298–300, 306
Hercules, 123
Hereford and cathedral, 209–14,
    illus. 210, 212, 213, 214
Hereward the Wake, 292, 302
hermits and hermitages, 171,
    180–1, 186, 238, 243–4,
    279–80, 289, 302, *illus.* 181,
    243, 279
Hetty Pegler's Tump, 201
Hexham, 244–7, *illus.* 245
Hieropolis, 105
Hilda, St., 15
Hill, Thomas, 280
hilltop shrines, 78–80, 120–2,
    135–6, 170–1, *illus.* 71, 78,
    79, 121, 136
Holy Grail, 134, 183
Holy Rood, 57–8
holy wells, 16, 31, 38, 44, 69, 71,
    79, 124, 138–9, 203, 221–2,
    228, 261, 265, 289, 301,
    305–7, 309, *illus.* 256
    of Cornwall, 172–4, 177–83,
      190–2, *illus.* 174, 177, 179,
      180, 181, 183
Housesteads, 232, *illus.* 233
Howel, King, 172, 190
Hoxne, 310–11
Hudson, Henry, 39
Hugh of Avalon, St., 286, 287
Hugh, Little St., 284–6
Huntingdon, Henry of, 101
Hurlers stone circle, 175 and *illus.*

Icarus, 154
Ice Age, 2

Ina, King, 112, 125
Iona, 15, 236
Ireland, 7, 15, 102, 173

Jacob's pillow, 23
James I, 23, 298
Jenkins, Bishop David, 260
Jeremiah, 6
Jerusalem, 48, 103, 105, 213
Jervaulx Abbey, 271–2
Jesus Christ, 130–1, 135, 151, 305
Jews, 41, 46–7, 164–5, 261, 284–5
John, King, 209, 214
John, St., 13, 104
Jordan's, 60–1, *illus.* 60
Joseph of Arimathea, 129–30, 134–5, 151
Julian, Mother, 308

Keats, John, 223
Keiller, Alexander, 95
Kelvin, William, 21
Kennet river, 89
   avenue, 89
   long barrow, 95, 96
Kestor Rock, 167
Keyne, St., 177–8, 183, 185, *illus.* 177
Kilpeck, 215–17, *illus.* 214–17
King, Bishop Oliver, 156–7, *illus.* 156
King's Lynn, 306
Knaresborough, 277–80
Knowlton, 111, *illus.* 112
Kwan Yin, 122

Lake District, 223–8
Lancaster, Thomas, Earl of, 282–3
Landor, Walter S., 157
Larkman, Brian, 260
Lawrence, St., 41
Lear, King, 18
Leland, John, 142
leys, 10, 51, 76, 107, 167–8, 260–1, 282
Lightfoot, Peter, 113, 148
Lincoln and cathedral, 284–9, *illus.* 285–8
Lindisfarne, 15, 235–41, 248, 274, 297, *illus.* 236
   Gospels, 237, 240
   Priory, 239, *illus.* 240
London, 17–52
   alignment of churches, 51–2
   cathedrals, 19–30, *illus.* 21–7, 29–31
   city churches, 30–46, *illus.* 31,

35, 36, 39, 40, 43, 44, 45, *map* 34
   early history, 17–19
   Fire of, 28, 31, 278
   plague of, 44
   Stone, 32
   synagogue, churches, chapels, 46–51
   Temple church, 47–8, *illus.* 47, 48–9
   Tower of, 49–51, *illus.* 50
Long Meg and her Daughters, 227–8, *plan* 227
lost Lyonesse, 186, 188
Lucius, King, 13, 19, 44, 68, 131, *illus.* 45
Lud, King, 17, 27, 38
Lutyens, Sir Edwin, 240

Madron well, 192
Maes Howe, 7
Maiden Castle, 119
Malmesbury, William of, 130, 132, 304
Malory, Sir Thomas, 231
Malthus, Thomas, 157
Maltwood, Kathryn, 141
Malvern hills, 194
Mappa Mundi, 212–13 *and illus.*
Marazion, 186
March, 301
Martha, St., 79–80, *illus.* 79
Mary, Queen, 25, 67, 110
Mary, Queen of Scots, 25, 298
masons and masonic lore, 51, 198–9, 294
Massachusetts, 117–18, 195
Mayflower relics, 61
maypole, 36, 123, *illus.* 35
mazes and labyrinths, 75–6, 293, *illus.* 76, 185
megaliths, 166–70, 174–8, 188–90, 200–2, 223–8, 282, *illus.* 90–2, 99, 169, 174, 175, 178, 189, 190, 192, 224
   and science, 7–10, 189, 224–8
Melbourne, Lord, 40
Mellitus, Bishop, 28
Mercury, 195
Merewether, Dean, 93
Merlin, 5, 102, 184
Merry Maidens circle, 190 *and illus.*
Mesolithic life, 4–5
Methodism, 47
Mexican pyramids, 103
Meyrick, J., 173
Michael, St., xiii, 43, 95, 134, 137–8, 170–2, 180, 185

line of sites, 89, 176
Milton, John, 39, 61–2
Milton Abbas, 115–17
Minerva, 154, 155
Molmutius, King, 17–18, 50, 68
Monmouth, Duke of, 113, 144
Monmouth, Geoffrey of, 101–2, 153
Montacute, 57
More, Sir Thomas, xi
Morwenna, St., 183
Morwenstow, 182–3
Mother Goose, 44
Mount Grace Priory, 272–3 and illus.
Muir, Richard, 5
Murray, Margaret, 73
music, 162, 194, 199, 207, 287, 295–6
Mycenae, 97, 100

Nash, "Beau," 152–3, 157
natural likenesses, 279–81, illus. 151, 168, 281
Nazareth, 305, 306
Nelson, Horatio, 26–7, 29
Newgate prison, 45
New Grange, 7
Newton, Sir Isaac, 21, 103
Nicholas, St., 71, 109, 120
Nightingale, Florence, 30
Norman Conquest, 19–20
Norwich, 51, 308
Nun, St., 179 and illus.

Odda, 206
Offa, King, 53, 66, 156, 211
Olaf, St., 44
Old Sarum, 106–8, 118, illus. 107
Orkney islands, 7
Osmund, St., 106, 118
Oswald, King, 236, 241–2, 248, 251, 297, 298, illus. 253
Oswy, King, 15
Oxford, Earl of, 186

Palmerston, Lord, 165
Pancras, St., 88
Parminter, Jane, 164–5
Patrick, St., 131, 132, 173
Paulinus, 255–6, 285
Penda, King of Mercia, 14, 218, 256
Penn, William, 35, 60–1, 63, 64, 144
Pepys, Samuel, 44
Peter, St., 14, 15, 154, 256, 306
Peterborough and cathedral, 292–301, illus. 297–300

Pilgrimage of Grace, 272
pilgrimages, xiii–xv, 77–9, 137–9, 186, 209, 221, 240, 297, 303–7
Piper, Edward, 66
Pitt, William, 21
Pitt-Rivers, General, 110
Plato, 6, 199
Plutarch, 9
Pocahontas, 45
Pole, Wellesley Tudor, xiii, 139
Potter, Beatrix, 195
Poynter, Edward, 59
Priddy, 151
proportion and measure, 48, 103–4, 163, 199, 224–6, 249, illus. 104, 135, 225, 227
Protestant Reformation, 3, 85, 208, 298–300
martyrs, 37
Purcell, Henry, 21
Puritans, 3, 54, 61, 118

Quakers, 60–1, 195, 308

radiocarbon dating, 7, 75, 93, 97
Raleigh, Sir Walter, 128
reincarnation, 12
relics, 20, 87, 131, 160, 241–2, 239, 251, 253, 256, 276, 292, 297–8, 308
Remigius, Bishop, 285
Renaissance, 33, 199
Revelation, 104
Richard III, 25
Rievaulx Abbey, 267–70, illus. 268
terrace, 269–70 and illus.
Rillaton Barrow, 175–6
Ripon and cathedral, 238, 264, 273–7, 281, illus. 275, 276
Robert, St., 279–80, illus. 279
Robin Hood, 265–6
Robins, Don, 9
Roche Rock, 180–1 and illus.
Roger, Archbishop, 257, 275
Roman Catholic shrines, 48–9, 65–7, 215, 280, 305–7
Romans, 13, 14, 43, 53, 83, 88, 102, 106, 117–19, 143, 155, 172, 194, 202–4, 228, 232–3, 284, illus. 202, 203
augury of, 216–17
Rosicrucians, 56

St. Albans, xv, 53–7, illus. 54, 55
St. Aubyn family, 187
St. Cleer, 173–5, illus. 174

St. Michael's Mount, 138, 172, 185–8, *illus.* 186, 187
St. Paul's Cathedral, 17, 27–30, 52, *illus.* 27, 29, 30, 31
Salisbury and cathedral, 106–10, *illus.* 109, 110
Samaritans, 46
Sancreed, 191 *and illus.*
sanctuaries, 27, 49, 246, 248–9, 274–5, *illus.* 249
Saxon churches, 159, 204–6, 311–12, *illus.* 159, 205, 311
Saxons, 15, 50, 69, 75, 102, 172, 292
Scone, Stone of, 23
Scorhill circle, 167
Scott, Sir Gilbert, 54, 70, 211, 219, 221, 293
Sedbar, Abbot, 272
Sewingshields, 232
Sexburga, 295, 298
Shaftesbury, Earl of, 165
Shakespeare, 18, 56
Sherborne, 106, 125–8, *illus.* 127
Shipton, Mother, 278–9
Silbury Hill, 89, 93–5, *illus.* 94
Simon Magus, 154
Sitwell, Edith, 66
Smith, Captain John, 45
Smuts, Jan C., 142
South Sea Bubble, 263
Southey, Robert, 177
Spinsters' Rock, 168–9, *illus.* 169
Stoke Poges, 62–5, *illus.* 62, 64, 65
stone circles, xi, 8, 69, 79, 89–93, 96–106, 119, 151–2, 167–8, 175–6, 178, 188–90, 223–8, *illus.* 90, 91, 92, 98, 99, 175, 178, 189, 190, 224, 225, 227
Stonehenge, xi, 11, 13, 16, 96–106, 108, 134–5, *illus.* 98, 99, *plan* 104
 dimensions, 103–4
 meaning, 103–6
Stonor Park, 65–8
Studley Royal, 264–6, *illus.* 264
Stukeley, William, 91–4, *illus.* 92
Swithin, St., 69, 72–3, 221

Tara, hill of, 23
Tennison, Alfred, 183
Tewkesbury, 204
Thom, Alexander, 8, 101, 224
Thompson, Ian, 52, 76
Thorney Island, 19, 303
Tintagel, 184–5 *and illus.*
Tintern Abbey, 262
Toplady, Augustus M., 151

Tothill, 19
Tree of Life, 148, 215
trees, sacred, 138, 142
Trevethy Quoit, 174 *and illus.*
Trojan dynasty, 17–19, 27, 153
Trollope, Anthony, 144
Tuck, Friar, 265–6
Turner, J. W. M., 97

Unknown Warrior, tomb of, 20–1
Uther Pendragon, 234

Vaughan Williams, Ralph, 21
Verulamium, 53–7
Victoria, Queen, 165
Vikings, 239, 255

Wales, 7, 172, 196, 221–2
Wales, Prince of, 172, 196
Wallace, Alfred R., 21
Walsingham, xii, xv, 297, 304–8, *illus.* 305, 307
Walsingham, Alan of, 294
Waltham Abbey, 57–9, 133, *illus.* 58
 Cross, 60 *and illus.*
Waltheof, Earl, 302
Walton, Izaak, 70
Warbeck, Perkin, 186
Warkworth hermitage, 243–4, *illus.* 243
Wellington, Duke of, 29
Wells and cathedral, 14, 144–52, *illus.* 144–9
Welsh Newton, 214–15
Wendreda, St., 301–2
Werburgh, St., 218–20
Wesley, John, 21
 chapel of, 47
Westminster Abbey, 19–27, *illus.* 20–6
 Poets' corner, 26
 Unknown Warrior, tomb of, 20–1
Whitby, Synod of, 15, 238, 274
Whitefield, George, 195
Whiting, Richard, 133
Whittington, Dick, 43
Wilberforce, William, 21
 Samuel, 70
Wilfrid, St., 15, 244–6, 274–6
 his crypts and chair, 245–6, 276, *illus.* 246, 276
William I, the Conqueror, 20, 50, 83, 106, 118, 206, 247, 284, 292, 302, *illus.* 258
William II, Rufus, 73–4, 156
William of Wykeham, 69, 75, *illus.* 69

Wimborne Minster, 111–14, 148, *illus.* 113, 114
    library, 113, *illus.* 114
Winchester and cathedral, 16, 68–75, 208, *illus.* 69–72
Winefride, St., 221–2
Wistman's Wood, 170
witches, 73–4, 111, 150, 278–9, *illus.* 151
Withburga, St., 309
Woden, temple of, 256
Wolfe, General, 24
Wolsey, Cardinal, 29, 278
Wood, John, 151, 153
Wookey Hole, 150, *illus.* 151

Worcester and cathedral, 206–9, *illus.* 207, 208
Wordsworth, William and Dorothy, 223, 268
Wren, Sir Christopher, 20, 28, 31, 33, 41, 46, *illus.* 31
Wulfstan, Bishop, 20, 206, 209
Wyatt, James, 63, 108–10, 210–11, 249

York and York Minster, 16, 51, 254–61, *illus.* 254, 256–60

zodiac signs, 59, 141

A Note about the Author

Over the last twenty-one years John Michell has become recognized as a major authority on ancient science, religion, and the symbolism of sacred landscapes. His books include *The View over Atlantis*, *The Earth Spirit*, *Secrets of the Stones*, and *Megalithomania*. He was born and lives in London.

A Note on the Type

This book was set on the Linotype in a face called Primer, designed by Rudolph Ruzicka (1883–1978). Mr. Ruzicka was earlier responsible for the design of Fairfield and Fairfield Medium, Linotype faces whose virtues have for some time been accorded wide recognition.

The complete range of sizes of Primer was first made available in 1954, although the pilot size of 12-point was ready as early as 1951. The design of the face makes general reference to Linotype Century—long a serviceable type, totally lacking in manner or frills of any kind—but brilliantly corrects its characterless quality.

Composed by Americomp, Inc., Brattleboro, Vermont. Printed and bound by R. R. Donnelly & Sons, Crawfordsville, Indiana. Book design by Marysarah Quinn adapted from a design by Christine Aulicino.